MW01110416

THE TRANSFORMATION OF LABOUR LAW IN EUROPE

The labour laws of European democracies all underwent major transformations in the seven decades after the Second World War. Following reconstruction, these laws became an essential element in the building of welfare states; in the 1980s and 1990s they were the target of neo-liberal deregulation; and at the beginning of the twenty-first century new 'flexible' labour laws have attempted to integrate economic and social policy. This book, a sequel to *The Making of Labour Law in Europe: A Comparative Study of Nine Countries up to 1945* (ed B Hepple), compares the similarities and differences in the ways in which EU Member States reflected and shaped these general developments, in the context of economic, social and political changes over the period 1945–2004.

Note: the Publishers are issuing a reprint of the first volume, *The Making of Labour Law in Europe: A Comparative Study of Nine Countries up to 1945*, to coincide with publication of the sequel.

The Transformation of Labour Law in Europe

A comparative study of 15 countries
1945–2004

Edited by

Bob Hepple

and

Bruno Veneziani

·H A R T·
PUBLISHING

OXFORD AND PORTLAND, OREGON
2009

Published in North America (US and Canada) by
Hart Publishing
c/o International Specialized Book Services
920 NE 58th Avenue, Suite 300
Portland, OR 97213-3786
USA
Tel: +1 503 287 3093 or toll-free: (1) 800 944 6190
Fax: +1 503 280 8832
Email: mail@hartpub.co.uk
Website: www.isbs.com

Hart Publishing Ltd, 16C Worcester Place, Oxford, OX1 2JW
Telephone: +44 (0)1865 517530 Fax: +44 (0)1865 510710
E-mail: mail@hartpub.co.uk
Website: http://www.hartpub.co.uk

British Library Cataloguing in Publication Data
Data Available

ISBN: 978-1-84113-870-1

Typeset by Forewords, Oxford
Printed and bound in Great Britain by
TJ International Ltd, Padstow, Cornwall

Preface

This book completes a project which was begun in 1978, when Thilo Ramm brought together a group of labour law scholars (the European Comparative Labour Law Group) who produced *The Making of Labour Law in Europe: A Comparative Study of Nine Countries up to 1945* (edited by Bob Hepple), published in 1986. This has long been out of print, and it is now reissued, with this volume, by Hart Publishing. The first volume was well received by reviewers, including two who had been members (with Thilo Ramm) of the Comparative Labour Law Group, established by Benjamin Aaron, the last of whose three works was published in 1978, just as the 'golden age' of labour law was coming to an end.[1] Lord Wedderburn described our first volume as 'a major contribution to comparative legal scholarship'[2] and Xavier Blanc Jouvan hoped it would serve as a model for later studies.[3]

It was always the intention of the European Comparative Labour Law Group to write a second volume bringing the comparative historical analysis of labour law in Europe up to the present. Some meetings of a reconstituted group were held in 1991, but unfortunately it proved to be impossible to continue at that stage because of the other commitments of the members. It was not until 2005 that Bruno Veneziani and Bob Hepple managed to assemble a group, including the present contributors, Eliane Vogel-Polsky (Emeritus Professor, Free University of Brussels), who had been a contributor to the first volume, and Philippe Hesse (Emeritus Professor, University of Nantes). Unfortunately, for health reasons, the latter two had to withdraw after undertaking some preliminary work on women in the labour market and health and safety, respectively. However, we had the benefit of Professor Vogel-Polsky's participation at our first meeting, and that of Professor Hesse at the second. Their withdrawal, at a fairly late stage, has meant that we have been unable to have a separate chapter on women and labour law (this is now integrated into chapter 3, Regulation of the Labour Market and chapter 5, Equality at Work), or one specifically devoted to health and safety (some aspects of which will be found in other chapters, particularly chapter 8, Workers' Representation on Plant and Enterprise Level).

Our method of work differed from that of the original group in that this time we did not first write national reports covering all the topics. The existence of a number of reference works relating to the modern period, such as *The*

---

[1] The work of the Comparative Labour Group was the subject of a symposium in 2005: see (2007) 28 *Comparative Labor Law and Policy Journal* 377-616.

[2] (1988) 17 *Industrial Law Journal* 131.

[3] (1989) *Revue Internationale de Droit Comparé* 262, 264.

Encyclopedia of Comparative Labour Law and Industrial Relations (edited by Roger Blanpain), the *International Encyclopedia of Comparative Law. Vol XV. Labour Law* (chief editor, Bob Hepple), the *European Employment and Industrial Relations Glossary* (European Foundation for the Improvement of Living and Working Conditions) and the European Commission's study of *The Evolution of Labour Law (1992-2003)* (edited and with a general introduction by Silvana Sciarra), made it possible for us to draw on these and other contemporary sources in the main European languages. Each contributor prepared a bibliography and a brief profile (see Appendix I, below) relating to the countries for which they took responsibility, and also answered questions and provided information to other authors as requested. At the first meeting, held in Bari in July 2006, outlines of each chapter were discussed. At the second meeting, held in Cambridge in September 2007, and the third, in Bari in April 2008, draft chapters were discussed. The drafts were prepared in English. Since this was not the first language of most of the authors, the drafts were revised and edited by Bob Hepple, hopefully without destroying the national idiom and meaning of each author. The book, like the first volume, is thus a co-operative effort, although individuals have accepted ultimate responsibility for particular chapters.

The aims, scope and comparative methodology of the authors are described in chapter 1 (Introduction). We hope that we have maintained the character of the first volume, which distinguishes it from other comparative labour law studies, by describing and analysing labour law as part of an historical process, and explaining the relationships between the development of labour laws in the 15 countries that were Member States of the European Union before 1 May 2004. We have taken that date, when the first eight former communist countries joined the EU, as our cut-off point, for the reasons explained in chapter 1.

Cambridge and Bari
February 2009

Acknowledgements

The authors wish to thank Eliane Vogel-Polsky and Philippe Hesse for providing information on Belgium and France respectively. We were fortunate to have advice from Aurora Vimercati, who was present at our meetings, and also from Mark Freedland, who participated in our Cambridge meeting. We are very grateful to Caroline Smith, Lara Blecher and Jessica Wiechert for highly efficient research assistance; Denise Milizia for help with translation of chapter 4, Michael Gotthardt, Antonio Le Faro, Silvaine Laulom and Taco van Peijpe for assistance with chapter 9; and Mary Coussey for advice on chapter 5.

We received financial assistance from a number of sources to cover travel and some research expenses. We express our gratitude to the Leverhulme Trust; the British Academy; the *Università degli Studi di Bari*; and the *Institutet för Rättsvetenskaplig Forskning*. We also wish to thank Clare College, Cambridge, and the *Università degli Studi di Bari* and its *Dipartimento sui rapporti di lavoro e relazione industriali* for providing facilities for our meetings.

We are grateful to Jelle Visser for permission to reproduce Tables 7.1 and 7.2.

Contents

The Authors

Niklas Bruun   *Professor of Private Law, University of Helsinki*

Jordi García Viña   *Professor of Labour Law, University of Barcelona*

Bob Hepple   *Emeritus Master of Clare College and Emeritus Professor of Law, University of Cambridge*

Antoine Jacobs   *Professor of Labour Law, Social Security and Social Policy, University of Tilburg*

Jonas Malmberg   *Professor of Private Law, particularly Labour Law, University of Uppsala*

Ulrich Mückenberger   *Professor of Labour Law and European Law, University of Hamburg*

Antonio Ojeda Aviles   *Professor of Labour Law, University of Seville; President of the European Industrial Relations Institute; President of the Spanish Association of Health and Social Security*

Robert Rebhahn   *Professor of Labour Law and Social Law, University of Vienna*

Bruno Veneziani   *Professor of Labour Law and Comparative Trade Union Law, University of Bari*

Table of Abbreviations

ACLV-CGSLB	Liberal Trade Union Movement (Belgium)
ABVV-FGTB	Socialist Trade Union Movement (Belgium)
ACV- CSC	Confederation of Christian Trade Unions (Belgium)
ANPE	National Employment Agency (France)
BDA	Federal Union of German Employers' Confederations
CBI	Confederation of British Industries
CEDAW	Convention on the Elimination of all Forms of Discrimination Against Women
CEEP	Centre Européen des Enterprises Publiques
CERD	Convention on the Elimination of all Forms of Racial Discrimination
CFTC	French Christian Workers' Confederation
CFTD	French Democratic Confederation of Labour
CGIL	General Confederation of Italian Workers
CGT (F)	French General Confederation of Labour
CGT (S)	Spanish General Confederation of Trade Unions
CGT-FO	French General Confederation of Labour-Workers' Force
CGTP-IN	Portuguese Confederation of Trade Unions
CIG	Wages Guarantee Fund (Italy)
CISL	Italian Confederation of Workers' Unions
CNV	Christian Confederation of Trade Unions (Netherlands)
CSR	Corporate Social Responsibility
DA	Danish Employers' Association
DGB	German Federation of Trade Unions
EC	European Community
ECSC	European Coal and Steel Community
ECHR	European Convention on Human Rights
ECtHR	European Court of Human Rights
ECJ	European Court of Justice
ECR	European Court Reports

EEC	European Economic Community
EES	European Employment Strategy
EMU	European Monetary Union
ESC	European Social Charter
EFTA	European Free Trade Agreement
ETUC	European Trade Union Confederation
EU	European Union
EWC	European Works Council
FNV	Federation of Dutch Trade Unions
FRG	Federal Republic of Germany
GSEE	Greek Trade Union Federation
ICCPR	International Covenant on Civil and Political Rights
ICESCR	International Covenant on Economic Social and Cultural Rights
ICFTU	International Confederation of Free Trade Unions
ILO	International Labour Organisation
INPS	National Institute for Social Insurance (Italy)
LO (D)	Danish Confederation of Trade Unions
LO (S)	Swedish Confederation of Trade Unions
NCFE	National Councl of Fench Emloyers
ÕGB	Austrian Trade Union Federation
OMC	Open Method of Coordination
PAYG	Pay as You Go
PES	Public Employment Services
PSA	Personnel Services Agency (Netherlands)
PTK	Private Salaried Employees' Cartel (Sweden)
SAF	Swedish Employers' Confederation
SAK	Central Organisation of Finnish Workers
SERPS	State Earnings Related Pension (Britain)
SMIC	Salaire Minimum Interprofessionel de Croissance (national minimum wage, France)
SSP	Statutory Sick Pay (Britain)
TCO	Central Organisation of Salaried Employees (Sweden)
TEU	Treaty of European Union
TNC	Transnational Corporation
TUC	Trades Union Congress (Britain)

TWA	Temporary Work Agency
UEAPME	International Association of Crafts and Small and Medium Enterprises
UGT (P)	Portuguese General Union of Workers
UGT (S)	Spanish General Union of Workers
UIL	Union of Italian Workers
UNICE	Union of Industrial and Employers' Confederations of Europe
WFL	World Federation of Labour
WFTU	World Federation of Trade Unions

1

Introduction

BOB HEPPLE AND BRUNO VENEZIANI

From 'Making' to 'Transformation'

The labour laws of European countries were transformed almost beyond recognition in the 60 years following the end of the Second World War.

Labour Law in 1945

The end of the war promised a new beginning for labour law. The totalitarian systems in Germany and Italy had been smashed, and with them disappeared the new orderings of labour relations based on the ideas of national socialism and corporativism. The Vichy French Charter of Labour suffered the same fate.[1] By 1949, with the adoption of the German Basic Law (*Grundgesetz*), democracy had been restored in most European countries. The exceptions were Franco's Spain and Salazar's Portugal, where authoritarian systems of labour law continued until the mid-1970s, and the communist countries of central and eastern Europe until the fall of the Berlin Wall in 1989. Greece, deeply divided by civil war, started as a democracy and ended as a democracy only after 1975, with a dictatorship in between. In the western democracies there were significant advances from the pre-war regimes, including the extension of the franchise to women in those countries, such as France, Italy and Belgium, where this had not occurred before the war. New constitutions, adopted after 1945, recognised to varying degrees not only the rights of property and the freedom to establish undertakings, but also the rights of labour.

Yet, despite these aspirations, the reality of the immediate post-war world was harsh for working people. Countries that had been involved in the conflict lay in ruins, 72 million people were casualties and millions more were displaced. For some in southern Europe the only escape was either emigration overseas or

---

[1] For details of these see Ramm (1986) 296–98.

work as migrant labourers in northern Europe. The labour laws and collective agreements that protected workers were almost exclusively national in origin—there was no 'European' system of labour law and social security. The typical worker covered by labour law was a male breadwinner under a 'standard' full-time contract of employment or 'service', hired through a public employment service. There were few, if any, legal controls over the powers of management to hire and discipline or dismiss workers either at will or on relatively short periods of notice. Women, who had replaced men in industries during the war, were usually expected to go back to their role as housewives and were discriminated against, sometimes under the guise of 'protective' laws on matters such as night-work in factories; when they did work, their average earnings were anywhere between 10 and 35% lower than those of men doing comparable jobs. There were no laws against discrimination in employment. Welfare and unemployment benefits, surviving from the pre-war systems, were generally confined to those who had made contributions while working under contracts of employment, so excluding those on the fringes of the labour market, the self-employed and most women.

The forces that wanted to improve the standard of life and to see the promise of democracy and social justice fulfilled were inspired by the ideas of solidarity and collectivism that had been required to defeat Nazism and fascism. This led, in some countries, to nationalisation of the banks and key industries, and a degree of economic planning. In the field of labour relations, the faith in collectivism was reflected in a steady growth in trade union membership and the extension of autonomous (usually sectoral) collective bargaining. Workers' representatives at plant level—whether on an informal basis (as in Britain and Italy), as a result of collective agreements (as in Sweden) or on a statutory basis (as in Germany and the Netherlands)—were, most of the time, the 'lubricants'[2] of systems of labour relations ensuring the trust and co-operation needed to promote productivity and efficiency. Laws and collective agreements were normally enforced through industrial relations systems rather than through individual judicial processes.

The advent of the cold war in 1946–47 meant that the predominant conflict was now seen to be that between capitalist, market-based western democracy and Soviet communism, which was based on state ownership, central planning and a one-party state. Except in the Nordic countries, the governments that shaped labour laws in the west were fiercely anti-communist and also predominantly conservative. As the 'iron curtain' descended 'from Stettin in the Baltic to Trieste in the Adriatic', in Churchill's famous phrase, the cold war not only divided Germany (until 1989) and split European political and economic systems, it also isolated the communist parties in countries such as France and Italy, where they enjoyed popular support. Moreover, the cold war divided the trade union

[2] The expression used by the British Royal Commission on Trade Unions and Employers' Associations (1968).

movements and the capitalist and communist systems of labour law. And within the former, there were significant divergences between those countries which developed co-ordinated economic, social and labour law policies and those where industrial relations were largely adversarial and fragmented.

Labour Law in 2004

Six decades later, Soviet communism had imploded and the cold war was over. Germany was reunited, and the former communist states of central and eastern Europe were expected to adopt a 'European social model' as one of the conditions for entry into the European Union (EU). The first eight of those states joined the Union on 1 May 2004, but the 'social models' of the then 15 Member States were very different from those of 1945. There was now a 'European' legal order that had evolved since the founding of the European Coal and Steel Community (ECSC) in 1951, and the European Economic Community (EEC) from 1957. From 1992 this was called the European Community (EC), one of the three 'pillars' of the EU established by the Maastricht Treaty in 1992 (the other 'pillars' being the common foreign and security policy, and police and judicial co-operation in criminal matters). It was Community (EEC/EC) law, rather than Union law, that was most relevant to domestic social and labour law, but the dimensions of what has come to be called 'European labour law' (or EC/EU/Community employment/labour law) are relatively modest, excluding, for example, collective bargaining and minimum wage laws. Sometimes national labour rights came into conflict with economic freedoms guaranteed by the Community treaties (see chapter 2 below). On the whole, Community interventions into domestic labour laws have mainly been in areas where they are thought to affect the economic functioning of the common market, and only in more recent years have these interventions also had a specific 'social rationale'.[3] But conceptions of 'fundamental human rights' have come to occupy an increasingly important role in labour relations under the influence of the EU, the Council of Europe and the International Labour Organisation (ILO). The most important of these human rights in employment is equality of status, irrespective of sex and sexual orientation, race and religion or belief, disability and age (see chapter 5 below). These rights have to be implemented through national courts and tribunals.

National labour laws and procedures were thus of continuing importance and, by 2004, these had changed dramatically since the immediate post-war period. The 'typical' worker was now likely to be a woman in a service industry working part-time or on a fixed-term contract, hired through a private temporary work agency. Women now had the support of anti-discrimination laws. The pay gap between women and men doing comparable jobs had been reduced but not

---

[3] Syrpis (2007) 61–75.

eliminated. Although many workers, both male and female, had come to enjoy a measure of job security, including protection against unfair dismissal, the growing number of workers in precarious or 'marginal' employment, such as work on call and telework, were often excluded from protection in response to employers' demands for 'flexibility'. Working time was regulated by EC law, but national laws could allow derogations from this by collective or works agreements or even by individual opt-out. The welfare states that had been built up over 60 years had undergone important changes, including the demise of the male-breadwinner model, affecting benefits in the case of parenthood and old age pensions; 'workfare' (benefits dependent upon active steps to find employment) had replaced 'welfare' for unemployed persons, single parents and some others. Active labour market policies, for example to increase the participation of women, young persons and older workers, were de rigueur. There were vigorous health and safety laws, minimum wages were widely prescribed and the principle of equality of treatment was the legal norm (although not achieved in practice) not only for women but also for ethnic and religious minorities, disabled people and older workers, gays and lesbians.

The most significant change from the 1980s onwards was the decline of collectivism. Trade unions suffered substantial losses of membership, apart from the Nordic countries and, to a lesser extent, Austria (see chapter 7 below). Strikes had become a rarity in most countries. Although collective bargaining remained the most important method of determining wages and hours of work, this was increasingly decentralised, or was supplemented by statutory methods of information and consultation with workers' representatives or works councils at plant or company level. Enforcement of employment rights was now typically through individualised judicial procedures. Labour relations had become highly juridified.

Historical Legacies

Over these 60 years, pre-war historical legacies (or, in modern jargon, 'path dependencies') continued to frame the development of labour law. Examples will be found throughout this book, including the concepts of 'subordination' and 'dependency' of the worker (see chapter 4 below); the survival of Bismarckian-type occupational social insurance systems in Germany and some other states (see chapter 6 below); the notion of freedom of association and the right to collective bargaining (see chapter 7 below); the influence of pre-war works councils systems (see chapter 8 below); and the special labour courts (see chapter 9 below).

A number of general principles continued to be important. The basic principle remained that labour is not a commodity. This reflected the ideas of human dignity and equal worth, that emerged in the Romano-Germanic systems as a result of the rejection of the concept of *locatio conductio* (letting and hire), which had implied that the value of labour is determined solely by exchange and not by substantive justice. This principle, as Veneziani has shown, was more or less accepted by the beginning of the twentieth century.[4] Even in the common law countries, where the status of master and servant persisted, the courts refused to 'turn contracts of service into contracts of slavery' and would not force a 'servant' to work for a particular employer or allow a 'servant' or to be transferred to another employer without his or her consent.[5] The Declaration of Philadelphia adopted by the ILO in May 1944 reiterated the Treaty of Versailles 1919 in stating that the first of the principles on which the ILO is based is that 'labour is not a commodity'. The source of this proposition seems to have been a speech by the Irish economist, Dr John Kells Ingram, to the British Trades Union Congress (TUC) meeting in Dublin in 1880, but it has echoes of Karl Marx's insight that capitalism turns labour power into a commodity, and was also later reflected in the 'Workers' Chapter' of Pope Leo XIII's Encyclical *Rerum Novarum* (1891).[6] It was an essential step in the movement towards equality in the labour market to assert the moral basis on which the relation between employer and worker should stand.

In the formative period of labour law, during the industrial revolution in Europe, the main expression of this principle was the struggle for contractual equality between the dependent or subordinated worker and the employer. It was the 'father' of German labour law, Hugo Sinzheimer, who argued that the special function of labour law—'the guardian of human beings in an age of unrestrained materialism'—was to ensure some kind of substantive and not purely formal legal equality between employer and employee.[7] Sinzheimer's conception became, in Kahn-Freund's words, a 'part of the common property of lawyers in Europe'.[8] This was realised in all European countries before the Second World War by protective legislation, initially for children, young persons and women. It was continued in the post-war period (see chapters 3 and 4 below). This has been described by van der Heijden as 'inequality compensation': 'the legislator has considered it useful and necessary to compensate the economic inequality existing between employer and employee through law'.[9] A critical aspect of contractual equality has been legal support for collective organisation, which was strong in the immediate post-war period but has declined since the 1980s (see chapter 7 below), to some extent eclipsed or complemented by the growing emphasis on forms of institutional workers' participation in the enterprise (see chapter 8 below).

Another principle, developed before the Second World War, was that of a uniform labour law—there must be comparable protection for all workers. This

[4] Veneziani (1986) 31–72.
[5] Hepple (1995) 53–54.
[6] O'Higgins (1997) 226–27.
[7] Hepple (1986) 6–12.
[8] Kahn-Freund (1981) 82.
[9] Van der Heijden (1994) 135–36.

was first stated in Article 158 of the Constitution of the Weimar Republic (1919), aimed at the particular problem of the barrier between public and private law. The idea of a uniform labour law was meant to remove the untenable distinctions between different categories of employee by linking public and private law. This principle was accepted in some post-1945 constitutions (eg Italy[10] and Spain[11]), and economic developments have led to the decline of some distinctions such as those between blue-collar (manual) workers and white-collar (non-manual) workers (see chapter 3 below). Comparable protection has become particularly important in the period since the 1980s, when 'new' forms of employment relationship such as part-time work, fixed-term contracts, teleworking and homework, so far from being 'atypical' or 'marginal', became the norm. The problem has been dealt with in various ways, such as by judicial or legislative expansion of the notion of 'worker' (see chapter 4 below), and by EC Directives that require part-time or fixed-term workers to be given comparable treatment to full-time or indefinite contract workers without discrimination (see chapter 3 below).

Convergence and Divergence

There were further processes of convergence towards generally accepted principles in the post-war period, for example in the development of job security laws, anti-discrimination legislation and polices of 'flexicurity' (balancing job protection and flexible working) in respect of new forms of work. However, important differences remained, for example in the use of public and private employment services and the role of public authorities in relation to termination of employment (chapter 3 below); the coverage of labour law and welfare systems (chapters 4 and 6); the adoption of universal benefit systems in preference to work-related insurance systems (chapter 6 below); procedures for collective bargaining, the effects of collective agreements and the right to strike (chapter 7 below); the diversity of methods of workers' representation at plant level (chapter 8 below); and the methods of enforcement of labour law (chapter 9 below).

  In part, these differences reflected differences in the national and regional labour markets, in which employment levels, the entry of women into the labour market and the availability of migrant labour varied considerably from country to country. Most important of all, though, was that some countries had inherited systems of labour relations and labour law from the pre-war period, or in the immediate aftermath of the war, that could be relatively easily adapted to the needs of post-war reconstruction and growth, and later to achieve the labour 'flexibility' demanded by firms who relied on technological innovation in order to improve productivity in the face of increased global competition. The leading

[10] 'The Republic protects labour in all its forms and applications': Italian Constitution 1948, Art 35(1).
[11] 'The law shall regulate a statute for all workers': Spanish Constitution 1979, Art 352.

examples were Germany, Austria, the Netherlands, Belgium and the Nordic countries. On the other side were countries where labour relations were fragmented and decentralised, making difficult any coordination of the actions of management and labour. Leading examples in this respect were Britain and Italy. Spain and Portugal (after democratisation) and France were in a more ambiguous situation.

The Aims, Methods and Scope of this Book

The aim of this book is to make a comparative historical analysis of the processes by which convergences and differences such as these developed. Legal history requires *diachronous* order, examining developments in stages or periods; legal comparison requires *synchronous* order, that, is a cross-evaluation between countries and their institutions in the same period. Comparative legal history requires both diachronous and synchronous orders. Within these orders, we have chosen to discuss developments thematically because this lends itself more readily than a straightforward historical narrative to a comparative analysis of specific aspects of the subject.

Chapter 2 (Bruun and Hepple) shows how the development of labour law has been influenced by the state of the economy and prevailing views on economic policy. Chapter 3 (Ojeda Aviles and Garcia Viña) analyses the main regulatory trends in labour markets, specifically in the regulation of labour supply, employment services, active labour market policies, employment contract strategies and job security. Chapter 4 (Veneziani) describes the evolution of the employment relationship and the social, economic, ideological and cultural factors that have conditioned its structure and essential functions. Chapter 5 (Hepple) discusses the recognition of the fundamental right to equality for workers who are disadvantaged by reason of their status in society, such as race and religion, sex and sexual orientation, disability and age. Chapter 6 (Rebhahn) traces the post-war evolution of social security systems in relation to wage labour. Chapter 7 (Jacobs) explores how the legal regulation of collective labour relations has developed since the Second World War. Chapter 8 (Mückenberger) explains how different structures of workers' representation and participation have developed. Chapter 9 (Malmberg) deals with changes in the procedural rules and institutional arrangements aimed at enforcing substantive rules of labour law.

Periodisation

We have found it useful to divide the post-war experience into five broad historical periods: (i) reconstruction (1945–50); (ii) the welfare state (1950–72); (iii) economic crisis (1973–79); (iv) restructuring and deregulation (1980–89); and

(v) the European response to global capitalism (1990–2004). This periodisation is used for the discussion of economic policy (chapter 2) and the regulation of labour markets (chapter 3), but in other chapters the periodisation is more closely linked to specific legal developments. So in chapter 4, the period of reconstruction is linked to the permanent legacy of the past, the welfare state to the impact of social legislation, economic crisis to the uncertainty about the meaning of subordination, and restructuring and deregulation to deviations from the standard contract, while the setting of minimum standards is seen as a European response to globalisation. In chapter 5, periodisation is framed in terms of the different stages of development of laws on status equality: first, the assertion of equality as a fundamental human right in international instruments and national constitutions (1948–58), secondly, the implementation of the principle of formal equality for women and ethnic groups (1957–75), thirdly, the focus on substantive equality through the concepts of indirect discrimination and positive action (1975–99), and finally, the apparent dawn of comprehensive and transformative equality (2000–4). In chapter 6, the development of social security is divided into two main stages: the construction and consolidation of welfare states (1945–78), and the stabilisation and restructuring of the welfare state (1979–2004). Chapter 7 links the period of reconstruction to building the pillars of collective rights and links the welfare state to free collective bargaining, neo-corporatism and industrial conflict, then examines the responses to economic crisis and the impact of global capitalism on labour relations. Chapter 8 examines continuity and change in workers' representation at the plant and enterprise levels through periods of reconstruction, the welfare state (including an excursus on health and safety representatives), economic crisis, restructuring and deregulation, and EC responses to globalisation. Chapter 9 uses three periods relating to enforcement of labour law: reconstruction and the autonomy of labour law (1945–70), juridification (1970–90), and alternative dispute resolution and Europeanisation (1990–2004). Appendix II contains a chronology of labour legislation showing when different countries adopted their most important laws.

The Countries Compared

The earlier volume on *The Making of Labour Law in Europe*[12] limited the comparisons to nine countries that were members of the EEC in 1980: Belgium, Britain,[13] Denmark, France, Germany,[14] Ireland, Italy, Luxembourg and the

[12] Hepple (1986).

[13] The word 'Britain' is used throughout this book as a shorthand for the United Kingdom of Great Britain and Northern Ireland, which includes England, Wales, Scotland and Northern Ireland. In some respects there are differences between the labour laws of each of the constituent countries.

[14] The description 'Germany' refers to the Federal Republic of Germany, which from 1949 to 1990 covered only the western part of the country. It excludes the German Democratic Republic (GDR), covering the eastern part until 3 October 1990, when unification of the two parts took place on the basis of the FRG Constitution.

Netherlands. In this volume we have expanded the comparison to another six countries that joined the Community before 2004: Austria (1995), Finland (1995), Greece (1981), Portugal (1986), Spain (1986) and Sweden (1995).[15] Profiles of all 15 countries are presented in Appendix I. The common denominator between them is their membership of the EU before 1 May 2004. Our study ends on 1 May 2004, when the former communist states of Poland, Hungary, the Czech Republic, Slovakia, Slovenia, Estonia, Lithuania and Latvia joined the EU, along with Cyprus and Malta. The reason for excluding the former communist states from our study is that the labour laws of those countries followed a different trajectory until the early 1990s. The ways in which they have had to change their labour law systems to the ideas of liberal democracy, and have adopted the *acquis communitaire*, is worthy of a study of its own. Developments after May 2004 belong to contemporary labour law and fall outside the scope of this book.

This book also does not seek to repeat the story of European economic, social and political integration, which has been told many times in other books.[16] However, it is essential to remember that the EEC and, since 1992, the EU and EC have never had exclusive competence in the field of labour law and social policy. Such integration as has occurred in these fields has not been aimed at total harmonisation, still less unification. There has been a 'variable geometry' in social and labour matters, with some countries seeking to avoid EC-imposed labour laws, such as Britain opting out of the Maastricht Social Chapter between 1991 and 1997, while others have wanted a deeper integration in the social field. Since the Lisbon process, started in 2000 (see chapters 2 and 3 below), the emphasis has been on a convergence of outcomes while leaving Member States free to decide on their own employment policies and labour laws within the framework of common objectives. In place of the ideas of harmonisation or a level playing field, there has been a trend towards establishing common minimum standards, such as those embodied in the Community Charter of Fundamental Rights of Workers (1989) and the Nice EU Charter of Fundamental Rights (2000).

Legal Transplants

In order to explain the convergences and differences between European systems of labour law, we examine two kinds of historical relationship. The first is that of direct legal transplants or cross-overs from one country to another. Examples of this before 1945 were the adaptation by many countries of nineteenth century British factory legislation, the extraordinary influence of the Code Napoléon in

---

[15] Denmark, Finland and Sweden are referred to in this book as the 'Nordic' countries. Norway has close ties the other Nordic countries but falls outside the scope of this book because it is not an EU Member State.

[16] See eg Kenner (2003); Hepple (2005) chs 8 and 9; cf Simitis and Lyon-Caen (1996) 1.

the development of contractual ideas in the employment relationship in continental Europe, the spread of Bismarckian schemes of social insurance and, after 1919, standard-setting by the ILO. Since the Second World War 'borrowing' and 'bending' of labour laws has become widespread partly, but not exclusively, as a result of the process of co-ordination and harmonisation within the EC (above).

The 'circulation' of different models between European labour law systems has been taking place at least since the 1970s, when a distinctive EEC labour law emerged.[17] For example, it was the German model of protection of acquired rights on transfers of undertakings that formed the basis for Directive 77/187/EEC on this subject, and the British anti-discrimination legislation of the 1970s that inspired the equality Directives (see chapter 5 below). Nordic family-friendly policies have been very influential in other countries (see chapter 6 below). It cannot be doubted that even the 'soft' law of the Community, such as the Open Method of Co-ordination introduced in 2000, has also contributed to changes in national law-making processes, not by laying down uniform rules but by giving Member States broad indications of the changes they need to make in domestic regulation. In these processes academic experts have played a 'remarkably prominent' role.[18] Non-European models, such as from the US, have also occasionally been transplanted, notably in the field of anti-discrimination legislation (see chapter 5 below).

However, it is important to note that Community Directives on subjects such as collective redundancies, acquired rights of employees on transfers of undertakings, protection in the event of bankruptcy, part-time and fixed-term contracts, hours of work (see chapter 3 below), discrimination (see chapter 5 below) and health and safety did not impose uniformity. They were binding as to the results to be achieved, but left the choice of form and methods to the national authorities. Each Member State had the freedom to adapt Community rules into its own system in a different way, so long as certain minimum conditions laid down in the Directive were followed. The European Court of Justice (ECJ), which was interested in promoting European integration, played a crucial role in developing Community-wide fundamental rights, but comparative research has shown that national courts and legislatures have generally insisted on translating these in their own way into their systems of labour law.[19] This has been justified on a variety of grounds, such as constitutional provisions, enforcement mechanisms, and the role of the social partners and collective bargaining in each system.[20] Institutional differences have resulted in a tension between divergence and convergence.[21]

Legal transplants of the kind described are not either rejected or domesticated. In Teubner's words, they 'unleash an evolutionary dynamics in which the external

[17] Sciarra (2001) 15.
[18] Sciarra (2004b) 203.
[19] Sciarra (2001) 15.
[20] Sciarra (2001) 14–15.
[21] Weiss (2007) 485.

rule's meaning will be reconstructed and the internal context will undergo fundamental change'.[22] A question with which this book is concerned is how the
transplanted rule or institution has been transformed in the new environment,
and what changes this has stimulated in the system as a whole. There is a
well-know thesis by Kahn-Freund that 'rules and institutions relating to collective
labour relations are usually too closely connected with the structure and organization of political power in a particular environment to be successfully imported
elsewhere'.[23] The evidence in this book (and elsewhere) would lead us to modify
that statement.

> Concepts and ideas—but not specific institutions—can be borrowed from another sys-
> tem of collective labour law, provided four essential conditions are met. These
> conditions are: (1) a social consensus between management and labour; (2) an organic
> relationship between a specific social need and the form of regulation adopted; (3) an
> internationalist and open-minded legal culture; and (4) the form of labour law
> adopted must contribute to improved national economic performance.[24]

A transplant that does not meet most, let alone all, of these conditions is likely to
fail, for example the unsuccessful adoption of the American Taft–Hartley model
in the British Industrial Relations Act 1971 (see chapters 2 and 7 below). Even if
the transplant takes root, the rule or institution takes on a life of its own in its
new environment. Examples include the Europeanisation of the works councils
model (see chapter 8 below), the different ways in which collective agreements
have normative effects on the employment contract (chapter 7 below) and the
use of alternative disputes settlement procedures (chapter 9 below). The structures and culture of each labour relations and political system determine how a
transplanted rule or institution develops.

Parallel Developments

The second kind of historical relationship with which we are concerned is the
'inner' social, economic and political relationships of parallel developments in
different countries. As in *The Making of Labour Law in Europe*,[25] we reject the
now largely discredited view that all national systems follow the same process of
development, and are sceptical of suggested universal trends. Our view is that the
development of legal systems in general, and labour law in particular, is the
product of a variety of factors which are neither 'natural' nor 'necessary'. The task
of the comparative labour lawyer is to examine the specific features of historical
change in each country. For example, in the first volume, we sought to explain
why the work book and police supervision were significant features of the labour

---

[22] Teubner (2001) 418.
[23] Kahn-Freund (1974) 635.
[24] Hepple (1999) 1.
[25] Hepple (1986) 3–4.

market in continental Europe but not in Britain, why in some countries the eight-hour day was achieved by collective bargaining and in others by legislation, and why 'workers' participation' took the form of shop stewards in Britain and Denmark but of works councils in Germany. In this book, we examine, for example, why some countries, such as France, regulated working time by legislation, while others, such as Britain and Denmark, left this to collective bargaining or individual agreement (see chapter 3 below), why some countries were slower or more resistant than others in adapting the contract of employment to economic and technological changes (see chapter 4 below), why some countries adopted equal pay and anti-discrimination laws before others (see chapter 5 below), why some adopted universal social security benefits and others work-related insurance (see chapter 6 below), why 'positive' rights to strike were embraced in some legal systems but not in others (see chapter 7 below), and why juridification has been more apparent in some systems than in others (see chapter 9 below).

The Changing Boundaries, Purposes and Sources of Labour Law

Boundaries

A comparative historical study of this kind rests on the assumption that a common definition of 'labour law' can be found. In *The Making of Labour Law in Europe*,[26] we showed that, with a few exceptions before 1939, studies of labour law were nearly all about the contract of employment and, less frequently, protective legislation. Collective labour relations tended to be neglected. The notable exceptions were Germany and Italy, where the legal nature of collective agreements had been discussed by scholars since the beginning of the twentieth century, and the Nordic countries following the landmark Danish September agreement of 1899 between unions and employers.[27]

German scholars of the Weimar period identified three special features of labour law. First, it was created not only by the state but also by autonomous groups, in particular employers and trade unions. The interaction between autonomous norms (self-help) and state intervention was thus for these scholars a central theme of labour law. When analysing state labour law they regarded it as important to distinguish between direct coercion (eg criminal law) and facilitative or power-conferring laws which allow or support the parties to make their own rules (private law-making), or even, on occasion, the opportunity to

[26] Hepple (1986) 6–10.
[27] Hasselbalch (2002)16.

bypass or derogate from state law. A second feature of labour law as it was developed in Europe before the Second World War was the notion of the contract of employment as distinct from the general principles of contract in the civil law systems, and its emergence from the law of 'master and servant' in common law systems. In both civil and common law systems, labour law was seen as the law of 'dependent' labour with the consequence that independent (self-employed) workers were excluded from its scope. A third feature, inferred from the idea of dependency, was that all forms of regulation of the worker's subordination to the employer's commands form the essential subject matter of labour law (see chapter 4 below).

The post-war period saw the consolidation and final breakthrough of labour law as a separate legal discipline in all European countries. The core subjects included collective labour relations, works councils (where they existed) and individual employment law, and often also trade union law and health and safety at work. In some countries, such as the Netherlands, the law on social security was seen as an annex to labour law; in its widest sense 'social law' came to describe both labour and social security law.[28] The starting point for most scholars in the period before the 1980s continued to be the inequality between the supplier and purchaser of labour power. Labour law was seen as serving primarily a social rather than economic function, providing institutions and processes, mainly collective, that created a fair balance between employers and workers.

Paradoxically, no sooner had labour law established itself in this way than its boundaries and rationale began to be seriously questioned. One challenge was the inability of traditional labour laws to protect the rapidly increasing number of workers in new work relationships that could not readily be defined as 'subordinate' or 'dependent' labour (see chapter 4 below). The new labour force included those on part-time and fixed-term contracts, on-call contracts and the like, and also those supplied as temporary workers through an intermediary. Even if not totally excluded from labour law, their protection was uneven, patchy and discriminatory (see chapter 3 below). An important part of our study is to compare the attempts made in different countries to extend the boundaries of labour law to all those under 'personal work contracts' in both the formal and informal economies.

Purposes[29]

A second challenge came, mainly after the 1970s as the post-war consensus broke down, from liberal and neo-liberal theories that tended to ignore the inequitable distribution of wealth and power in society (see below). Some scholars argued that it is no longer appropriate to focus on the 'protective' features of labour law.

[28] Van der Ven (1986) 147–48.
[29] This section draws extensively on Hepple (2003) 181.

They suggested that the subject should be reconceptualised around its advantages and disadvantages to employers, the economy and society at large.[30] Their starting point was regulatory theory. For example, Collins remarked that

> The regulatory agenda for the traditional field of labour law commences with a disarmingly naïve question: Why regulate the employment relation? . . . Why should we exclude ordinary market principles such as the general law of contract and property from employment relations in favour of special rules?[31]

He said that there is a 'heavy burden of proof' on advocates of employment rights to 'establish the superiority of regulation over ordinary market rules', and that 'the special regulation must be demonstrated to be efficient in the sense that its costs do not outweigh the potential benefits or improvements'.[32] Not surprisingly, in view of the presumption in favour of private law rules, regulatory theory was used to justify deregulation of the employment relationship. 'Deregulation' was not infrequently portrayed as an absence of regulation; in fact, it meant leaving regulation to ordinary market rules, to the private law of property and contract.

Alternative versions of regulatory theory were also applied to labour law from the late 1980s onwards. In these versions, special regulation of the employment relationship could be justified on two grounds. The first is market failure—that is, where there is a significant deviation between the ideal outcomes that would result from perfect competition and the actual operation of the labour market. So when the labour power of some is undervalued, this leads to productive inefficiency, hampers innovation and encourages short-term strategies and destructive competition. Only employment rights (eg to a minimum wage, equal pay for women and men) can correct this market failure. The second justification for regulation is to correct unacceptable distributive outcomes; for example, regulation may be necessary to enable those who wish to enter the labour market to do so by providing better education, training and childcare. However, even in this version of regulatory theory, there remains a presumption against regulation unless it can be shown that it will not harm those whom it was designed to help: for example, increasing the job security of workers is justifiable only if this leads to better selection and training, and monitoring of performance of workers which outweighs the risk that the employer will hire fewer workers. Some advocates of this version of market regulation argue that labour market institutions that encourage 'high trust' or co-operation lead to superior economic performance. This leads them to support more legal provision for information, consultation and other forms of workers' participation in the enterprise.[33]

---

[30] Davidow and Langille (2006) 3–4.
[31] Collins (2000) 4.
[32] Ibid.
[33] Deakin and Wilkinson (2000) 56–61.

Another variant of regulatory theory that has been influential since the 1980s regards 'competitivity' of the enterprise and 'flexibility' of work practices as of central importance in the context of globalisation. The liberalisation of trade and investment within the EC, by removing barriers on the free movement of capital, goods, services and labour, is said to throw the labour law and welfare systems of the Member States into competition with each other. This leads to a process of market selection by which states adopt the most efficient forms of regulation. Countries with low labour costs attract investment; this in turn leads to greater demands for wages, higher wages, and improved working and living conditions. This kind of argument has frequently been used against harmonisation of labour laws and the setting of minimum standards.

Even those who reject some or all of these regulatory approaches have sought to shift the traditional focus on the 'protective' purposes of labour law (which implies that this is given by a paternalistic state to vulnerable individuals or groups) towards an emphasis on 'rights' to decent conditions of work, fair pay, job security, participation in trade unions and collective bargaining, and so on. Rights, rather than 'protection', are increasingly seen as a means of redressing the inequality in bargaining power between employer and worker. In this labour movements have won allies in the human rights movement since the Second World War; sometimes the human rights movement has been ahead of trade unions in pressing for change, such as in respect of equality for ethnic minorities and migrants at work (see chapter 5 below). A distinctive feature of rights discourse in the employment context in recent decades has been the individualisation of these claims: it is the individual, not the collective group, that becomes the subject of labour law, as seen, for example, in the rights under Article 11 (freedom of association) of the European Convention on Human Rights (ECHR) (see chapter 7 below).

One must agree with Klare[34] is that the law regulating work cannot be fitted into a single overarching paradigm. In this book, we examine the ways that different perspectives—'protective', 'deregulatory', 'rights-based regulation', 'competitive regulation' and 'human rights'—have shaped labour law in different periods.

Sources

International Human Rights

The International Labour Organisation was founded at the end of the First World War.[35] By 1939, the International Labour Conference had adopted 67 conventions and 66 recommendations, many on subjects already familiar in European countries, such as hours of work, minimum age for employment, employment of

---

[34] Klare (2002) 3.
[35] Ramm (1986) 279–84.

women and health and safety. After the Second World War, the ILO became a specialised agency of the UN, preserving its independence and unique tripartite structure in which governments, employers and workers (2–1–1) were all represented. The standard-setting system was improved, but proposals to tilt representation in favour of workers, or for equal representation of government, employers and workers (2–2–2), were rejected. The Declaration of Philadelphia, adopted at the 26th annual conference in 1944, which was appended to the ILO's revised constitution, reaffirmed the 'fundamental principles' on which the ILO is based, in particular that:

— Labour is not a commodity;
— Freedom of expression and of association are essential to sustained progress;
— Poverty anywhere constitutes a danger to prosperity everywhere.

The Declaration went beyond the Treaty of Versailles by recognising social justice as a distinct objective in its own right. Article II(a) stated that 'all human beings irrespective of race, creed or sex, have the right to pursue their material well-being and their spiritual development in conditions of freedom and dignity, of economic security and equal opportunity'. This was expressed as 'fully applicable to all peoples everywhere', significantly not limited to workers (Article V). All 15 countries in this study are members of the ILO, and were parties to the ILO's Declaration of Fundamental Principles and Rights at Work (1998). They have all ratified the 'core' conventions on freedom of association and collective bargaining (C.87 and C.98), forced labour (C.29 and C.105), non-discrimination (C.101 and C.111) and minimum age in employment, and the prohibition and elimination of the worst forms of child labour (C. 138 and 182), as well as a large number of other conventions.[36]

The UN Declaration of Human Rights, adopted by the UN General Assembly in 1948, upheld not only civil and political rights, such as freedom of association, but also listed social and and economic rights. These included the right to social security (Article 23), the right to rest and leisure (Article 24), the right to a standard of living adequate for the health and well-being of the worker and his family (Article 25), the right to education (Article 26), and the right to participate in the cultural life of the community and to share in scientific advancement and its benefits (Article 27). The inclusion of these rights was supported by the US delegation (led by Eleanor Roosevelt) but opposed by Britain and some other Commonwealth countries (notably Australia and white-dominated South Africa).[37] It was contemplated that all these rights would be elaborated in a single human rights instrument, but in the atmosphere of the cold war, western countries became less enamoured of the idea of enforceable economic and social rights. The result was that two separate instruments were adopted by the UN in

---

[36] On the work and effectiveness of the ILO, including the Declaration of Fundamental Principles and Rights at Work, see Hepple (2005) 25–67.
[37] Steiner and Alston (1996) 260.

1966 (in force 1976): the International Covenant on Civil and Political Rights and the International Covenant on Economic, Social and Cultural Rights. These were ratified by the 15 countries in this study.

The Council of Europe's Convention for the Protection of Human Rights and Fundamental Freedoms, adopted in 1950 (ECHR), was also confined to civil and political rights, and it was left to the much weaker European Social Charter (ESC), adopted in 1961 (revised 1996), to deal with economic and social rights. These instruments were also ratified by all 15 countries in this study.

The separation of economic and social rights from civil and political ones was to have lasting effects. The former came to be regarded as merely aspirational, and inferior to civil and political rights.[38] This has been a particular obstacle to the development of rights to equality at work (see chapter 5 below), and of the 'right to work' (see chapter 3 below). It also pervades the approach to enforcement of social rights (see chapter 9 below).

Mutliple National Sources

The legal structure of labour law has become increasingly complex because of the multiplicity of sources of regulation. The task of comparison is made exceptionally difficult by the different hierarchies and relationships between these sources, such as constitutions, statutes, collective agreements, work rules and implied contractual terms, in each country.

As already noted, new constitutions adopted after 1945 recognised the rights of labour in varying degrees. The rights included the freedom of trade unions and collective bargaining and the right to strike (see chapter 7 below), and also social rights, including the 'right to work' (see chapter 3 below). The presence of a written constitution or a bill of 'fundamental' rights must be understood, in a formal sense, as a law 'higher' than the one laid down in an ordinary statute within the hierarchy of norms. The comparative panorama offers different trends and models of the ways that constitutional rights have an influence on a labour law. For example, in Italy, the Constitutional Court has recognised their indirect effect. In Germany the same results have been achieved with a different technique, construing fundamental rights as *boni mores* clauses in the law of obligations. The doctrine of *Drittwirkung der Grundrecht* served to protect freedom of speech and the privacy of the employee in the employment relationship. The case law has focused on certain basic principles, particularly those relevant in areas such as the abolition of forced labour and non-discrimination, and the 'rule of law' in the 'social state'. In France, too, the 'constitutional block' (Constitutions 1789–1946–1958) has had a strong effect on labour law through the decisions of the Council of State, for example on the right to strike.[39]

The importance of constitutions is, of course, conditioned by their content. The Danish Constitution promulgated in 1953 does not contain any explicit

[38] Fredman (2008) 9.
[39] Pélissier et al (2006) 72–73.

social rights.[40] The limited impact of fundamental rights in the Netherlands was because the Constitution contained almost exclusively civil and political fundamental rights, while the social rights were included only later by the reform in 1983 (Articles 1–23).[41] Above all, in the Netherlands there is no constitutional control of statutes. However, certain fundamental rights have been imported by the judicial strategy that recognises the direct applicability of the Articles of the ESC on the right to strike, and Article 26 of the UN Treaty on civil and political rights (general prohibition of discrimination). But this has proved to be a weak strategy because most of the provisions of international treaties do not lend themselves to direct application to individual employment contracts. This made it more attractive to integrate the international texts into domestic labour law through the good faith (*bona fides*) or public policy (*bonos mores*) principles.

Britain has no written constitution, though since 2000 civil rights (such as freedom of association and non-discrimination) under the ECHR have been incorporated into domestic British law, enabling courts to invalidate subordinate legislation and administrative acts in conflict with convention rights. However, Acts of Parliament cannot be invalidated, and the court can do no more than make a declaration of incompatibility with convention rights which Parliament is free to ignore in theory, although it has not done so in practice. In other legal systems there is a pyramidal structure placing at the top public legal sources (international or national bills of rights, codes or statutes, regulations), followed by the autonomous sources (collective agreements, individual contracts of employment, works rules, custom and practice). The strongest example is Belgium, where the hierarchy of labour law sources has been laid down explicitly by Article 51 of the Law of 5 December 1968 (mandatory legal provisions—generally binding collective agreements—written individual agreements—sectoral collective agreements that are not generally binding—works rules—supplementary legal provisions—verbal individual agreements—custom). Austria also has a clear hierarchy (see Appendix I below). On the other hand, the hierarchy of labour law sources is less clear in the Netherlands, being dependent on general principles of civil and public law.

The entire hierarchical order is affected by the principle of applying the law 'most favourable to the worker', which can be based on different legal techniques. This principle, once highly disputed, was affirmed in 1996 by the French Court of Cassation,[42] which stated that it is a 'fundamental principle of labour law, according to which, in a case of conflict of rules, the most favourable to the worker must be applied'. In some systems, such as Austria, a collective contract deviating to the detriment of the worker is void, and an individual contract may deviate from a collective agreement only in a way favourable to the worker. In this respect, the common law approach differs from the civil law systems. The common law allows judges to intervene radically in shaping the content of the

---

[40] Hasselbalch and Jacobsen (1999) 7–8.
[41] Jacobs (2004a) 32.
[42] Pélissier et al (2004) 134, note 1.

contract because of the way in which external sources can be made effective within the employment relationship. The sources include terms imposed by or under statutes, and terms presumptively implied under the rules of common law.[43] More generally, common law distinguishes between terms implied in law (held by judges to be essential to a particular relationship) and terms implied in fact (derived from the ascertainment of the intention of the parties as emerges from the context), but the optional nature of implied terms (including custom) and the absence of imperative norms means that implied terms can always be replaced by express ones even if these are less favourable to the employee.[44]

The widespread use of collective agreements in most western European states in the 1950s and 1960s (see chapter 7 below) meant that this relatively new source of law had to be incorporated into the framework of legal sources, and had to be protected from all derogations *in pejus* (less favourable) made by private parties. In this respect, the Italian Civil Code gave, and still gives, an extremely strong effect to the collective agreement as 'the automatic replacement' of provisions in an individual contract, pre- or post-dating the collective agreement, that is inconsistent with the collective agreement (Article 2077). This juridical effect was regarded a consequence of the quasi-public nature of collective agreements in the fascist regime. After the restoration of civil and social liberties, the same rules were interpreted as a surviving technical device to be applied to collective agreements, since this was an expression of private collective autonomy. In the period of economic restructuring, this protected collective bargaining in its function of distributing incomes and conditions of work equally among the labour force.

Generally speaking, freedom of contract itself between individual parties is heavily conditioned in countries where collective bargaining is the main source of regulating the terms and conditions of work. The rule that it is impossible to overrule the terms laid down by collective agreement is the backbone of the Danish bargaining system.[45] The juridical principle of 'inderogability' was also observed in other civil law systems, which consider that normative clauses in the collective agreement should not be excluded, varied or adapted by the individual parties. The scenario changed from the late 1970s onward when, because of the economic crisis and oil slump of 1973–79, high rates of inflation and public expenditure deficits in some countries (Italy, Germany), statutes began to allow derogations *in pejus* by way of individual contracts of employment. This became a feature of EC legislation prescribing minimum standards (eg on working time) in the 1990s (see chapter 7 below).

The term 'inderogability' does not belong to the British vocabulary because it is 'deeply offensive' to the classical common law of contract.[46] In common law, collective agreements are also presumed not to be enforceable between

---

[43] Freedland (2003) 115.
[44] Hepple and Fredman (1986) 94.
[45] Hasselbalch and Jacobsen (1999) 41.
[46] Wedderburn (1992) 249.

the collective parties. This meant that, in comparison with civil law countries, British labour law left workers doubly exposed to aggressive employers: the unions could not legally enforce collective agreements, and employers could usually end the incorporation of collective terms into individual contracts by the simple expedient of giving due notice to terminate the individual contract and offering re-employment on less advantageous terms. This was mitigated to some extent by the introduction of statutory protection against unfair dismissals from 1972 (but even then, employers could often justify the changes on economic grounds) and also, after 1975, by EC legislation requiring consultation before collective dismissals.

Another controversial question has been whether constitutional rights merely serve to protect the individual in relation to the state or whether they also operate between citizens, such as the parties to a contract of employment. It should be kept in mind that many legal provisions—like those included in the Italian Civil Code of 1942 and the German Civil Code of 1900, concerning contractual relationships—originated in a different cultural atmosphere and, in the second half of the twentieth century, were no longer compatible with the basic post-war constitutional principles. The German Federal Labour Court, for example, decided, on the basis of Article 3.2 of the Bonn Basic law, that the constitutional principle of equal rights of men and women also governs collective agreements.[47]

Factors Influencing the Transformation of Labour Laws

Indicators of Comparative Development

A traditional approach in comparative legal studies is to divide legal systems into just a few large groups of 'legal families'.[48] There are different views about which criteria should be used to distinguish between these families: should it be the historical sources of law, the general structure of systems, their legal techniques, their substance or their ideology, or a combination of these factors? The approach that we favoured in *The Making of Labour Law in Europe*[49] was to concentrate on the substance of labour laws over time, having due regard to the factors which had shaped that substance, such as economic and social development, the changing nature of the state, the character of employers' and labour movements, and ideology. We suggested a number of indicators by which to measure the comparative development of labour laws in different European countries. These ranged from the earliest forms of law, such as the protection of children, young persons and women, up to measures to promote self-regulation

[47] Kahn-Freund (1976a) 269.
[48] Zweigert and Kötz (1998) 63.
[49] Hepple (1986) 11–12.

by workers' and employers' organisations and to facilitate workers' participation at the plant and enterprise level and the integration of workers' representatives in the administration of the economy and of the state. By 1945, these indicators had been reached, in different forms, in nearly all the nine countries studied, and the process continued after the Second World War.

The 'transformation' of labour laws involves changes not simply in form, but of substance. The distinction may be made between 'path dependence', when changes follow the path of previous laws and policies, and so are generally changes in form, and 'path departure', when a juncture is reached at which substantively different laws and policies begin to be followed. It is possible to draw up another list of indicators of the comparative extent of 'transformation' of labour laws since 1945, in the sense of 'path departures'. Among these are the following:

1. The classification within the sphere of labour law of personal work contracts beyond the classic model of subordinate employment relationships (see chapter 4 below).
2. The regulation of new forms of personal work contracts, such as part-time, fixed-term and agency work (see chapter 3 below).
3. The privatisation of employment services and the legitimation of temporary work agencies (see chapter 3 below).
4. Individual rights against unfair dismissal, and for payment of compensation in the event of redundancy (see chapter 3 below).
5. Protection of acquired rights of workers on the transfer of undertakings (see chapter 3 below).
6. Mandatory information and consultation with workers' representatives in the event of collective (economic) dismissals and transfers of undertakings (see chapter 8 below).
7. Active labour market policies to promote high levels of employment, particularly for vulnerable groups such as women, young persons, ethnic minorities, older workers and disabled persons (see chapter 3 below).
8. Laws against discrimination in employment on grounds of sex and sexual orientation, race and religion, age and disability, and positive duties to promote equality of opportunity (see chapter 5 below).
9. Enforceable social welfare rights in cases of important needs; means-tested social assistance in cases of poverty or unemployment; access to charge-free health care, at least in severe cases financed by the community or by insurance; and provision for old-age benefits above the level of social assistance (see chapter 6 below).
10. The 'containment' of freedom of association, the right to collective bargaining and the right to strike (see chapter 7 below).
11. Rights of workers' representatives at the plant and enterprise level to information and consultation on management decisions affecting employment, and some rights to co-determination on social matters (see chapter 8 below).

12. 'Social dialogue' between employers' organisations and trade unions at the European, national and sectoral levels (see chapter 7 below).
13. Individualised and juridified procedures for the enforcement of labour laws (see chapter 9 below).

This list of indicators of 'transformation' is not exhaustive but, in similar fashion to the earlier indicators of 'making', provides a guide to the extent of 'transformation' in each labour law system. In seeking explanations for the transformations that have occurred, the contributors have considered a number of factors, including socio-economic developments and policies, the changing nature of the state, the character of workers' movements and civil society, and ideology. This approach does not exclude the relevance of other factors such as legal techniques: for example, in explaining the development of the concept of the contract of employment, the differences between the legal methods of civil law systems and the common law ones are very important (see chapter 4 below). However, the practical effect of our approach is to make historical comparisons specific, rather than to fit labour law systems into traditional families such as Romanistic, Germanic and Anglo-American. The comparative substance of labour laws cuts across these categories.

Economic Developments and Policies

The connection between labour laws and economic development and policy merits a chapter on its own (see chapter 2 below). Here we simply note that while the 'making' of labour law was the product of the industrial revolution, of the shift from an agrarian handicraft economy to one in which machine manufacture in mills, mines and factories (including the Fordist system of production) dominated, 'transformation' has been the outcome of the shift to a post-Fordist, service- and information technology-based society. The 'new' systems of labour law have been a response to global competition and the decentralisation and fragmentation of work and the workforce, but, as we found in respect of 'making',[50] there is no mechanical connection between an economic 'base' and a 'superstructure' of labour law. The 'timing of changes in legal institutions can and does materially affect the pace and character of economic development',[51] but equally the transformations in labour laws may come well after the economic changes. Several contributors point to the paradox that the golden age of labour legislation and the welfare state occurred in most countries in the 1970s and 1980s, when the period of economic growth had already slowed down or ended, and there was stagflation and slump (see eg chapters 2 and 8 below). The deep explanation for this may lie in the contradiction between political freedom and

---

[50] Hepple (1986) 14–15.
[51] Landes (1969) 199.

economic subordination and the inequality of power and wealth.[52] Demands for greater job security and welfare came from enfranchised workers, including women who demanded equal treatment in the labour market. These demands had to be met by democratically elected governments as the price for continuing economic subordination, even when they had become less affordable.

The Changing Nature of the State

This kind of interaction between political democracy and economic subordination is underlined when one considers the changing nature of the state since the Second World War. The form of state under which labour law was 'made' was liberal constitutionalism (with some notable exceptions, such as the German Empire before 1914), characterised by the active promotion of laissez-faire, which meant giving almost uncontrolled power to property owners, particularly the owners of capital. Moreover, the 'public' sphere of the state and the private sphere of economic life (civil society) were separated. Key to the 'making' of labour law was the participation by workers in the 'public' sphere in order to improve their situation in the economic sphere. This led, even before the Second World War (eg in the Weimar Republic), to the recognition of some social 'rights' of citizenship: labour laws, instead of being the 'gift' of an enlightened ruling class, became the 'rights' of workers and their collective organisations, who could exercise pressure on the state.[53]

This process was accelerated, after 1945, by the building of neo-corporatist social democratic welfare states, which were based on steady economic growth and rising levels of employment until the 1970s. Under the welfare state there was a trade-off between economic dependence and social rights. In return for continuing to be subject to hierarchical management organisation, it was understood that there would be a guarantee of job and income security.[54] The dominant task of the state in relation to labour relations, which remained relatively stable, was to maintain 'balanced' industrial pluralism. The 'principal purpose of labour law' was seen by Kahn-Freund as being 'to regulate, to support, and to restrain the power of management and the power of organised labour'.[55] The welfare state aimed to provide the institutions and processes, mainly collective, that created a 'fair' balance between employers and workers. The focus was on subordinated workers within the employment relationship and not on the wider labour market. 'Rights' were of increasing importance in order to end the distinction in liberal states between the 'private' sphere of economic life and the 'public' sphere of what was now directly controlled by the state. The new rights, such as the 'right to work' (see chapter 3 below), were different from the rights of the

---

[52] *Cf* Desai (2005) 310.
[53] Hepple (1986) 15–22.
[54] Supiot (2001) 151–55.
[55] Kahn-Freund (1972) 5.

individual proclaimed in the French Revolution and in most liberal constitutions. 'They were claims on the state to provide work and economic security and to recognize the collective interests of workers through the rights to organize, to bargain collectively, and to strike.'[56] However, not all democratic states created legal 'rights'; for example, the British approach 'was to defend social and organisational "rights" won through industrial struggle, using the law on a pragmatic basis only when voluntary means were inadequate',[57] although from the 1960s onwards there was also a growing 'floor of rights' for individual employees in Britain. Moreover, in all the western democracies the desire to emphasise the priority of political rights and freedoms, in contrast to the communist countries' claims that their workers had greater job security and social protection, led to artificial distinctions between political and socio-economic rights (above).

When the post-war welfare state consensus broke down in the 1980s, the character of European states became increasingly 'deregulatory' based on neo-liberal theories (see above). Britain took the lead in this under the Thatcher (Conservative) government, elected in 1979. The downsizing of the British state in controlling the economy began with the deregulation of capital movements, so removing 'a basic building block for the state's control over the economy'.[58] One consequence of this was that the state could no longer run large deficits, and economists ceased to believe that such deficits could achieve full employment. State intervention in the economy and welfare spending declined. This was accompanied by privatisation and the breaking of collective union power through legal restrictions, and by crushing strikes, such as that of the miners in 1984 (see chapters 2 and 7 below). By contrast, the French socialists (led by Mitterand), who came to power in 1981, followed aggressive Keynesian policies, increasing public expenditure and the budget deficit in response to the crisis of profitability and rising unemployment. At the same time, they strengthened labour laws (eg *lois Auroux*). This 'competition' between the French welfare state and the British neo-liberal one was 'won' by Britain, whose economy began to revive, while that of France declined and the new measures had to be severely modified after 1983. This was not a true competition because of the many differences in starting points, but Thatcher's success (and that of Reagan in the US) led the continental states to become increasingly neo-liberal in respect of the labour market of the late 1980s and 1990s. Italy, after experiencing a new burst of pro-worker legislation in the early 1990s, moved by the turn of the century to greater privatisation and individualisation. The Nordic countries, however, managed to retain strong collective organisation as the basis of labour law while modifying labour legislation, which was regarded as being too restrictive, or made the legislation open to deviation by collective agreement.[59] In Germany, too, deregulation never became mainstream and the collective labour law

[56] Hepple (2005) 259.
[57] Ibid.
[58] Desai (2005) 298.
[59] Hasselbalch (2002) 34.

framework was left largely untouched, but flexibility was introduced by opening up collective agreements to plant agreements and, after 1998, by attempts to 'reform' the social security system.

In fact, most states did not go as far as the neo-liberal advocates of de-collectivisation and deregulation of employment rights would have liked. For example, all states maintained their laws against unfair dismissal and for compensation in the event of redundancy (see chapter 3 below). Most striking of all was the enactment of comprehensive anti-discrimination legislation, partly in response to the changes in the labour market (feminisation, migration, ageing population, etc), but also due to the pressure of feminist and other human rights movements (below). Towards the end of the 1990s, most European states came to espouse the ideas of 'fundamental human rights'—including labour rights— although some, like Britain, were more reluctant than others to do so. The states were increasingly characterised by 'rights-based' regulation of the labour market. Two consequences of this were the growing individualisation of employment rights and dispute-settlement procedures, and the juridification of labour relations (see chapter 9 below). Human resource managers and trade union officials turned increasingly to their lawyers.

The Character of the Employers and Labour Movements and the Growing Influence of Civil Society

In the 'making' of labour law, before the Second World War, the relationship between the trade unions and political parties was a crucial factor.[60] The depoliticisation of most European trade unions after the war, and the weakening of their links with communist, socialist and liberal parties, reduced their direct influence on labour legislation. France, Italy, Spain and Portugal were exceptions. The end of the cold war in 1989 narrowed the ideological and political gap. European unions were able to join in a single confederation (the European Trade Union Confederation). Trade unions in most countries continued to exert pressure, and were particularly successful in periods of neo-corporatist co-operation, such as the social dialogues in Austria, Belgium and the Netherlands, which effectively gave law-making powers to the social partners (see chapter 7 below), and the 'social contract' between the Labour government and the Trades Union Congress in Britain in the 1970s, which promised wage restraint in return for employment protection legislation (see chapters 2 and 7 below). In the former dictatorships—Spain, Portugal and Greece—the contribution of trade unions to the struggle for democracy was rewarded by extensive modern legislation supporting trade unions and the rights to collective bargaining and to strike.

The decline in union membership was reflected in the increasing number of mergers and a concentration into a few relatively large organisations. Their

---

[60] Hepple (1986) 22–26.

weakness, in the wake of changes in the labour market, from the 1980s onwards made unions more reliant than ever before on the 'method of legislation'; in particular, EC legislation was favoured as a means of counteracting the 'social dumping' resulting from globalisation. The new forms of legislation gave a role to trade unions in negotiating derogations from statutory standards. This was a recognition of their weakness rather than their strength because they were put on the defensive against employers' demands for greater 'flexibility'. The character of employers' organisations also changed, including the ending of the divisions between 'economic' and 'social' bodies (see chapter 7 below). Decentralisation of collective bargaining meant a loss of central organisational control, although in some countries, such as Germany, local agreements continued to be integrated into national and sectoral arrangements.

Perhaps the most significant change has been the growing importance of civil society organisations and action. For example, the rise of the feminist movement had a direct impact on anti-discrimination legislation and family-friendly policies, as did activists seeking rights for ethnic minorities and migrants, disabled people, homosexuals and older workers (see chapter 5 below). The students' and workers' demonstrations around May 1968 in France and elsewhere produced changes in cultural attitudes (see chapter 2 below), and also on issues such as workers' representation at the plant and enterprise level (see chapter 8 below).

Ideology

In the 'making' of labour law, no single ideology predominated; the law was the outcome of struggles between conflicting ideologies, including the ideologies of the market and self-help, of state-help, socialism and social Christianity, and of patriarchy.[61] In the period after 1945, new or recast ideologies became important. The most significant clash was between the supporters of liberal capitalist democracy and the supporters of one or other form of democratic socialism or social democracy. Confessional divisions based on Christianity declined. Soviet-style socialism had only a very limited appeal in the western countries, apart from France and Italy in the early post-war years, and by the 1980s had become widely discredited both ideologically and in practice. There was a revival of feminist ideas and a new landscape of human rights. To many in the labour and socialist movements in Europe, who remembered the Great Depression, Keynesian economics had solved the problems of unemployment and had pointed the way to steady economic growth, on the basis of which workers could get a larger share of income and better conditions, and public expenditure could expand the welfare state. This could ensure a harmonious equilibrium between capital and labour within a framework of labour laws that enhanced collective organisation as a countervailing force to the power of capital.

[61] Hepple (1986) 26–30.

This ideology came under increasing criticism, both academically and politically, as economic crisis reappeared in the late 1970s. There was a revival of nineteenth-century liberal ideology. This, as Desai points out, is somewhat misleadingly labelled neo-liberalism.[62] We need to distinguish, in his view, between 'mere conservatism' (such as that of the World Bank and the transnational corporations), which retains a large role for the state, trade unions and workers' protection, and 'liberalism' or 'libertarianism', which takes the view that the state and other agencies cannot control civil society and the economy, and should not try to do so; it rests on an almost unquestioning belief in the power of markets and the profit motive. This liberal ideology—espoused especially by Mrs Thatcher's government in Britain—was reflected in the work of Hayek, who argued that trade unions used labour law to cartelise the market, so that in the British context they had to be stripped of their 'special privileges' which protected them from the operation of the ordinary law of obligations.[63] In relation to individual rights, such as against unfair dismissal and discrimination, Epstein, of the University of Chicago, claimed that such legislation interferes with the efficient incentive structures provided by the law of contracts.[64] Political parties and social partners in European countries varied in their addiction to these ideas, but none of them went as far as the liberal ideologues might have liked.

As prosperity and stability began to return to Europe in the late 1990s, the ideology of the 'Third Way' began to permeate labour law policy. This took many forms, but, as Fredman explains, had several common themes.[65] First, it rejected the liberal faith in free markets and hostility to the state, but its supporters also rejected the traditional social democratic state, arguing for a new 'balance' between the individual and the state within a competitive market economy. Secondly, the idea of individual responsibility (which in an earlier age might have been called 'self-help') was given renewed importance. While rejecting the complete 'hollowing out' of the welfare state, supporters of the 'Third Way' emphasised that individuals should take primary responsibility for themselves. Thirdly, equality of opportunity is a central tenet (see chapter 5 below). Finally, the 'Third Way' stressed the importance of social inclusion, active citizenship and democracy. At the time our story ends, this was an influential ideology of labour law in most European countries. But this will not, as some have forecast, be 'the end of ideology' in shaping labour law.

The Future

There are two underlying socio-economic factors that bring into question the very survival of the labour and social law systems of regulated capitalism as

---

[62] Desai (2005) 297–98.
[63] Hayek (1980) 89–90.
[64] Epstein (1984, 1995).
[65] Fredman (2004) 10–18.

they have developed in Europe since 1945, and more particularly since 1990 in the face of globalisation. The first is the pace of technological change. The traditional social models in most of continental Europe have been co-ordinated market economies, dependent on low labour turnover, strong job security, workers' participation, social security and the protection of income. These models were a source of comparative institutional advantage at the time of stable Fordist production systems with long-term investment, the development of in-firm skills and incremental technical innovation. They have, however, proved to be less well placed when radical innovation is required in a highly competitive globalised market. The more 'flexible' British model, although not as liberal as the American and Japanese ones and itself constrained by regulation in some areas by the EU, appears to have given better opportunities to develop new technologies in rapidly changing industries, such as biotechnology and information technology. This is because firms wanting to develop new products can hire and fire workers with relative ease, using non-standard forms of employment relationship, and placing a premium on transferable industry skills, with relatively little involvement of workers' representatives.[66] The Nordic countries have moved furthest in providing a mix of social protection and labour market reforms, which are believed to be necessary to improve productive efficiency, while maintaining collective workers' participation. The other European countries will have to make more progress in the same direction if their labour law systems are to adapt to new technologies and become more effective in facing global competitition.

The second question mark which hung over the future of European social and labour models in 2004, and approached a tragic climax in 2008–9 (as this book was being completed), was whether the traditional bank-based financial system could survive the growing competition from new markets in securities.[67] Banks were increasingly under pressure to provide quick profits and were becoming less willing to finance long-term corporate investments and the development of human resources, including on-the-job training. This threatened to make it harder for firms to offer employment security and other forms of labour protection. The collapse of the global banking system, as later events have shown, has not only resulted in mass unemployment but has also deeply threatened the gains of labour over the period since the Second World War.

As a general proposition, we continue to take the view that labour legislation is the outcome of struggle between different social groups, and of competing ideologies. As Abrams said, 'what any particular group of people gets is not just a matter of what they choose, but whether they can force or persuade other groups to let them have'.[68] In other words, in the future, as in the past, the crucial element in both the making and the transformation of labour law will be the

---

[66] Hepple (2005) 252–53.
[67] Foreseen by Eichengreen (2007) 419–23.
[68] Abrams (1982) 15.

power of capital, and the countervailing power of organised labour and civil society—workers, consumers and active citizens. In offering this book and its predecessor to those who may be involved in future transformations, we recall the words of Milon Kundera: 'the struggle of man against power, is the struggle of memory against forgetting'.

2

Economic Policy and Labour Law

NIKLAS BRUUN AND BOB HEPPLE

Introduction

The development of labour law is profoundly influenced by the state of the economy and by prevailing views on economic policy. Labour law is judged not only by the protection it might offer to individual workers, but also by how it interacts with the functioning of the labour market and the economy. Many of the institutions of labour law are aimed at binding labour and capital together so as to achieve wage moderation and to ensure that profits are earned and go to shareholders or back into investment.

In the first three decades after the Second World War, those countries which developed co-ordination of economic, social and labour law policies appear to have been more successful in raising labour productivity and achieving economic growth than those with adversarial and fragmented systems of industrial relations. However, as Eichengreen points out,[1] the corporatist arrangements proved to be a hindrance to innovation and growth in the last quarter of the twentieth century, when increases in output became primarily dependent on rapid technological change. In that new era, systems with flexible production and decentralised work organisation proved to be the most effective in raising labour productivity and reducing unemployment.[2]

In all these periods, market-driven branches of law have not infrequently come into conflict with labour law. Nineteenth-century ideas that trade unions were a restraint on trade and cartelised the labour market were revived. Employment protection legislation was criticised for interfering with the incentive structures provided by the individual contract of employment. State intervention to protect workers was seen as a source of economic inefficiency and a cause of unemployment. The alleged 'rigidities' created by labour legislation led to varying degrees of action in different countries to 'deregulate' or remove the

[1] Eichengreen (2007) 270.
[2] Ibid, 257.

legislation of the welfare state. By the end of the century, however, labour law was being reinvented across Europe as a form of labour market 'regulation', which could be structured so as to be 'smart' or 'efficient' from an economic viewpoint. The underlying issue was seen to be how could economic integration in a Europeanised and increasingly globalised market economy be reconciled with social and labour rights?

In this chapter, the development of post-war labour law is discussed from the perspective of its relationship with changing economic policies. This relationship is difficult to describe on a general level because there have been different national ways of making the link between economy and law. In spite of these national divergences, we also find many similarities. Both regulatory competition and economic integration within the EU have resulted in significant con-vergences of national labour laws and economic policies.

Reconstruction (1945–50)

Economic Priorities

Before the human rights and labour law aspirations expressed in post-war European constitutions and international labour standards (see chapter 1 above) could be achieved, it was necessary to overcome the economic dislocation and damage caused by the war. Industrial production on the continent in 1945–46 was only one-third of the 1938 figure and in agriculture production was down to half the pre-war figure. Factories, mines, cities and communications had been extensively damaged. In Britain damage was largely restricted to the cities and ports, but machinery and buildings were run down, and war had turned Britain from the second-largest creditor in the world in 1939 into the largest debtor as a result of the liquidation of one-third of its overseas assets to pay for the costs of conflict. All countries involved in the war had suffered irreplaceable human losses, not only from direct casualties of war and bombardment, but also the millions of civilians who had been transported to concentration camps or placed in forced labour, many never to return to their homes (see chapter 3 below).

On the other hand, the US had emerged from the war as the world's major power, exporting more than three times as much in 1945 as in 1938. European recovery was made possible by the Marshall Plan, under which nearly US $13 billion was channelled to 17 European countries outside the orbit of the Soviet Union (which declined to participate and stopped its client states from doing so) from 1948 to 1952. Even Sweden and Ireland, which had remained neutral during the war, shared the benefits. The enormous demand for goods from labour-intensive industries at a time when labour costs in Europe were relatively lower than those in the US had 'multiplier' effects and led to rapid economic growth and high rates of employment in all western democracies, especially Germany, where the gross national product increased by 300% between 1947 and 1950. Trade grew on the basis of a stable currency (the US dollar) and the support given by the World Bank and the International Monetary Fund. The General Agreement on Tariffs and Trade of 1947 provided a framework for the development of world trade. Politically, the Marshall Plan moved the balance of power to moderate centrist parties, who could point to the benefits of close alliance with the US, and who supported the system of private ownership.

Co-operation and Conflict

In the countries occupied by Germany during the war trade unions had been dissolved, but after the war there was no comprehensive replacement of the pre-war labour law systems. The British, French and American liberation forces were keen to promote a pluralist model of politics and collective bargaining in their sectors of occupied Germany and elsewhere. New demands for social security and equality were reflected in the Beveridge Report (1942) in the UK, and this had a profound influence on political leaders, employers and unionists in exile, who had begun to plan together for the future of their countries. Examples are the programme of the French National Resistance Council, the Belgian *Pacte de Solidarité Sociale* and the Dutch Van Rhijn Scheme, which was worked out by the Dutch government in exile in London. These schemes were wholly or partly implemented after the end of the war.

In the countries which did not fall under Nazi control—notably Britain, Ireland and Sweden—and also in Finland (which had been at war with the Soviet Union), labour and union leaders were taken into government. In the Nordic countries, the Netherlands, Belgium and Austria tripartite (government–employers–unions) systems of national social and economic policy-making were developed, and principles of social partnership were implemented at the company level. On the other hand, in Mediterranean countries unions were weaker and more divided. They tended to be excluded from government policy-making, in which employers had considerable influence, and at company level there was significant anti-unionism. This led to industrial conflict on a scale not experienced in countries with stronger unions that were participating in government and enterprises.

In Britain, a well-developed pluralist system of voluntary collective bargaining was already in place. In 1946, when repealing anti-union legislation enacted after the 1926 General Strike, a Labour government offered the unions virtually any labour legislation they wanted. The unions declined the offer on the ground that it was unthinkable that any future government would take away what had been achieved by their industrial strength—a belief that was to be shattered 40 years later by the Thatcher government. When the wartime ban on strikes and lockouts was ended in 1951, there was a return to full-scale 'collective laissez-faire' in

Britain—Kahn-Freund's characterisation of the largely voluntarist system in which there was de facto freedom to organise, to bargain collectively and to strike.[3]

The Welfare State (1950–72)

Economic Growth and Full Employment

The picture in the western democracies by the early 1950s was one of growing ideological consensus between the major political parties based on the ideas of Keynesian economics, with a greatly increased role for the state in stimulating economic growth and productivity, stabilising prices and maintaining an equilibrium in the balance of payments. There were, however, differences of emphasis. For example, in Germany (by persuasion) and the Netherlands (by law) the stress was placed on price controls so as to prevent inflation, while in Britain unsuccessful attempts were made to develop a permanent framework for incomes policy as a feature of economic management by the state in order to restrain inflation. Overall western European unemployment rates fell from an average of 7.5% in the 1930s to just under 3% in 1950–60 and 1.5% in the 1970s.

The rate of economic growth in many countries was spectacular in comparison with the pre-war period. Between 1913 and 1950, per capita growth in western countries had averaged 1% a year; between 1950 and 1970, this rose to an unprecedented 4%. There were important national variations, with growth being highest in Greece (9.5%), West Germany (8.3%), Italy (7.7%) and France (6.0%) and lower in the Netherlands (4.9%), Belgium (4.5%), Denmark (4.0%) and Ireland (3.7%), with Britain trailing behind (2.8%). One reason for these differences is that the continental countries had suffered the greatest war damage and so had the opportunity to invest in modern technologies. More generally, countries with a low starting point tend to grow at a faster rate than those at a high level of affluence. There were also significant regional variations; for example, in Italy the south continued to display the characteristics of an agricultural and undeveloped region while the north became industrialised. Agricultural labour also remained significant in Spain, Portugal, Greece and Ireland, but the general trend was a decrease in the need for workers in agriculture and an ongoing movement from the countryside to cities.

A second factor that influenced growth was migration. The population of western Europe grew by 25% between 1945 and 1970, and chronic shortages of labour in the north and west stimulated an influx of immigrant workers and their families, for example into Germany from Turkey, southern Italy, Greece, Yugoslavia, Spain and Portugal; into Britain from her former colonies in the

[3] Kahn-Freund (1959) 224.

Caribbean, Africa and the Indian subcontinent; into France from the North African colonies; and into the Netherlands from Indonesia and Surinam. New ethnic minorities had become a significant and permanent part of the labour force by 1970, suffering racial discrimination and disadvantage (see chapters 3 and 5 below). The migration to leading industrialised countries was extensive, and continued throughout the 1970s. The rapidly growing labour force reduced pressure on wages and allowed revenues to be put into investment. At the same time, the competition for labour was an incentive to increase employment security and to make open-ended contracts the main form of employment. A significant feature for the movement of labour in Europe at this time was that the employees were usually hired directly by the employers in the receiving countries.

A third factor influencing growth, and the most important of all from our perspective, was the structure of industrial relations and labour law. Eichengreen sums this up as follows:

> [N]eo-corporatist societies were most successful at limiting increases in unit labour costs and devoting resources to capital formation . . . In contrast, societies lacking national unions, cohesive employers' associations and governments capable of harmonising wage bargaining saw co-ordination break down as each craft- or industry-based union attempted to leapfrog the wage gains of others, and owners uncertain about the future paid out profits rather than plowing them into capacity expansion and modernisation. Such countries, of which the United Kingdom and Ireland are examples, were characterised by low rates of investment and productivity growth.[4]

Germany, with national unions now organised on industrial lines in 'social partnership' and with strong unified employers' associations, was the leading example of a successful neo-corporatist society in this period, with co-ordinated wage regulation and stable unit labour costs. It was also characterised by the dual system for workers, relatively strong autonomous works councils co-existing with trade unions and collective bargaining (see chapter 8 below). The Netherlands, too, achieved wage moderation, low unit labour costs and a high degree of flexibility on the basis of neo-corporatist institutions such as the Labour Foundation (*Stichting van de Arbeid*) and the tripartite Social and Economic Council (*Sociaal-Economisch Raad*). In Austria, a single trade union federation and universal employers' organisation co-ordinated wage-setting across the country. In Sweden, the Rehn–Meidner model for solidaristic wage policy and collective bargaining set a framework for successful industrial relations.

In contrast, Britain's poor economic performance in the 1950s, reflected in the stagnation of productivity growth,[5] can be partly explained by the decentralised system of industrial relations, the conflict between the formal system of

---

[4] Eichengreen (2007) 90.
[5] For details, see Eichengreen (2007) 88, Table 4.1.

voluntary sectoral collective bargaining and fragmented shop steward bargaining at the plant level outside the control of national and regional union officials, which resulted in chronic wage inflation. However, one must be careful not to pin the entire explanation on industrial conflict. In Italy, where co-ordination was difficult because of rival union confederations and decentralised bargaining had become increasingly prevalent in the 1960s, there was rapid economic growth. This was due to a number of non-institutional causes, such as tariff protection, inflation stabilisation resulting from reserve requirements on bank lending, and high levels of capital investment.[6] Moreover, in Italy the fascist legacy meant that many economic activities were under state control. State ownership and state shareholding were used in failing industries and to support the economy of southern Italy.

State Intervention

More generally, none of these countries was a fully free market economy. There was substantial state intervention. One form this took was nationalisation. In Britain, the first post-war Labour government (1945–51) nationalised the Banks of England and Scotland (the central bank), the coal mining industry, the railways, road transport, electricity, gas and water supplies, and iron and steel.[7] The form of nationalisation was much different from that which pre-war syndicalists had desired. In particular, while there was a duty to 'consult' trade unions and extensive voluntary collective bargaining arrangements were made, this was different in character from the 'joint control and administration by the workmen and the state' that unions such as those of the miners had demanded since the First World War. Nationalisation in Britain did not involve systematic planning, as in France (see below). Not surprisingly, rates of return in the British public sector were low, and industrial conflict remained a problem.

In other western democracies, nationalisation was seen to be necessary only in those situations where private ownership clearly could not operate effectively. In France, the government felt compelled to nationalise the mines to end severe industrial conflict and to expropriate industries, such as the Renault car firm, whose owners had collaborated with the Nazis. France also nationalised air transport and aircraft manufacturing, the banks and 32 insurance companies. By May 1946, one-fifth of industrial capacity was in state hands. In contrast, in Belgium the socialist members of the government supported economic reforms that could be achieved by private owners. In Denmark, like other Nordic countries, the social democrats saw the issue not as one of state ownership but rather of state regulation through a variety of institutionalised mechanisms in which employers

---

[6] Eichengreen (2007)115–16.

[7] Iron and steel was returned to private ownership by the Conservative Government in 1952, renationalised in 1966 and again denationalised under the Thatcher administration in 1980.

and trade unions collaborated. In countries like Germany and the Nordic states, where industrialisation had taken place under strong government action, this was the more natural path than in Britain, where the industrial revolution had occurred under laissez-faire conditions, and political adversaries took as their starting points a stark choice between extensive state ownership and unbridled laissez-faire.

Economic Planning

Another approach to economic development that had implications for the character of the labour laws was that of comprehensive national economic planning. Rigid bureaucratised centralised planning was introduced in the countries in the Soviet sphere of central and eastern Europe. The explicit aim of labour law was to help raise productivity and 'to strengthen state and work discipline'.[8]

In the western democracies, France, with its General Planning Council (*Commissariat general du Plan*), and Belgium, with a Central Council on the Economy, went furthest in producing national economic plans, but these were not based on coercion. Unlike the Soviet plans, they set only indicative targets, not rigid production quotas. In both France and Italy, plans were focused on capital investment in industries, rather than on improving domestic consumption. This led to strikes and demonstrations by trade unions and left-wing parties. In part, these plans were a response to the condition attached to the receipt of American aid, that effective institutions should plan the use of aid and administer it. On the other hand, in Germany the idea of national planning was unpopular because it reminded people of the Nazi era. The idea of economic democracy through different kind of works councils was more acceptable. Workers' participation in the management of undertakings in Germany was regarded as important even by the Americans, who believed that the councils would reduce union power at enterprise level. Works councils and *Mitbestimming* had a role to play in the process of economic and social planning (see chapter 8 below).

Generally, governments remained firmly in control of economic strategy. The state continued to exercise many of the large competencies to regulate the economy it had acquired during the war. It also played an important role through public contracts. This is reflected in the International Labour Organisation (ILO) Convention 94 (1949), concerning labour clauses in public contracts. Eight of the European countries covered in this study ratified the Convention: Austria (1951), Belgium (1952), Denmark (1955), Finland (1951), France (1951), the Netherlands (1952), Italy (1952), Spain (1971) and Britain (1950, denounced under the Thatcher government in 1982). The state in these countries in effect undertook the role of ensuring that wage levels agreed upon

---

[8] Batygin (1972) 73.

in collective agreements were followed by private contractors that were fulfilling public contracts.

Building the Welfare States

There was a political consensus in the western democracies in this period that governments should build up the welfare state (see further, chapter 6 below). This had three basic features: first, the provision of free or almost free public services, such as education, health care and social care; secondly, income maintenance or social security in respect of risks such as unemployment, illness, disability and old age; and thirdly, a commitment to secure full employment by means of macroeconomic policies. The growth of social spending was seen as part of the Keynesian policy of securing full employment. The welfare state was the corollary of the policy of greater investment and growth. The new welfare states were directed not just at the poorest sections of society, like much pre-war welfare provision, but aimed to provide security for all citizens from cradle to grave. Everywhere the standard of life seemed to be improving, with a dramatic increase in consumer goods, health care, educational opportunities and social provision. The peoples of the western democracies came to expect an ever-expanding welfare state and no government could afford to ignore these demands.

The Role of Labour Law and Social Policy

Labour law was regarded as a tool for organising the labour market in order to ensure industrial peace. The growing trade union and labour movements were promised concessions regarding social policy, pensions and the like. Direct social obligations were also put on private employers to protect persons with a reduced working capacity, in particular those disabled by the war. The idea of creating protection for workers who were hit by the consequences of restructuring appeared on the European agenda. One example is the European Coal and Steel Community Treaty 1951, the predecessor of the 1957 Treaty on the European Economic Community (EEC). This provided for funding when coal mines closed down in order to make it possible for employees to move to other jobs or at least have a decent period to adapt to change.

However, the evolution of collective labour law took place mainly on a national basis and without any attempts for European harmonisation, although the employers and unions maintained close ties to international organisations. Different organisational patterns in various countries led to a diverse picture, but the collective bargaining level became very important for wage-setting in all countries (see chapter 7 below). This period was also a golden era for pensions policy, and here the link between economic policy, the need for the accumulation of a large amount of capital and social (old age) security found various combinations of pension policy and participation in working life. The link between labour market participation (work) and earning of pensions became important all over Europe. The participation of labour market organisations in the administration of big pension funds was also a way of democratising economic decision-making.

In some respects, economic policies and labour laws tended to diverge. Wage and price levels were clearly important to economic planning. In the 1960s a number of attempts were made to implement economic policies as part of a broad strategy for distributing the national income. In 1945, the Netherlands, followed later by Sweden and Austria, achieved agreement with employers and unions on incomes policy, and in 1961 the Organisation for Economic Co-operation and Development (OECD) recommended that its members should follow this example. Only Denmark acted immediately, and by 1965 incomes policy had been abandoned by its originator, the Netherlands. By the late 1960s, the post-war consensus of wage restraint in return for high capital investment was breaking down. As the risk of long-term unemployment seemed to be receding, wage demands became intense.[9] In the larger countries with an adversarial tradition of labour relations, like Britain, France and Italy, it was difficult to achieve a consensus on wage restraint. Britain continued to experience a 'stop–go' cycle of recession and boom; a statutory wage freeze lasted only one year (1966–67). There were recessions in Italy and France in 1963–64, and in 1966 there was a slump in much of Europe, including Germany. Despite this, governments, in collaboration with employers and unions, continued to tolerate higher real wages, wage indexation and a huge expansion in welfare costs, in the belief that Keynesian techniques could be used to sustain economic growth. They also responded to demands for greater employment protection, increased rights for trade unions and an expansion of workers' participation. Examples are the controls on termination of employment, starting with protection against unfair dismissal in Germany (1951), prohibitions on temporary work (1949) and labour-only subcontracting (1960), and strict controls over fixed-term contracts in Italy (1962) (see chapter 3 below); the introduction of equal pay for equal work for women and men (France 1957, and for the then six-member EEC in the Treaty of Rome 1957; see chapter 5 below); the strengthening of collective bargaining laws (Belgium 1968); and minimum wage laws (the Netherlands 1968; see chapter 7 below). In other countries, similar labour law developments occurred even after the period of growth had been halted.

In general, there was a profound mismatch between economic policy and labour laws in nearly all western democracies. This was reflected in the upsurge in industrial conflict in many countries in the late 1960s. Centralised and formal

---

[9] Eichengreen (2007) 219.

collective bargaining systems were challenged in different ways. In some countries, workers expressed dissatisfaction with wages and price inflation by wildcat strikes; in others, they resisted rationalisations by employers which fell outside the scope of collective bargaining. Wages began to rise faster than productivity, profits were squeezed and the incentive to invest was weakened. In most western democracies, governments tried to dampen the unrest by strengthening central union leaderships and union discipline, enhancing trade union status and rights, and extending statutory employment rights. In return, they sought the co-operation of unions in incomes policies to restrain the inflationary potential of collective bargaining.

The Challenges from Below

By the mid-1960s it was possible for sociologists to depict western Europe as being on the threshold of a 'post-industrial' society, with a convergence of neo-corporatist 'planning' in conditions of political stability. A symbol of this was the new EEC, established by six nations (Belgium, France, Germany, Italy, Luxembourg and the Netherlands) in the Treaty of Rome in 1957. This contributed to annual growth rates of 4–7% in the six countries until the oil crisis of 1973–74. As the free trade area and common external customs tariffs developed, there was significant restructuring and growth of industry; at the same time, the common agricultural policy entrenched the position of small farmers in France, Germany and Italy, who supported political conservatism.

The belief in stability was to be questioned by the youth culture, which rejected the new acquisitive society and instead emphasised communal self-sufficiency and individual liberty. In 1968, a politicised student movement was the spark that lit widespread social unrest in France, Italy, Spain and Germany. It was less important elsewhere, but everywhere it presaged a new preference for direct action and alternative forms of popular participation. Associated with this youthful rebellion was the revival in Europe of feminist movements, which vigorously took up issues such as equal rights and equal pay for women and men, the legalisation of abortion, pre-school nursery provision, and greater participation by women in trade unions and the political system. The older male working-class political and trade union culture was being called into question by radical student and feminist critiques of the neo-corporatist welfare state. The end of this era was paradoxically marked by the 1968 'revolutions' and their demands, one of which was for economic democracy. Suddenly issues concerning power and decision-making at the workplace were once again on the agenda. The conflicts of interest between the social parties came into focus in the labour law debate.

It was in this changing political climate that economic growth and the welfare states were to be shaken by the oil crisis of 1973–74.

Economic Crisis (1973–79)

Recession, Unemployment and the New World of Work

In 1973, as a result of the Yom Kippur War between Israel and the Arab states, the price of oil was quadrupled and the Arab states imposed an oil embargo on states which they believed to have supported Israel, notably the US and the Netherlands. In the period that followed, western Europe experienced the new phenomenon of 'stagflation'—a combination of increasing inflation, rising unemployment and declining economic growth (see chapter 3, Table 3.1 below). Governments were compelled to introduce deflationary measures, but this meant even higher unemployment, with growing demands on public expenditure.

The oil crisis of 1973 made transparent deep-seated economic problems. Many of the most important industries were facing increased competition from Japan and rapidly industrialising countries outside Europe. These industries—like steel, engineering, shipbuilding and textiles—were beset by poor productivity and declining markets. Labour markets were expanding as a result of high birth rates in earlier years and more women seeking employment. At the same time, new technologies were undermining the dominant system of production, of which the automobile industry is the leading example, known as Fordism. The elements of Fordism have been summed up as: (i) a male full-time breadwinner; (ii) long-term service in the same firm doing one or similar jobs; (iii) a homogeneous and standardised working style; (iv) a clear-cut separation of working time from leisure or private time, as well as collective and objective working time; (v) a relatively short term of life expectancy after retirement; and (vi) predominantly industrial—sometimes enterprise—union and industrial collective bargaining.[10] This system was geared towards semi-skilled workers producing standardised goods for mass markets in large factory production lines. This organisation of production assisted the rise of mass trade unions and collective bargaining, which could provide stability and predictability in employment relationships. Labour laws were designed to support this institutionalisation of labour relations and presupposed a workforce largely composed of men working a standard 40-hour week. In turn, the welfare states provided a deal in which workers accepted their subordination to management in Fordist enterprises in return for the guarantees of job protection and social security provided by the state.[11] This was the golden age of the so-called standard employment relationship that, in various ways, became institutionalised in the labour laws of the countries studied (see chapter 4 below).

In the post-Fordist world that emerged in the 1970s, there was growing segmentation of product markets, microprocessor-based innovations rapidly

---

[10] Igwami (1999) 692.
[11] Deakin and Wilkinson (2005).

changed production lines, there were far smaller and more decentralised units of production, and new technical skills were required. Managers had to be able to respond quickly and effectively to changes in demand and to international competition. This engendered new conflicts over what came to be known as 'flexibilisation' of labour markets (see chapter 3 below). New types of jobs, new forms of employment and the growth of the services sector were also associated with the increased feminisation of the European labour market. Women, however, were generally concentrated in lower-paid, part-time and temporary jobs, with continuing gender pay gaps (see chapter 5 below). The segmentation of labour markets was also a feature of the absorption of increasing numbers of workers from outside the EEC.

The Expansion of Labour Law and Collective Bargaining

One of the curious features of the economic crisis and the rise of new technologies, in many ways unprecedented in European history, was that both political and industrial relations remained favourable to labour. In Britain, the Labour Party ruled from 1974 to 1979 and in Germany the Social Democrats governed in coalition with the Free Democrats from 1969 to 1982. In France, from 1971 a vigorous Socialist Party, led by Mitterand, came to replace the communists as the leading party of the left. In Italy, the Communist Party continued to grow in influence in the 1970s, reaching its high point in 1976. In the Netherlands, the middle years of the decade (1973–76) saw a centre-left coalition. In the southern countries where democracy was restored (Greece and Portugal in 1974, Spain in 1975) there were initial successes for the conservative parties, but there was a consensus to secure trade union freedoms in all these countries.

In the new and old democracies, trade unions made important gains, neo-corporatist tendencies (or 'social contracts') grew and protective labour laws were expanded. Eichengreen has compiled an index of employment protection legislation that shows that France, Germany, Ireland, Portugal and Sweden all significantly increased the stringency of their employment protection in the period 1973–79.[12] The 1970s were indeed the high water mark of employment rights, for example the Workers' Statutes of 1970 in Italy and 1980 in Spain, controls over dismissals in Britain from 1972 and in France from 1973, protection of workers' acquired rights on the transfer of undertakings in Germany in 1972, the wide-ranging Employment Protection Acts in Britain in 1975 and Sweden in 1974, and the Co-Determination Act in Sweden in 1976.

Many governments adopted a promotional role towards collective bargaining and other forms of co-operation between the social partners at various levels. There was a high degree of recognition of trade union rights and of the central role of collective bargaining (see chapter 7 below). This period also saw the

[12] Eichengreen (2007) 273, Table 9.6.

development of so-called semi-mandatory minimum legislation, where a deviation from the legislative standard is only possible through a clause in a collective agreement. This not only showed acceptance of the social partners, but also reflected a legislative policy of making legislation more flexible, especially from the point of view of employers, and created incentives for them to participate in such bargaining. Legislation with derogation clauses was in effect seen as an effective way of both promoting collective bargaining and introducing more flexibility (see chapter 7 below).

Institutions for co-operation between the state, employers and unions were strengthened in countries where they were already well established (notably Austria, Belgium, Denmark, the Netherlands and Germany), despite some tensions. The outstanding example of this was Italy, whose industrial relations had been characterised by delayed development of the industrialisation process, accompanied by a heavy dependence on the state economy. From the second half of the 1970s, an important role was played in Italian industrial relations by the intervention of the state as a direct participant in the various episodes of social concertation (*concertazione sociale*).[13] After the 'recentralisation' (*recentralizzazione*) of collective bargaining in the 1970s, mainly with the inter-confederal agreement on labour costs and productivity, the first experience with triangular bargaining was the 1983 Scotti Protocol, which declared the principle of co-ordination between different bargaining levels. In Britain the Heath (Conservative) government had tried to bring about a more co-ordinated and orderly system by enacting the Industrial Relations Act 1971, giving unions significant legal rights in return for far-reaching legal responsibilities. This broke down in the face of union resistance and a miners' strike in 1974. The Heath government fell and the new Labour government tried to achieve co-ordination through a 'social contract' with the TUC, restoring and improving traditional collective laissez-faire, underpinned by extensive new rights for individual workers.[14] This 'contract' ultimately failed in the 'winter of discontent' in 1978–79, leading to the election in May 1979 of the Thatcher (Conservative) government, committed to the ideals of Hayek and Friedman.

The EEC Social Dimension

During the first 15 years of the EEC, labour law and social policy were seen as almost exclusively national functions. There was considerable diversity in these matters because of the different economic, social and political evolution of the Member States. There was little pressure for harmonisation or intervention at the Community level. It was only in October 1972, on the eve of the enlargement of the Community to include Britain, Ireland and Denmark, that the Heads of Government declared that they 'attribute the same importance to energetic

---

[13] Giugni (2001) 158.
[14] Davies and Freedland (1993) ch 8.

proceedings in the field of social policy as to the realisation of the economic and social union'. By the time the first Social Action Programme was unveiled in 1974, the economic boom was beginning to fall apart and a wave of strikes and wage explosions were sweeping across the Member States. Not surprisingly, the main measures adopted under the Social Action Programme were designed to harmonise the raft of national laws which sought state intervention and workers' participation as ways of mitigating the impact of mass redundancies, the growing concentration of enterprises and the insolvency of employers. Community labour law came to life with three employment protection directives, on rights in respect of redundancy consultation (1975), acquired rights (1977) and rights on the insolvency of the employer (1980). The EEC rules in this period sought to provide a 'level playing field' for collective dismissals, transfers and insolvency, with the aim of equalising costs and so improving economic competition, but they did so only to a limited extent, allowing for the different national traditions to survive, resulting in significant differences in the way collective dismissals and transfers were regulated in the Member States (see chapter 3 below). In this period, the provisions of the Treaty of Rome on equal pay for women and men were enhanced and implemented by EEC directives on equal pay (1975) and equal treatment (1976), and some landmark decisions of the European Court of Justice (ECJ) (see chapter 5 below).

The strong formulations concerning some economic aspects of European integration in the Rome Treaty also laid the base for a potential conflict between competition law and labour law, between rules on state aid and employment policy, and between rules on economic freedoms and social policy. These conflicts did not, however, come to the surface before the early 1990s, when the internal market project really gained momentum and the economic articles were interpreted in a strict way (see below).

Restraining the TNCs

In international terms, the focus of economic power shifted in the 1960s to transnational corporations (TNCs), whose decision-making centres were often in the US. By 1970, a British TUC paper could state that 'the international company is rapidly replacing the nation state as the basic operating and accounting unit in the international economy'.[15] These companies penetrated not only into the former colonies but also into western Europe. This changed the character of collective labour relations because trade unions now frequently faced managers who themselves were subject to decisions made in another country. The TNCs could adjust their production and profits to suit an international strategy, while trade union strength remained largely national, or even regional or local. In time, this was to lead to increasing pressures for international labour regulation.

[15] Cited by Wedderburn (1972) 12.

During this period the issue of social clauses in trade agreements was debated. This led the OECD to adopt the OECD Guidelines for Multinational Enterprises in 1976. These Guidelines encompassed many areas, but one important area was employment and industrial relations. Among the Guidelines was an obligation for multinationals to fulfil the minimum labour law standards in the host country. The host country in turn was required to treat these companies on an equal basis with the treatment of national companies. The multinationals were expected to respect trade union rights and to enter into collective bargaining with representative trade unions. The Guidelines were and are not legally binding, but certain implementation structures are nevertheless in place.[16] One year later, in 1977, the Tripartite Declaration of Principles Concerning Multinational Enterprises and Social Policy was adopted by the Governing Body of the ILO.[17] This instrument had drawn inspiration from the OECD instrument, but dealt only with social policy issues and referred very much to ILO instruments. In 1981 a special procedure was initiated by the ILO in order to solve disagreements over the application of the declaration.

By the end of the 1970s it was true to say that industrial relations everywhere had become more politicised because of the growing tensions between economic policies, including wage restraint, which limited the role of collective bargaining, and labour policies that tended to promote trade union and workers' rights. There continued to be divergence, however, in the ways in which the continental countries, on the one hand, and Britain, on the other, resolved these tensions. This was to lead to profound disagreements between these countries within the EEC in the 1980s.

Restructuring and Deregulation (1980–89)

Neo-liberalism Takes Control

The 1980s witnessed a transformation of the economies and labour markets of western Europe. In all these countries the overriding need was to overcome the effects of the recession and to make the economies better able to meet growing international competition. During this phase financial markets were opened in Europe. Restrictions on the operations of foreign-owned companies were lifted. Provision of services across borders was increasing. This had the important implication that the labour market was no longer only a national market; many types of production could be removed to other areas in the world and employers could operate across borders.

There was fierce debate about the contribution of employment protection

---

[16] Hepple (2005) 78–85.
[17] Ibid.

laws and welfare policies to inflation and unemployment. Many argued that relatively generous benefits encouraged workers to stay out of the labour market, but
there was also agreement that it was the slowdown in productivity, the increase in
oil price and the rise in real interest rates that were the primary causes of rising
unemployment.[18] Governments aimed to curb inflation and cut public expenditure drastically. Managements of private enterprises, too, needed to adopt
technological innovations and restructure their businesses. There were significant
differences in the success of various countries in this process of adaptation. At
first, Germany was the most successful, with the newly democratic Spain and
Portugal also achieving impressive growth, bearing in mind their backward
starting point.

   In all the economies there was persistent unemployment, with Spain, Ireland,
Belgium, the Netherlands, France and Britain having the highest rates in the
1980s (over 10%), and Denmark, Finland, Italy, Sweden and Germany the lowest
(below 7%).[19] The changes in the labour market (described in chapter 3 below)
led to a growing segmentation between a shrinking permanent 'core' of workers
protected by collective bargaining and labour law and a growing 'periphery' in
precarious employment without trade union or legal protection. These changes
reflected not only the need for enterprises to employ more flexible workforces,
but also the changing aspirations of the young, old and female workers, who
wanted new forms of working and family life.

The Changing Role of the State

The 1980s also witnessed a changing role for the state, both in the economy and
in labour relations, under predominantly conservative governments. There were,
however, fundamental differences between the British and continental European
approaches. The Christian (Catholic) traditions of the continent revolved around
ideas of reconciliation and a harmonious society. This was reflected in welfare
states that depended on social institutions, such as the trade unions and
churches, and in neo-corporatist industrial relations structures, such as
board-level workers' participation, works councils in the enterprise and collective
bargaining arrangements, in which wages were linked to labour productivity
rather than prices. In Britain, on the other hand, the traditions were those of free
market liberalism and adversarial industrial relations. Mrs Thatcher famously
declared: 'there is no such thing as society'. Her brand of neo-liberalism was
based on an idea of competitive individualism, which was seen not only as the
way to maximise economic efficiency, but also as the guarantee of individual
freedom and democracy. The thrust of her policies was to reduce the responsibility of the state for dealing with welfare and to encourage private sector
insurance in its place. State-owned industries were to be privatised and a

---

[18] Eichengreen (2007) 272–76.
[19] Ibid, 264, Table 9.3.

competitive market introduced for the delivery of public services. She embraced Hayek's view that trade unions and labour laws cartelise the market, so in the British context unions had to be stripped of their 'special privileges' and exposed to the ordinary common law, which treats combinations of workers or employers as unlawful 'conspiracies' and restraints on trade.[20] She was willing to face ideological turmoil and violence (such as the miners' strike of 1984) of a kind which contemporary continental leaders, such as Kohl in Germany and Mitterand in France, studiously avoided.

The differences in British and continental approaches were reflected in labour laws. The Thatcher government was openly hostile to trade unions and, through a series of legislative and administrative measures, taken against a background of declining manufacturing industry and unemployment, succeeded in seriously weakening the unions. In France, by contrast, the Socialist government introduced the Auroux laws (1982) to extend plant level bargaining, which it achieved, though with only limited success, while at the same time implementing an incomes policy that restrained bargaining. In Spain and Portugal unions were helped by legislative intervention. Distinctive forms of concertation were developed in Austria, the Netherlands and Belgium, Italy and the Nordic countries (see chapter 7 below). At the same time there was growing pressure from employers for greater flexibility in labour contracts and legislative rules. The rigid requirements of legislation on part-time, fixed-term and temporary work were relaxed in most countries, and private employment agencies were allowed to operate in countries where they had previously been prohibited, such as Sweden and Italy (see chapter 3 below).

One of the main reasons for the reconsideration of the role of the state was that the evolution of the welfare state had made the public sector the employer of a large group of employees essentially funded by the taxpayers. Public sector employees became highly unionised in most European countries. During this period there were an increasing number of labour market conflicts in which unions in the public sector took part. There was a growing tension between public sector militancy and the needs of government to reduce budget deficits by limiting the size and costs of the public sector.

Social Market v Neo-liberalism

The conflict between continental 'social market' ideas and British deregulation came to a head in the EEC from 1980 onwards. European employers' organisations and several American TNCs campaigned vigorously against the European Commission's proposals for the harmonisation of employment rights and for industrial democracy. The requirement for unanimity on the European Council enabled the British government (with the active or tacit support of some other

[20] Davies and Freedland (1993) ch 9.

governments) to block these proposals. The only new Council directives adopted in the 1980s were in the fields of sex discrimination and health and safety. The governments were, however, all agreed on the need to complete the single market. In order to achieve this, the Single European Act was adopted in 1986 (even Mrs Thatcher gave her reluctant support), introducing qualified majority voting in the Council in certain areas, including health and safety.

Free movement of capital encouraged relocation in areas of the EEC with low social and wage costs, but this was hindered by low productivity, lack of skills, energy and resources, and weak infrastructure in those areas. The removal of the remaining technical, physical and fiscal barriers to free movement of capital, goods and services was thus seen as essential to the lowering of real labour costs. The debate about 'flexibility' also became central to the future of the EEC. This was driven by the desire to reduce unemployment, the need to adapt to new technologies and the competitive models of labour 'flexibility' in the US, Japan and newly industrialising countries. These pressures were reflected in a raft of Commission proposals vigorously opposed by the Thatcher administration. The difference between Thatcher and the majority of European leaders was not over the direction of change—reducing the real costs of labour and enhancing employers' ability to respond effectively to new markets and processes—but in the methods which could best achieve this. In particular, while Thatcher wanted to change the balance of bargaining power and reduce both Community-level and national regulation, the Commission emphasised greater workers' involvement and an expanded 'social dimension' as the ways to achieve flexibility.

In an attempt to break the deadlock, the Commission, led by President Jacques Delors, in 1989 proposed a Community Charter of Fundamental Rights of Workers. This was adopted by the Heads of Government of all the Member States, with the notable exception of Britain. Although it had only the status of a political declaration, the Charter became the inspiration for an action programme that resulted in 13 new directives, including those on proof of the employment relationship, health and safety of fixed-term and temporary workers, safety and health of pregnant workers and a revision of the collective redundancies directive, as well as a series of directives on specific safety hazards. The breaking point came at the meeting of the European Council at Maastricht in December 1991. When John Major, Thatcher's successor as British Prime Minister, made it clear that he would not support a new Social Chapter that would widen EEC (renamed EC) competence in labour and social matters, Ruud Lubbers, the Dutch President of the Council, negotiated a deal by which the Social Chapter was taken out of the Treaty. A separate Agreement on Social Policy was accepted by 11 Member States, excluding Britain. The result was to create two parallel European social policy regimes, one for the Community of 12 (later 15) and the other for the Community of 11 (later 14) who subscribed to the Maastricht Agreement on Social Policy. This unsatisfactory state of affairs continued until Tony Blair's New Labour government agreed to the reintegration of the Social Chapter into the Treaty by the Treaty of Amsterdam (1997), and accepted the four directives (on parental leave, part-time work, European Works Councils and burden of proof in sex discrimination cases) that had been adopted under the Agreement on Social Policy. This was the signal for a major rethinking of labour and social policies throughout the EU.

Global Capitalism: the European Response (1990–2004)

The End of Communism

The fall of the Berlin Wall in November 1989 symbolised a new beginning for Europe: German reunification, the independence of the Baltic states, the fall of communist regimes all over central and eastern Europe, the dissolution of the Soviet Union and its replacement by the Russian Federation, the Ukraine and other successor states. These countries embraced capitalism and democracy and entered the globalised market economy. By 2004, when our story ends, eight of these 'transition states' were deemed ready to become Member States of the EU, and more would follow. The new (transition) market economies in Europe had to rearrange their welfare and labour law systems. They introduced new welfare models, new low tax strategies, and a labour law model based on basic ILO and EU standards. The export of versions of the European Social Model to these countries was in some cases more successful on paper than in practice. In particular, structural difficulties such as the lack of effective employers' associations, trade unions and other civil society actors made it difficult to establish genuine collective bargaining.

The 'Third Way'

Profound changes also occurred in the older European democracies. In place of the individualist neo-liberal free market ideology hostile to state intervention in general and labour laws in particular, there emerged a variety of policies that attempted to reconcile the free market with social justice. These have been described as a 'Third Way' between market individualism and social democracy. There is no single 'European social model', as sometimes claimed. There are many inconsistencies within states, and important differences between them. 'Third Way' policies emerged most clearly in Britain under Blair's New Labour after 1997. In its first major policy statement on labour relations, the new government set out as its major goal the creation of a balance between fairness and efficiency.[21] Fairness was seen as a means to achieve efficiency: so collective representation of workers was seen as a way of helping 'employers to explain the

[21] White Paper, *Fairness at Work* (1998).

company's circumstances and the need for change',[22] laws against unfair dismissal were described as facilitating labour mobility, and anti-discrimination and family friendly laws served the business objective of widening the pool of qualified workers. Co-operation (or partnership) between employers and workers was promoted in order to improve business competitiveness. Among the measures taken in this direction were laws enabling unions that had substantial support to compel employers to recognise them for bargaining over pay and hours of work (earlier legal measures of this kind had been repealed under the Thatcher government) and individuals were given the right for the first time to be accompanied by a union official in company grievance procedures even where the union was not recognised. At the same time, the restrictive anti-strike laws of the Thatcher period were retained to prevent a return to the industrial disorder of the late 1970s (see chapter 7 below).

In other European democracies, in which institutionalised forms of workers' participation were well entrenched (see chapter 8 below) and trade unions had not suffered the same neo-liberal onslaught as in Britain, there was greater continuity with the past. Nevertheless, all these countries were undergoing profound economic and social changes. In 1994, the European Commission issued a White Paper on Growth, Competitiveness and Employment,[23] which identified a deep structural crisis. Over a 20-year period, the EU's global competitiveness had worsened in comparison with the US and Japan. While the rate of employment of the population of working age was 60% in the EU, it was 70–75% in the US and Japan. Similarly, the EU's share of export markets, research and development and investment ratio was significantly lower than in the US and Japan. The EU's rate of growth had shrunk over the 20-year period from about 4% to 2.5% per year, and unemployment had risen. It was against this background that, in the early 1990s, the flexibilisation of labour law became a central issue in many Member States (see chapter 3, below).

The Impact of the Economic and Monetary Union (EMU) on Collective Bargaining

The establishment of the EMU and the European Central Bank system in 1999 marked a far-reaching historical change in the EU towards a common centralised monetary system and a true co-ordination of economic policies in the Member States. This development presented a huge challenge for the different national systems of collective bargaining that had been built up in the various European countries during the twentieth century.[24] Could collective bargaining continue to take place on a national level as before? One classic example of the European integration of collective bargaining at the intersectoral level is to be found in

---

[22] Ibid, para 4.3.
[23] European Commission (1994b).
[24] Magnusson (2000) 9.

Belgium. After the national labour market organisations in Belgium had failed to reach an intersectoral agreement in 1996, the Belgian government enacted a 'law on competitiveness', which included the introduction of a legal wage norm for the years 1997–98. Under this wage norm, pay increases in Belgium were not to exceed the average wage increases in France, Germany and the Netherlands. The explicit goal in this legislation was to meet the conditions for fulfilling the economic performance criteria, the so-called EMU convergence criteria.

An example of wage co-ordination on the part of trade unions in order to respond to the EMU challenge is the so-called 'Doorn initiative' taken by the Belgian, German, Luxembourg and Dutch trade union confederations. These organisations met in the city of Doorn in September 1998 and adopted a joint declaration emphasising the need for close cross-border co-ordination of collective bargaining under the EMU in order to prevent possible competition on wages and working conditions with the prospect that this raises of a downward spiral. The essential content of the 'Doorn declaration' is the definition of a formula for national bargaining, according to which trade union negotiators should seek collective agreements that provide at least the equivalent of 'the sum total of the evolution of prices and the increases in labour productivity'. The European Trade Union Confederation (ETUC) welcomed the Doorn initiative, adding that such initiatives must be extended to the entire euro zone.[25] The ETUC adopted a resolution at its congress in Helsinki in 1999 aimed at promoting a strategy for co-ordinated European collective bargaining at the sectoral and cross-sectoral levels. A committee for the co-ordination of collective bargaining policies was established that, in the year 2000, formulated a guideline for co-ordinating collective bargaining at European level.

Two different approaches to collective bargaining in the shadow of the EMU were emerging in the early twenty-first century. The first of these approaches is defensive, and argues that the traditional national collective bargaining process will be endangered if it is polluted by an international element; the second approach favours greater co-ordination at European level. In the Nordic countries there are fears that weaker trade unions in southern Europe will not be able to keep up a reasonable level of minimum protection. In the southern part of Europe there is a fear that the northern countries will not give due consideration to productivity differences but will try to maintain a high level of costs throughout Europe. This creates problems for low productivity enterprises. The huge differences in traditions, mechanisms and enforcement of collective agreements have also been used as an argument against any co-ordination of collective bargaining.

On the employer side, where deregulation and decentralisation have been key words for a long time, co-ordination of collective bargaining at sectoral level is of little interest. Against this background, it is not surprising that the proponents of

---

[25] Towards a European System of Industrial Relations. Adopted by the IXth Statutory Congress in Helsinki 29 June–2 July 1999 (www.etuc.org).

collective bargaining co-ordination at the European level have been quite cautious. They emphasise that the intention of a co-ordination-based approach is not to approximate arrangements in order to produce a homogeneous European system of collective agreements. Instead, co-ordination should take account of regional diversity and develop a complementary European level.[26] By the end of our period, however, we do not yet see much of transnational collective bargaining, although many have predicted that such bargaining must evolve if the trade union movement wants to survive as a bargaining force in Europe.

The New Integration of Economic and Social Policy

At the EU level, the major change in thinking and action occurred in the period between the coming into force of the Maastricht Treaty (1993) and the Treaty of Amsterdam (1997).[27] The European Commission rejected miracle cures such as protectionism, reduction in working hours and severe wage reductions. They favoured active labour market policies, including job creation, the development of a Community labour market with a high level of skills, greater flexibility in the organisation of work and the distribution of working time, and reduced non-wage labour costs. The Directorate-General on Employment, Industrial Relations and Social Affairs initiated a major debate on the future of social policy,[28] and at the same time an ad hoc *Comité des Sages* proposed the integration of civic and social rights as a basis for social policy.[29]

There was a growing consensus for a European-wide 'Third Way' that would combine economic and social integration. There were four main features of this consensus. The first was employment growth. The so-called 'Essen principles' (after the European Council meeting of 1994 at which they were agreed) involved promoting investment in vocational training, reducing non-wage labour costs, avoiding measures that negatively affect availability for work and improving the position of groups most affected by unemployment, such as young and older workers and the long-term unemployed. Secondly, the emerging European model was to be 'social' rather than narrowly focused on labour. The emphasis was no longer primarily on labour laws but also on social protection. There was massive pressure to dismantle the welfare state, so increasing inequalities between the shrinking elite protected by labour law and the 52 million Europeans living below the poverty line—the 'socially excluded'. The alarming rise of racism and xenophobia against third-country migrants and visible minorities had exacerbated this social divide. Not surprisingly, therefore, the social policy White Paper emphasised the need to combat social exclusion. The idea of the 'European citizen'—an individual whose social standards are guaranteed in and out of work by

---

[26] See Mermet and Hoffmann (2001).
[27] Hepple (2005) 209–10.
[28] European Commission (1993, 1994b).
[29] European Commission (1996, 1999).

indivisible social and civic rights—became a central concept. Equality of opportunity for women and men required measures to desegregate the labour market, to reconcile employment and family life, and to accelerate the participation of women in decision-making. Social integration was to be promoted by fighting against poverty and social exclusion.

Thirdly, the White Paper on social policy emphatically rejected total harmonisation of labour laws as an objective of social policy. It was the

> convergence of goals and policies over a period of time by fixing common objectives that is vital, since it will permit the coexistence of different national systems and enable them to progress in harmony towards the fundamental objectives of the Union.[30]

The role of the EU was to be mainly programmatic and goal-setting within a framework of minimum standards. However, certain social and labour rights were to be regarded as 'fundamental'. The EEC started the process of constitutionalisation of rights with the Community Charter of Fundamental Rights of Workers (1989) (above). This was followed by the Treaty of Nice (2000), which proclaimed a Charter of Fundamental Rights that included a relatively clear and systematic statement of social and labour rights.

Fourthly, the creation and implementation of this 'Third Way' social model was increasingly to be through the social dialogue between management and labour at EU level, first institutionalised in the Single European Act 1986 and given new legitimacy by the Treaties of Maastricht and Amsterdam. This was described as a 'European model of social consensus reconciling economic efficiency and social solidarity',[31] but in practice it was relatively little used (see chapter 7 below). This dialogue at EU level must not be confused with the many systems of autonomous collective bargaining that have developed in European countries. Those systems rest on the freedom of association, including the right to strike and the negotiation of agreements between representative organisations of workers and employers. The 'right of association and the right to strike or the right to lock-out' are expressly excluded from the EU's legislative competence, and European-level unions lack the membership and social power which is essential to effective collective bargaining. While the EU social dialogue is consonant with the Third Way idea of democratic legitimacy, it differs from national collective bargaining in that it is not supposed to be adversarial.

The Treaty of Amsterdam (1997) created the institutional framework within which economic and social integration could be achieved. Title VIII (Employment) was a legal and constitutional, as well as a social and economic, turning point in the evolution of EU labour law. In place of centralised harmonisation, the new approach has been based on the principle of subsidiarity. This principle, according to Article 5 EC, is that the Community should take action

---

[30] European Commission (1994a) 12.
[31] Ibid.

only if and so far as the objective of the proposed action cannot sufficiently be achieved by the Member States and can therefore, by reason of the scale or effects of the proposed action, be better achieved by the Community.

The Open Method of Co-Ordination—a decentralised process involving the exchange of best practices, the use of benchmarking, national and regional target-setting, periodic reporting and multi-lateral surveillance—emerged as an intergovernmental (rather than supra-national) means of fiscal, economic and employment co-operation. In 2000, the EU adopted the Lisbon strategy for employment and growth.[32] This was linked to employment policy and the 'flexicurity' agenda, the aim of which was to achieve flexibility for employers without undermining the security of workers (see chapter 3 below).

Free Competition v Labour Law and Collective Bargaining

Market rules of free competition have always contained a threat against trade unions and collective bargaining when those social institutions are viewed as being in restraint of trade and so undermining the workings of the free market. European countries have sought to resolve these conflicts in different ways. We can distinguish between three groups of countries by the way in which they regulate the relationship between competition law, labour law and collective agreements.[33]

First, in the Nordic countries we find statute-based immunity for collective agreements explicitly confirmed in national competition law. For instance, in Denmark, Sweden and Finland the national Acts on competition contain a clause saying that the legislation as such is not applicable to the labour market. Secondly, in continental European countries such as Austria, Belgium France, Germany and Italy national law defines no anti-trust immunity for collective agreements. Such immunity has, however, been derived in several countries from constitutional rights or freedoms pertaining to collective bargaining. In other words, the perceived autonomy of the collective agreement protects it from competition law. Moreover, trade unions have usually not been regarded as undertakings and therefore they have fallen outside the scope of competition law. Thirdly, we have the common law tradition, in Britain and Ireland, where doctrines of restraint of trade in principle apply to the entire sphere of labour law, so that freedom to organise in trade unions and to bargain collectively has had to be protected, since 1871, by a series of negative immunities from actions in common law against unions and employers. In Britain, since 1956 specific legislation on restrictive trade practices has excluded restrictions related to terms and conditions of employment, but these exceptions are rather weak and judges have interpreted them narrowly, being reluctant to give up their power to strike

---

[32] Ashiagbor (2005) 139–90.
[33] See Bruun and Hellsten (2001) 70.

down agreements which they consider to be against 'the public interest' even though they relate to employment conditions.[34] Furthermore, there are no fundamental or constitutional rights in Britain against which collective agreements can be assessed.

Since 1957, national competition rules have had to be remodelled in accordance with Community rules, implying the possibility of scrutiny of collective agreements where they appear to breach Community law. The 1957 Treaty of Rome set up EEC competition rules as core elements of a common market that was meant to promote the harmonious development of economic activities within the Community. This first came into focus with the Community public procurement regime, where the issue at stake was the extent to which individual public purchasers may prescribe that bidders are to apply a particular collective agreement.[35] Another issue that drew extensive attention concerned the applicability to collective agreements of Articles 81 (formerly 85) and 82 (formerly 86) of the EC Treaty. The first of these provisions controls anti-competitive behaviour by cartels, the second controls the abuse of market power by dominant undertakings.

Neither of these provisions was drafted having regard to their applicability to collective agreements, but the issue arose several times in the ECJ and also the EFTA court. The ECJ first examined these issues in 1999.[36] Without any clear guidance from the EC Treaty, the Court expressly established the basic anti-trust immunity of sectoral collective agreements. The Court held that the negotiating (sectoral) social partners do not fall under competition rules when seeking jointly to adopt measures to improve conditions of work and employment. The ultimate reason was that falling under those rules would seriously undermine the social policy objectives of collective agreements. Nevertheless, any provision of a collective agreement could be tested under competition rules. The nature and purpose of a provision has to be justified, either as improving 'conditions of work and employment' or by 'social policy objectives'. The basic anti-trust immunity was found to apply to inter-professional and European agreements, and to company-level agreements. The judgments in these cases also affirmed the validity under European competition law of the *erga omnes* extension of collective agreements. Joint bodies established by a collective agreement are regarded as undertakings subject to competition rules if operating on a market.

The national disparities at the sectoral and inter-professional levels in defining the co-existence of collective agreements and competition law were therefore somewhat alleviated by the effect of these ECJ judgments. In particular, an analysis of EC competition rules demonstrates that collective agreements falling only

---

[34] Wedderburn (1995) 371.

[35] See Krüger et al (1998).

[36] Case C-67/96 *Albany v Stichting Bedrijfspensioenfonds Textielindustie* [1999] ECR 5751; Joined Cases C-115–117/97 *Brentjens'Handelonderneming v Stichtungbedrijfsoensioenfonds voor de handel in bouwmaterialen*; Case C-212/97 *Drijvende Bokken v Stichtungpensioenfonds voor de vervoer-en havenbedrijven* [1999] ECR 5751; discussed by Bruun and Hellsten (2001).

under national law are none too common. Nationwide agreements normally fall under EC law, but even merely regional agreements may qualify. On the other hand, the issue is complicated where a contradiction between the EC law immunity and national immunity of collective agreements might arise.

The tension between the market freedoms enshrined in the Treaty and national labour law systems also arose in the context of industrial action at the national level, which hindered the free movement of goods.[37] In one case, where there had been violent destruction of imported fruit and vegetables from Spain by French farmers, the ECJ held that the French Republic had failed to fulfil its obligations under the EC Treaty 'by failing to adopt all necessary and proportionate measures in order to prevent the free movement of fruit and vegetables from being obstructed by actions of private individuals'.[38] The Court did not specifically stress the fact that the actions in the case were of criminal character, which raised some doubts regarding the relevance of the judgment to obstacles to trade resulting from industrial action. These doubts were reinforced by the presentation by the European Commission of a proposal for a Council Regulation giving the Commission competence to intervene in national procedures when obstacles to the free movement on goods occurred at the national level (the Monti proposal). According to its explanatory memorandum, this proposed regulation was clearly intended to cover at least some industrial action. Article 2 of the Regulation eventually adopted gave clear guidelines for interpretation in conflict situations[39]:

> This regulation may not be interpreted as affecting in any way the exercise of fundamental rights as recognised in Member States, including the right or freedom to strike. These rights may also include the right or freedom to take other actions covered by the specific industrial relations systems in Member States.

Like so much else in the ongoing conflict between EC rules and national labour law, this was not the end of the story. It was not until after the end of the period covered by this book that the status of the right to strike in Community law was seriously brought into question, with potentially far-reaching implications for national systems of collective bargaining.[40] But that is a controversial issue that belongs to contemporary labour law.

---

[37] See Bruun and Veneziani (1999).

[38] Case C-265/95 *Commission v France (Spanish strawberries)* [1997] 1 ECR 6959

[39] Regulation 2679/98/EC (7 December 1998).

[40] Case C-48/05 *International Transport Workers' Federation and Finnish Seamen's Union v Viking Line* (judgment of 11 December 2007); Case C-341/05 *Laval v Svenska Byggnadsabetareförbundet* (judgment of 18 December 2007).

Conclusion

At the beginning of the new century, a group of experts, led by Alain Supiot and set up by the European Commission, concluded that the socio-economic regulatory model that had underpinned labour law since the beginning of the twentieth century was in the throes of a crisis.[41] That framework depended on a standardised form of subordination of workers, the widespread nuclear family and the institutionalisation of the parties who have an interest in collective bargaining, all within a national state. The model could be seen as a triangle, the three sides of which were Fordist companies, engaging in mass production of standardised products; trade unions, focused around business sectors; and a Keynesian state, aiming primarily to maintain domestic demand (at a risk of inflation) and protect its domestic markets from foreign competition. The group's report showed that all three sides of the triangle were collapsing. Post-Fordist companies were engaged in producing more non-standard goods and were increasingly in the services sector; technological change and fierce foreign competition demanded a flexible, skills-based workforce; and the wide-scale entry of women into the labour market was eroding the patriarchal model of employment, with greater emphasis on part-time and temporary work. Trade unions were in decline and had begun to redefine their role to deal with issues such as employment growth, company survival and gender equality. Nation states (many of them devolving power to regions) were abandoning their Keynesian policies in favour of anti-inflationary strategies and budgetary control; they were greatly affected by the forces of international competiton and, at the political level, by the shared sovereignty of the EU.

The most significant new developments in the period since 1989 have been at EU level. Those developments have gone in two, not always compatible, directions. On the one hand, the challenges of globalisation have led to attempts at greater harmonisation and co-ordination of the economic, social and labour policies of the European states. On the other hand, EU intervention has been limited to certain areas of labour law, continuing the freedom of nation states to diverge in other areas in order to build on their own competitive institutional advantages. Strike laws, collective bargaining institutions and some other key aspects of labour laws will continue to diverge for the foreseeable future, although they may increasingly come into conflict with the economic freedoms guaranteed by the EU Treaties. This continuing tension between social rights and economic freedoms is set to become a dominant theme of twenty-first-century labour law.

---

[41] Supiot (1999b, 2001).

3

Regulation of the Labour Market

ANTONIO OJEDA AVILÉS AND JORDI GARCÍA VIÑA

Labour Market Policies and Right to Work

Comparing Labour Market Policies

This chapter analyses the main regulatory trends in labour markets. From this perspective, five main sets of policies will be examined and compared as they have developed in significant periods of recent European history. The policies are: (i) regulation of labour supply; (ii) employment services; (iii) active labour market policies; (iv) employment contract strategies; and (v) job security.

An obstacle to comparison is the lack of a common definition of 'worker' or 'employee' in the labour law systems studied; indeed, some countries do not even have a consistent definition of these terms. For our purposes, the critical distinction is between dependent or subordinated workers and autonomous workers. The conceptual problems and how they have been affected by social changes is more fully examined in chapter 4 below. The distinction is of importance to us, not because some countries draw a clear division between the concepts while others do not, but because of what Freedland has called 'a false duality'[1] between them. The pressure for flexible labour markets has created mixed situations and made the distinctions even less obvious than before. As a result of mid-twentieth-century social and labour legislation, European countries have closed the gap between manual and non-manual workers—or, in the terminology of Fox, low-trust relationships and high-trust relationships[2]—and elaborated a unitary concept of the contract of employment[3] that rested on the standard stable employment relationship. But 'large developments have falsified the unitary conception'.[4] Subordination has been blurred in a gradient, and the red line between dependent and independent workers has become increasingly

---

[1] Freedland (2003) 18; see also Pedrazzo (1999) 743.
[2] Fox (1974).
[3] For Britain, see Deakin (1998) and (2001) notes 71 and 72.
[4] Freedland (2003) 18.

deceptive.[5] The real problem, from our point of view, is that the concept of 'labour market' no longer refers exclusively to dependent workers, and—what is worse—in some countries there is no clear field for these. In other words, there is no presumption of subordination, so that autonomous work competes with dependent work on equal terms as alternative ways of doing jobs. For some lines of our study this confusion will not affect the analysis, but when we come to explain certain employment policies or contract 'engineering', the division between those countries with highly formalised (juridified) employment relationships and those with 'open' collective agreements regulating labour relations will feature strongly. The same diversity lies behind proposals by British scholars for an enlarged domain for employment law, comprising not only 'the family of personal work contracts', but also that of personal work relations,[6] and the cautious continental approaches to an enlargement of labour law in certain, measured aspects and for the regulation of certain kinds of autonomous work. Examples of the latter are the application of collective agreements to certain semi-independent workers in Germany, application of certain protections to quasi-subordinate status (*parasubordinazione*) in Italy and the recognition of a set of rights for economically dependent workers in Spain.[7]

The Right to Work

The right to work had already been recognised during the French Revolution of 1789,[8] the Parisian Revolution of 1848[9] and the German Weimar Constitution of 1919.[10] The UN, in its Universal Declaration of Human Rights of 10 December 1948, stated this right in its Article 23.[11] This was followed in European constitutions after the Second World War, as in Belgium,[12]Denmark,[13] France,[14] Italy,[15] Luxembourg,[16] the Netherlands,[17] Finland,[18] Greece,[19] Sweden[20] and Ireland.[21] The Federal Republic of Germany made no reference to the right to work in the

---

[5] See chapter 4 below.

[6] Freedland (2007) 12.

[7] See Ojeda Aviles (2002) 469ff.

[8] Declaration of Rights of Man and the Citizen, 23 June 1789. The General Code of the Prussian State, of 5 February 1794, also declared the state obligation of procuring adequate work for the needy.

[9] Decree of the Provisional Government of 25 February 1848; however, the Constitution of 29 August 1848 failed to declare the right to work.

[10] Art 163.II.

[11] See Stuby (1978) 75ff.

[12] Art 23.

[13] S 75, soft wording.

[14] Preamble, 5.

[15] Art 4.

[16] Art 11.4.

[17] Art 19, soft wording.

[18] Art 18.

[19] Art 22.5.

[20] Art 2(2).

[21] Art 45.2.

Bonn Basic Law (1949), but the constitutions of the *Länder* repeatedly cited the right to work as a social right. Britain, without a written constitution, proclaimed no such legal right, but did ratify the European Social Charter (1961), which recognises the right to work in Article 1.[22] By the end of the twentieth century, the dominant opinion about the enforceability of this right was that it involves only a mandate to the state to introduce active employment policies, not a clear individual right to obtain a job. Such an individual right would only be possible in a state economy.[23] In other words, as the German labour courts[24] and the Spanish Constitutional Court[25] have recognised, the constitutional provisions are programmatic declarations marking a general guideline for the country's administration. The idea that the state must take measures against unemployment entered consistently into the socio-political heritage of all European countries. Recently, Deakin and Wilkinson have refined the dominant opinion by describing the linkage between employment policies and unemployment benefits as a twofold compromise by the state. First, 'social insurance and full employment policy together sought to guarantee access to a wage capable, at a minimum, of supporting subsistence'.[26] Secondly, the compromise comes with a string attached to it, a worker's duty to work,[27] which is a feature of new theories of the workfare state, discussed below. This refinement has to take into account a third element to describe the entire idea of a right to work as it developed in the second part of the twentieth century. There was an extensive effort in the European countries to find jobs for their citizens through employment measures or, alternatively, to give them means of subsistence. However, we must not forget that a strong part of the right to work was composed of a diversity of legal and collective bargaining rules around what is called job security. Full employment policy, social insurance and protection against unfair dismissal constitute in our opinion the three feet of the table and, in this sense, the right to work, together with comprehensive social security and a permanent social dialogue, had by the end of our period become a feature of the 'European Social Model'.

Reconstruction (1945–50)

Regulation of Labour Supply

The aftermath of the Second World War was acute in countries which had

[22] Hepple (1981) 68ff, (1982) 657.
[23] Wank (1980) 66.
[24] Däubler (1994) 523.
[25] Spanish Constitutional Court Decision 22/1981 of 8 April 1981.
[26] Deakin and Wilkinson (2005) 149; see also Van Parijs and Vanderborght (2006) *passim*.
[27] Freedland et al (2007) 196.

suffered many human losses during the conflict.[28] The great majority of the 72 million casualties were Europeans, mainly from East European countries, but also from Germany (7,293,000 deaths, 10.47% of the population), France (562,000; 1.35%), Austria (105,500; 1,59%), Belgium (86,100; 1.02%), Finland (97,000; 2.62%), Denmark (3,200; 0.08%), Greece (311,300; 4.31%), Britain (450,400; 0.94%), Italy (454,500; 1.02%) and the Netherlands (202,800; 2.32%). However, employment was not an easy issue, since firms across the continent suffered many physical losses as well. The reconstruction had to be fostered by the states, which assumed the responsibility through several measures.

Macroeconomic measures aimed to reduce unemployment. Several International Labour Organisation (ILO) recommendations had insisted on the importance of public works to cope with unemployment (1919, 1937, 1944), and the US had undertaken a successful initiative in this way, in the form of the Tennessee Valley Authority Act of 1933. These measures were discussed in chapter 2, above. Internal migrations in Italy and other southern countries to their more industrialised northern regions re-emerged in this period. Other nations restored external migration, like France, with its traditional African labour sources[29]; Britain and the Netherlands, with their Asian and Afro-Caribbean immigrants; and Denmark, with its seasonal agricultural workers from eastern Europe.

Strategic companies and industries came into the hands of the state through a wave of nationalisations which secured the survival of their activities and, with them, jobs, as we saw in chapter 2 above. Reconstruction took place at different speeds in the western countries, signalling what, during the next phase of welfare state, would become two vertical Europes: that of the north and that of the south. On the one hand, Italy, Spain, Portugal and Greece formed the sources of migrant workers, accompanied at that time by Ireland. These could be described as secondary players in economic growth. On the other hand, countries located largely in the north needed foreign labour immediately. At the same time, emigration from Europe to other parts of the world remained powerful for several years. For instance, between 1946 and 1958, almost two million Europeans went to work in the US, headed by the Germans (377,378, 20% of the total emigrants), British (282,360, 15%), Italians (212,050, 12%), Irish (75.957, 4%), French (52,279, 3%) and Dutch (51,421, 3%). But emigration co-existed with pronounced immigration. As early as 1948, Alfred Sauvy said about France that 'after three years of full employment, immigration has been very much below the demand', and that 'the National Immigration Office acted more as a brake than as a motor'.[30] International migrations operated more or less freely, and a report from the International Labour Office detected a simultaneous manpower

---

[28] Gregory (1951); Steinberg (1991).
[29] Sauvy (1948) 134.
[30] Ibid.

shortage in certain industries of some countries and a general surplus in others[31] in western Europe after the Second World War.

Chaos in labour exchanges finally provoked, at the end of the period, the flourishing of bilateral agreements to facilitate interstate migrations, like that signed by Italy, Germany, Belgium, France, Luxembourg, the Netherlands, Britain, Switzerland and Sweden, which mainly sought labour for agriculture and construction, and that by Spain, Belgium and France. These agreements became even more important in the period after 1950 (see below).

Employment Services

The huge need for managing unemployment in a devastated continent led to a radical change in the role of the public employment offices. Many efforts were made in the early post-war period to cope with abuses by private agencies and the inefficiency of unions and charitable organisations that provided placement services, at times subsidised by the administrations. A number of public offices and networks were organised, mainly by local authorities but always under the subsidiarity principle, since it was thought that the 'market' ought to regulate the employment relationship, including the recruitment of the worker. ILO Convention No 2 (1919) proposed national systems of public and free employment agencies, under the control of a central authority, and coordination plans to link free private agencies to the public network. Some years later, ILO Convention No 34 (1934) proposed the prohibition of profit-making offices, but obtained only 10 ratifications. Consequently a new version followed in 1949 with Convention No 96, which gave the states two options: either to prohibit profit-making agencies or to bind them by tight regulation.

Countries reacted in different ways. Some prescribed regulation of profit-making agencies without prohibiting them, and gave vigorous support to the public offices, not only by creating a nationwide set of them, but also by giving them a monopoly of placement, and bound the remaining private agencies to the supervision of the public service.[32] Following that trend, the French Ordinance 45-1030 of 1945 established a state monopoly and permitted associate agencies and union-employers services to operate temporarily, as well as those profit-making agencies established before 1945.[33] Sweden, Denmark, Germany, Greece, Spain and a number of other countries also declared a state monopoly. A 'highly centralised system' had been created in the Netherlands in 1940, under German occupation, and was maintained after the war. Britain continued the system of labour exchanges, first established in 1909, co-ordinated and paid for by a national authority. [34] In other countries, too, the state network took

---

[31] ILO (1959a) 206.
[32] ILC (1994) *passim*; Servais (2005) 175.
[33] Péllisier et al (1998) 102; *Droit Social* 4 (1948) 144ff and 6 (1948) 225ff.
[34] Vogel-Polsky (1986) 162–63.

advantage of the regional, provincial and local services created in previous decades, centralising their direction, and opening their management to the participation of unions and employers' associations, which played a substantial role during the reconstruction period.

Three divergences from the common type should be mentioned. The first was in Germany, divided into four zones by the victors, with different approaches to the labour market until 1949, when the Russian zone became the German Democratic Republic and adopted a Soviet-style planning and employment system. Secondly, Italy kept some features from earlier times of the state monopoly, especially the *richiesta numerica* (request by the employer to the employment office specifying only the number, category and skill level of the workers needed, as distinct from the *richiesta nominativa* to take on a specific worker), obliging the employment office to select the specific workers using objective criteria.[35] Other mandatory requirements in Italy, like labour quotas in agriculture (Legislative Decree 929/1947), were declared null and void by the Constitutional Court in 1958. Thirdly, southern countries with dictatorships, like Spain and Portugal, did not open their systems to the unions and employers' organisations, which had been forbidden and superseded by state-imposed 'vertical' organisations.

Job Security

Job security measures had a difficult birth because of the liberal doctrine of equality of the parties. Both common law and civil law systems viewed employer and employee as free and equal contracting parties, ignoring the obvious discrepancy in their bargaining power and the fact that the employment relationship provided income to a family unit for one party and constituted a cost of production for the other.[36] There had been many inroads into this liberal approach in the period before the Second World War, by both case law (such as the doctrine of *l'abus de droit* in France), and by legislation, most notably in the Weimar Works Councils Act 1920, the Spanish Labour Contract Act 1931, the Basic Agreement between the Swedish Employers' Confederation and the Swedish Confederation of Trade Unions in 1938, and the Italian Civil Code of 1942.[37] However, it was only during the post-war years that protection against unfair dismissals became widespread. Among the measures adopted in Europe at different times in those years were requirements of notice to terminate employment, remedies for unfair dismissal, requirements for prior administrative authorisation, and requirements for consent of the works council or negotiations with trade unions.[38]

---

[35] Decree 1934/1938, and after the war, Act 264/1949.
[36] Anderman (1985) 3.
[37] For details see Vogel-Polsky (1986) 185–89.
[38] Blanpain (1973) 156.

Of these measures, the most striking in the immediate post-war period was the Extraordinary Decree on Labour Relations adopted in the Netherlands in 1945, which became a permanent feature of Dutch labour law, but was not copied elsewhere. This Decree provided that an employer may not dismiss any regular worker without previous express permission by the regional Labour Office (*arbeidsbureau*). As a result, the Labour Office became involved in almost every collective dismissal (*collectief ontslag*) involving 20 or more workers, and also in individual dismissals for economic or non-economic reasons. Bakels concludes that the Director of the District Labour Office came to fulfil much the same function as the conciliation service does in Britain.[39] Havinga has shown that it is the employers who have the strategic advantage of determining what issues are brought up for discussion during the dismissal procedure at the Labour Office, and the officials are mainly concerned with the selection of individual employees rather than the general grounds of dismissal.[40] This system of administrative authorisation 'may have endured because of the Dutch traditions of participatory and consensual labour relations at many levels, including institutionalised co-determination by the works council and the informal character of Dutch legal culture in comparison with for example, neighbouring Germany'.[41] Post-war Germany in fact revived and extended the Weimar requirement that before any dismissal the employer must consult the works council. Failure to do so would make the dismissal null and void.

The Welfare State (1950–72)

Regulation of Labour Supply

Economic growth in post-war Europe was accompanied by structural change, for which labour market adaptability was a prerequisite. But this adaptability could no longer be guaranteed without active manpower policies. A further reason for this was growing awareness of the possible problems posed by the persistence of large-scale immigration, which, in the earlier years, had provided a crucial element of flexibility in the labour market. Already by 1965, migrant workers accounted for 3.5% of the west European labour force, and were concentrated in specific industries and regions, like the construction and motor vehicles in France.

Immigration provided a source of mobility and flexibility in many European countries. The existence of administrative controls on the number of immigrants, on their subsequent jobs and on their duration of stay in host countries

[39] Bakels (1981) 538.
[40] Havinga (1994) 270–77.
[41] Hepple (1997) 215.

should have ensured that immigrants only took jobs when and where there was a demand, but some industrial occupations were increasingly taken over by immigrants. This concentration of immigrant workers in particular industries and regions necessarily had far-reaching social consequences, and provoked two main responses: first, the protection of disadvantaged groups, beginning with the Black and Asian ethnic minorities in Britain and the Netherlands (discussed in chapter 5 below), and secondly, the management of flows of migrant workers.

External missions for recruitment were established in the southern countries, like that created by France in Italy and Spain, which contracted 83,000 Italians and 18,000 Spaniards in 1956, or another one established by Germany in Italy. From 1950 onwards, the preference was for multilateral agreements with migration as the unique subject or as part of extensive labour regulations. In this connection, mention must be made of the convention of the European Defence Community in 1950, as well as the regulations on the common labour market of the Nordic countries (1954), the Labour Treaty for the Benelux countries and the European Coal and Steel Community (1954).[42] Germany signed its first migration agreement with Italy in 1955, followed by similar instruments with Spain and Greece in 1960, with Turkey in 1961, with Morocco in 1963, with Portugal in 1964 and with Tunisia in 1965. In 1964, one million *Gastarbeiter* worked as foreigners with resident permits, which allowed them to stay in the country and open the way to a second generation. Generally speaking, countries envisaged migration as a fertile but delicate device which needed strict regulation, through the use of work permit systems. The total number of immigrant workers grew from 4 million to 10 million between 1950 and 1970, mainly in Britain, Belgium, France, Germany and the Netherlands. Southern countries, for their part, sent 5 million to the north.[43] By the beginning of the 1960s, laws of the host countries drastically limited free immigration flows, as Britain did with its Commonwealth workers from 1962 onwards.[44] It must be remembered that the issue became deeply affected by the formation of the European Economic Community (EEC) in 1957 and its basic principle of free movement of workers who were nationals of the Member States. Thus Italians could travel freely to Germany or France, but not to Britain, Ireland or Denmark until the accession of the latter to the EEC in 1973, and Greeks, Spaniards or Portuguese could not travel freely to work in the EEC until their accession in 1981 and 1986 respectively.[45] For the third country nationals, from outside the Community, the work permit system involved strict control with some exceptions.[46] The main distinction between citizens of the Member States and third country nationals was that the former could not be

[42] ILO (1959a) 207–12.

[43] Dolado (2002) 14.

[44] Commonwealth Immigrants Act 1962, followed by Commonwealth Immigration Act 1968, superseded by the Immigration Act 1971.

[45] Austria, Finland and Sweden entered in the EU in 1995 and their nationals then enjoyed free movement rights.

[46] Macdonald and Blake (1995) 287.

discriminated against on grounds of nationality, while the latter could be and were the subject of widespread discrimination (see chapter 5 below).

Southern countries saw the question from a different angle. Influenced by the history of oceanic migrations to America,[47] these countries introduced new legislation that considered mass departures as an aspect of employment policies and as involving rights of citizenship. This meant not only taking care of the human aspects, like travel protection, repatriation assistance and family reunification, but also administrative co-ordination issues, vested social security rights and mediation with host employers.[48] Southern countries spoke only of 'emigration', and created a specific bureaucracy under this name.[49]

Employment Services

Extensive immigration and the state monopoly of employment services did not solve the shortages of labour, in particular short-term jobs. Differences by sectors, regions and groups of workers increased the unemployment rates in certain niches. In Belgium, for instance, in 1959 the regions showed quite disproportionate amounts of total unemployment, with 66% in the Flemish part, 21% in the Walloon part and 13% in Brussels, although the active population corresponded to 47, 35 and 18% respectively.[50] Profit-making agencies returned—if ever absent—to the stage.

During the 1960s temporary work agencies (TWAs) grew rapidly everywhere, and in practice, as Vergara observes, the state monopoly of employment services was overcome by private intermediaries.[51] The first law regulating TWAs came in the Netherlands (1965), followed by Denmark (1970), Ireland (1971), France and Germany (1972), and Belgium (1976). The other countries in this study followed from 1989 onwards (see below). The British Employment Agencies Act 1973 regulated both recruitment through a fee-charging agency and placement with a user of a person employed by a fee-charging employment business, irrespective of whether the work was temporary or indefinite. Agency work, in the sense of temporary work provided through an intermediary (*travail intérimaire*), is the product of a less stable economy and of varying market demands, which expose companies to unpredictable planning in their production schedules and also to changing needs in selecting skills. At the same time, agencies providing temporary workers responded to the employers' increasing need for flexibility. Trade union opposition achieved some success in achieving workers' guarantees, like information, representation or dual responsibilities of both the agency and the user business for failure to comply with the employer's obligations. Even before

---

[47] Sec, eg Spanish Emigration Law of 20 December 1924.
[48] See, eg Spanish Emigration Law of 22 December 1960.
[49] Eg Spanish Institute of Emigration, created in 1956.
[50] Reneau (1960) 484–85.
[51] Vergara Del Rio (2005) 11.

legislation, labour courts in France and Germany were indulgent towards the phenomenon of temporary work through an intermediary. Camerlynck expressed the reality in France in 1969, three years before legislation:

> [I]t is remarkable that collective bargaining preceded law. Indeed, on 9 October 1969, an agreement was made between Manpower France and the CGT. The legislator to a large extent took it into consideration in 1972, especially in introducing the 'allowance for precarious employment'.[52]

By way of contrast, the British unions, although relatively powerful at the time, refused to discuss the issue of private temporary work services with employers or the agencies, and wanted them abolished.[53] Experience showed unsuspected capacities of TWAs related to cross-border flows very early in time: for example, in 1970 the European Court of Justice (ECJ) had to decide a case which dealt with a French TWA sending workers to Germany taking advantage of different national regulations.[54] This decision formed part of the background to EC regulation of posted workers in 1996 (Directive 96/71/EC).

Most laws of the 1960s and 1970s enacted strict requirements of authorisation, usually called a licence, and subjected agencies to a strict public control, linking the worker to the TWA with a written employment contract containing a minimum content. In some countries, agencies could only be devoted to supplying labour as an intermediary (*travail intérimaire*), or could provide workers only in sectors or areas where there were shortages, or could do so only for specific reasons. In some countries, employment contracts did not have to be formalised, but a contract for services (self-employed, independent workers) between the supplier firm and the temporary worker could be used instead. Two main models were later followed by other countries. The French model permitted employment contracts to be adapted to the duration of the task, but the temporary worker was entitled to the same remuneration as paid to workers of the host, user company. The German model permitted the standard earnings prescribed by a TWA collective agreement to be paid, but required the workers to be engaged for an indefinite duration—not connected with a particular mission—so that they retained salaries during interim periods of inactivity. The following decades saw the evolution of these models in search of flexibility, by permitting adaptations of contracts to missions but requiring that the temporary workers be entitled to the same earnings as those of permanent workers of the user company. The activities of TWAs conflicted with one of the principles of labour law in this period: the stability principle, or property in jobs. Courts in several countries created the presumption of an indefinite relationship when the contractual parties did not express their opinion about duration, and declared that the employer had to exhibit an objective ground to make a contract of fixed

---

[52] Camerlynck (1978) 457.
[53] Hepple and Napier (1978) 196.
[54] Hepple (2005) 165–72.

duration.[55] Some Acts required a written contract, including a termination clause. Italy approved Act No 230/1962, limiting the justification for temporarily contracting in the form of six 'exceptions' to the presumption of indefinite duration. This was followed by similar Acts in Portugal,[56] Spain[57], France[58] and some other states.

Active Labour Market Policies

One aspect of active labour market policies that surfaced in this period was the principle of equal treatment of disadvantaged workers (see chapter 5 below). This principle included equal remuneration for women and men. However, equal earnings was just one aspect of a many-sided problem. Segmentation of the labour market brought difficulties for several sectors of the population when searching for jobs—not only for women, young people, disabled or senior workers, but immigrants as well, who did not enjoy the national workers' mobility upwards to more skilled occupations and were concentrated in occupations with below-average pay. It was in this period that the EEC Social Fund (Regulation 9/1960/CEE) became responsible for about 50% of the investments in vocational training, devoted to three targets: professional re-education, relocation of the unemployed and subvention payments during temporary reductions of employment as a result of restructuring of firms to another activity.[59] France created *Fonds National de l'Emploi* (1963), and other countries followed suit, such as the Spanish National Fund to Protect Work (*Fondo Nacional de Protección al Trabajo*).[60]

Rapid technological and economic changes and the trend from manufacturing to services[61] opened a gap between the classic learning of skills and the new demands of firms. Vocational training had to be reformed, and to be accompanied by continued training. One of the most relevant measures to cope with the transition of young people from learning to employment was the German 'dual system'. The Vocational Training Act 1969, revised in the 1970s, laid down the lines for simultaneous theoretical and practical teaching in schools and industries, under the coordination of the Federal Institute for Vocational Training.[62] Other countries, like France with its training

---

[55] Gumpert (1961) 645; Blomeyer (1967) 408.

[56] Labour Contract Act 49408/1969, Art 10: justified cause or compensation.

[57] Labour Relations Act 1976, Art 15.

[58] Several Acts and Regulations since 1982, and Art L 122-1 and L 122-2 Code du Travail. See Pélissier et al (1998) 247ff.

[59] A positive approach to the Fund in De Riemaecker-Legot (1960) 161. Other European employment and vocational training incentives in Servais (2008) 164ff.

[60] Act of July 21, 1960, ss 13–16.

[61] For automation and the 'new working class' at the beginning of the 1960s, see Mallet (1963).

[62] See Tremblay and Le Bot (2000) 2.

and employment contract (*contrats d'insertion en alternance*), followed the example.[63]

In this period, new types of training institutions emerged in many countries. They were nearer to the world of work than were the old vocational schools. In countries like Denmark and France, alternatives were developed of training workers in centres and in large companies. This apprentice was bound to the employer by an apprenticeship contract and thereby received wages from the employer, but he or she was trained entirely at the centre. Of course, the concept of an apprenticeship contract had been changing because different systems were appearing, integrated with policies and programmes of continuing education.

It was made clear over a long period that the needs of workers for employment security could no longer be primarily ensured through employment protection, but must involve giving employees the abilities and possibilities, through education, training and lifelong learning, for staying attractive to employers in a changing labour market. It is important as well to take note of the trends to convert apprenticeship and/or young workers' contracts into non-labour relationships, whatever they are called.

Disabled workers benefited to a certain extent from war veterans' legislation in the post-war period but, when reconstruction had finished, new legislation tried to modify the integration techniques from subvention measures to training and rehabilitation under the aegis of the three ILO recommendations devoted to the subject, as, for instance, Belgium did with an Act of 1958 (see further chapter 5).

Job Security

Job security measures were a response to growing union demands for employment security and for workers' participation in management decisions affecting them, at a time when unions were at the height of their membership and power. The lead came from the German Dismissals Protection Act 1951, which was the outcome of a basic consensus between the central employers' and union organisations, and 'so from the outset enjoyed a very specific legitimacy and authority'.[64] It required a 'socially justified cause' to dismiss, with only three kinds of reason possibly justifying dismissal: those concerning the worker's personality (ie which make the worker incapable of fulfilling the requirements of the job); reasons concerning the worker's behaviour; and economic reasons. The German law can only be understood if the works council's role is taken into account. Building on the Weimar law (see above), the Works Constitution Act 1972 obliged the employer to consult the works (or staff) council, informing them of the reason for dismissal. In the case of an ordinary dismissal, the works council could agree, it could do nothing, it could declare a written reservation or

---

[63] Act No 130 of 1984 developed an excessive regulation of it, which hindered its effectiveness: Javillier (1996) 159. It was replaced on 4 May 2004 by the so-called 'professionalisation contract'.
[64] Weiss and Schmidt (2000) 104.

it could object to the dismissal in writing. Although an objection would not prevent dismissal, it would place the worker in a strong position when fighting the case in court. The approach of the 1951 Act had a major influence in other European countries in the period of the welfare state.

Another major influence was ILO Recommendation No 119 (1963) (later replaced by Convention No 158 (1982)), which stated that termination of employment should not take place unless there is a valid reason connected with the capacity or conduct of the worker or based on the operational requirements of the undertaking. The issue formed part of central collective agreements in several countries like Sweden, where the Basic Agreement of 1938 was revised to require valid reasons for dismissals. The three- months miners' strike in 1969–70 was followed by a new spirit of cooperation ("Saltsjøbaden spirit") that facilitated legislative interventions, in particular the Employment Security Act 1974, which required a long period of notice for lay-offs (2–6 months) and previous notification to the established local unions, as well as written notice to the worker.[65] Other Nordic countries went in a similar direction. The Finnish Labour Contract Act 1970 distinguished between dismissals for a reason connected with the individual employee (individual termination) and a termination for lack of work (collective termination). An individual dismissal required an especially weighty reason.[66]

In Britain, a government consultation document in 1970[67] reported that:

> Britain is one of the few countries where dismissals are a frequent cause of strike action. It seems reasonable to link this with the fact that in this country, unlike most others, the law provides no redress for the employee who suffers unfair or arbitrary dismissal, if the employer has met the terms of the contract, eg on giving notice.

Britain entered a new era of job security in 1963, with the introduction of what proved to be the first in a long line of individual employment protection statutes, in the form of the Contracts of Employment Act, which provided minimum periods of notice.[68] There followed quickly the Redundancy Payments Act 1965, which provided for a system of severance pay (redundancy payments). Then the Industrial Relations Act 1971, part of an attempt to use law as the main means of re-ordering British industrial relations, came into force with a 'very modest protection' against unfair dismissal. This protection was extended in 1974, with the qualifying period being reduced from 2 years to 6 months (only to be raised again to 1 year by the Thatcher government in 1980). However, the remedies of reinstatement and re-engagement never proved to be successful in practice, and compensation (limited in amount) remained the main remedy. Perhaps the most

---

[65] Adlercreutz (1976) 100 and 103.
[66] Suviranta (1976) 26.
[67] Industrial Relations Bill Consultative Document, 5 October 1970, para 52, cited by Anderman (1985) 4.
[68] Anderman (1985) 3.

important consequence of unfair dismissal laws in Britain was the formalisation of disciplinary and dispute procedures, so that by the mid-1980s it was estimated that most firms, especially larger companies, had such procedures.

The spark in France was the social unrest of May 1968, leading to the Grenelle agreements, which resulted in statutes on union rights in the enterprise (1968), professional training and retraining (1971), and reforms of the law of dismissal (first in 1973, then in respect of economic dismissals in 1975). It was in Italy, however, where the spirit of the period reached its height in the 'hot autumn' of 1969. Before this, an Act of 1966 had introduced the notion of invalidity of unjustified dismissals with Act 604/1966, which should have meant worker's rein-statement, but the doctrine of unenforceability of personal obligations prevented the judges from implementing it.[69] However, the significant section 18 of the Workers' Statute 1970 made enforceability possible: the judge who declared the dismissal unfair could order the employer to reinstate the worker and to pay him or her compensation corresponding to no less than 5 months' salary. The law provided for an injunction (*inhibitoria*),[70] and, despite the long delays of Italian justice, that sanction transformed the paper right to have a dismissal rendered invalid into a real assertion of 'job property'—the worker's right to retain his or her specific job.[71] Ten years later, in the period of deregulation (below), a reform softened the impact by excluding firms with fewer than 15 workers on the payroll.[72]

Economic Crisis (1973–79)

Regulation of Labour Supply

The turbulence triggered by the oil crisis had dramatic consequences on Euro-pean industrial relations in general and collective bargaining in particular, notably through unemployment, redundancies and restructuring.[73] A sharp fall in real earnings and productivity began in 1974 and did not level until 1986.[74] Unemployment went up from 2–3% in 1966 to 5% in the following decade (Table 3.1) and to 11.1% in 1986, but it must be remembered that Greece, Spain and Portugal, with relatively high unemployment rates, joined the EEC in the 1980s. Ireland and Italy had the highest figures at the beginning of the crisis, but at the end of it, Spain had reached 22% in 1985. There emerged what would later be called social dumping, with competition on wage costs, health and safety, and

[69] D'Antona (1979) 2.
[70] Ibid, 125.
[71] Molitor, cited by d'Antona (1979) 1; Napoli (1980) 42–54.
[72] Act 108/1990.
[73] Pélissier et al (2004) 23.
[74] European Commission (1989) 49, 55.

Table 3.1: Unemployment, Prices and Wages, EEC 1965–81

Country	% unemployment			% price rise			% wages rise		
	1965	1975	1981	1965	1975	1981	1965	1975	1981
Belgium	2.2	5.0	11.6	3.1	6.8	7.5	7.6	12.3	8.8
Denmark	1.2	3.3	8.2	5.0	9.7	11.2	10.2	11.6	9.9
Germany	0.9	2.5	4.8	2.6	5.3	5.8	7.6	9.5	5.6
Greece	–	–	3.3	–	11.7	24.1	–	–	22.5
France	0.8	3.3	7.8	4.2	8.6	13.5	9.6	13.5	15.6
Ireland	4.5	7.1	9.7	3.9	12.8	20.0	9.3	18.1	18.4
Italy	5.5	5.6	8.6	3.5	13.2	19.5	10.3	17.8	19.3
Luxembourg	0.1	0.2	1.0	2.3	6.3	8.0	6.2	10.4	9.0
The Netherlands	0.9	3.0	7.3	4.0	7.5	7.5	10.4	11.7	4.3
UK (Britain)	1.8	4.0	10.2	3.5	12.3	11.8	6.1	15.1	12.1

Source: European Commission (1981) 19–29. Figures for years 1965 and 1975 are averages of 1960–69 and 1970–79, respectively.

other working conditions. Unemployment had stabilised by the summer of 1986 and slipped downward from 1988, when western Europe seemed to be split in three blocs of countries: those with low rates of unemployment, between 5 and 10% (Britain, Portugal, Greece, Germany and Denmark); those with medium rates, around 10% (the Netherlands, France and Italy); and those with high figures, 17–18% (Ireland and Spain).[75]

Different approaches to the crisis and economic restructuring were adopted (see chapter 2 above). Macroeconomic measures were implemented with stricter restrictions on immigration, accompanied by tripartite coordination on employment and measures concerning the restructuring of companies. Immigrants, probably to a greater extent than young people, women, senior workers and disabled persons, suffered from the crisis not only because of entry restrictions, but also because redundancies punished them dramatically. The crisis also aggravated the discrimination against established ethnic minorities, such as the Roma communities in continental Europe, people from Surinam and the Antilles in the Netherlands, and Asian and Afro-Caribbean groups in Britain (see chapter 5 below). Hundreds of thousands of migrants returned to their southern countries, aggravating the economic situation there. Nevertheless Spain, Italy, Portugal and Greece had undergone a turnaround from being countries of emigration to countries of immigration during the previous few decades. Southern European migration can be distinguished in three stages[76]: (i) emigration (overseas, until the 1950s; to northern Europe, from the 1950s to the mid-1970s); (ii) return

[75] Ibid, 113–14.
[76] Rodríguez Garcia (2005) 1.

(from the mid-1970s); and (iii) immigration (1980s–1990s, first in Italy, from 1972, then in Spain and Greece from 1975 and Portugal from 1981). The increase in international immigration and the new issues of multiculturalism would challenge the social and political structures in southern Europe (see chapter 5 below).

Employment Services

Placement of workers continued under the guidance of public services, but the turbulences of mass dismissals and restructuring convinced governments of their limits, principally in the fields of temporary (short-term) placement and of reactive employment policies, giving rise to more indulgent treatment of temporary work agencies and the exploration of proactive policies. Rather than evaluating the rationale of the economic choices behind agency work and regulating the contract between the agency and the user, labour law attempted to address agency workers with some specific measures. The relationship between agencies, employees and users became the object of regulation by provision for joint liability of agency and user to pay remuneration and social security, as well for other typical managerial obligations, such as the delivery of health and safety measures and the duty to inform.

Active Labour Market Policies

The crisis highlighted the vulnerability of older workers. A distinction should be made here between workers aged 45–60, and workers aged 60 or more. The first group were the subject of special measures in the 1970s during the recession following the oil crisis. Those workers were the first to be fired and found serious difficulties in finding re-employment. The measures implemented in European countries concentrated more on facilitating early retirement than on reintegration. Legislation granting them long periods of unemployment benefits and pre-retirement pensions started during the 1970s. The result was that large numbers of mature workers left the production system, so creating a danger to the financial stability of social security, until the energetic reaction of the 2000 Lisbon European Employment Strategy (see chapter 6 below). Two apparently contradictory approaches were taken in the 1970s: the first one promoted the exclusion of older workers as a means of labour market policy and the second promoted their maintenance in the 'active ageing' population as a means of sustainability of the social security system.

Employment Contract Strategies

Distrust of temporary (short-term) and part-time contracts changed when some countries proved that they could be a source of job creation. Spain, Greece and

Portugal began subsidising a policy of temporary contracts for the young and senior unemployed,[77] and Britain, the Netherlands and Denmark achieved good results in reducing unemployment by promoting part-time work,[78] despite the initial bad experiences related to subsidising it in the Netherlands in 1978–79. In the Netherlands, not only did employers support this kind of contract, but the unions also saw the advantages for disabled and senior workers and those with family responsibilities, and considered that employers needed organisational flexibility more than wages flexibility. Legislation excluded part-time workers from several benefits under the 'one-third' criterion: if a person worked for less than one-third of normal working time they were excluded from benefits such as minimum wages, minimum holidays and representation on works councils. Collective agreements left out part-time employees from several benefits, such as complementary pension schemes, and did not apply the *pro rata temporis* principle with regard to wages, etc. Neither general definition nor legislation avoided the problem. Although the bilateral *Stichting van de Arbeid* fought against differences, many claimed that it was precisely the discrimination between full-time and part-time workers that explained the expansion of part-time work during the1970s. By 1983, 21% of employed people in the Netherlands belonged to this category (this had risen to 30% by 1993).[79] It was only in 1996 that the equality principle was applied to these workers in the Netherlands. Britain (with the second highest proportion of part-timers in the EC) did not do so until after the EC had enacted a Directive aimed at discrimination between part-time and full-time workers (Council Directive 97/81/EC)). In Belgium, where there was a high rate of part-time work, an Act of 1981 required a written form to contract, and works councils had to be informed of the number of part-time workers every 4 months. A French Act of 1973 placed some limits on part-time work, but restrictions on the justification for temporary contracts had to wait until the next period to evolve (below).

Another labour contract policy aimed at promoting employment, in France, was the reduction of working time. France tried to convince other countries about the advantages of 'working less to work for all'. The 1968 Grenelle Agreements had reached the compromise of gradually bringing down work duration, from 40 weekly hours, won in 1936, to a target of 35. It was believed, in that decade, that a reduction of working time meant much more to workers than welfare. Steps towards the target of 35 weekly hours were the Act of 1982 on collective negotiation of working time, followed later by the (Aubry) Acts of 1998 and 2000 on bargained reduction with financial support. However, the reduction of working time to promote employment was not backed as a common rule by the Essen Council of the EC when adopting the European Employment Strategy

---

[77] See Ojeda Aviles (1980) 471ff, on Decrees 3280/1977, 3281/1977, 41/1979 and 42/1979.
[78] European Commission (1993) 87.
[79] Dederichs and Kohler (1991) 37; Jacobs (1995) 53. In 1993 some of the exclusions were forbidden, and in 1996 the equality principle arrived for these workers.

(see below). Gradually France developed a more sophisticated method of working time reorganisation (*aménagement du temps du travail*) (below).

Job Security

In the period of crisis, termination for economic reasons (redundancy in Britain and Ireland, B*etriebliche Gründe* in Germany and Austria; *licenciement économique* in France; *arbedjmangel* in Denmark, etc) moved away from the rules relating to breach of contract and dismissals for disciplinary reasons. Much earlier, during the reconstruction period, Germany had begun to introduce measures that made a differentiation between individual dismissals and collective dismissals for economic reasons. The 1951 Dismissals Protection Act dealt with mass terminations due to serious 'economic, technical or organizational reasons'.[80] Almost the same wording was later adopted in other countries, such as Article 51 of the Spanish Workers' Statute 1980, which referred to 'economic, technical, organisation or productive' reasons. In Germany, judicial control of the seriousness of the economic and other reasons was not possible, but the labour courts insisted that the employer had to disclose all necessary information. The relevant collective dismissals were defined in Germany as affecting a minimal number of workers (6, 26 and 50, for small, medium-sized and large undertakings respectively) in a period of 1 month. These had to be notified to the Labour Administration, which could authorise them. The Netherlands (Decree of 1945, above) and Spain (Decree of 1944) had introduced the authorisation requirement after the Second World War. The Labour Administration could accept the proposed restructuring, refuse it, award part of the proposal or concede short-time working. The notification, moreover, had to be transmitted to the works council, which had to state its position. The novelty consisted in the distinction between the individual and the collective impact of undertaking's crisis.

Several countries had already followed this distinction, before Directive 75/129/EEC on collective redundancies made notification to a public authority a Community rule. However, largely as a result of British opposition, the Directive did not require prior authorisation by a public authority. In the period of deregulation (below), the trend was to diminish, and ultimately to remove, the powers of the administration. The emphasis was on the introduction of a social plan for the workers and obligations to negotiate this with workers' representatives, as in Germany (1952) and France (1975). The bridge between employment promotion and corporate co-determination was made through the medium of social plans. These were aimed at mitigating the economic disadvantages that workers would suffer as a result of a company crisis.

---

[80] Hueck and Nipperdey (1963) 639.

There was also some relaxation in the number of affected workers required to activate the legal obligations, and in the length of periods of notificiation. A number of structural problems arose for countries without works councils. In the case of Britain, the Employment Protection Act 1975, implementing the EEC Directive of 1975, conferred on recognised trade unions a number of significant legally enforceable rights, such as disclosure of relevant information and the right to be consulted about proposed dismissals for redundancy.[81]

The Collective Redundancies Directive was part of a wider package of measures following the EEC Social Action Programme of 1972 based on three principles that were to guide Community action: full and better employment, improvement of living and working conditions, and greater workers' participation in social and economic decisions. Another element in this package was the Transfer of Undertakings Directive 77/187/EEC. The justification for this Directive was said to be the rapid increase in the concentration of undertakings—there had been a ninefold increase in the founding six Member States between 1962 and 1970—and this had 'far-reaching consequences on the social situation of the workers employed by the undertakings concerned', though the legislation of the member states 'did not always take sufficient account of the interests of the workers'.[82] The primary purpose of the Directive was to enable workers to maintain the rights acquired prior to the transfer of an undertaking. This was to be achieved by automatic transfer of the employment relationship from the transferor to the transferee, ie from the old to the new employer; the protection of workers against dismissal due exclusively to the change; and information, consultation and negotiations with representatives of the workers affected. The stringent nature of the principles contained in the Directive often made the actual integration of the various undertakings or parts of undertakings quite difficult. Practical problems with outsourcing also occurred in the area of putting workers at the disposal of other companies; this was a very common practice in outsourcing deals. Externalisation may involve different ways of regulating the relationships between the various components of an enterprise. In France, the creation of a satellite company posed the problem of identifying who the actual employer was in terms of establishing contractual responsibility towards employees, especially in deciding which legal provisions to apply when the reason for dismissal was based on economic grounds. In Italy, the legislation created different legal conditions for workers of both small and large-sized companies. In Belgium, in order to safeguard the rights of the employees, a few sectors of industry concluded a collective sector level agreement determining the rights of the employees in case of the takeover of an economic activity; for example, it determined that in case of loss of contract, in some sectors of industry the new contractor had to take over a percentage of the old workforce, or at least to offer them contracts.

[81] Grunfeld (1980) 39.
[82] European Commission (1974) para 4.

Some countries responded to economic crisis and restructuring by compensating workers, such as Britain (1965), where those employees with at least 2 years' continuous employment with the same employer were compensated, the amount depending on age and length of service. Additionally, payment in lieu of notice had to be paid, with a minimum of 1 week per year of service, up to a maximum of 12 weeks. Other countries followed the path of introducing a duty to give notice to the works council and to negotiate 'social plans' (above). In practice, it became clear that the agreements and compensation payments provided for in the social plans were not sufficient in periods of mass unemployment. The prospect of finding a suitable job was more important. This is where employment plans took the place of social plans. They provided for those affected, helped companies with training to develop new products and open up new markets, regulated the introduction of new technology, or made money available to create employment and training.

Restructuring affected entire industrial branches, hit by the international competition from the cheap labour in developing countries. Governments supplied funds to dissuade unions and workers from social unrest. In Italy, industrial restructuring (*riconversioni industriali*)—a planned process of reducing or adapting the production capacity of the industrial sector or of any of its components and assisting the circulation of labour—was facilitated by Act 675/1977. This gave priority to the regional dimension but with unified coordination.[83] For example, in Spain, the *reconversiones industriales*, from 1973 to the mid-1980s—somewhat later than other countries—involved state intervention to fund modernisation of companies and reduction of payrolls, the latter being obtained by means of early retirements, special unemployment measures (employment promotion funds) and job security techniques.

Restructuring and Deregulation (1980–89)

Regulation of Labour Supply

The economic downturn of the 1980s hastened incipient shifts in the structure of the economy, notably the decline of manufacturing and large-scale manual employment. The employment question became high on the agenda. Growing rates of unemployment lasted until the second part of the decade, but the figures were considerably worse in Europe than in the US and Japan,[84] and had an ideological impact: neo-liberal ideas, which had been developing in the academic literature of the 1970s, captured the imagination of politicians at the beginning of the 1980s in the form of Thatcherism in Britain and Reagonomics in the US,

---

[83] d'Antona (1979) 105.
[84] See European Commission (1990) 20.

and remained dominant well into the 1990s (see chapter 2, above). At least from 1986 onwards, the search for flexibility[85] focused on 'rigidities' in the labour market. There were pressures to ease restrictions on working time and on working practices such as part-time work, temporary work and sub-contracting. At the same time, technological changes caused substantial transformation in labour demand,[86] which renewed the search for adaptation and continuing training.

The response to these pressures revealed an ideological and political rift between Thatcherite Britain and most of the continental countries. The Thatcher Administration's position was that flexibility 'involves not just working patterns and hours' but 'a better balance of bargaining power in industry', and that there needed to be a great reduction at Community level, as well as national level, on 'the burdens on the regulation of business'.[87] Most of the continental countries, however, took the view that 'flexibility' is not synonymous with 'deregulation', and that the objective was both to improve the functioning of the labour market and to maintain the social values of justice and security.[88] Moreover, those countries favoured a role for workers' participation (albeit in the attenuated form of 'information and consultation' rather than negotiation and consent) in the management of change. This was also reflected in their support for the 'social dialogue' at European level (see chapter 7 below). Despite the weakening of employment protection in some countries, the EEC Action Programmes—especially those of 1984 and 1988[89]—and the anti-discrimination legislation (see chapter 5 below) became important sources of regulation. The enforcement of the EEC employment Directives directed at collective dismissals, transfers of undertakings and protection of workers in the event of bankruptcy slowed down, with an 'effectiveness vacuum'.[90] However, under the Belgian, French and Spanish presidencies of the Community there were attempts to revive workers' protection, in particular by the non-binding Community Charter of Fundamental Rights of Workers adopted in 1989 by all the Member States except Britain (see chapter 2, above).

Employment Services

Several national legislatures made efforts to expand the protective scope of labour law to employees working under the direction of a user-employer, even though formally employed by another entity, be it a legal or illegal subcontractor, or another commercial firm. This period was marked by a tendency not to maintain all core and peripheral activities within the firm. Externalisation and

---

[85] Treu (1992) 533.
[86] European Commission (1990) 9.
[87] Department of Employment (1985), cited by Hepple (2005) 203.
[88] Hepple (2005) 203.
[89] Rocella and Treu (1995) 17 and 20.
[90] Ibid, 17.

outsourcing of entire areas of the production process, while being the result of deep changes in the structure of the firm, also involved different ways of selecting and acquiring the workforce. Temporary work agencies flourished across Europe during the decade. There was growing intervention of third, subordinated companies in the production process as a part of the outsourcing phenomenon. Subcontracting became one of the substantial methods of manufacturing products or goods during the 1980s, and not all the countries had labour regulations devoted to it. In Britain, temporary workers could be considered as either dependent employees (under a 'contract of service') of the employment business or the user, or self-employed, leaving it to the common law tests to verify whether there was a mutuality of obligations, and there was no limit on the length of placements with a user employer.[91] In Ireland, because of court decisions suggesting that temporary workers were not employees, the government decided to amend the unfair dismissals legislation in 1993. In Germany, the most important changes relating to TWAs were made gradually, in particular in conjunction with the reform of employment promotion law. During the 1980s the maximum time limit for employee placement remained at the 3 months prescribed in 1972, only being extended to 24 months in 2002.

Active Labour Market Policies

Although the neo-liberal positions were dominant in this decade, under the leadership of Britain, its neighbour Ireland tried an original form of reform under the name of 'social partnership' and became a model of employment and economic growth and adaptability. Social dialogue between government and representatives of employers' and farmers' organisations, trade unions and representatives of the community and voluntary organisations[92] resulted in several big central agreements, beginning with the 1987 Programme for National Recovery, which resumed centralised bargaining of wages, and, as compensation for wage discipline, key economic and social decisions referred to active labour market policies and related matters. There were successive agreements from 1987 until 2000. Although the Irish model and social dialogue seemed isolated, there were also new models in the Netherlands and Denmark.

Employment Contract Strategies

During the 1980s, there was considerable pressure to make labour legislation more flexible. This led to a series of reforms affecting part-time and fixed-term employment. These measures had one and the same goal: to increase the scope for flexible management of company workforces in response to the perceived

---

[91] Freedland (1976) 19; Freedland (2003) 129ff.
[92] Ó Móráin (2000) 87.

rigidity and excessive protection that had stymied firms' competitiveness. The decade was rich in initiatives regarding part-time and temporary contracts. The most significant reforms were in Germany, in particular the Improvement of Employment Opportunities Act 1985, which represented the spirit of the time. The Act provided minimum standards for two controversial forms of part-time work: work on call (*Kapovaz*)[93] and job sharing. The first implies that the employee is used only as and when the employer's demand for labour so dictates. The Act laid down minimum terms and conditions for this practice as a special form of part-time work, requiring the contracting parties to specify in advance the amount of working time due over a specified period. The employer could then call on this agreed time (at least 10 hours per week unless the parties agreed otherwise) according to need, provided that the worker was given 4 days' prior notice of every call. In respect of job sharing, the Act of 1985 provided that job sharers have no legal relationship with each other, nor do they have joint and several responsibility for the work. If one of the job sharers is unable to work (eg due to illness), the employer cannot call on the others to act as replacements unless agreed for the particular case, or unless there are urgent operating reasons and they can reasonably be expected to undertake the additional work. If one job sharer leaves, the employer cannot use this as a justification for dismissing the others.[94] In the same year, the Protection against Dismissals Act excluded from dismissal protection part-time workers working for less than 10 hours per week or 45 hours per month. The Act on Part-Time Work on Grounds of Age 1989 eased the transition to retirement of workers between 58 and 65 years in the form of a reduction of working hours to not less than 18 a week.[95] Other countries, like Spain with its Act 32/1984, created the notion of partial retirement, whereby the senior worker could enjoy a partial pension while working less time, provided that the employer contracted simultaneously with an unemployed person to fulfil the rest of the hours. Spain, like Italy, required part-time and fixed-term contracts to be in writing. The more stringent Italian Act 863/1984 required that the document stipulate the relevant activity and the distribution of working time, and a copy of the contract had to be kept by the provincial labour inspectorate. Between these two models, Portugal required the contract to be in writing only when doubly precarious, that is, both of a part-time and of a temporary nature.

Regulation of the duration of working hours as a means to create employment was floated in union–employer debates, but without reaching any definite shape. After the French and Finnish[96] legislation for a 40-hour week, several other countries also applied this limit, but even when Directive 93/104/EEC required a 48-hour weekly maximum throughout the Community it was difficult to find a consensus. There was a preference for a sectoral and collectively agreed limit. An important step in the development of labour relations and labour law in the

---

[93] An acronym standing for *kapazitätsorienttierte variable Arbeitszeit*; see Weiss (1992) 193.
[94] Weiss (1992) 189.
[95] Dederichs and Kohler (1991) 29.
[96] Suviranta (1976) 78.

Netherlands then took place in 1982 with the Wassenaar Agreement, through which the social partners agreed to start with working time reduction and promotion of part-time contracts in order to fight unemployment. During the 1980s maximum working hours were 38 per week, but in return for this reduction automatic compensation for inflation was abolished.

Denmark and Britain, on the other hand, represented the group of countries with full freedom of contracting, without legal definition and no specific legislation, although many important collective agreements introduced some regulation. In Denmark there was centralised bargaining between the employers' and unions' confederations which resulted, from 1990, in weekly working hours of 37 hours, or 35 hours for night shifts, implemented through collective agreements.[97] In Britain, which with Denmark had the highest levels of part-time work in the EEC, there were very few legal restrictions on hours of work and on part-time work. Measures affecting part-time work were inconsistent: on the one hand, the threshold to qualify for various employment rights, such as protection against unfair dismissal, was 16 hours (in some cases 8 hours), but on the other hand, from 1985 onwards national insurance contributions were altered to make lower-paid and part-time work more attractive. Collective bargaining practice in Britain with regard to hours of work and part-time work was also inconsistent, largely because agreements were negotiated at plant and company level: some agreements provided for equal treatment of full- and part-timers, but most denied the latter access to occupational pension schemes.[98] Discrimination between full- and part-time workers (the majority of whom were women) was, however, attacked by use of the concept of indirect discrimination in sex equality law, first introduced in Britain in the 1980s and later by decisions of the ECJ (see chapter 5 below).

Job Security

High unemployment in the 1980s shifted the balance of power in favour of the employers, but they found it difficult to keep down labour costs in the face of increasing global competition because of noticeable shortages of skilled labour. Moreover, there was a growing contradiction between the continuing need for flexibility on the one hand and the demands for job security for employees on the other. Countries tried two approaches to resolve these issues. The first was to hand over the problems to the collective parties. Restructuring labour in the enterprise already had been dealt with by bargaining between companies and unions during the 1970s, but now the state in some countries financed and actively backed *inter partes* solutions. For instance, so-called 'solidarity contracts', or job creation contracts, were used in France and Italy. In the former, an Ordinance of 1982 offered an agreement between state and company to subsidise

[97] Hasselbalch and Jacobsen (1999) 92.
[98] Hepple and Hakim (1997) 665, 685.

vocational training of young people.[99] An Act of 1989 required an agreement between state and enterprise for every *contrat emploi-solidarité*, with the state assuming responsibility for all or part of the wages and detailing the duration, weekly working time and job description. In the 1990s there emerged the *contrats de reinsertion* to recruit unemployed people following an agreement between the enterprise and social security authorities. In Italy, an Act of 1984 allowed a state-financed agreement between the firm and the most representative unions to reduce working time in order to avoid dismissals. Prior to this Act, in 1983, a trilateral solidarity agreement was signed under which supplementary payments amounting to 60% of lost wages for a period of up to 4 years (5 years in southern regions) were made by the state. Another kind of solidarity collective agreement consisted of an 'external' or 'expansive' project, promoting employment by reducing working time and wages while at the same time recruiting new workers, preferably young ones, whose engagement generated a subsidy to the employer of 15% of the first year of wages.[100] Other countries took inspiration from these models, like in the German Pact on Jobs and Training, October 1998, fostering agreements between unions and employers' associations around new kinds of part-time work.[101] The second approach was for the state to retreat from the control of collective dismissals. Controls and administrative authorisations disappeared, as in France in 1986, or were reduced, as in Spain some years later.[102] Only the Netherlands remained an exception. In their place there was increased individualisation of dismissals. However, transferring the decision to the labour courts and tribunals was not always the best solution, since judges were not prepared for financial or economic problems, and this led to a notorious degree of uncertainty.[103]

Global Capitalism: the European Response (1990–2004)

Regulation of Labour Supply

During this period, the fight against unemployment was a key government objective. General education policy was viewed as an important element in the government's strategy to increase employment. Investment in public education was considered to be the basis for lifelong learning and thus for increased adaptability, leading to improved growth. Those efforts had a result. Data revealed a great reduction in unemployment rates in Ireland, Spain and Finland, and rates also diminished significantly in Britain, Denmark, Sweden and the Netherlands,

[99] Domerge, in Pélissier et al (1998) 44–45.
[100] Ghera (2000) 670, 714.
[101] Zachert (1999) 27–28.
[102] Art 51-6 of the Workers' Statute as reformed in 1994.
[103] See Brunhes (2003) 41.

although the situation did not improve much in Italy, France or Germany (see Table 3.2).[104]

National employment policies converged in these years with strong coordination when the EU decided to intervene actively in the process and revised its objectives in the Maastricht Treaty 1992 to include employment promotion; the Amsterdam Treaty 1997 adopted a new Title on employment, and in 1998 the EU began the European Employment Strategy (EES), with guidelines to the Member States[105] and an open method of coordination based on five principles. These principles are subsidiarity (EC to take action only if objectives cannot be sufficiently achieved at national level); convergence (concerted action); mutual learning (exchanging good practice); integrated approach (structural reforms extended to social, educational, tax, enterprise and regional policies); and management by objectives. The Open Method strongly influenced national policies in several ways, among them the following.

First, changing the approach from a negative to a positive one. Until Maastricht, most of the countries fought against unemployment with a set of

Table 3.2: Unemployment Rate, 1990–2005

Country	1990	1994	2005
Austria	–	3.8	5.1
Belgium	6.6	9.8	8.4
Denmark	7.2	7.7	4.8
Finland	3.2	16.8	8.4
France	8.5	11.7	9.5
Germany	4.8	8.3	9.5
Greece	6.3	8.9	9.8
Ireland	13.4	14.3	4.3
Italy	8.9	10.6	7.7
Luxemburg	1.7	3.2	5.3
The Netherlands	5.9	6.8	4.8
Portugal	4.8	6.9	7.6
Spain	13.0	19.5	9.2
Sweden	1.7	9.4	6.4
UK (Britain)	6.9	9.3	4.7

Source: OECD (2006) 382.

[104]   OECD (2006) 41.
[105]   States must answer with national reform programmes, after which comes an EU annual progress report and a joint employment report.

defensive policies and measures, principally with social security benefits. Now the intention became to reach a high rate of employment, and the means to this was percentile targets. The Lisbon (2000) and Stockholm (2001) summits set down different numerical benchmarks to be reached by 2010—70% as the total employment rate, with more than 60% for women and 50% for older people— and compared the situation in the various countries. At the end of the period analysed here, the differences were as set out in Table 3.3.

The EES expressly backed active employment policies in the guidelines rather than defensive policies, such as simply compensating the unemployed with subsidies or giving economic incentives to employment. In 1990, the Organisation for Economic Co-operation and Development had reported that the great majority of programmes were in the form of subsidies for at-risk groups of the unemployed, especially the long-term unemployed, but that these programmes were generally as expensive as training programmes.[106] In their place, the main active measures adopted were vocational training, personal orientation, help with the search for employment, etc, which were all captured in the sobriquet 'employability'. The Lisbon strategy endorsed the policy of active ageing, which, at that

Table 3.3: Employment Ranking in the EU, 2005

Country	Total employment rate (70%)	Female rate (>60%)	Older people's rate (50%)
Denmark	75.9	71.9	59.5
The Netherlands	73.2	66.4	46.1
Sweden	72.5	70.4	69.4
UK (Britain)	71.7	65.9	56.9
Austria	68.6	62.0	31.8
Finland	68.4	6.5	52.7
Ireland	67.6	58.3	51.6
Portugal	67.5	61.7	50.5
Germany	65.4	59.6	45.4
Luxembourg	63.6	53.7	31.7
Spain	63.3	51.2	43.1
France	63.1	57.6	37.9
Belgium	61.1	53.8	31.8
Greece	60.1	46.1	41.6
Italy	57.6	45.3	31.4

Source: European Commission (2006) 29.

---

[106] OECD (1990) 88.

time, was at marked variance from policies of early retirement that had been applied by many European countries as a means to create jobs for young people, and whose impact was to severely increase the unemployment rate, and pensions burden, of older workers.

Towards the end of the period, the new buzzword in the EU was 'flexisecurity'.[107] Everywhere, Member States tried to combine flexibility with security. Examples are the Dutch Act of 1998 Act on Flexibility and Security at Work, devoted to atypical forms of work like temporary work, freelance work, work on call, home working and distance working, the Spanish reform in 1994 of the Workers' Statute, the Italian legislation of 2003 on employment and labour market (*Legge Biagi*) and the new Portuguese Labour Code of 2003, which includes provisions for flexibility in the employer–worker relationship and the simplification of collective bargaining, directed at increasing productivity.

Globalisation and the fall of the Berlin Wall meant a serious growth in immigration flows, now coming from the eastern European countries as well as Asia and Africa. Although European countries have had different approaches to the subject, there is a trend towards convergence, both in respect of equal treatment and integration of migrants and also in controls over migrant flows within the Community and of those coming from outside. Those who were EU citizens (nationals of the Member States) enjoyed rights to free movement. Third country nationals did not, and they suffered considerable discrimination on grounds of nationality as well as race (see chapter 5 below). An example of the integration policies that began to spread across the EU is that of Denmark, which in 2000 launched a programme aimed at integrating immigrants by more intense and effective use of three tools: more training, support to enter the labour market and the teaching of Danish language within companies. The efforts to integrate immigrants had a counterpart in the controls to reduce illegal immigration. One of the more controversial policies has been regularisation of the status of those already working in the country for some period of time. In spite of increasingly stringent rules to stop undocumented immigrants from working, regularisation is practised by almost all the European countries, sometimes permanent, sometimes on a case-by-case basis, as in Britain, or a mass procedure, as in Belgium, France, Greece, Italy, Portugal, the Netherlands and Spain.[108] There was also Community-wide regulation in respect of posted workers through Directive 96/71/EC, which requires all Member States to apply to workers posted to their territory certain core terms and conditions of their own labour laws.[109]

---

[107] See, eg European Commmission (2006) ch 2.

[108] Casado Lopez (2005) 30ff. Some of these figures referred to periods of years ending in that stated in text.

[109] Hepple (2005)165–72.

Employment Services

The 'hollowing out' of the welfare state[110] encouraged a network of institutions to be created by municipalities and unions to cope with unemployment. In some cases, these institutions traced their origins to legislation on masters and servants, and the poor laws.[111] But a stronger reason for the deeply rooted position of these local institutions is the historically strong commitment of unions to systems for mutual assistance. This was particularly true in countries with high union density, such as the Nordic countries and Belgium. The move to decentralised administration of employment creates confusion and weakens responsibility patterns, but on the other hand has some advantages. As Roberts and Devine point out, cities now compete with each other through partnership networks in order to attract funding from various regional, national and pan-regional bodies. The establishment of new governing bodies has meant that the policy needs of specific local populations can be targeted and met.[112]

Local employment agencies existed but were seriously reformed in Belgium in 1994. Creation of local employment agencies in municipalities had a twofold target: on the one hand, to find a solution for activities that could not be found in the normal labour market; on the other hand, to find work for long-term unemployed persons. In France in 1986, the French National Employment Agency (ANPE) had some adjustments made to its monopoly as a public service agency for the placement of job-seekers. While ANPE retained control, the municipalities were permitted a certain degree of intervention and, later, the right to obtain a list of job-seeking residents.[113] During the 1990s the monopoly status of PES came to an end in Portugal (1989), Spain (1995), Italy (1997) and Greece (2001).[114] Indirectly, the EEC had recognised them in 1991,[115] and the ILO adopted Convention No 181 in 1997, which allowed private employment agencies to operate while protecting the workers concerned from possible abuse.[116] The only exception in the period of our study is France, where the monopoly continued until 2005.[117] In France, a fine distinction had previously been drawn between job placement, which was unlawful if provided by a private fee-charging agency, and recruitment, which was lawful and frequently entrusted to specialist private agencies. The French Social Cohesion Law 2005 represented an example of modernity, since it not only abolished the state monopoly, but also created 300 job houses (*maisons de l'emploi*), gave incentives for training

[110] Rhodes (1991) 137ff.
[111] For Britain, see Deakin (2001) footnote 45; Fox (1974) 183; Hay (2000) 227.
[112] Roberts and Devine (2003) 313.
[113] Domerge in Pélissier et al (1998) 102–03.
[114] Albeda et al (1978) *passim*; Vergara Del Rio (2005) 11.
[115] Directive 91/383/EEC, on health and safety in temporary work and temporary employment agencies.
[116] The definitions included TWA as well: Servais (2005) 176.
[117] Javillier (1996) 176.

contracts for 800,000 youngsters at risk and stated new obligations for jobseekers.[118]

In the Netherlands, the legislature proved to be particularity inventive. In the Flexibility and Security Act 1999, a wide range of measures provided for agency workers, who were assigned to a standard contract of employment with the agency for the first time. The Act reformed Civil Code provisions by excluding the first 26 weeks of the 'dispatching work contract' from protection against unfair dismissal. In the same year, a collective agreement on temporary work extended the period of exclusion to 1 year. Apparently neo-liberal, this was, however, considered less liberal than the previous situation, when full employment was attributed here, as it was in Britain, to the absence of any restrictions on temporary work.[119] In any event, the Dutch 'Polder' or 'Tulip' model has taken shape around these ingredients, as we shall see later.

Germany offered a prime example of the colonisation of public services by the private sector. A deep reform brought two Acts on the promotion of modern labour market services in 2003, and job centres became agencies providing temporary work, ensuring that those jobless for more than 6 months were placed by the agencies in private firms to perform temporary work at a pre-determined pay rate.[120] The *Personalserviceagenturen* (PSAs) were to be established on the basis of public tenders in which private employment agencies were to be given priority, and regional offices of the Federal Employment Service were to sign 'free agent' agreements with PSAs to cooperate in the placement of unemployed people.[121]

The 'hollowing out' process co-existed with simplification of the PES, in the form of the 'one-stop-shop'[122] in the administration of jobseekers' demands. By the 1990s, most of the countries had some kind of dual system where, for instance, one public entity administered 'defensive' policies (unemployment benefits, etc) and another assumed responsibility for active labour market measures. The rationale for this was that defensive issues absorbed all the energies of personnel in the offices, impeding proper attention to the active measures. This happened in France and in Spain, where the response was to assign active labour market policies to the regions, so that benefits payments were placed in the hands of the state. In some cases the division led to specialisation, like the Italian distinction between the National Institute of Social Insurance (INPS) and the Wages Guarantee Fund (CIG). Germany distinguished between PES for contributory benefits (*Arbeitslosengeld* and *Arbeitslosenhilfe*) and municipalities for non-contributory care. Denmark marked a line between the insured and the non-insured and the respective competences of Ministry of Employment and Ministry of Social Affairs. In theory, hollowing out processes made dual

---

[118] Rojot and Plotino (2007) 376–77.
[119] In this sense, Van Voss (1999) 419; Visser et al (2004) 226ff.
[120] Freedland et al (2007) 217.
[121] Di Pasquale (2002) 1.
[122] See Freedland et al (2007) 255–57.

structures redundant, but in reality even more complexity was introduced in central institutions. For example, there are consortia in Italy and Germany between PES and municipalities, and in Spain competences have been distributed between several ministries.

Active Labour Market Policies

Neo-liberal tendencies in the labour market persisted during the 1990s, and even deepened with the 'workfare state' and supply side measures. The *acquis* of right to work in European countries, conditioned as we saw by some basic duty to work, was inverted. Now the important question became how to fulfil the civil duty or responsibility to work. The 'workfare state' placed the focus on the employability of workers rather than on grants and subsidies to the employers. Gradually all the countries hardened the conditions of entitlement for unemployment benefits and compelled workers to accept jobs in what was called the 'activation' of unemployed persons, measuring results and not merely processes. The ability of companies to compete on the global marketplace was seen to lie in vocational training, efficiency in placement and development of capabilities. The responsibility to work permeated public policy in the labour market.

The following are examples.

1. Restrictions on unemployment benefits, including longer qualification periods and more stringent control of them, and lower amounts or lower duration of benefits, were common features of social security legislation during this period (see chapter 6 below).
2. Jobseekers' agreements, obliging jobseekers to actively seek work and to accept and fulfil the guidance of employment services. For example, the British Jobseekers Allowance Regulations 1996 spelled out an exacting list of steps to be taken by persons actively seeking employment, and a list of requirements for the jobseeker to attend interviews, employment programmes or training schemes.[123] The requirements in other countries appeared more vague, as for instance Spanish Social Security Law 1/1994, Article 231.
3. Reasonable job offers had to be accepted by jobseekers if they were adequate to their abilities, income and location, although after a certain period of time the requisites might gradually disappear. The minimal regulation was expressed by Danish Supreme Court doctrine of 2002, stating that a jobseeker cannot reject an offer on the grounds that the proposed salary is much lower than previously received, or because the proposed job did not fall within the person's area of competence.[124] More welfarist legislation, instead, considered offers to be unreasonable if the workplace was more than 30 kilometres distant from the worker's residence or involved travel taking more than 25% of daily working

[123] Ibid, 211.
[124] Ibid, 214.

time, or the cost of travel was more than 20% to the salary, and, of course, if the job did not correspond to the skills of jobseeker.[125]

4. Sanctions were applied against free-riders. In this way, German jobseekers refusing proper job opportunites could be downgraded in the next offer to places of lower categories. Other countries preferred to withdraw or to suspend unemployment benefits.

5. Personalised training plan. The paradigm was the Danish model. The Labour Market Reform Law of 1994, which reduced unemployment benefits from four to two years, followed by an educational and vocational training period of three years.[126]

The Dutch and Danish models also utilised social dialogue to implement the activation of jobseekers, and consequently recognised the virtues of giving something in return for compulsion. The techniques employed made small contributions to reducing the numbers of long-term unemployed and jobless youngsters, women and disabled persons. These techniques included internships, training contracts, study holidays, personal plans and a personal itinerary to employment. Similarly, in Finland, a system of training agreements was developed and the number of places increased significantly. As far as other educational initiatives are concerned, measures have to a great extent been tailored to the needs of different groups. Legislation requires an action programme to be drawn up for each individual employee, and various forms of training are a key element of these action programmes. The demand for educational initiatives also increased in line with improvements in the level of education of the workforce. Local employment initiatives converged towards common standards and rules, as happened, for instance, with 1993 British Training for Work programme and the Danish job-rotation schemes in the 1990s.

The economic activity of young persons is closely linked to their participation in education and training. In an open EU, with free movement of labour, diversities among states could lead to a double disadvantage for those in a country with poorer skills than those of the migrants. In Portugal, under Article 58 of the Portuguese Constitution, the right to work includes an undertaking by the state to promote cultural and technical training and vocational development for workers. Decree-Law 401/91 established the vocational training system, which was to remain in force for most of the decade, regulating the vocational training to be promoted within the education system and in the labour market, schools and companies. However, vocational training in Portugal, like in Spain, appeared at the beginning of the 1990s to be underdeveloped, poorly administrated and marginalised because of the emphasis on academic education,[127] and progress in this respect seems to have been minimal in practice despite the legal enactments.

---

[125] Spanish Social Security Act 1/1994, Art 231. Similarly, Italian Laws 223/1991 and 350/2003. In the same way, but vaguer, French Law 91-1405.

[126] Freedland et al (2007) 205.

[127] Rhodes (1993) 314.

Similarly, during the 1990s Greece tried to create new structures and systems for vocational education, but all the mechanisms and systems were established in an unco-ordinated manner. The result was that, by the end of our period, Greece had still not developed a cohesive strategy for lifelong learning, and initial vocational training was not yet linked to continuing education and employment. The Fund for Employment and Professional Training in 1996—as an innovative intervention body of the social partners funding in-company training for workers and programmes to improve employability of the unemployed, including subsidised programmes for older workers or for those close to retirement—appears to have had relatively little impact.

The extent of labour market participation among young people declined, particularly during the 1990s, as the expansion of further and higher education persuaded many to delay their entry into paid work. Compared to other countries, youth unemployment in Germany over this period was relatively low. An important reason for this was the established dual system of vocational training in a public technical school and at the workplace. But reunification of Germany gave rise to problems, with a lack of on-the-job training places.[128] One way to encourage youth employment is to reform training contracts. A positive example of such reform was the Belgian Act of 1999 to enhance employment. This introduced the system of first job contracts and abandoned the internships for young people that had been in existence since 1983. Belgium was also innovative in its system of paid educational leave, which was simplified in 2001. In this system, employees receive extra leave hours for training attended during their free time or are granted leave if the training takes place during normal working hours. The employee receives normal remuneration for these hours. The employer can claim a reimbursement for this expense from the Ministry or Employment and Labour. Both Belgian regions organised a system of training cheques. Employers could buy training cheques from the regional government. With these they could pay for the training of their employees in a recognised training institution. Similarly, in Luxembourg, the provisions concerning young people, revised in 1995, refer either to helping young people to achieve basic qualifications or to helping them enter the world of work on leaving their educational establishments. Luxembourg also had regulations that allowed students to work during the two summer months, similar to the Italian Legislative Decree 276/2003 on summer stages for orientation in companies, with limited employment rights.

Employment Contract Strategies

Precarious employment found a means of self-perpetuation through successive fixed-term contracts, which could leave the employee excluded from job security for decades. Following a lead given by the courts, Dutch legislation tried to

---

[128] Heidemann and Rademaker (2004) 358.

limit abuses when employers entered into successive fixed-term contracts to avoid dismissal protection: fixed-term contracts of more than 3 years or a chain of more than three contracts became considered as a single contract for an indefinite period.[129] The German labour courts had already declared that such a series of contracts was as a fraud of law when not sustained by different causes, but legislation in 1985 and 1996 introduced a threshold of 2 years during which the employer could enter into fixed-term contracts without judicial control.[130] The Belgian legislature reformed the Labour Contracts Act by introducing a presumption of indefinite contracts when there was a chain of successive fixed-term contracts, unless the employer could demonstrate a justification for them.[131] The Spanish Parliament passed an Act to treat as a single contract a chain of fixed-term ones with duration of more than 24 months in a period of 30.[132] Eventually, a Framework Agreement concluded between the European Trade Union Confederation, the Union of Industrial and Employers' Confederations of Europe and the European Centre of Employers and Enterprises on 28 June 1999 was implemented by Council Directive 1999/70/EC. This required all Member States to ensure that fixed-term workers be treated no less favourably than workers on contracts of indefinite duration. To prevent abuse from the use of successive fixed-term contracts, Member States have to take measures limiting the maximum total duration of fixed-term contracts or the number of permitted renewals, or establishing objective reasons justifying renewals.

Thresholds were frequently used to avoid employment protection. For instance, in Germany, part-time workers with less than 15 hours of weekly work and earning less than 630 DM were considered 'marginals' and excluded from social security contributions; this affected between 3 and 5.5 million workers, mostly women,[133] until the Law of 1 January 1999 required employers to pay a global contribution amount and conceded retirement protection to part-time workers (*Altersversorgung*). This, like the earlier British legislation, was a response to rulings of the ECJ on indirect sex discrimination against part-time women workers (see above, and chapter 5 below).

One of the most significant developments from early 1990s was the regulation of new forms of work whether performed by dependent or autonomous (self-employed) workers. There was an increase in the number of self-employed workers operating on the margins of companies, often involved in outsourcing activities. Some voices criticised what they considered to be discriminatory treatment of 'false' autonomous workers as compared to dependent workers, and they proposed some balance between social protection and free enterprise.[134] The

---

[129] Van Voss (2000) 140–41; Jacobs (1995) 54.
[130] Zachert (1999) 25.
[131] Humblet and Rigaux (2004) 65.
[132] Royal Decree-Law 5/2006, on Improvement of Growth and Employment.
[133] Zachert (1999) 25–26.
[134] Engblom (2001) 211.

paradigm here was the Italian Legislative Decree 276/2003 on Employment and the Labour Market, which not only regulated private employment agencies and recruitment co-operatives, but also provided a set of rules on contractual typology, outsourcing, posting and semi-autonomous work.

In general, however, autonomous work grew during the 1990s to such an extent that it could compete with dependent work. The European Commission recommended support for self-employment,[135] in line with measures already adopted by countries such as Britain, France, Greece and Spain. These countries provided assistance to unemployed people wishing to enter self-employment. The approach varied over time and location, with advice, training, grants, loans and income support being available for unemployed people.[136] At the same time, unemployed people were able to access assistance through mainstream government business support agencies.

From the 1980s onwards, the British government vigorously opposed attempts by the European Commission for Community-wide measures to regulate hours of work, on the grounds that this would add to costs and inhibit job creation, and also on the legal ground that the Community lacked competence in this field. The traditional British system, unique in Europe in the second half of the twentieth century, was to regulate only the hours of work of vulnerable groups, such as women, children and young persons. The Commission, upheld by the ECJ,[137] managed to treat the Working Time Directive (93/104/EC) as a health and safety measure within the legal authority conferred on the EC by Article 118a (later 137) of the EC Treaty. The implementation of the Directive marked a turning point in employment law in Britain because for the first time the working time and holidays of all workers were regulated. However, in practice, the effect of the Directive on working time in Britain was limited because Article 22 of the Directive, inserted at British insistence, allows individual derogations to be made from the maximum 48-hour working week.

Job Security Policies

During this period, the protection against individual dismissals for economic reasons tended to diminish, be it in the quantitative thresholds, in the compensation levels or in the procedures. In contrast, the regulation of collective dismissals was improved in several ways, at times achieved via collective agreements. That was the case with so-called outplacement, defined, in the Belgian national agreement No 51 of 1992, as a set of services and orientation advice supplied after the employer's payment to permit a worker to find a job or develop his or her own business. Another example is the preventive managing of jobs and skills, which consists in France and other countries of an annual report to the works council

---

[135] European Commission (1993).
[136] See Meager (1992) 24ff.
[137] Case C-84/94 *United Kingdom v EU Council (Working Time)* [1996] ECR I-5755.

on employment forecasts in the undertaking.[138] German labour courts and collective agreements sporadically regard reduction of working time as a milder means than dismissals for coping with economic crisis, and consequently do not permit dismissals when other alternatives have not first been considered. However, many doubts have been expressed about this *ultima ratio* principle.[139]

A mixture of legal regulations and collective agreements were used to implement the Community Directives on collective dismissals (75/129/EEC and later 98/59/EC). While some countries preferred the achievement of an agreement between the firm and the workers' representatives, others were content simply to observe the procedure of information and consultation. Among the former, Germany encouraged agreement by requiring a social plan. Spain gave administrative authorisation only after a social plan. If agreement was not reached, the authorisation could be refused or could be partial.[140] Italian employers needed a social plan in order to avoid litigation and administrative intervention.[141] In the Nordic countries there were no such regulations, but in practice their co-determination philosophy reached a similar result. By way of contrast, France spent several reforms of its Labour Code trying to improve the consultation procedure, but the consequences seemed only to be a delay in going through a procedure that sceptical workers' representatives could obstruct.[142]

Conclusion

Regulation of Labour Supply

We have seen that in the period of reconstruction macroeconomic policies and nationalisation had a significant influence on labour markets, and that two vertical Europes, one of labour demand in the north and other of labour supply in the south, emerged. Bilateral and later multilateral labour agreements between European countries were common until the Treaty of Rome established the principle of free movement of workers within the Community. Free movement of citizens of the Member States provided a source of flexibility in Member States. This was supplemented by relatively large-scale migrations from third countries, in particular from the former colonies of Britain, France and the Netherlands, and from Turkey to Germany. In the period of economic crisis after 1973 there were dramatic rises in unemployment, shared unequally between the countries, with the highest rates by the early 1980s being in Ireland and Spain, medium

---

[138] French Law of 1989, reformed in 1990: Rousseau (1993) 8; Merlin (1993) 33; Bertrand et al (1993) 67.

[139] Däubler (2008) 167–68; Kittner et al (2008) 1544ff.

[140] Art 51.6 Workers' Statute.

[141] See Brunhes (2003) 42.

[142] Brunhes (2003) 41ff sets out the delaying tactics.

rates in the Netherlands, France and Italy, and the lowest rates in the other Member States. Among the measures adopted were controls on migration, tripartite co-ordination and controls on the restructuring of companies. The southern countries experienced a turnaround from being countries of emigration to countries of immigration.

The decline of manufacturing and manual employment, technological changes and continuing high rates of unemployment until the second half of the 1980s provided fertile ground for the radical neo-liberal ideas of Thatcherism and Reagonomics, which focused on 'rigidities' in the labour market. This included pressures to reduce restrictions on working time, and to remove barriers to part-time and fixed-term contracts. But there were important differences between Britain, which sought to change the balance of bargaining power between employers and workers in favour of employers, and the continental countries, which continued to favour a role for workers' participation and trade unions. In that situation, Community regulation of collective dismissals, transfers of undertakings and bankruptcy protection was to some extent a compensation for the weakening of workers' power.

It was only in the 1990s, however, that the fight for high employment became a common European strategy. This was the result of active intervention by the EC, particularly through the European Employment Strategy, which provided guidelines to Member States on reaching employment targets. There was a transformation from a negative or defensive approach to reduce unemployment to a positive approach to achieve the targets. Instead of financial subsidies and incentives to maintain jobs, there were schemes to improve 'employability', such as improved vocational training, personal orientation and help with searching for jobs. Attention was paid especially to older people, moving away from policies of early retirement to extend the availability of part-time jobs for older workers, and to create combined work and training contracts for young people. 'Flexicurity'—combining flexibility and security—was seen as a way to improve productivity and profits and to reach the goal of full employment. At the same time, fresh restrictions were imposed by all countries on immigration from outside the EU, and to integrate long-term migrants into the countries where they had settled.

Employment Services

Public employment services generally enjoyed monopoly conditions in most of the countries studied at the beginning of the period, and private employment services were either prohibited or restricted. However, these controls did not solve the shortages of labour, particularly for short-term jobs, which became acute in the period of economic growth and the welfare state. Moreover, there remained huge regional disparities in unemployment, even within a single country, such as Belgium. As a result, temporary work agencies grew rapidly, and were controlled by licensing and regulation. Some countries, like France and

Germany, were indulgent towards the phenomenon of temporary work through an intermediary, and unions were willing to negotiate with them. By way of contrast, British unions, which were relatively powerful at the time, refused to discuss the issue of private temporary work services with either employers or agencies, and there were no legal controls over the kind of contracts the agencies and employment businesses could offer. In other countries, restrictions were imposed on these contracts: the French model permitted short-term contracts but insisted on non-discrimination between short-term and indefinite contract workers, while the German model required contracts of indefinite duration. Some legislation required justification for departing from a presumption that the contract was of indefinite duration. A combination of these models formed the basis of the agreement between the social partners, translated into an EC Directive on fixed-term work in 1999.

In the period of economic crisis after 1973 there was further regulation of the agencies, but they flourished across Europe in the 1980s, a time when there was also a growth of sub-contracting and outsourcing, work-on-call, job sharing and distance working. The 'hollowing out' of the welfare state led to growing decentralisation of employment services. During the 1990s the state monopoly came to an end in all countries, with the exception of France (until 2005). The private employment services predominated, with the public services having a guiding role to promote employment and to ensure the efficiency of the private services. Temporary work agencies were the real winner.

Active Labour Market Policies

The period studied begins with the predominance of demand side measures, evolving until there was paramount attention to supply side measures. Those who suffered from the segmentation of the labour market, such as women, young people, disabled persons and migrants, were helped in the years of economic growth by social funds, investment in vocational training and some special measures. The economic crisis after 1973 highlighted the needs of older workers who were caught between two contradictory policies: on the one hand, that of early retirement and priority for redundancy, to promote the entry of young people into the job market; and on the other hand, the beginnings of an 'active ageing' policy, to maintain the sustainability of the social security system. Neo-liberal positions in the 1980s stood in the way of active labour market policies in many countries, but some, like Ireland, Denmark and the Netherlands, persisted in forms of social partnership in making key economic and social decisions, including active policies for employment growth. In the 1990s neo-liberal tendencies persisted with the trend towards the 'workfare state', which focused on the duty rather than the right to work that had been proclaimed in many post-war constitutions. All countries hardened the conditions to receive welfare benefits, required jobseekers actively to seek work and applied sanctions against so-called free-riders. Vocational training and the development of capabilities, particularly of young people, were seen as the key to improving the comparative advantages of European countries in the face of global competition.

Employment Contract Strategies

The growth of non-standard or atypical employment contracts, for instance part-time and fixed-term contracts, as well as experiences with the reduction of working time and training contracts, provide a fascinating perspective on contract engineering as a tool of regulation. One of the most significant developments, especially from the 1990s, was the regulation of new forms of work, whether performed by autonomous (self-employed) or dependent workers. Self-employment was actively encouraged by governments, and these workers—sometimes actually dependent workers under disguised or false labels of self-employment—were able to compete with the traditional 'core' of workers under contracts of employment. This had an impact on classical notions of subordinated and dependent employment, which is discussed in chapter 4 below. It was in the period of economic crisis after 1973 that many countries that had previously distrusted temporary and part-time contracts saw their value as a means of job creation and labour flexibility. In some countries, such as the Netherlands and France, unions were quicker to embrace these non-standard forms of working than in other countries, such as Britain. There is no doubt that temporary and part-time workers suffered from abuses and discrimination in comparison with full-time workers on indefinite contracts. The most significant reforms were in Germany, starting with an Act of 1985 regulating forms of contract such as work-on-call and job sharing. Other Continental countries also sought to formalise and regulate the new forms of contracting through legislation and collective agreements. However, Denmark and Britain continued with full freedom of contracting, without legal definition and with no specific legislation. The principle of equal treatment was applied by the ECJ to protect women part-time workers, who were disproportionately affected by discrimination against part-timers (see chapter 5 below), but the principle did not extend to men as well until there were social dialogue agreements at the EC level, implemented by Directives in 1997 in respect of part-time workers, and in 1999 for fixed-term contracts.

Another labour contract strategy aimed at job creation was that of reduction of working hours. This had been most keenly advocated in France ever since the 1968 Grenelle agreements, although the target of 35 weekly hours was not reached in legislation until the end of the twentieth century. Other countries also regulated working time and aimed to reduce working hours. From the 1980s onwards, the government in Britain, which had the longest working hours in the Community, vigorously opposed attempts by the European Commission for Community-wide of measures to regulate hours of work, but in 1993 a Directive

(93/104/EC) was adopted as a health and safety measure within the legal competence of the EC. The implementation of the Directive marked a turning point in employment law in Britain because for the first time the working time and holidays of all workers were regulated, although the impact was limited because individual derogations could be made from the maximum 48-hour working week.

Job Security Policies

One of the main tools of labour market regulation is job security policies. These include consultation with works councils, control of the unfair dismissals and notice of dismissal, transfer of duties, restrictions on temporary work, protection in lay-offs or redundancies, and unemployment benefits.[143] The main trends during the period studied were the disappearance (except in the Netherlands) of requirements for administrative authorisation of dismissals and the growing diversification between individual and collective dismissals, with specific duties in the second case, standardised by the so-called 'crisis' Directives of the EC in the 1970s (amended in the 1990s) on collective redundancies and transfers of undertakings. Protection against unfair dismissal became an important part of the European *ius commune* especially in the welfare state period, but was already recognised before the Second World War in some countries, in particular Germany. Many of the post-war instruments applied by legislation in the bright decades may be discovered in the jurisprudence and collective agreements of many years before, as the decisions of Italian *probiviri*,[144] French *conseils de prud'hommes* or collective bargaining of the Nordic countries[145] testify. In Britain, legislation in force from 1972 was seen as an alternative to shop steward bargaining and wildcat strikes.[146] Despite the individualisation of regulation of dismissals and the juridification which accompanied this, information and consultation with workers' representatives, and in some cases even agreement with them, became the norm in the case of dismissals for economic reasons.

---

[143] Peijpe (1998) 170.
[144] Redenti (1906) 162; Napoli (1980) 66.
[145] Adlercreutz (1976) 101.
[146] Hepple (1992) 86–88.

4

The Employment Relationship

BRUNO VENEZIANI

The aim of this chapter is to describe the evolution of the employment relationship and of the social, economic, ideological and cultural factors that have conditioned its legal structure and essential functions. It is not an historical analysis of the content of the contract of employment or the 'standard employment relationship',[1] ie of terms and conditions as they have been enriched by statute and other labour law sources, such as constitutions, collective agreements, and work rules. Rather, the chosen perspective is to discover if, how and when all those factors have transformed the structure and original function of the contract of employment into a modern economic and social institution of the labour market.

Reconstruction: the Permanent Legacy of the Past (1945–50)

The nineteenth century undoubtedly witnessed the rise of freedom of contract in general, and this was seen as the reaction of liberal laissez-faire societies to the closed autarchy of economies of a guild society based on status. In post-revolutionary Europe the Napoleonic Codes celebrated the freedom of contract and private ownership as essential elements in the protection and full realisation of the individual will.

However, it has been observed that the paradox of this type of freedom lies in the fact that freedom itself is a commodity that is consumed right from the start. Indeed, in stipulating any contract a free person becomes subject to legal obligations. The sanctity of freedom is thus transformed into a sanctity of the obligations arising from the contract. The inevitable corollary of this dogma was

---

[1] Mückenberger and Deakin (1989) 157.

the rigour of the principle of contractual responsibility (Article 1147 of the Napoleonic Code) and of culpability (Article 1382) as a source of liability.[2]

This was a widespread phenomenon and was also a consequence of the diffusion of economic liberalism in nineteenth-century society, involving civil law and common law countries alike. While the sanctity of contract was codified by law in the former, support for this expression of laissez-faire ideology came from the legal culture in the latter. The contract as an essential means of exchange of a commodity was not aimed at bringing about substantive justice. It was the expression of individual dominion, the concrete realisation of a person's will, with which true justice was identified.[3] But the idea of freedom of contract in liberal societies hid an ambiguity when the principles and theoretical constructions that raised contract to the status of an article of faith were applied to the working world and industrial society. The legal equivocation consisted in the fact that freedom of contract could justify its social function in a society of equals, where goods, capital and people are free to circulate and to engage into freely accepted work. But this presupposes the affirmation of a general principle of the right to work seen as a freedom to work.[4] This right to work (or equivalent expressions) appeared in some constitutions (France, some German *Länder*, Italy) at the end of the Second World War and in other countries in the second half of the 1970s (Greece, Spain, Portugal) (see chapter 3 above).

It must also be emphasised that traditional legal institutions and culture have affected the evolution of the law of employment relations and labour law in general. In Britain there was a continuing legacy of the master and servant laws. For example, the doctrine of 'common employment' under which the courts held that a master was not responsible to a servant for the tortious acts of a fellow servant continued until 1948, when it was abolished by legislation. German labour law continued to be influenced by the Empire's legislative activity. Ramm maintains that the theoretical construction of the employment relationship is still today full of traces of the conflict between liberal and paternalistic–conservative ideologies reflected in the two concepts of a duty of care and of fidelity in the employment relationship.[5] Furthermore, the duty of the employee to 'cooperate' with the firm, as stated in Article 2094 of the Italian Civil Code of 1942, was strong evidence of the fascist ideology of 'community of interests' embedded in the structure of the contract. The authoritarian regimes during the 1940s in Germany, Italy and Vichy France considered that the contract of employment was founded on the idea of the 'interests of the firm' and the 'higher interests of national production'. That was the guiding principle behind the Italian Civil Code and the Vichy French Charter of Labour of October 1941. The connection between 'work' and 'enterprise' was used by the Italian fascist dictatorship, in order to strengthen the principle of authority also expressed by the *Führerprinzip*

---

[2] Savatier (1959) 7.
[3] Atiyah (1979) 103.
[4] Veneziani (1986) 35.
[5] Ramm (1989) 39.

in Germany and in the laws of the Spanish Franco regime. In these experiences the legal technique, used to support the predominance of the employer in the firm, was inspired by the idea of a delegation of powers from the state, the only law-making authority in the field of the contract of employment.[6] So it would have been quite difficult to characterise the employment relationship as a freely stipulated social phenomenon between equals having a real contractual origin.

This weighty heritage of the recent past influenced legal opinion at the dawn of the new era in Europe. The expression 'contractual regime of work' was used in the Programme of the National Council of Resistance of Free France (1946) and a rough definition was included in the two Portuguese laws of 1931 and 1944 on the specific labour contract.[7] Legal scholars in some countries had debated the nature and origin of employment relationship. There was a lack of a legal definition of 'employment contract' in some civil codes. Although the Dutch Civil Code 1907 contained a clear definition of the category of contract of employment, Germany, Italy and France did not: the *Bürgerliches Gesetzbuch* of 1 January 1900 qualifies the employment contract as a sub-category of the contract of service (*Dienstvertrag*) (Article 611ff) and some criteria of distinction have been formulated later on (Act 6.8.1953) in the Commercial Code (Article 84 al.1, section 3), but only for a special category of workers (commercial agent). The Italian Civil Code does not refer to a 'contract' but provides for a mere definition of 'subordinate employee' (Article 2094), whose discipline is contained in a special Title II under the heading 'work in the enterprise'. Both examples show how heavy the weight of the ideology permeating both codifications was, reinforced by the presumption of the purely formal equality of the two parties. The inevitable submission of the employee would have been tempered or balanced with his duty to cooperate with the employers.

The German 'communitarian' theory, according to which the employment relationship was considered a 'community relationship of persons' living in the establishment, resembled the former law on domestic servants and revived the duties of loyalty and of welfare. This relationship was an alternative to the opposite notion of the contractual relationship of reciprocal obligations, under which the employee has the duty to perform 'promised services' (Article 611), enhanced by the general restoration of liberalism and recognition of individual liberty. Nevertheless, the 'communitarian' doctrine was present in Germany even after 1945 and in the 1950s and 1960s. It has been present in some decisions of the Federal Labour Court due to some continuity of the culture of judges after 1945.[8] In many countries, such as Portugal, the social legislation on the contract of employment, enacted in the early1940s, lasted until the 1960s, due to the slow adaptation of economic and social structures[9] or, as happened in Spain, to the cultural heterogeneity and different economic structures of the regions, 'far from

---

[6] For Spain, see Valverde et al (1991) 71.
[7] Ibid, 354 note 1.
[8] Sefert (2003) 33.
[9] Monteiro Fernandes (2004) 39.

the decisions of political milieu'.[10] The dispute between 'communitarian' and 'contractual' views of the origin of the employment relationship in Germany was rooted in the contrast between the liberal concept of the *locatio conductio operarum* and the pre-liberal concept realised in the former law on domestic servants, and is still extant in the law of state officials (*Beamte*).

The weight given in Greece, Portugal, France, Belgium, Luxembourg and Italy to the civil law of obligations as a framework for the employment relationship is a mirror of the principle of freedom to work, a theoretical pillar of socio-economic liberalism that pervaded most European countries after 1945.[11] The enactment of a constitutional right to work in these countries influenced legal opinion. The close linkage between freedom to work and freedom to enter into a contractual relationship is a crucial feature for the development of a coherent system of employment relations and systematic labour law in these countries. Moreover, the presence in the legal systems of continental Europe of civil codes has given a framework of positive rights to the individual parties moving from the general theory of obligations. The birth of the notion of the contract of employment and the distinction between autonomous and dependent employee are the results of this legislative technique.

This marks the striking difference with the evolution of British law, which has used a different technique to analyse the same phenomenon. On the one hand, the British system has suffered from the heavy burden of the past, which slowly conceptualised the legal category of the contract of employment on a case-by-case basis, utilising the pre-industrial conception of 'service'. On the other hand, the repeal in 1875 of the Master and Servant Acts removed a major impediment of the concept of freedom of contract guaranteed by civil sanction alone.[12] British scholars stress the relative slowness of the evolution of the employment contract due to its foundations in the master and servant relationship, which has had a 'lasting impact' on modern law.[13] A further reason for this sluggishness is linked to legislative technique. Labour legislation enacted piecemeal was never coordinated into a comprehensive system. It was without general principles or uniform legal concepts.[14] British labour law has been marked by the exclusion of those without a 'contract of service' from the scope of protective legislation. In fact, British labour law is much more the history of step-by-step legislation enlarging its personal scope than the evolution of a unitary model of the contract of employment. The latter 'only came into being when further reforms were enacted to social legislation, in particular the extension of social insurance after the Beveridge report of [1942]'.[15] A slightly different analysis is that the British concept of the employment contract is the product of the system

---

[10] Valverde et al (1991) 56–57.
[11] Jamoulle (1994) 71–72; Monteiro Fernandes (2004) 39.
[12] Hepple and Fredman (1986) 40.
[13] Ibid.
[14] Kahn-Freund (1966) 515.
[15] Deakin (1998) 221.

of uncodified case law. As Kahn-Freund wrote in 1951, the nature of the contract of employment and its distinction from the contract for work and labour 'is not altogether clear'. It depended on the permanent legacy of the past, where the distinction between 'servant' and 'independent contractor' was developed in the law of tort to ascertain the liability of the employer, who was responsible only for the wrongs of a 'servant' and not generally for those of an 'independent contractor'.[16]

The differences between common law and civil law countries was grounded in the different legal perspectives and the legal techniques. The common law term 'servant' did not contain any element referring to the nature of the services assumed. Conversely, the expression 'contract of employment' indicates the inner essence and the content of the employee's performance within the framework of the general law of obligations, as is clearly indicated in the Greek (1946) and Italian Codes (1942) and in the French *Code du travail* (Book 1, Articles 19, 23a, 24 and 29).

In both common law and civil law systems the contract of service or employment is the legal device and the social parameter that represents the sphere of application of individual and collective labour law. The contract of service was described by Kahn-Freund as the 'cornerstone' of British labour law. The same was true of the contract of employment in civil law systems: after surveying the sources of the civil law, Camerlynck concluded that the employment contract, as implying a mutuality of obligation and exchange of work and wage, is 'a generally accepted foundation for the individual employment relationship'.[17] The prevalent models in the period of reconstruction are represented by the contract of subordinated employment stipulated for an indefinite period of time or for a fixed term, inherited from the previous codes or regulated and updated by special legislation. Both models were present and functional in the post-war economy. The first step was to temper the consequences of the war on pre-existing contracts of employment. For example, a French Ordinance of 1945 was intended to restore the workforce to the industrial system. A Dutch Decree on Employment Relations 1945 obliged the employer 'to reinstate the employee in his former employment' (Article 4). Other nations had similar legislation. The second step was to renew previous legislation. So a Spanish decree of 1944 represented for that country the first comprehensive text containing a precise definition of the contract of employment as a pure exchange obligation dealing with different categories of workers (seamen, home workers, apprenticeship, young persons). The same path was followed for domestic and agricultural workers (eg Austria, 1948). The third step was the intervention of the state to guarantee equal opportunities for all the unemployed to enter into contracts of employment by having access to the labour market through a public placement service (France, 1945; Luxembourg, 1945; Italy, 1949) (see chapter 3 above).

---

[16] Kahn-Freund (1952) 193.
[17] Camerlynck (1962) 21.

Welfare State: the Impact of Social Legislation
(1950–72)

The legacy of the past did not suddenly disappear in the period of evolution of the welfare state. The new laws were still pervaded by the models inherited from the past. For example, the Belgian Act on the contract of employment of 1960 was a slight modification of the previous ones made in 1900 and 1954; the Luxembourg law on the private employee of 1962 recalls the ones of 1919 and 1937; and the Dutch law on contracts of employment, inserted in the Civil Code 1907, has never been repealed but only amended on various occasions. The Italian law on the contract of employment of private employees of 1924 was collateral to the more general discipline of Book V of the 1942 Code and is still in force today. In the Austrian Industrial Code (*Gewerbeordnung*) of 1973 the employment relationship of employees in industrial or commercial enterprises doing manual work continued to be governed by old versions of 1859 and 1885.

A similar path was followed by legal systems that have suffered from alternation between authoritarian and democratic regimes, like Spain and Portugal, where the modernisation of the law came in in the late 1960s without repealing the previous laws, the survival of which was caused by the influence, at least in Portugal, of legal opinion coming from other European countries.[18] These laws on the contract of employment are evidence of the efforts made by all states to confer autonomy on the employment relationship through different legal techniques mirroring the characteristics of the national legal culture. This goal was attained through specific laws on the contract of employment or specialised codification. The construction of the French *Code du travail* lasted almost 40 years, starting in 1910 and ended provisionally only in 1956, and is still in force today.[19] The Danish legislation on private employees started in 1938 and lasted until 1987, and the body of rules regarding the employment contract is contained in a general framework Basic Agreement of 1898, which was amended in 1960 and 1973 without any major modification.[20]

A different path was followed by common law countries, like Britain and Ireland. The repeal of the Master and Servant Acts in 1875 removed a major impediment to the development of the notion of freedom of contract between equal contracting parties protected by civil sanctions alone. However, the form of contract that emerged in the nineteenth and early twentieth centuries guaranteed the rule-making power of the employer. The trade unions were content to rely on their considerable political and economic power during and immediately after the Second World War, rather than on legislation, to counter the power of the employers. The first significant legislation since 1875 was introduced by the

---

[18] Monteiro Fernandes (2004) 39.
[19] Durand and Rouast (1957) 37.
[20] Hasselbalch and Jacobsen (1999) 61.

Conservative government in 1963 'and received without enthusiasm by the unions'.[21] The bulk of British legislation (much of it followed in the Republic of Ireland) in the 1960s and 1970s dealt with the termination of employment (minimum period of notice, 1963; redundancy payments, 1965; unfair dismissals, 1972), but also began to introduce fundamental human rights into the employment relationship (racial discrimination, 1968; equal pay for women and men, 1970; sex discrimination, 1975). Nevertheless, this legislation did not introduce a unitary legal concept of the 'contract of employment' or 'employment relationship'. It was left to the courts to conceptualise 'the contract of employment on a case-by-case basis utilising pre-industrial conceptions of "service"'.[22] In other words, British and Irish law followed the opposite trend from the civil law systems, which moved from the general theory of contractual obligations to a specific notion of the autonomy of the contract of employment as a legal 'shell' for the social phenomenon of employment.

The reasons are not limited to the legacy of the past but also to different legal techniques in making labour law. There was a lack of an 'alphabet of concepts'[23] in the English common law and systems derived from it which could resemble the legal category defined by the Italian, Belgian, Greek, Dutch, German Civil Codes and the French *Code du travail*. This tendency 'has become even more pronounced in the [late twentieth century]'.[24] The early body of social legislation developed extracontractual liability on employers and did not contain any uniform definition on what an 'employee' or a 'workman' is. The consequence was that 'when the major expansion of statutory individual employment rights took place, it was usually seen as obvious and uncontroversial to confer these rights on employees working under a contract of employment, but not upon other workers', with the exception of the anti-discrimination legislation, which came from a different institutional setting.[25]

All European countries developed a network of social legislation whose aim was to ensure an embryonic welfare protection of people engaged in an employment relationship. The main feature of this trend was a diversity of regulation—progressively amended—for different categories of workers in different economic sectors (from 1910 to the Industrial Code 1973 for *Angestellte*; agricultural workers, 1948, domestic workers, 1962 and janitors, 1969 in Austria; maritime workers in France from 1926 to 1955; Finland, 1955; Germany, 1952; Norway, 1953; Belgian commercial agents, 1956 and domestic workers, 1970) or according to their professional status as blue-collar (manual) or white-collar (non-manual) workers. A second trend was the progressive extension of the personal scope of welfare legislation to all the people engaged in a 'contractual relationship'. A similar evolution was followed by the common law countries,

---

[21] Hepple and Fredman (1986) 46.
[22] Ibid, 75.
[23] Kahn-Freund (1966) 512.
[24] Hepple and Fredman (1986) 75.
[25] Freedland (2003) 19.

which, from 1875 to 1946, gave a more comprehensive definition of the personal scope of welfare legislation; extension to all categories of wage earners only occurred when further post-war reforms were enacted, in particular the extension of social insurance which took place in the National Insurance Act 1946.[26]

A third trend during the 1960s was continuing state control of the labour market through the prohibition of fraudulent use of contract of employment, that is, by hiding a subordinate relationship under the mask of an independent one (eg home work) or continuous employment under the mask of a succession of fixed-term contracts. This explains why legislation tried to limit the use of all forms of work relations not functional for the stability of employment: on the one hand, a severe regulation of fixed-term contracts (Italy, 1962; and prohibition subcontractors or intermediaries, 1960) and home work (Germany, 1951; France, 1957; Austria, 1954–59), and on the other hand, strict provisions regarding individual dismissals (Germany, 1951; the Netherlands, 1953; France, 1958; Greece, 1955; Italy, 1966, 1970) (See chapter 3 above).

The story of the evolution of the various statutes concerning the contract of employment indicates the progressive extension of their scope to cover all professional categories of workers. An example of this tendency is to be found in the 1970s, with a rapid growth of the distributive sector of the economy and, perhaps more importantly with an even more rapid technical development of industry, 'a steadily increasing proportion of the working population has become engaged on non manual work whether clerical or technical'.[27] The building of the welfare state in the period from 1945 until the 1970s blurred the distinction between blue collar and white-collar workers. It must be remembered that the first comprehensive statutes on specific categories of workers were those on apprenticeship and white-collar workers. The Italian law of 1924, which is still in force, the Belgian law of 1922, the Luxembourg laws of 1919, 1937 and 1962, the Finnish laws (1949, 1973, 1978)[28] and—albeit only for employees with top functions (*leitende Angestellte*)—the German Acts 1952 and 1972 on co-determination were based on the distinction between work that is totally or mainly intellectual for white-collar workers and manual for blue-collar workers. This distinction and its different kinds of terms and conditions were based on the political strategy to consider white collars as part of the intellectual class useful to the ruling establishment. The evolution of society with the emerging class consciousness of white-collar workers as part of a larger working class and the transformation of work started to blur the distinction in the 1970s. The change in composition of the labour force also encouraged unionism among these workers. This led to even more attention by the state to this social class through protective legislation on the contract of employment of white-collar workers.

[26] Deakin (1998) 221.
[27] Kahn-Freund (1972) 40.
[28] Suviranta (2000) 70.

This is evidenced by the Danish legislation on white-collar workers, which enlarged its sphere of application from 1938 to 1974, embracing a different approach to white-collar workers and also containing terms and conditions of their contracts of employment, one of the most comprehensive statutes in Europe. The reform of the Belgian Code in the 1960s included blue collar and white-collar workers; from the beginning, both categories were covered by the Dutch law of 1907 and the Spanish law of 1931. This process of standardisation was not completed everywhere: for instance, although the British employment protection legislation of the 1960s and 1970s introduced important guarantees in the area of income security and termination of employment for both manual and non-manual employees, its impact was limited by qualifying conditions that allowed for the exclusion of certain types of relations to which the notion of contract of employment could not readily be applied.[29]

An historical–comparative analysis reveals how the provisions of the most important labour law statutes contain exceptions which either enlarge or restrict their personal scope. Finland and a few other countries, such as Denmark (1973),[30] also enacted special statutes applicable only to certain enumerated branches of employment according to their relative importance in the national economic and social context, such as seamen (1978) in Finland.[31] Also, in the Netherlands there are many specific rules for the contracts of employment of seamen, dating back to 1838, reformed in 1931 and amended numerous times subsequently.

However, in most countries there is no clear distinction between a contract of subordinate employment and autonomous employment. The common law system has developed a distinction between those under a contract for services (self-employed workers) and those under a contract of service (employees). Yet this distinction—as has been observed—does not exactly correspond to the civil law distinction between *locatio conductio operae* and *locatio conductio operarum*. The common law category of employee has frequently been interpreted as narrower than the range of persons under a contract of employment in civil law systems.[32]

As we shall see shortly, in both common law and civil law the traditional dichotomy between a contract of services and contract for services has been considered controversial. In academic debates it has been disputed whether and how to redraw the borders of conceptual definition in its application to employment legislation.[33]

Most civil codes have not defined the category as they did in Belgium.[34] In France, for example, the notion was virtually non-existent in the *Code du travail*.

---

[29] Ibid, 224.
[30] Hasselbalch and Jacobsen (1999) 34.
[31] Suviranta (2000) 27.
[32] Hepple and Fredman (1986) 75.
[33] Freedland (2003) 23ff.
[34] Horion (1965) 166.

Some civil codes have preferred to designate the employment relationship as one in which one party—the employee—undertakes to perform work in the service of the other for remuneration for a given period (Italy, Article 2084, 1942). This is a definition somewhat similar to that in the Greek (Article 648, 1946) and Dutch (Article 7:610) Civil Codes. The lack of a precise formula indicating a list of the individual rights and obligations has meant that the shortcomings of a specific codification have been filled by the interpretative activity of academic writers and the courts. A process started at the beginning of the twentieth century was in continuous evolution and, by the 1970s, progressive and refined intellectual arguments helped to resolve disputes taking place in court.

Economic Crisis: the Uncertain Meaning of Subordination (1973–79)

The expansion of the personal scope of regulatory legislation reflects the growing insight that the contract of employment expresses a special 'human bondage' linking the parties that must be focused, clearly ascertained and legally evaluated. The Italian Civil Code uses the term 'subordinate' activity but does not clarify the concept, and Italian academics and the courts have tried to analyse the role this legal category plays within the contract. In civil law countries subordination is considered as an 'effect' of the formation of the employment contract. It is an essential component of its internal structure and of its social function. This function has changed considerably in the course of history and has been the element that has revealed how fragile the idea of the freedom of contract affirmed in the post-French revolution era was. The concept of subordination moved from the idea of the personal and complete availability of the worker to the will of the 'master' to dependency on the power of control and direction of the work. This reflected the era of expansion of large-scale industry, where the commitment to work lasted for a relatively long period of time, thus presuming a certain stability in the contractual linkage. A further step and shift of meaning occurred during the Nazi and fascist regimes in Germany and Italy, where subordination acquired the 'ethical' flavour of personal loyalty expressed by the duty to co-operate in the interests of the firm and the state.

The new idea which pervaded the post-war period—interpreted in the light of constitutional values (see chapter 1 above) and imperative provisions of the statues and codes—was to give a purely 'technical' meaning to a subordination, which is 'functional' to the task the employee must perform. Many statutes of the 1970s reveal this new process of 'depersonalisation of subordination'. The status of employees requires full protection of their 'personality'. The human values embedded in a contractual link are guaranteed by special imperative rules, contained in quasi-constitutional laws, like the Italian (1970) and Spanish (1980)

Workers' Statutes. More recent constitutions, enacted during the age of economic crisis—like those of Spain (1978), Portugal (1976) and Greece (1975)—also expressed this trend. The process of 'constitutionalisation' of labour law (see chapter 1 above) includes the modernisation of the contract of employment, with a new function to protect the employee no longer as a weaker party, but as a social citizen of the enterprise with full rights.

Nevertheless, the intervention of the law still did not clarify the meaning of subordination. The two classic types of work—dependent and autonomous—still predominated in the 1970s. Statutes and codes were vague, and the criteria used to enlighten the concept of subordination were insufficient to cover the profound transformation of professions and skills of the modern labour market that emerged in this period. The expansion of the personal scope of regulatory legislation reflects the growing insight that the relation of subordination between employer and worker is the same 'whether the worker is employed on the assembly line or in the office'.[35] EC law made little contribution in this respect because, except in some specific cases (eg migrant worker regulations), the definition of the concept was left to individual Members States. According to the European Court of Justice, the essential nature of subordination is the power of command stemming from the internal structure of the contract.[36] This notion is too vague and insufficient to focus on the complexity of the concrete features of dependence.

No German statute defines the concept of employee, but there is a statutory definition of the 'self- employed' as one 'who is essentially free in organizing his work . . .' (Article 84 of the Commercial Code).[37] The amended Dutch Civil Code (Article 7:610, former Article 1637 a) did not alter the anodyne definition of employment contract of the past. More clearly, but not sufficiently precise, the Finnish Employment Contract Act (1970, section 1) stated that the employee undertakes to perform work under 'direction' and 'supervision' of the employer. An analogous trend is observed in the Italian (Article 2094, Civil Code 1942) and Spanish laws (1978), which describe some elements for a useful interpretation (Article 1.1).[38] A more exhaustive and complete definition of the contract of employment is to be found in the recent Portuguese *Codigo do Trabalho* (Title II, Book 1 l.99/2003), which uses the words 'authority and directions' to represent the powers of the firm. Much British legislation (eg on unfair dismissal) was confined to 'employees', that is, those under subordinated contracts of service. But the anti-discrimination legislation (Equal Pay Act 1970, Sex Discrimination Act 1975 and Race Relation Act 1976) covered not only 'employees', but also a wider category of 'workers' who personally perform work, thus including many

---

[35] Kahn-Freund (1972) 41.
[36] Case 66/85 *Deborah Lawrie-Blum v Land Baden-Württemberg* [1986] ECR 1986 212.
[37] Weiss and Schmidt (2000) 41.
[38] Valverde et al (1991) 354.

of those who are self-employed, but specifically excluding those who work for a professional client (eg lawyers and doctors in private practice).[39]

All these formulae reproduce the idea that the notions of command and subordination are strictly inherent and are almost exclusively to be found in the contract of employment. The Italian Code and the Dutch Code and statutory law clearly lay down the model of 'juridical subordination', according to which the employee must observe the technical rules governing performance of work and directions about order and discipline within the firm, provided that these rules stay within the limits of general provisions of the Code or of the contract. The notion of 'juridical subordination' is closely linked to the idea, inherited from the past, of the stringent correspondence between the contract of subordinate employment and statutory protective labour laws. However, the common trend of civil law and common law has been that legislation has delegated to the courts the task of elaborating the notion of subordination applicable to all kinds of employment contracts.

The ideology of interpretation has been the same in that the socio-economic tendency of the labour market has become similar throughout Europe since the economic crisis from 1973 onwards. The predominance of the archetypical model of the employment relationship has changed considerably, and the pattern of full time and continuous employment in the core of the labour market has been neither prevalent nor unique.

The evolution of the criteria to identify subordination has demonstrated how similar the new technological, social and cultural values of dependent work in all western societies are. In general terms it can be said that the attempt to describe the 'substance' of subordination has evolved from an analysis of 'inner' features of the notion to its more 'external' profile. From the end of the nineteenth century to the twentieth, and particularly in the last 60 years, the emphasis has shifted from the inner elements, like command (Germany), direction and control (Portugal, Belgium, Finland, France, Greece, Italy, the Netherlands and Britain), to the entire activity of the worker. This reflects the passage from a pre-industrial to a Fordist industrial context, and towards more up-to-date insights, like the 'continuity and availability' of the legal obligation of the employee (Italy).[40] In this last theory the main idea is that subordination must be present in the quality and intensity of the linkage between persons (both workers and employees) and the organisation of the firm. It starts from the assumption that the profound transformation of the European economy after the two oil crises in 1973–77 has obliged enterprises to undergo different kinds of restructuring processes such as outsourcing, sub-contracting and externalisation.

The theory that emerged in civil law systems is that the contract of employment is a legal device to 'organise' the resources and the structure of the enterprise through the recognition of the subjective right of property and of

[39] Carby-Hall (2003) 249.
[40] Ghera (2003) 49ff.

connected powers. The inner sense of subordination is to be found in the linkage between the 'quality of the organisational structure' and the role played by the work of the employee. This linkage has been closely investigated by the Italian *Corte di Cassazione*, according to which the subordination appears, in a conceptual perspective, different from the past, as a performance 'functionally coordinated' to the productive organisation (Cass 6 July 2001, no 9167; Cass 26 February 2002, no 2842).[41] The same perspective was expressed by the Spanish Supreme Court interpreting the Workers' Statute[42] and the French *Cour de Cassation*,[43] developing the link between work and enterprise in the light of the theory of organised work (*service organise*) that can arise even when the firm does not interfere with the worker's performance.

The judicial development of criteria in Britain is paradigmatic. The 'control test' has remained an important factor[44] and has permeated the minds of judges as the basis to hold the employer vicariously liable for the employee's negligence where the employer has ultimate authority over the dependent's work.[45] Its applicability derives, in fact, from the organisational power of management in the firm, including the power of selection, control of the method of work, and the right to suspend and dismiss, even though some of these indicia are altogether absent or are present in an unusual form. British judge-made law suggested the different criterion of integration into the organisation (ie how the employee integrates into the firm's structure). This is helpful, although still not exhaustive or comprehensive, 'particularly in cases where the workers provide some equipment or is paid on a piece-rate basis'.[46] Another criterion which has been used is that of 'economic reality', whereby the ownership of tools and the bearing of financial risks (the 'chance of profit' and 'the risk of loss') are incompatible with the position of an employee under a contract of service.[47] The general observation is that judges and academic doctrine in all countries have realised that no single criterion is able to resolve the question of definition in an exhaustive manner. If the control test is still used in Britain, it has lost most of its adequacy for distinguishing the contract of employment from other contracts where the essential requirement is the content of the obligation of one of two parties.[48]

A trend common to all legal systems is the debate as to whether the classification of a contract is a question of fact or law investing the judge-made law with the task, on a case-by-case basis, of looking for the criterion that appears to be more consistent with the substantive profile of the case. Italian courts have decided to ascertain if all the criteria are present in the particular case[49]

[41] Ibid, 66.
[42] Ojeda Aviles (2002) 464.
[43] Chauchard (2003) 14–15.
[44] Carby-Hall (2003) 304, note 445.
[45] Ibid, 251–52.
[46] Hepple and Fredman (1986) 76.
[47] Carby-Hall (2003) 256–57.
[48] Jacobs (2004a) 47.
[49] Ghera (2003) 64.

according to the 'typological' method whereby the judge analyses which feature of the facts are closer to the functional basis of the contract (*causa negotii*) and makes a final determination on the basis of the consistency between a 'set of factual indicia' and a 'typical model of subordination', according to the judge's own instincts. The Portuguese courts have also followed this approach.[50]

This evolution mirrors how much the contract of subordinate employment has changed its original function of the pure exchange of mutual obligations (work and remuneration) to become a legal base for social relations not exclusively between persons but between persons and a complex organisation's structure. More precisely, the passage from subordination as command to a model of subordination as 'functional coordination' was a consequence of the movement away from the Fordist division of labour and the emergence of a complex structure of the firm no more hierarchically ordered and no longer ruled by commercial law. Consequently, this approach involved a new theoretical perspective and a new notion of economic subordination. This modern profile of the concept justifies a need for legal protection by the state to temper the inequality of powers between the parties to the contract, above all if the substantial and effective identity of the employer is not clear and labour law seems 'polluted' by the commercial law.

The basic assumption is that in recent times the spheres of influence of commercial law are more restricted than labour law for two reasons. First, there has been a substantial reduction in the economic autonomy of employers, who have become more strongly subjected to the decisions of a wider network of corporate entities. Secondly, the constraints of the economic crisis and the need for flexible production obliged employers to limit their activity to some of the core functions of their enterprises while other functions were dispersed or decentralised outside the enterprise. Commercial law and the contract of employment law follow opposite trends. Employers lose their economic autonomy and employees acquire more independence in performing their subordinate employment. Both processes generate risks and difficulties for protective labour law.

The vertical disintegration of the enterprise and the substitution of small entities only apparently independent could mean that the contract of subordinate employment is frequently fragmented or interrupted. Furthermore, in some cases it loses, at least formally though not substantially, its original shape and profile of subordination. This is particularly the case where one or both parties to the employment relationship choose to place themselves in one category rather than another in order to reap the benefits of a particular tax or social security regime.

From the viewpoint of strict contract theory, the private agreement is conclusive in respect of the intention of the parties. This is clearly expressed by the Italian Civil Code (Article 1362), which states that the content of the contract must be determined by 'reconstructing' the common intentions of the parties.

[50] Monteiro Fernandes (2004) 143.

However, it is increasingly clear that Italian,[51] Belgian,[52] Dutch[53] and French courts[54] tend to intervene and look at the 'realities' of the relationship rather than at its form or the name given by the contracting parties to their agreement. The judge of the case is requested to investigate the effective content of the obligations and the real linkage existing between subordination and social powers of the employer. This judicial behaviour is shared by both common law and civil law systems. In both, the judges try to discover whether or not employers, by reducing the cost of labour, hide a subordinate employment disguised under the mask of autonomous work. The use of atypical contracts of employment to escape from labour law became pronounced in the period of economic crisis (see chapter 3 above). In both common law and civil law systems the judges responded by refusing to allow the parties to mask their real intention using a contract scheme that did not correspond to the effective development of envisaged social relations.[55] Their freedom in respect of employment contracts was thus more limited compared to the other contractual obligations, where the parties were totally free to produce the desired effects. In English case law[56] employers have not generally been able to escape liability for breach of statutory safety duties to a building worker by pleading that the worker had agreed to be self-employed simply in order to mislead the Inland Revenue.[57] The emerging model in this period, as defined by a Portuguese scholar, was composed of economic dependence without subordination, ie continuous work done exclusively for one client or autonomous work as part of a production process ruled by others.[58]

The reaction of the state was an attempt to harmonise different legal regimes, enlarging the scope of labour law and social security systems. The category of parasubordinate employees, invented by the Italian law (1973), is a meaningful symptom of the existing grey zone within the traditional dichotomy between autonomy and subordination upon which labour law was built. The parasubordinate employee in the condition of economic dependence was thought to be entitled to enjoy the same protection as other workers as regards health and welfare, as happens in Spain and Germany, where the 'person similar to salaried people' is covered by national social security and collective agreements. Furthermore, according to the German doctrine, they should enjoy protection against unfair dismissal.[59] In general, the employment contract or social relationship involving work was being considerably enlarged, affecting the original meaning of subordination and the structure of the 'classical' model.

---

[51] Ghera (2003) 68.
[52] Jamoulle (1994) vol I, 194.
[53] Jacobs (2004a) 42.
[54] Pélissier et al (2006) 330.
[55] Constitutional Court, 31 March 1994, no 115; 29 March 1993, no 121.
[56] Carby-Hall (2003) 262.
[57] Hepple and Fredman (1986) 78.
[58] Monteiro Fernandes (2004) 136.
[59] Sobczack (2003) 316.

Restructuring and Deregulation: Deviations from the Standard Contract (1980–89)

The contract of subordinate employment has been and still is central to the regulation of individual employment relations but is no longer the only one at the core of the legal regulation of the labour market. Originally it reflected a market-based economy in the process of industrial development. It was fairly straightforward: it covered the working life of an adult male who worked in a firm belonging to his employer, who required that the worker should perform a specific task for an unspecified length of time.

The classic model, what we might call the 'Aristotelian rule of labour law' of a pre-technological society, was based on the unities of place and work (work performed on the premises of the firm), of time and work (work carried out in a single temporal sequence), and of action and work (a single occupational activity).

These assumptions, upon which both statutory law and collective bargaining were built, have been undermined. In the period since the 1970s, the contract of employment has carried out an increasing set of functions reflecting the change in duties and obligations of the parties. The structure and dynamic of standard contracts of subordinate employment has been strongly challenged by social and economic changes. All European countries were obliged to face the same variables as labour market internationalisation, high levels of unemployment, transformation of the composition of the labour market (such as feminisation) and counter-inflationary state policies. The traditional scheme of the employment contract was no longer a viable model in terms of representing all the various forms of the employment relationships, such as part-time and fixed-term contracts and home-based telework, that were needed to satisfy the economic demands of employers and social demands by the 'new' workers for flexibility. The increasing shift from industrial society into an information/communication society, challenging the old paradigms of social protection and stable jobs, have multiplied, and continue to multiply, the use of the so-called 'atypical' forms of work, often outside the realm of protective statutes and collective bargaining. From the perspective of labour market policy, this economic approach requires functional 'deregulation' of labour relations, removing (eg Britain) or re-writing (eg Italy) employment rights in the name of a 'market paradigm', that is, the idea that a developed system of stringent rules is an obstacle to productivity and in some way responsible for mass unemployment. This approach affected not only tax and incomes policy and the post-war universal social security schemes, as happened in Germany and Britain for instance (see chapter 6 below), but also provisions regarding employment relations. The effects here were on a secondary segment of labour markets where we find a mixture of employment relations still using the contractual links inherited from the past and new types where one can identify the deviations from the archetypal. We shall consider five of these deviations.

The First Deviation: the Duration of the Contract

The contract of specified duration (for a fixed period) has been around for a long time and was inherited in the civil law systems in the form of *locatio operarum* from the Napoleonic Codes, where it was a predominant and unique model, the only one capable of protecting the freedom of the parties. The trend was reversed in favour of the contract for indefinite duration in all the civil codes and special statutes in the 1950s and 1960s, as a way to guarantee stability in the social context of mass unemployment and by the needs of post-war reconstruction. The use of fixed-term contracts was rigidly limited to certain sectors and to specific objectives in order to prevent fraudulent use of this typology. This model was widespread—especially after 1974—and found its highest acceptance in France, Germany, Spain and Portugal.[60]

The need to guarantee a flexible use of the workforce in industry and other sectors accelerated the evolution of the typology of fixed duration contracts. In some countries, it was in the direction of extending their applicability to sectors of the economy where this was not previously possible. However, contractual freedom was still limited by legislation or case law demanding the existence of an 'objective' and 'practical' reason, that is, 'reasonable' motive and justifiable by the facts (German case law), 'legitimate' reason (Belgian case law), unusual and exceptional job (Spanish Workers' Statute 1980), and temporary character and nature of work (France).[61] During the 1980s and 1990s the movement was precisely towards the easing of the ties that used to restrict the use of the contractual model. It could be said that legislation restored the will of the parties to the contract, thus squarely putting bargaining back into the free market. The legislative technique was sometimes based on the model of 'collectively negotiated flexibility', ie on the attribution to the trade unions of regulatory powers over the fixed-term labour market.[62] This model acquired importance in the period of crisis and signified a trend to limit freedom to resort to it only through the scheme of collective authorisation agreements. The function of the fixed-term contract was more and more to create a flexible workforce, but on the conditions agreed by collective social partners in the face of weak legal guarantees. Their weakness is reflected, for example, in uncertainty over the notion of objective cause (Germany), inefficiency of state control (Italy), limited enjoyment of union rights (Portugal) and the vagueness of the notion of fraudulent use of contract (Greece). From the beginning, a trend in all civil law countries was to impose the sanction, where there were frequent renewals of the fixed-term, of conversion of

[60] Kravaritou (1988) 23.
[61] Veneziani (1993) 206.
[62] Italy, Law 56/87; Zappalà (2004) 103.

the contract into an open-ended one. In Britain and Ireland, by contrast, it was only after EC intervention in the late 1990s that such sanctions were imposed.

A further variation in the fixed-term contract is an agreement whereby it is stipulated that the employer must provide for the worker's training. Generally speaking, the worker traditionally entered the enterprise in order to invest his or her skills in a given job. The agreement to provide job plus training marks the advent of a new kind of labour law, one that acts as an incentive to flexible employment and is no longer limited to guaranteeing the security of an existing post.

In the early 1980s, a new era started when the ideology of reconciliation or compromise between conflicting interests arose out of the economic crisis. The legal system faced the problem reconciling two spheres of interests—that of the workers and that of the firms—since, on the one hand, it sought to promote employment, while, on the other, it permitted reduction of costs and taxation by excluding atypical workers from being considered as part of the firm. This meant that there were no guarantees in terms of social security. In a 1993[63] survey, such cases were found in France, Spain, Portugal, Belgium and Italy. In Italy, job plus training contracts were confined to public employment. The most striking characteristic of such contracts lies in the rights and duties of the parties. Importance is attached both to job performance and to the obligation of the firm to train the young worker. Training alternated with periods of actual work; in France this was described as a 'contract of qualification', and in Spain and Belgium, training–job agreement. Being regarded in Spain as a modern-day equivalent to apprenticeship, the contractual model has a strong component of job creation[64] and is a way to implement Article 40.2 of the Spanish Constitution, which obliges the public authority to 'promote a policy guaranteeing occupational training and retraining'. The Spanish constitutional provision of a right to training shows that training is regarded as a 'personal value' to be included into the contractual scheme. From 1992 onward in France, lifelong training has acquired a status of an 'obligation' of the firm.

The contract of employment is called on to perform a new function to improve the skills that have a genuinely vocational value for the trainee. This is a function which differs from the typical contracts of the mercantile economy, such as apprenticeship. The legal technique has been enhanced by the French *Cour de Cassation* in its innovative rulings,[65] arguing that *adaptation et reclassement* are implicit obligations in the structure of the employment contract. Observers argue quite rightly that the mechanism is twofold because from one side it tries to combat unemployment while, from the other, it constructs an inventive notion of stability in employment. In the absence of the 'adaptation practice', a dismissal lacks a just cause.[66]

---

[63] Veneziani (1993) 208.
[64] Rodríguez-Pinero Royo (2004) 18.
[65] Moreau (2004) 10.
[66] Sciarra (2004a) 9.

The Second Deviation: the Duration of Work

The duration of performance (content of the legal obligation of the worker) as distinct from the duration of the 'contractual tie' may deviate from a standard contract even though the worker is still subordinate to the firm for an unspecified length of time. A reduction in working hours does not modify the nature of the contract. The need for flexibility requires the reduction of the overall time of performance. Normally we are dealing with new jobs and (where they are regulated by law or collective agreements) contractual formulae based on the principle of solidarity between employed and unemployed workers.[67] The increase in the volume of part-time work is due to different causes: on the one hand, the changing composition of the labour market due to the increase of female labour and of young persons, and, on the other hand, technological innovation (work at videoterminals, etc). In most cases the contract of employment is now shaped so as to serve as a legal instrument of a labour costs-saving policy. The aim is, on the one hand, to guarantee the protection of the physical person of the worker and, on the other, to ensure that the reorganisation of work is not rigidly structured, which explains the success of this alternative structure of the contract in all countries. It matches the organisational requirements of a firm while also satisfying the needs of certain sectors of the labour market (such as women, students, and older people) that would not be able or willing to accept full-time employment.

Contractual freedom rules supreme as regards the content and ways to organise the contract. This is shown by the variety of forms it may assume. It may be constituted by a reduction in normal working hours (horizontal part-time), by full-time work carried out on alternate days (vertical part-time) or by job sharing, job alternation or early retirement, combined with the part-time job of an unemployed worker with the support of public funds. Between the 1960s and the 1980s some limits were imposed by the law to the freedom of contract—by the courts or by collective agreements and statutes—like a requirement of objective motive (German Federal Labour Court), 'reasons of a technical and economic nature' (Belgian Collective agreement 1972) or necessity not to unbalance 'the employment conditions of a particular profession or branch' (French *Code du travail* Article L.212–4 and 7).[68] Collective agreements have tried to reduce the risks involved in using this kind of flexibility, indicating, even at the plant level, the maximum percentage of part-time workers who may be engaged as compared to the number of full-timers, classified by skills, or fixing the maximum number of working hours for part-time work in order to gain access to social benefits.

---

[67] Blanpain and Kohler (1988) 79.
[68] Veneziani (1993) 211.

The Third Deviation: the Personal Availability to Work

The progressive diffusion of deviations from the pre-existing contractual frame-work of employment relations, as analysed in 1985–6,[69] was evidenced by job performances that were not continuous but alternate, intermittent, cyclical or interspersed with periods of vocational training courses. Here we are dealing with the most sensitive features of the contract of employment, ie the worker's promise to engage his physical energies at a given moment. Of course, when he or she enters into the contract the worker pledges to supply his or her actual ener-gies, which he or she does in concrete terms through the performance of the job; however, it is commonly assumed that subordination consists largely in the worker's legal, and not simply physical, availability. His or her juridical tie remains in force even when he or she is not materially working (eg because of illness). In more recent forms of work, the worker promises a 'potential job' that he or she will perform in the future when the employer decides to 'call' him. Here we are dealing with a sophisticated contractual scheme where subordination is not of a technical–juridical nature but is only socio-economic.

In this case, the contract suffers from alteration of its classic feature and loses its protective function: the worker has no decision-making power over (i) the time of work and life; (ii) the length and continuity of the obligation and its material performance; or (iii) the nature of his obligation (a promise of future performances). The phenomenon became common in the period of deregulation in commerce, service industries, air transport and tourism.[70]

The Fourth Deviation: the Triangular Relationship

The structure of the traditional contract of employment reflects the bilateral rela-tionship between the worker and the employer whose juridical entity is known. Since the early 1970s there has been an increase in the number of socio-economic relationships of a triangular nature involving the employer by whom the worker is employed, the worker, and a third legal or natural person who actually receives the latter's services The first anomaly of this structure lies in the fact that job performance may be detached from the original contract where it has its roots. Various types of legal links are possible, among which it is worth mentioning the work carried out by a worker employed by a firm (the supplier) for the benefit of another firm (the user).

The singularity of the scheme is that the worker is juridically dependent on the firm that has, so to speak, provided or lent his or her services to the second firm at the latter's request. A further anomaly, from the legal viewpoint, is that the worker works for the firm with which he entered into an agreement whose

[69] Cordova (1986) 715.
[70] Kravaritou (1988) 60.

content is his or her promise is to be available to carry out a given task. In fact, from the moment he or she takes on the employment he or she pledges to be available to the other party to the agreement.

We may group together, in the model described above, the contract of employment through an intermediary (*travail intérimaire*), the sub-contracting of the workforce and the lending or temporary attachment of workers, including labour pooling. Undoubtedly, one of the most widespread forms is temporary work through an intermediary. This atypical contract is the clear evidence that there can be a grey zone where labour law meets commercial law, although the respective philosophies are still different. The employment contract is a 'container' of protection of human personality, while commercial law provides for the exchange of commodities or services. The risks involved were understood in legal systems that considered the phenomenon of intermediation in making the employment contract as unlawful. Lawmakers have clearly been on their guard, because of the fear of evasion and fraud in respect of existing protection. The changing regulation of temporary work agencies, from prohibition in some countries, to more limited forms of regulation is examined in chapter 3 above.

The Fifth Deviation: the Work Place

Here we are dealing with a major phenomenon whereby the work is performed outside the central place of production, ie the factory or office. The novelty in this social relationship is relative because home work has existed since before the industrial revolution. In short, it could be said that it constitutes the original economic organisational form of work that was to become factory work. However, the contract has undergone a process of renewal and has become widespread, in no small measure through the contribution of technological developments. Nevertheless, what we are interested in here, from the legal stance, is the performance outside the firm of the productive cycle that normally belongs to the organisation of the firm, and the effect of this on the contractual subordination of the worker. The technological revolution made it possible to decentralise certain functions, such as planning, research, supervision of accounts and know-how. Externalisation may involve different ways of regulating the relationships between the various components of the enterprise. The mere creation of a satellite company in France has posed the problem of identifying who the actual employer is in terms of establishing contractual responsibility towards workers. French case law and the Italian Workers' Statute have both confronted this problem because they are countries where there is no barrier against the decentralisation of parts of undertakings.[71]

Telework provides a good example. This is a form of work that makes use of telecommunications and can be carried out either inside or outside the firm. This

---

[71] Veneziani (1993) 216.

is a kind of work outside the sphere of most protective legislation which aimed at regulating home work for manual activities for the production of quantifiable and fungible goods and material services. German, Belgian and Italian experiences and laws support this conclusion.[72] One problem that would seem to be common in all cases, both in common law countries and in those with specific ad hoc legislation, is the identification of the criteria characterising the employment relationship that is based on actual experience and on the concept of subordinate employment. According to British and Swedish legislation, home work may be considered, depending on particular circumstances, as a form of either self-employment or of subordinate employment on the basis of whether it is connected to a specific organisation of work under an employer. Italian law, German law and the Belgian Court of Cassation, in deciding on the provision to be applied to teleworkers, resort to the 'nature of work' and the 'stable economic, technico-functional connection with productive cycle of the client firm'.

Another problem with the evolution of the contract of employment in the technological era concerns the change in the role of the parties and the content of their respective subjective rights. In the early capitalist economy the employer is both manager and technical expert, and his or her power of control concerns what, how and when the work is performed. In the modern age, managerial prerogatives, because of the high skills and expertise of the subordinate employees, have rather to do with the way in which a highly skilled worker belongs to the organisation of a firm. The orders of the employer concern when and if, rather than how, the work should be done; this constitutes the substance of the new subordination. In the technological era the power of command does not lose its intensity but its scope is reduced. Thus, according to the Belgian *Cour de Cassation*, the law of July 1978 on the contract of employment could be applied to teleworkers.

Certainly the contract of employment still remains the formal wrapping covering the relationship of the worker to the organization. However, major influences have been derived, especially in northern countries, from statutes and collective bargaining, both of which are concerned with ensuring that the workers have the power to intervene in determining the content of their jobs and also to understand their position within the organisational network. The tendency of collective bargaining is to favour a right of influence by workers coupled with a degree of autonomy far greater than in the past.

The socio-economic function carried out by the contract of employment in these cases is no longer one of mere mercantile exchange between work and remuneration. The agreement now includes the function of control by the individual over his or her performance. However, there is a further problem, namely that technology, especially informatics, potentially threatens the personality of the individual. Statutory law (Italy, Spain) and case law (Germany) have tried to reduce the risks by 'depersonalising' job performance and by banning the use of

---

[72] Ibid.

sophisticated surveillance machinery on workers at a distance. The function of the contract of employment is that of allowing the organisation of work through 'depersonalised job performance'.[73]

Global Capitalism: Setting Minimum European Standards (1990–2004)

Before 1990, the risks of these contractual schemes never disturbed the EC, which was convinced that multiple contracts of employment represented a good way to promote flexibility. However, the abuse of the various forms and the danger of unjustified differences and competitive advantages led to attempts to fix a legal threshold of fundamental principles, such as equal treatment for part-time and fixed-term workers with full-time and permanent ones. Although a weak panacea for social dumping, Directives 97/80/EC on part-time work and 99/70/EC on fixed-term work, and a draft Directive on temporary work in 2002, were seen as providing a minimum base for a European integration policy. This was a path that was also followed by ILO Convention No 181 (1997) in reversing the previous hostility against temporary work agencies (see chapter 3 above). Generally speaking, the EC Directives have led to a more flexible legal framework in the civil law countries, but to greater regulation of part-time and fixed-term contracts in Britain and Ireland.

In fact, the trend since the 1990s, even though not generalised, is towards a progressive relaxation of the legal prerequisites and of the most significant pillars against a distorted use of the atypical contract. On the one hand, Belgium has allowed the stipulation of successive fixed-term contracts without having to give reasons and without having to consider them as permanent contracts; on the other hand, the vagueness of the formula indicating objective reasons—'technical, productive, organisational and other substantive reasons'—adopted by the Italian conservative government in transposing the Directive 97/81/EC (law 6.9.2001, no 368) has widened the scope allowing a major flexibility in the use of the workforce. Objective reasons are not necessary for such contracts for German workers over the age of 52 (2003), and the limit on renewal can be derogated *in pejus* by collective parties. This legal strategy was adopted also by regulations under the British Employment Act 2002, which provide that the conversion of subsequent fixed-term contracts after 4 years into open-ended ones can be overcome by collective or workforce agreements.

It seems that state control on the excessive use atypical contracts is as difficult as it was in the past, because of a deliberate policy of weakening guarantees. However, it also depends, even in the context of rigid protection, on political and

---

[73] Veneziani (1993) 62ff.

financial reasons—as happened in Greece—or on the deliberate attempt to erode the centrality of the traditional classical model. This happened in Italy under a right-wing coalition government, where the ambiguity of the formula (see above)[74] offered a space manoeuvre for discretionary powers of the firm. This trend stands in opposition to the ideological essence of the European Framework Agreement 1999 on fixed-term contracts, which specifies that the absence of objective reasons constitutes an 'abuse'.[75] According to the EC Directive 99/70/EC, which gave legal effect to the European Framework Agreement, contracts for an indefinite period remain the prevalent form in labour market negotiations.

Limits to the structure of part-time jobs were imposed by Greek legislation, influenced by Directive 97/80/EC. This was extended, as it was in Italy, to the public sector. The minimum guarantees were the prohibition not to exceed a certain number of hours a week, the limited duration of the contract (lasting up to 24 months) and renewal after a given interval. The extraordinary success of this kind of contract gave an impulse to a different trend appearing in the Netherlands and in Germany in the 1990s, under the auspices of Directive 1997/80/EC, in the direction of promoting the use of this model. Both countries encouraged workers to voluntarily go part-time and fixed the obligation on the employer to give reasons for a refusal to accept the employee's request for part-time work, indicating the organisational reasons impeding the reduction in working hours. German laws (Act on part-time work and fixed-term contracts of 1 January 2001 implementing Directive 97/80/EC) reflected, amending some parts, the previous Act of 1985, providing for minimum guarantees. It tries, in effect, to avoid the employer's risks being transferred to the employees and gives protection against discriminatory practices. However, by the end of the period of this study the question remains whether or not 'it will contribute to an increase in the quality of part-time work'.[76]

Many doubts were also generated by the collateral trend towards establishing additional flexibility by individualisation of the right to reduce or extend the agreed working time. Britain secured a provision in the EC Working Time Directive to allow for individual contracting-out of the prescribed maximum 48-hour week because of fears that the Directive would undermine Britain's competitive advantage of a long working-time culture (see chapter 3 above). Similar risks of individualisation of the contractual regime are to be found in Germany and Italy. In the latter country the legislative Decree 2003 no 276 (amending. Decree no 61/00 of 25 February 2000) is the result of a policy whose ideological background (contained in the conservative government White Paper on Labour Market Reform, 2000) pays less attention to the request for quality from the supply side than the requests for flexibility from the demand side. The rationale of the two statutes enacted by the same right-wing coalition between 2000 and 2003 is to

---

[74] Art 1 of Legislative decree 368/01 and decree 2003/368, Zappalà (2004) 107.
[75] Vignaeau et al (1999).
[76] Schmidt (2004) 97.

disregard collective forces and discipline by giving room to individual autonomy to be deployed beyond the collective limits, worsening guarantees dating from 1984. The restoration of individual consent is a device to overcome trade union control. The most evident example is the idea of 'elasticity clauses', ie individual contractual arrangements giving the employer the power to change the time of performance, even in the absence of a collective agreement. The low level of guarantees in Italian statutory regulation and the risk of individualism in labour law for the employee were clarified by the Italian Constitutional Court in 1992 when it judged the compatibility of elasticity clauses with the freedom of the worker. The Court underlined how, in an era of flexibility, the function of the employment contract is not a pure exchange of flexible work for economic remuneration. It involves the freedom of the worker 'to organise his life', which could be severely limited if a contract placed him or her under the power of the employer to alter the work schedule that is or had been previously established by the contract (Constitutional Court 210/1992). The Irish Part-time Act Work 2001 moved in this protective direction as part of family-friendly labour law policy started in that country in 1997.[77]

Excessive flexibility through unilateral modification of working time has an upsetting impact on the original and 'natural' function of the contract. It loses its essential function to plan and make foreseeable all 'personal' costs involved in employment relations. The more fragmented the temporal continuity of the activity and the juridical continuity of the obligation, the more the worker is exposed to the risk of avoidance of any kind of labour and social security protections. National experiences show how sensitive and politically debatable the introduction of work through an intermediary is because of the huge amount of risk for the worker. The job on call is an extreme form of part-time work introduced for the first time in Italy by decree in 2003, and renewed in Germany in 2001, following an earlier law of 1985, where the employer determines unilaterally if and when the employee has to work in the areas of production indicated by collective agreements with the consequence of transferring the employer's risks to the worker. The Italian legislative measure still expresses 'a precise philosophy of individualisation in the employment contract' and the whole equilibrium between collective agreement and individual agreement is jeopardised.[78] The same impression derives from the German model because the reform of 2001 has restricted the employer's flexibility but it still encourages an individual trade-off between contracting parties, ie the possibility to derogate from some provisions unfavourable to the worker on condition that weekly and daily working hours are specified and a period of prior notice is given.[79]

To enhance the weak position of these workers the Dutch system has proposed a framework of legal regulations inspired by the 1999 'flexicurity' strategy that modified the civil code. The philosophy behind the statute is connected to one of

---

[77] Kerr (2004) 4; for England, see Davies and Freedland (2006) 210.
[78] Sciarra (2004a) 28.
[79] Schmidt (2004) 80.

the pillars of the EC Lisbon strategy calling for adaptability in the labour market (see chapter 3 above). 'Flexicurity' meant a coordination of measures coupling accepted flexibility and social welfare reform to increase security in the market. The legal technique is based on a web of different sources of law: statutes and deregulated bargaining policies.[80] The rationale of Dutch reforms of jobs on call is that the original and natural function, to provide work in a specific case for particular and temporary needs of employers, is materially changed by the employer's abuse (repetition of calls, vagueness of working time, violation of minimum wage rate) (Article 7:667–68(a) and Article 7:628(a) Civil Code). The legislative changes were a result of a political compromise: to discourage employers from the use of precarious contracts, such as freelance jobs, jobs on calland zero-hours agreements. This is clearly stated by the Italian law of 2003 (amending a 1997 Act) in the rule that in case of non-compliance with the obligation to sign the contract in writing and lack of detailed information, the worker is considered legally dependent on the user.[81] The hostility of unions to new forms of work can be explained as a reaction to a practice that can exclude them from the control of the labour market. This shows why, in most countries, when the needs for flexibility emerged all interventions of the legislator were preceded by the unions' consent. This happened in France in the case of enactment of laws in 1972,[82] 1985 and 1990. The same happened in the Netherlands where the Flexibility and Security Act 1999 was anticipated by the national agreement reached in the *Stichting van de Arbeid*.

The framework of rules contained in the Directive 91/83/EC aimed to complete and promote the health and safety of workers on fixed-term contracts and temporary contracts of employment. It describes the relationship existing between the temporary work agency, the user and the worker, where the latter is made available to work for or under the control of a beneficiary firm or plant (Article 2). It is a wide and rather vague definition that crosses various models. The French system has progressively legalised *travail intérimaire* (see chapter 3 above).[83] The statutory provisions tried to guarantee equal treatment between temporary workers and permanent employees of the user and to limit the cases of permissible use of this kind of contract. The point of contact between the commercial contract (agency/user) and the employment contract (agency/worker) is represented by the joint liability of the two employers for the payment of remuneration and of social security provision of health and safety measures etc.

Compared to the French, Italian and German schemes, the British system seems more open to flexible work arrangements. The British law does not specify the contractual nature of the relationships with the supplier and hirer. This ambiguity gives rise to a casuistic common law trend in which the courts have a wide

---

[80] Caruso (2004) 27.
[81] Ghera (2003) 341.
[82] Agreement Manpower-CGT 1969, in Verdier et al (2007) 67–70.
[83] Ibid, 67.

discretion to decide whether or not the worker is subordinate, under a contract of service, or autonomous, under a contract *sui generis*. On this point a clear legal framework is present in the Italian context, where temporary workers are legally subordinate to the agency by an open-ended or fixed-term contract. In this kind of atypical work the main deviation from the classical prototype does not concern the structure of the contract but the 'multiple' content of the employee's obligation deriving from the split of powers between agency and user. In fact, the worker has promised 'permanent availability' to his or her legal employer (the agency) and to give 'temporary performance' of the job to his real counterpart (the user). The agreement between the original contracting parties (agency and temporary worker) should make it easier to establish an employment relation between the worker and a different party (user).

The parasubordinate employee in the condition of economic dependence enjoys the same protection of workers as regards health and care, as happens in Spain and Germany, where the person 'similar to salaried people' is covered by national social security and collective agreements. Furthermore, according to the German doctrine, they should also enjoy also protection against unfair dismissal.[84] The concept of 'worker' used by British statutes, such as the National Minimum Wage Act 1998, the Working Time Regulations 1998 and the Employment Relations Act 1998, seems to 'broadly correspond to civil law notions of parasubordination'.[85] Common law countries offer a significant lesson on the survival of the legal distinctions and the permanence of the old functions of the employment contract. Some scholars question the labour law attempts to shift the boundary of the legal category of dependent labour so as to encompass those apparently self-employed. They suggest that, while these workers may lack a contract of employment based on mutuality of obligation, they are not genuinely in business on their own account (the so-called dependent self-employed).[86] The Italian labour market reforms of 2003 clearly show how thin the border between autonomy and subordination is. A new 'contract for work by project or by programme' (*contratto a progetto e a programma*) is a special agreement stipulated in writing where a simple project or programme is the content of the obligation carried out by the self-employed instead of continuous and coordinated collaboration, as in the previous legal definition. It has become clear to commentators and in the first case law how important it is to carefully investigate the factual dynamism of the mutual obligations. In this perspective, a special measure has been introduced by the law to prevent abuses. This was also the goal of the 1999 German law on the promotion of self-employed work.[87] The Italian system of 'certification' is an administrative act issued *erga omnes* at the end of a voluntary procedure, involving a special public (administrative) or private (unions and employers) bilateral commission. The commission provides for a

---

[84] Sobczak (2003) 316.
[85] Deakin (2002) 191.
[86] Ibid.
[87] Contouris (2007) 66.

preventive analysis of the real and concrete intention of the parties in forming or modifying the employment contract. The body is not bound by the legal title of the contract given by the individual parties, but indicates all the legal consequences (civil, administrative, of social security) attached to it. The idea underlying the system is the attempt to clarify this 'grey zone' of the atypical labour markets.

Conclusion

The range of the employment contract has been considerably enlarged, and this has affected the original meaning of subordination and the structure of the 'classical' model. The model of the contract of subordinate employment for an indefinite period of time emerged as a prevalent model in post-war European societies. The model was largely functional to a developing economy that needed a stable workforce. The employment relationship, as a contractual category of civil law, was intended not only to be a tool for employers to acquire a workforce but also as a legal device for the working of the enterprise.

Welfare state statutes, like the British National Insurance Act 1946 (covering 'employed earners', including but not limited to those 'being employed under contract of service'),[88] provide the evidence of the linkage between the contract of employment and the larger phenomemon of the ideology of the welfare state which dominated the post-war period until the beginning of the 1970s, when employment relations and the contractual 'shell' had become strongly influenced by protective legislation enriching its function, if not its structure.

The contract of subordinate employment has provided the social and legal parameters for the sphere of application of labour law and social security systems. In the civil law countries, constitutional rules have promoted the position of the subordinate worker as 'citizen of the enterprise' without touching the traditional structure of the contract. Special statutes in both civil and common law countries have done the same. The traditional 'organisational' function—to link human effort to the organisation's needs—has been coupled with the protective function of treating the worker as a human being. This can be described as a process of 'depersonalisation of subordination' tempering the dominant and intrusive presence of the employer's power of command and control. Statutes against unfair dismissals protecting a sort of 'ownership of the job', banning discriminatory practices and promoting equal pay policies, corroborate this trend towards a more balanced position of the contracting parties. The contract of employment thus becomes a container of a less asymmetrical quality of the employment relationship.

[88] Deakin (2002) 185.

The same trend was followed by statutes and the constitutions enacted in the 1970s in the new EU Member States (Spain, Portugal, Greece) because of the radical changes of their labour laws and political framework. Nevertheless, throughout the 1970s, a new process of transformation of the economies, induced by the economic crisis, started, along with substantive changes of the enterprise (vertical disintegration, outplacement, outsourcing, etc). This produced a move away from the Fordist model of production of goods and services, given to the acceleration of technological changes and the growing competition in labour intensive industries from low-wage producers in the Third World.

The new labour law system reshaped the structure and functions of the employment contract. It marked the passage from an idea of contract as a source of 'technical depersonalised co-operation' of the employee to the contract as a means of greater adaptability to the changing complex physiognomy of the firm's organisation. The new function required a new structure and a new form of availability of the worker. The key elements of the structure are the place of work, the skills required and the bilateral obligations as to time. The changes involved the different and alternative notions of the duration of the legal obligations (through the diffusion of fixed-term contract) and the different distribution of working time through part-time contracts and reductions in working hours. This exposed the paradox of the classical model of the employment contract, regarded as a container of social citizenship and, at the same time, as a legal instrument for saving labour costs. It was in the name of competitivity and promotion of employment that state labour policy in the 1980s started to deconstruct the classical scheme and adapt it to perform a plurality of functions mainly in the interests of the company. The contract contained a new trade-off: availability over a more or less continuous period without material subordination against a reduced wage. The distinction between internal and external flexibility becomes quite clear: the former is about the pursuit of productive efficiency (good organisation, innovation); the latter deals with allocative efficiency.[89] The two kinds of flexibility were reached consciously by all European countries from the 1980s onwards, cultivating the segmentation of the labour market and using different kinds of workers as a part of a 'core–periphery recipe'.

A segmentation of the labour market is a common European trend. The suggested therapy is not to enhance but rather to circumvent the protective legislation on individual dismissals that exists in all European countries (see chapter 3 above) by resorting to atypical contracts that fall outside the sphere of protection. The strategy to reach numerical flexibility touches the nature of the law and its relations with individual and collective agreements deeply: the wave of contracting-out clauses is designed to facilitate possible derogations from statutes by collective parties. France, Italy, the Netherlands, Sweden, Britain and Germany

---

[89] Dore (2004) 26.

follow this path, which underlines the function of employment contract as a 'soft' instrument for a deregulation policy.

In its more extreme forms the rationale of strongly neo-liberal labour market regulation can shift towards a more precarious methodology of individualising and liberalising the contract *à la carte*, as an even more direct instrument for a deregulatory policy. The risk is the deeper separation between standard employment relations and marginal personal work relations that could be projected towards grey and peripheral zones of the law or towards an area outside the law affecting the of whole civil society.[90]

All the indicated trends have resulted in demands for a more stable and solid bulk of principles and a floor of fundamental rights that preserve the individual contract of employment from deteriorating from its true protective mission. The road is indicated by several international texts: the elimination of discrimination 'in respect of employment and occupation' is the message of ILO and of EC Directives against discrimination, so as to ensure equal treatment in employment and working conditions (see chapter 5, below). However, the trust in the contract as a source of regulation for every worker is to be found in a precise statement of the Community Charter of Fundamental Social Rights of Workers 1989: 'The conditions of employment of every worker of the European community shall be regulated in laws, a collective agreement or a contract of employment' (point 9). The Nice Charter of Fundamental Rights 2000 enlarges and specifies the scope of the protection. This is a programme for the future work of unions, governments at national and European level, and also presents a challenge for labour lawyers who wish to develop the contract of employment into a guarantee of fundamental rights.

[90] Davies and Freedland (2006) 240; Freedland (2007) 12; Jeammaud (1988) 176.

5

Equality at Work

BOB HEPPLE

Introduction

One of the most significant developments in labour law since the Second World War has been the recognition of the fundamental right to equality for workers who are disadvantaged by reason of their status in society, such as race and religion, sex and sexual orientation, disability and age. The moral basis for this development lies in the ideas of human dignity and the equal worth of all individuals, reflected in labour law in the notion that that 'labour is not a commodity' (see chapter 1 above).

Before the Second World War, the concept of a legal right to equality of status, irrespective of race, sex, disability, age and other personal characteristics not relevant to job performance, did not exist outside of the written and largely unenforced constitutional provisions. The idea of status equality in the public sphere had not entered the sphere of private employment. The great transformation in this respect occurred in stages after the Second World War. The first was the assertion of equality as a fundamental human right in international instruments and in national constitutions. Broadly speaking, this was a product of the period of reconstruction—for the purposes of this chapter dating from the Universal Declaration of Human Rights (1948) to the International Labour Organisation (ILO) Conventions No 100 (1951) on Equal Pay for Men and Women and No 111 on Discrimination in Employment (1958), although there were also some later international treaties and constitutional provisions. The second stage centred around implementation of the principle of formal equality or consistent treatment between men and women and between members of different racial groups. Broadly speaking, this was a feature of the building of welfare states in Europe—for the purposes of this chapter dating from the adoption and implementation of Article 119 of the Treaty of Rome (1957) on equal pay for men and women, and building on earlier French laws on the subject. It was in this period, too, that the American model of anti-discrimination employment legislation was transplanted first in Britain in 1968 and

1975–76, and then throughout western Europe. By about 1975, the principle of formal equality of status in employment was well established, even if not fully achieved in practice.

The third stage was one in which the failure of formal equality to bring about significant changes in the position of women, ethnic minorities and other disadvantaged groups led to a new focus on substantive equality or, in Community jargon, 'full equality in practice'. This started with the transplantation of the American notion of indirect or 'adverse impact' discrimination into British law in 1975 and, through dialogue between British and German courts with the European Court of Justice (ECJ), into European Economic Community law in 1981. In this period, too, there was a development of special measures (positive action) to compensate for disadvantages in the labour market suffered by women and ethnic minorities, and there were family-friendly policies, starting in the Nordic countries. Measures of 'reasonable accommodation' to help disabled people in the labour market were adopted. Broadly speaking, these attempts to achieve substantive equality were a reaction to economic crisis and deregulation of the labour market, which had exacerbated social and economic inequalities.

The fourth stage is one in which the focus is moving towards comprehensive and transformative equality. Starting in the Netherlands in 1994 and Ireland in 1998, and given a major impetus by EC Directives in 2000, under Article 13 of the Treaty of Amsterdam, legislation in the countries studied aims to end the 'hierarchy' of inequalities and to cover all grounds of unfair discrimination. Moreover, public measures to remove defined systemic inequalities and to achieve social and economic equality have begun to be implemented. Broadly speaking, the struggles for comprehensive and transformative equality have been a response to the growing social and economic inequalities between and within states under the impact of global capitalism.

These four stages are not precise historical periods; rather, they represent a progression or general trend of policies and laws, in response to fundamental economic, social, political and cultural changes. The changes included the growing culture of human rights, which treated equality as a fundamental right even for previously marginalised groups such as disabled people, homosexuals and transgender people; feminisation of the labour force, the extension of the full franchise to women in countries where this had not occurred before the war, the rising expectations of women and the re-emergence of feminist movements; the need to support free movement of labour of EU citizens by the prohibition of discrimination on grounds of nationality, and the attempts to integrate new settled communities of third-country migrants irrespective of race or religion, while maintaining a 'Fortress Europe' to keep out unwanted immigrants; and the pressure to keep older people in the labour force because of labour shortages and the pressure of an ageing population on public finances.

These pressures were not present at the same time or to the same extent in all countries, with the result that legislation on status equality in employment was introduced slowly and at different times in respect of specific issues, starting with discrimination on grounds of sex, race and (sometimes) religion. Once it was established that there was no reason to exclude people on these grounds, attitudes began to change to other forms of status inequality, such as age, disability and sexual orientation.

Human Rights in the New World Order (1948–58)

The United Nations and the Council of Europe

In the new world order after the Second World War, equality was elevated into a fundamental human right. The first article of the Universal Declaration of Human Rights (UNDHR), adopted by the new United Nations (UN) on 10 December 1948, proclaimed that 'all human beings are born free and equal in dignity and rights'. Article 2 stated:

> Everyone is entitled to all the rights and freedoms set forth in this Declaration without distinction of any kind, such as race, colour, sex, language, religion, political or other opinion, national or social origin, property, birth or other status . . .

This meant that not only the civil and political rights but also the extensive economic and social rights recognised in the UNDHR (see chapter 1 above) were to be available without status discrimination. However, two separate instruments, which included the right to non-discrimination, were adopted by the UN in 1966 (in force 1976): the International Covenant on Civil and Political Rights and the International Covenant on Economic, Social and Cultural Rights. Separate Conventions were adopted on the Elimination of All Forms of Racial Discrimination (CERD) (in 1965) and on the Elimination of All Forms of Discrimination against Women (CEDAW) (in 1979). These instruments were ratified by all 15 countries in this study.

The 1950 European Convention for the Protection of Human Rights and Fundamental Freedoms (ECHR), confined to civil and political rights (including the freedom of association), contained a complementary right to non-discrimination on grounds of status in the exercise of convention rights. The much weaker European Social Charter 1961 (ESC) contained provisions on equal pay for men and women workers for work of equal value, the right of employed women and of mothers to protection, the rights of disabled people to vocational training and rehabilitation, and the rights of migrant workers. However, it was not until an Additional Protocol to the ESC in 1988 that the right to equal opportunities and equal treatment in matters of employment and occupation without discrimination on grounds of sex was recognised. A revised ESC in 1996 widened the scope of the original provisions on disadvantaged groups, adding the elderly and workers with family responsibilities, and specifically declaring that the rights under the ESC were to be secured without discrimination on specified grounds of status. The ECHR and ESC (1961) were ratified by all 15 countries in this study, and with the international treaties on discrimination, these instruments set out their common aspirations.

The separation of rights to non-discrimination in respect of economic and social rights from civil and political ones, and the fragmented approach to different grounds of discrimination, was to have lasting negative effects on the development of equality as a fundamental human right in the sphere of labour law (see chapter 1 above). Moreover, the separation of discrimination against women in CEDAW from that on racial grounds in CERD fragmented the struggle for equality and introduced a hierarchy of rights to equality, with many inconsistencies. Moreover, action against discrimination in employment and other fields was separated from the mainstream struggle for human rights, weakening both movements.

National Constitutions

This split between equality in respect of civil and political rights and economic and social ones also featured in written constitutions adopted after the Second World War. In some constitutions there is an emphasis on equality as the sharing of 'common humanity' or 'equal worth'. An example is Article 23 of the Belgian Constitution (1994), which provided that 'everyone has the right to lead a life worthy of human dignity'. The German Basic Law (1949), under the shadow of the Holocaust, placed public authorities under a duty to respect the 'dignity of man', which is 'inviolable'. Article 2 of the Greek Constitution similarly speaks of 'respect and protection of the value of the human being' as the 'primary obligation of the state'. The constitutions diverge, however, in the amount of detail they provide as to how human beings are to be treated with equal humanity in the social and economic spheres. The most extensive were those of Italy and Germany. In the Italian constitution of 1948 the principle of equality before the law was combined for the first time with a general prohibition on discrimination in respect of the right to work (Article 4) and the rights to equitable wages, hours of work and holidays (Article 36), social assistance (Article 38) and participation in management (Article 46). The Bonn Basic Law (1949) also had a general prohibition against discrimination on a number of grounds, and section 51 of the German Works Constitution Act 1951 had made the employer and the works council responsible for all persons in the establishment being treated in conformity with the principle of justice and equity, in particular prohibiting discrimination by reason of descent, religion, nationality, origin, political or trade union membership or union activities or views, or on account of sex. In Spain, Article 9.2 of the 1979 Constitution instructed public authorities to promote conditions for an effective and real equality between private persons and groups, but treated these as 'guiding principles of social policy' rather than as legally enforceable rights. The Nordic countries' constitutions required judicial and executive discretion to be exercised without discrimination, but left the private sector alone.[1]

The International Labour Organisation

The most important and far-reaching international developments affecting equality in labour law were not at the level of the UN and the Council of Europe, but in two ILO Conventions, No 100 on Equal Remuneration of Men and Women for Work of Equal Value (1951) and No 111 on Discrimination in Employment (1958). These were both ratified by all the 15 countries in this study over a prolonged period, starting with Belgium (1952) in respect of Convention No 100,[2] and ending with the UK and Ireland (1999) and Luxembourg (2001) in respect of Convention No 111.[3] The principle that 'men and women should receive equal remuneration for work of equal value' had been stated in Article 41 of the ILO Constitution (1919) and repeated in the Declaration of Philadelphia (1944). Convention No 100 elaborated this principle. By using the notion of 'equal value', the ILO went beyond the concept of 'equal work', used in the UNDHR (Article 23(2)), and later in Article 119 of the Treaty of Rome (1957). This was a controversial issue during the debates on the draft Convention, and was strongly opposed by the International Organisation of Employers and some governments. The British government took a different stance from the Trades Union Congress (TUC), which had campaigned for equal pay since 1888,[4] on the grounds that equal pay could not be afforded at a time of huge national debt occasioned by the war. In 1946, an all-male majority of a British Royal Commission on Equal Pay had opposed the introduction of equal pay because of probable adverse effects upon the demand for female labour and because, in their view, existing differentials reflected real differences in efficiency.[5] On the other hand, France, which had accepted the principle of equal pay in minimum wage legislation since 1944 (see below), was in favour of a Convention.[6] Sweden and Denmark had reservations because of their policies of non-intervention in wage negotiations.[7]

Convention No 111 (1958) was even more far-reaching, well ahead of national

---

[1] Eg Swedish Constitution, Art 8.

[2] Austria, 1953; Belgium, 1952; Denmark, 1960; Finland, 1963; France, 1953; Germany, 1956; Greece, 1975; Ireland, 1974; Italy, 1956; Luxembourg, 1967; the Netherlands, 1971; Portugal, 1967; Spain, 1967; Sweden, 1962; Britain, 1971.

[3] Austria, 1973; Belgium, 1977; Denmark, 1966; Finland, 1970; France, 1981; Germany, 1961; Greece, 1984; Ireland, 1999; Italy, 1963; Luxembourg, 2001; the Netherlands, 1973; Portugal, 1959; Spain, 1967; Sweden, 1962; Britain, 1999.

[4] Creighton (1979) 90.

[5] Ibid 94.

[6] ILC (1951) 32, 35.

[7] ILC (1951).

laws in Europe at the time, apart from Italy and Germany. While the British government agreed 'that equality of opportunity and treatment in employment and the avoidance of discrimination on irrelevant grounds are in principle desirable', it nevertheless doubted 'whether an international instrument . . . would be realistic and practical'.[8] Britain wanted no more than a Resolution; Austria, Belgium, Denmark and the Netherlands wanted only a Recommendation, but Finland, France, Sweden and Italy supported a Convention.

The Convention as finally adopted was surprisingly broad in scope for its time, embracing substantive and transformative equality. It provides that all persons are entitled to equality of opportunity and treatment in respect of employment, training, collective bargaining, and participation in workers' and employers' organisations; it imposes positive obligations on public authorities to promote equal opportunities and treatment (including making eligibility for government contracts dependent on observance of the principles); and supports 'special measures' to meet the particular requirements of persons who, for reasons such as sex, age, disablement, family responsibilities or social or cultural status, are generally recognised to require special provision or assistance. The approach to discrimination (which has been interpreted to cover both its direct and indirect forms)[9] is comprehensive and universal, including (but not limited to)

> any distinction, exclusion or preference made on the basis of race, colour, sex, religion, political opinion, national extraction or social origin, which has the effect of nullifying or impairing equality of opportunity or treatment in employment or occupation (Article 1).

In a sense, the history of discrimination law in Europe since 1958, has been an exercise in levelling countries up to the standards laid down in the two ground-breaking ILO Conventions.

Formal Equality (1957–75)

The Meaning and Scope of Formal Equality at Work

The principle of formal legal equality (*égalité de droit*)—that 'all men are and will be born free and equal before the law'—found its early expression in the French declaration of the rights of man and the citizen in 1789, and entered into the written constitutions of all continental European countries in the nineteenth and

---

[8] Ibid, para 8.
[9] Rubin (2005) para 6.03.1.1.1.

twentieth centuries.[10] This version of equality was embedded in the circumstances of eighteenth-century France, and continues to influence French attitudes today (see below). 'It was in the first place, legal privilege, not inequality of wealth, which was the object of attack.'[11] A distinction was drawn between formal or legal equality and practical or economic equality (*égalité de fait*). It was thought that once legal impediments to economic enterprise were removed, in other words once legal equality of opportunity was established, individuals, by acting in their own self-interest free from arbitrary constraints, would maximise the welfare of society. France is often contrasted with Britain in this respect. Britain had little time for resounding proclamations of rights such as legal equality ('so much bawling on paper' or 'nonsense upon stilts', said Jeremy Bentham)[12] because there were no legal barriers differentiating the different strata of society. The English, Welsh, Scots and Irish relied on custom and convention, not positive enactment, to maintain the inferior social status of the lower classes. It was not until the 1960s that legal equality was actively asserted in Britain, and then only in very specific contexts where abuses could be shown, such as race or sex discrimination.

All the European democracies proclaimed formal equality before the law (above), but apart from a few limited exceptions, upheld social, cultural and economic discrimination. However, specific economic, social and political pressures led these countries, at different times and in different ways, to address the problem of direct discrimination on grounds of sex and race. Direct discrimination means treating one person less favourably than another on one of these grounds.

Sex Discrimination[13]

Female labour force participation increased strongly from the 1960s onwards in most European states, starting with the Nordic countries, followed by some Northern European ones (eg Belgium, Britain, Germany, Luxembourg and the Netherlands), with the lower income countries (eg Greece, Ireland, Italy, Portugal and Spain) joining the trend only from the 1980s.[14] However, cross-country differences persist into the twenty-first century, with participation rates below 60% in the southern European countries, apart from Portugal, and as high as

---

[10] France, Preamble to Constitution of 1946, Arts 2 and 3 and Constitution of 1958; Belgium, Constitution of 1994, Arts 10 and 11; Austria, Treaty of St Germain 1919, Arts 66 and 67; Germany, Basic Law of 1949, Art 3(1), (3); Greece, Art 4(1) of Constitution; Italy, Constitution of 1948, Art 3; Luxembourg, Art 111 of Constitution; The Netherlands, Art 1 of Constitution; Portugal, Arts 13 and 60 of Constitution; Spain, Constitution of 1979, Art 14.

[11] Tawney (1964) 92–93.

[12] Bentham (1843) II,489.

[13] The term 'sex' discrimination is used in this book because it was used in anti-discrimination legislation throughout the post-war period. For arguments that the newer concept of 'gender' discrimination is confusing when constructing social and political goals, see Browne (2006) 2.

[14] OECD (2004) 52.

80% in the Nordic countries. Public policy has been geared towards increasing female participation for a number of reasons, in particular to meet increased demand for labour in times of economic growth and to reduce child poverty, especially among the growing number of single-parent families. Increased female participation has been seen as one way to resolve the pressures of an ageing population on labour supply and on public finances.[15]

Sex discrimination in pay and opportunities for promotion has a negative effect on female participation. The pay gap between men and women (the difference between men's and women's gross hourly wage as a percentage of men's average gross hourly wage excluding overtime) varies significantly between countries. In most European countries, however, the long-term trend has been for the gap to decrease. In France, for example, the average pay of women relative to men's rose from 64% in the 1960s to 82% in 1996. In Germany it increased from 59.9% in 1950 to 73.3% in 1991, but fell to 71.2% in 2004. Even in Britain, which has the largest pay gap, the pay ratio between women and men rose from 72% in 1982 to 82% in 2001. However, among part-time workers (four-fifths of whom are women) the increase was considerably lower, rising from 56.8% in 1982 to 59% in 2001.[16] The evidence suggests that individual differences, like education, experience and age, play a relatively minor part in the persistence of the pay gap, which seems more related to the level of occupational segregation and the wage structure.[17]

Occupational sex segregation has two forms, horizontal and vertical. The former indicates that men and women are segregated into different jobs. If they were all paid the same and enjoyed the same working conditions, there would be no inequality in employment terms, but in reality separate is never equal. Vertical segregation refers to the disproportionate concentration of women in the lower grades with lower pay and worse working conditions.[18] Among the reasons for vertical segregation are social norms and stereotypical assumptions regarding men and women, family responsibilities, taxation and social security; the structure of the labour market (for example, the extent to which the public sector is an employer); and discrimination at entry and in work.[19] Occupational segregation tends to be greater in countries with high levels of female participation in the labour market, mainly because of high levels of part-time and temporary work by women.[20]

The problems of unequal pay and opportunities were highlighted during both world wars, when women replaced men in many occupations and large numbers of women were drawn into the labour market. The demands for equal pay by male-dominated trade unions was a way to protect men's wages from being

---

[15] Ibid, 53.
[16] Plantegna and Remery (2006) 22–23.
[17] Ibid, 25–27.
[18] Browne (2006) 4–5.
[19] Anker et al (2003) 1.
[20] Hakim (1996) 170.

levelled down by employment of women at lower rates. The distinction between 'men's jobs' and 'women's jobs' was fostered by men to protect their jobs, and collective agreements perpetuated these distinctions.[21] Notable exceptions were the interconfederal (all sector) collective agreements reached in Italy in December 1945 and May 1946, providing for equal pay for women if they performed jobs on the same terms and with the same productivity as men. In practice, however, as a parliamentary inquiry found, such provisions were rarely applied.[22] Article 37 of the Italian Constitution specifically provided for the same rights for women as for men, and 'for equal work, the same remuneration as for the man'. But, in the 1950s, the courts justified the practice of underpaying women performing equal work on the grounds that women's work was less productive than the corresponding work performed by men, and they gave a narrow interpretation to the concept of 'equal work'.[23]

The legislative reaction to sex discrimination was hesitant and patchy. A French law of 1946 provided that women having a trade certificate (*certificat d'aptitude professionel*) had a right to equal pay to men in the same occupational category. An earlier Decree of 24 August 1944, immediately after liberation, had established equality as regards the minimum wage, but a differential of 10% was allowed against women employed in the same job as men. It was claimed by employers that this was justified because women did 'lighter' work than men. This differential was abolished in 1946, but it still remained possible for collective agreements approved by a public authority to provide for a differential in earnings above the minimum wage. In Britain, collective agreements and wages councils orders (the latter in industries where there was no effective collective bargaining) generally differentiated between 'men's jobs' and 'women's jobs' and set a lower rate for women doing work of equal value to men. In Belgium and Luxembourg, the minimum rate for women was around 80–90% of the men's rate.[24] In most countries there were restrictions on the hours of work of women in mines and factories, and on night work by women, and men were given priority for overtime working. Family responsibilities led to a higher degree of absenteeism among women than among men. Factors such as these depressed women's pay relative to that of men.

A turning point came in 1957 with the adoption of Article 119 of the Treaty of Rome, which provided that '[e]ach Member State shall . . . ensure . . . the application of the principle that men and women should receive equal pay for equal work'. At the time of the Treaty negotiations, four of the six founding Member States (Belgium, France, Germany and Italy) had ratified ILO Convention No 100, but only France had specific legislation requiring equal pay.[25] The French government argued that France would be at a competitive disadvantage,

[21] ILC (1951), Report VI (1) passim.
[22] Barnard in Hervey and O'Keeffe (1996) 326.
[23] Ibid.
[24] ILC (1951) Report V(1).
[25] This account draws on Hepple (1996) 241–42.

especially compared to Italy, which also had a large female workforce in industries such as textiles and electrical goods, if France alone had to bear the costs of
equal pay. At the time differentials between the remuneration of men and women
was 7% in France, compared to 20–40% in the Netherlands and Italy.[26] Germany
and the Benelux countries, on the other hand, maintained that the harmonisation of indirect or social costs would be the inevitable outcome of the
establishment of the Common Market. This was similar to the position taken by
a Committee of Experts established by the European Coal and Steel Community
(ECSC) in conjunction with the International Labour Office.[27] The Committee
distinguished between the general level of labour costs, which were said to reflect
different levels of productivity, and inter-industrial patterns of costs, where it was
said that intervention was justified in particular industries with exceptionally low
wages or social costs that gave them a competitive advantage. The Title on Social
Policy (Title III) of the 1957 Treaty was a compromise between the German and
French positions. On the one hand, the exhortatory Article 117 of the Treaty,
circumscribed by Article 118, declared that improved working conditions and an
improved standard of living 'will ensue from the functioning of the Common
Market, which will favour the harmonisation of social systems', and also referred
to the 'approximation of provisions'. On the other hand, Article 119 sought to
pay lip service to French demands for protection against 'social dumping'. The
commitment to achieve 'equal pay for equal work' was weaker than the ILO standard of equal pay for work of equal value. The objective of achieving equal pay by
the end of 1962, extended to 1964, was, in Warner's words, 'either made without
conviction or was remarkably naïve'.[28]

Steps to implement Article 119 were taken only after a Evelyne Sullerot, a
French sociologist, had pointed out in a report to the European Commission in
1972 that there was still widespread sex discrimination in the Member States.
One outcome of this was Council Directive 75/117/EEC, which introduced the
ILO standard of equal pay for work of equal value into Community law. Another
was the Equal Treatment Directive 76/207/EEC, which introduced the principle
of equal treatment as regards access to employment, vocational training, promotion, working conditions and termination of employment. The main pressure for
these Directives and also those on equality for men and women in social security,[29] were demands from the European Parliament, where there was a strong
feminist group who highlighted the rising expectations of women. Ellis
comments that, by acceding to these demands, the European Commission and
the Council were able to appease women voters and be seen to be committed to
social progress, while at the same time ignoring the Parliament's advice on sensitive issues like reproductive rights and violence against women.[30] This had the

[26] Barnard (1996) 325.
[27] ILO (1956).
[28] Warner (1984) 143.
[29] Council Directive 79/7/EEC.
[30] Ellis (1991) 40; (1998) 62.

support of the centre-left governments that held the balance of power in the European Council in the mid-1970s.

These legislative initiatives coincided with a series of actions for equal pay brought by Gabrielle Defrenne, a Belgian air hostess, advised by Professor Eliane Vogel-Polsky, who had been compelled by her employer to retire at the age of 40 while men cabin crew could work to the normal retiring age and claim full pension rights. Three of her actions alleging sex discrimination were referred by the Belgian court to the ECJ during the 1970s.[31] These actions resulted in the ECJ making the historic ruling that Article 119 was capable of being enforced both vertically against the Member State and horizontally against her employer. The ruling was, however, qualified in two ways. First, the ECJ accepted arguments submitted by the British and Irish governments that it would be unduly burdensome to back-date equal pay claims, and stated that the principle of equal pay could not be relied on in the national courts before the date of the ruling (8 April 1976) unless the claim had already been started in the national court before that date. Secondly, the decision was said to apply only to 'direct and overt discrimination', which could be identified solely with the aid of criteria based upon equal work and equal pay. The Court held that Article 119 could not be relied upon in relation to 'indirect and disguised discrimination'. That could be done only by further legislation going beyond Article 119, either at the Community or national level. It was not until the 1980s that the Court, in further rulings, made it possible to rely on indirect discrimination, so opening the way towards substantive equality for women (see below). The actions pre-dated the Equal Treatment Directive, and the Court held in *Defrenne (No 3)* that working conditions relating to retirement ages did not fall within the scope of Article 119. However, the Court, drawing its inspiration from the ILO Conventions, pointed the way forward by stating that

> respect for fundamental personal rights is one of the general principles of Community law, the observance of which it has a duty to ensure. There can be no doubt that the elimination of discrimination based on sex forms part of those fundamental human rights.[32]

The result of the *Defrenne* cases, as well as domestic pressures from the feminist movements, was that equal pay laws spread throughout the Community, with a variety of enforcement mechanisms (see Table 5.1; on enforcement, see chapter 9 below).

While equal pay for work of equal value addresses one long-standing inequality, it does not prevent, indeed on its own may even encourage, occupational segregation and the denial of equal opportunities in access to employment, promotion and other aspects of work. In the early post-war period there were

[31] Case 80/70, *Defrenne v Belgian State (no 1)* [1971] ECR 445; Case 43/75 *Defrenne v Sabena (no 2)* [1976] ECR 455; Case 149/77 *Defrenne v Sabena (no 3)* [1978] ECR 1365.
[32] Case 149/77 [1978] ECR 1365, para 26.

Table 5.1: Equal Pay Regulation, 1957–86[a]

Country	Year	Source	Enforcement
Austria	1979	Act on equal treatment of men and women in wage payments	Commission; Labour Court
Belgium	1971	Art 47*bis* introduced into law of 1965 on workers' pay	Labour courts
	1975	National Labour Council collective agreement no.25,mandatory by royal decree	Collective bargaining parties; Ministry of Labour; labour courts
Britain	1970 (in force 1975)	Equal Pay Act	Industrial tribunals; Central Arbitration Committee
	1984	Amended 1984	
Finland	1970	Employment Contracts Act	
	1986	Act on equality between women and men	Equality Ombudsman, Equality Delegation; civil courts
France	1972/1983	Act No 72/143 on equal remuneration for men and women; strengthened 1983	Ministry of Labour; delegation on the status of women; labour courts
Germany	1980	Equal Treatment Act amended Code of Civil Procedure,§612	Ministry of Labour; labour courts
Greece	1984	Law No 1414/84 on equality between sexes	Ministry of Labour
Ireland	1974	Anti-discrimination (pay) Act amended by Employment Equality Act 1998	Employment Equality Agency; labour courts
Italy	1960/1964	Equal Pay Agreement for industrial sector/agricultural sector	Collective bargaining parties/Ministry of Labour
Luxembourg	1974	Grand-Ducal Regulation on equal pay for work of equal value	Civil courts
Netherlands	1975	Equal Pay Act	Civil courts
	1980	Equal Treatment (Civil Servants) Act	
Portugal	1969	Equal pay for equal work: Article 116, Decree No49408	
	1979	Decree No392/79 on equality in work and employment, extended to public administration 1989	Equality Commission; Labour Inspectorate

Table 5.1: continued

Country	Year	Source	Enforcement
Spain	1980	Workers' statute	Labour tribunals; Labour Inspectorate
Sweden	1977, 1983	Collective equality agreements	Collective bargaining parties
	1979	Act on equality between women and men at work	Equal Opportunities Commission and Equal Opportunities Ombudsman; Labour Court

[a]Source: Meulders *et al* (1993) 110, with additions and amendments.

still marriage bars in several countries requiring women to resign or allowing them to be dismissed on marriage or pregnancy. Sweden was the first country to prohibit dismissal in the case of marriage or pregnancy, as one of several measures to stop the downward trend in the population.[33] This law was revised in 1945 and replaced in 1976 as part of a more far-reaching reform on parental leave (see below). An Italian Act of 1963 is the counterpart of the Swedish legislation of 1939 and 1945.[34] In the 1960s, the French courts ruled that requirements that air hostesses had to be single (*clauses de célibate*) were void as violations of both the freedom of marriage and the freedom to work.[35] In Germany, dismissal of a woman on grounds of marriage was 'socially unjustified' under the Protection against Dismissal Act 1951, but discrimination was still possible in the case of selection for lay-offs on the assumption that a married woman, because of support by her husband, would be less likely to suffer harm than a married man with a large family.[36] In Britain, the Sex Disqualification (Removal) Act 1919, which followed the extension of the franchise to most women, had removed the disqualifications by reason of sex or marriage from, among other activities, 'carrying on any civil profession or vocation'. However, the Act was little used, and did not help married women teachers, who sought to have the policy of dismissing them to make way for unmarried women or men declared unlawful. It was not until 1966 that the English Court of Appeal controversially declared that a policy of refusing a licence to a horse trainer on grounds of her sex was an unlawful breach of her common law 'right to work'.[37]

In several countries, the early approaches to discrimination on grounds of sex were based on the criminal law. So in France, the Penal Code, under which racial

[33] Schmidt (1978) 155.
[34] Ibid.
[35] Dalloz 1963 J 428.
[36] Schmidt (1978) 156.
[37] *Nagle v Feilden* [1966] 2 Queen's Bench 633; for the Act generally, see Creighton (1979) 66–77.

discrimination had been criminalised in 1972, was extended to sex discrimination. Although this made it possible for the injured party to sue for damages, including damages for moral loss (*dommages intérèt en reparation du prejudice moral*), the criminal law approach generally resulted in weaker enforcement than in countries where the remedies were civil ones. This is why Britain preferred an American model of individual civil remedies coupled with administrative enforcement. The Sex Discrimination Act 1975 made both direct and indirect discrimination on grounds of sex and marital status unlawful. Individuals could bring proceedings in industrial (later called employment) tribunals, and strategic enforcement was entrusted to an Equal Opportunities Commission (EOC) (see further chapter 9 below). The Equal Treatment Directive 76/207/EEC, was heavily influenced by the British model. It was only after this Directive that most other Member States implemented the equal treatment principle.

Equal pay and equal treatment began to be integrated into national collective bargaining contexts. In France, a law of 13 July 1983 made it obligatory for those agreements capable of extension to include provisions concerning equal treatment in employment and for pregnant and nursing mothers. These were in addition to clauses in existing legislation requiring application of the principle of equal pay for equal work. The *Commission Natonale de la Negotiation Collective* was given the duty of securing the elimination of discriminatory elements in collective agreements. In practice, however, relatively few agreements included equal pay and equal treatment, and when there were references to these principles they were brief. The contribution of the 1983 law to equality bargaining appears to have been modest.[38] In Italy, the interconfederal agreement of 1960 had maintained an explicit wage gap of 10% between men and women, but this was annulled by the courts on the basis of the principle of equal pay in Article 37 of the Constitution (see above). In practice, the absence of job evaluation and the difficulty in downwards classifications that infringed guaranteed legal protections meant that relatively little progress was made.[39] In Germany, despite the Federal Labour Court having annulled directly discriminatory provisions in collective agreements, the equal pay principle was avoided by agreements that distinguished between 'easy or light work', usually jobs done predominantly by women, and 'employees of full worth', done by men.[40] In Britain, a term in a collective agreement that applied specifically to men only or to women only could be referred to the Central Arbitration Committee for amendment or to remove the discrimination, but this jurisdiction was repealed by the Thatcher government, as part of its deregulatory policy, in 1986. Pay bargaining in Britain was very decentralised and there were relatively few attempts by unions to provide centralised co-ordination of equal pay claims, an exception being agreements in respect of one million local government workers. Reliance tended to be placed on claims to industrial tribunals by individual workers, with union assistance, against a few

[38] Bercusson (1996) 189–91.
[39] Ibid, 192–93.
[40] Ibid, 193–94.

large employers, but the legal procedures were complex and time-consuming, and had little impact in reducing the overall pay gap between men and women.

By the mid-1980s, sex equality had emerged as a fundamental human right and general principle of Community law, and had been introduced by legislation and collective bargaining into all the Member States. However, enforcement was, in practice, normally limited to direct discrimination or formal equality between men and women. Unequal pay and occupational sex segregation was condemned in theory but remained a practical reality.

Racial Discrimination

The second major pressure for action against discrimination in employment arose from the increasing presence of migrants and ethnic minorities in western European countries. These groups tend to be disproportionately unemployed, and to suffer from racial discrimination and disadvantage. Direct comparisons between the countries studied is difficult because of their different histories of immigration and their different concepts of migrants and minorities.[41] Broadly speaking, however, they fall into three main groups. First, there are those with a history of colonial immigration, particularly from the 1950s to 1970s, where a large part of the minority population stems from their former colonies (Britain, France, the Netherlands) Most of these migrants, their families and descendants have citizenship status and are generally referred to as 'ethnic minorities' (Britain), or *allochtonen* (in respect of those not born in the Netherlands or with one parent not born there). In France, an egalitarian concept of citizenship meant that traditionally the only distinction in official statistics was between citizens and foreigners, although a new category of immigrant origin (*issue d'immigration*) was introduced from the 1990 census onwards to refer to persons born abroad and with foreign citizenship at birth. In this group of countries, legislation and other policy measures have tended to be directed at issues of racial equality and racism. By the end of the twentieth century about 7.1% of the British population (4 million) belonged to ethnic minorities; 17.5% of the Dutch population (2.75 million) were classed as 'immigrants', 9% of them born abroad; and 'foreigners' by nationality or origin (5.6 million) comprised 9.6% of the French population.[42]

The second group of countries are those which actively recruited so-called 'guest workers' from the 1950s to the 1970s (Austria, Belgium, Denmark, Germany. Luxembourg, Sweden), and who refer to them as 'foreigners' or 'aliens', with the result that only immigrants with a foreign nationality can be traced in labour market statistics, and inequalities affecting naturalised immigrants and their descendants cannot be measured. There is some refinement of this in Denmark, where a distinction is drawn between 'immigrants' (whose parents are

---

[41] Jandl et al (2003) 5–9.
[42] Ibid, 95–96, Table A1.

both foreign citizens or born outside Denmark) and their 'descendants' (who are born in Denmark by parents neither of whom are Danish citizens born in Denmark), and Sweden, where the concepts 'foreign-born' (person born abroad) and 'foreign origin' (person who has migrated to Sweden or at least one parent has done so) are used. Integration policies in this group have tended to be less focused on equality issues than in the first group. By the end of the twentieth century, the percentage of foreign citizens in these countries ranged from 37.3% (Luxembourg) to 8.9% (Austria and Germany), and the 'foreign-born' were 11.5% of the Swedish population.[43]

The third group of countries (Greece, Italy, Spain, Portugal, Finland and Ireland) are those which began to experience significant immigration only from the 1980s or 1990s onwards (see chapter 3 above), and the majority of the immigrants were, therefore, foreign citizens. The legal and administrative framework for developing equality policies, accordingly, tends to be less well developed than those in the first and second groups. In all these countries, however, there are also historic minority ethnic groups (eg Irish travellers, Pontian Greeks, Thracian Muslims, Roma and Sinti) who have traditionally suffered from extensive discrimination in society and in the labour market.

In view of the different bases on which statistics are collected, it is not possible to make a direct cross-country comparison of inequalities affecting all these groups. However, research makes it clear that the unemployment rates of these migrants and minorities have remained persistently higher than those of nationals or majority populations; that labour markets continue to be segmented along national or ethnic lines; and that there are marked income differences between nationals/non-migrants and immigrants/ethnic minorities, with the working conditions of migrants/ethnic minorities often being worse than those of their non-migrant/majority group counterparts.[44] Econometric and other studies provide ample evidence that these disadvantages, at least in some countries and for some groups, are due to factors beyond education and skills, language proficiency, age, employment experience etc, but have their origin in racial discrimination.[45]

The national responses to this discrimination have tended to reflect the three groupings mentioned above, but there have been important divergences within these groups. Britain was the first European country to legislate against racial discrimination in employment, and this was closely tied to immigration policy. Commonwealth citizens lost their rights of entry (as British subjects) into Britain, but the Labour governments of the 1960s were keen to match this with domestic policies that encouraged integration of settled ethnic minorities. There was a prolonged campaign, from 1950 onwards, by human rights and anti-colonial groups, who had to overcome the widespread reluctance of politicians, business leaders and many trade unionists to accept that there was

[43] Ibid.
[44] Ibid, 26, 30, 40, 43.
[45] Ibid, 50; Wrench and Modood (2000).

widespread racial discrimination, until extensive research proved that this was the case. There were many reasons why British law, before 1965, provided no redress against racial discrimination. These included an absence of constitutional guarantees, judicial reluctance to extend common law doctrines to racial discrimination, the unsuitability of ordinary employment law remedies and the practical difficulties in proving discrimination to the satisfaction of a court of law.[46]

The campaigners sought their inspiration in the North American models of administrative enforcement of anti-discrimination legislation by Fair Employment Commissions. The main advantages of administrative enforcement were thought to be that strategic action in the public interest was more likely to change behaviour than ordinary adversarial criminal or civil proceedings, and that a specialised expert body independent of government would be able to investigate complaints against public sector employers. The Race Relations Act 1968, for the first time, made direct racial discrimination in employment unlawful, but placed the main responsibility for enforcement in the hands of voluntary procedures in some 40 industries, with an administrative agency, the Race Relations Board (first set up in 1965), as only a backstop. Where conciliation failed, proceedings could be brought by the Board in specially designated county courts, but this rarely happened. The reliance on voluntary procedures, run by employers and unions—the very people most likely to discriminate—was a compromise agreed by the Labour government in the face of concerted opposition from the TUC and the main employers' body (the Confederation of British Industry) to legally enforceable remedies. Not surprisingly, these procedures, which relied entirely on complaints by individuals and did not investigate systemic discrimination, proved to be ineffective. In 1976, the precedent of the Sex Discrimination Act 1975 (above) was followed. Both direct and indirect discrimination on racial grounds were made unlawful. Individuals were given the right to bring proceedings for compensation in industrial tribunals, and a new Commission for Racial Equality was given powers of strategic enforcement, similar to those of the EOC, which dealt with sex discrimination (see further chapter 9 below).

The Netherlands, another first group country, also developed a legislation against racial discrimination prior to, and independent of, the Race Directive 2000/43/EC, in the Civil Code, the Collective Agreements Act (amended in 1971) and the Act on Works Councils. However, in France, also in the first group, there was reluctance to recognise racial discrimination as a legal category that could cut across the citizen/foreigner divide. Legal responses were focused on a penal approach against racism (*racisme*), in particular in hate speech and racist organisations. The law of 1 July 1972, Article 7, amending the Penal Code, did provide that than any person who refused, without a legitimate reason, to hire a person or who dismissed a person because of their origin, membership or non-membership in an ethnic group or race etc could be imprisoned from 2 months to 1 year,

---

[46] Hepple (1970) 144; Lester and Bindman (1972) 107ff.

or fined, or both imprisoned and fined, but this law was little used in practice because of the difficulties of proof. It was not until the Labour Code (L 122–45) was amended in 1982 that civil sanctions were provided against racial discrimination in employment.

Countries in the second and third groups were not all slow to act against racial discrimination in employment. For example, in Italy, Article 13 of Law 903/1977, amending Article15 of the Workers' Statute of 1970, prohibited racial, religious and language discrimination, as well as political discrimination, at the workplace, and this was enforceable by the Labour Inspectorate, but it appears that only a small number of cases were brought under this law. More important was Law 943/1986, which established the principle of equality of opportunity, including equal treatment at the workplace, between national and non-national workers, and the 'Martelli Law', Law 391/1990, which granted rights to equal pay and working conditions to migrant workers. In Spain, the Workers' Statute 1980 (amended 1984), conferred on all private sector workers a right to freedom from discrimination on grounds of race, although it was unclear whether this was limited to direct discrimination. In Sweden, the Criminal Code was amended in 1970 to make it a crime for an entrepreneur to discriminate in trade or business on racial grounds, but the primary purpose was to prevent discrimination in the offering of public accommodations, and there was no specific reference to employment discrimination.[47] In 1986, the office of Discrimination Ombudsman was created with the task of preventing racial discrimination, but it was not until 1994 that racial discrimination in employment was prohibited. In other European countries, effective legislation against racial discrimination in employment came only in response to the EC Race Directive 2000/43/EC of 29 June 2000 (see below).

Substantive Equality (1976–99)

Critiques of Equality

In the period of economic crisis and deregulation from the 1970s onwards, there was intense criticism of anti-discrimination laws from opposite ends of the political spectrum. A 'frontal intellectual assault' on these laws was made by Epstein and some other liberal economists,[48] who argued that the common law doctrine of freedom of contract, including the refusal to deal with others on grounds such as race, sex or disability, achieves a Pareto efficient allocation of resources. A distribution of resources is said to be 'Pareto-efficient' if no change in that distribution can be made that leaves no one worse off and at least one person better

---

[47] Aaron (1978) 59.
[48] Epstein (1995).

off. Epstein argued that the black or female worker with whom an employer refuses to deal is not worse off because he or she can simply move on to the next potential employer. A variant of this, proposed by the Chicago School, is that if an employer pays lower wages to women than to men this is 'wealth maximising', and hence cost-effective, provided that the men, whose work is overvalued, earn enough to compensate for the loss suffered by the women, whose work is under-valued. According to this argument, it is irrelevant that the women are not compensated. The employer's decision maximises wealth and so is cost-effective. So long as women are free to search for jobs, they will be taken on by employers, who will have a competitive advantage. Wage rates will rise and there will be eventual equalisation of conditions of employment between women and men.

The social democratic and welfare ideologies, which had developed in Europe, proved to be sufficiently strong to resist these and other extreme liberal views. Even the Thatcher government in Britain, despite its neo-liberal agenda, accepted and extended laws on sex discrimination in the 1980s. From an economic view-point, it was generally not questioned that the freedom of black workers and women to search for jobs does not lead inexorably to parity of wages or common terms of employment. There are too many imperfections in the labour market for this to happen. Governments throughout western Europe were in agreement that individuals do not have free choices, precisely because of differences of wealth, socio-economic status, race, gender and disability. From a political view-point, as mentioned above, formal equality for women was a way to win electoral support; on the other hand, governments were more reluctant to take action against racial discrimination because of entrenched racist and anti-immigrant attitudes among the majority populations.

Formal equality was criticised by human rights activists as being inadequate to achieve genuine equality. It was pointed out that the concept of direct discrimi-nation necessitates a comparison between two individuals who are alike in relevant characteristics. This begs the central question: when are two people sufficiently similar to qualify for equal treatment? In reality, no two individuals are identical and the differences between them are shaped not only by genetic endowments and other biological factors but also by the very fact of ongoing discrimination. A woman is not the same as a man because only a woman can become pregnant and give birth; to apply a male norm means taking for granted the existing values in a male-dominated society. For example, women with family responsibilities are simply unable to conform to working patterns that assume a male breadwinner and a female housewife. The comparison between a member of an ethnic or religious minority with a member of the dominant culture becomes a requirement for assimilation or conformity rather than respect for individual dignity and diversity. One cannot simply extend the principle of formal equality to disabled people who do not share the same capacities as able-bodied persons. Arguments such as these led to the development of the principle of *substantive* equality, or 'full equality in practice'. The two main examples developed in the period before 2000 were the concept of indirect discrimination and positive action measures.

Indirect Discrimination

The concept of indirect, or adverse impact, discrimination, first formulated by the US Supreme Court in *Griggs v Duke Power Co* (1971),[49] was reconstructed in the European context and developed a life of its own.[50] It was not a wholly alien idea, because *discrimination indirecte* had first appeared as a concept (undefined) in the International Declaration of Human Rights in 1929,[51] and, after 1957, in the ECJ case law on 'overt' and 'covert' discrimination against nationals of the Member States on grounds of nationality.[52] The novelty of the *Griggs* case was that it gave a specific definition of 'covert' or 'adverse impact' discrimination. The Court held that:

> Under the [Civil Rights] Act, practices, procedures or tests, neutral on their face and even neutral in terms of intent, cannot be maintained if they operate to 'freeze' the *status quo* of prior discriminatory employment practices . . . The Act proscribes . . . also practices that are fair in form but discriminatory in operation. The touchstone is business necessity. If a business practice which operates to exclude Negroes, cannot be shown to be related to job performance, the practice is prohibited . . .[53]

This was translated into somewhat restrictive statutory language in the British Sex Discrimination Act 1975 and Race Relations Act 1976, and in the Irish Employment Equality Act 1977. It then found its way, through a dialogue between the British courts and the ECJ, into the case law under Article 119 EEC.[54] The early attempt by the ECJ, in *Defrenne v Sabena (No2)*[55] (1975), to distinguish between 'direct and overt' discrimination and 'indirect and disguised' discrimination was confusing.[56] However, by 1981 the ECJ had redefined the concept, in the context of Article 119 EEC, to bring it closer to British, Irish and American anti-discrimination law. The concept proved to be capable of far-reaching results that profoundly affected the employment conditions of women in the new labour market of precarious work. For example, equal treatment of part-time workers (the majority of whom were women) and full-timers was required; employers had to justify 'objectively' relatively large pay differentials between women and men in the same grade, where a system of pay was not transparent; and practices that obliged single parents (most of them women) to

---

[49] 40 US 424 (1971).
[50] Hepple (2006) 623.
[51] Schiek et al (2007) 334.
[52] Bell (2002) 33–42.
[53] 40 US 424 (1971), 433.
[54] Kilpatrick (2001) 31.
[55] Case 43/75 [1976] ECR 455.
[56] Ellis (1998) 111.

work anti-social hours incompatible with their child care responsibilities had also to be objectively justified.[57]

It was not until the EC Burden of Proof Directive 97/80/EC that the definition of indirect discrimination was codified. This, like the ECJ case law and the Anglo-Irish-American approach, placed the emphasis on statistical comparison between the consequences of an apparently neutral requirement (eg to work full-time to get a higher rate of pay) on members of each sex. This produced problems for the French legal system, among others, in relation to indirect racial discrimination because the republican ideal involved a prohibition on collecting statistics of ethnicity. Some even saw the application of the concept of indirect discrimination as a dividing line between the French and Anglo-Irish approaches to racial discrimination.[58] However, as we have seen above, in some other countries the problem was partly overcome by relying on statistics of birthplace or parents' birthplace. The concept of indirect discrimination came into German labour law through a series of important references by the labour courts to the ECJ, but significantly the Federal Labour Court justified its use on the basis of traditional German constitutional law going back to a judgment on the funding of political parties in 1958.[59]

The broadest approach to indirect discrimination was found in the Nordic countries. A Swedish Act of 1991, in language reminiscent of ILO Convention No 111 of 1958 (see above), defined sex discrimination as occurring 'when someone is disadvantaged in situations where the disadvantage has a direct or indirect connection with the person's sex'. The Finnish Equality Act was similarly broad. This Nordic approach, as Schiek comments, 'allows a more holistic approach than a definition focusing on a single requirement', and considers 'whether a bundle of rules used by an institution impacts negatively on the situation of women or ethnic minorities'.[60] In the Netherlands, while an Anglo-Irish-American approach has been influential, the Equal Treatment Commission has tended to take a broader and less formal approach to indirect discrimination than the courts and tribunals in Britain.

The introduction of the concept of indirect discrimination was a major step in equality law, with the potential to overcome many aspects of institutionalised inequality by removing apparently neutral barriers that have an adverse impact on disadvantaged groups. However, in most countries, it was applied almost exclusively to sex discrimination before the implementation of the Race Directive 2000/43/EC and Employment Directive 2000/78/EC (below), and in many countries it was scarcely used at all. The forces behind the activation of sex equality law, and indirect discrimination in particular, varied: in Britain, the EOC and trade unions took the lead in supporting test cases; in Denmark, trade unions were crucial but they played only a marginal role in Italy, Germany and France; in

---

[57] Ibid, 111–24.
[58] Geddes and Guiraudon (2004) 334.
[59] Schiek et al (2007) 369–70.
[60] Ibid, 368.

North West Germany it was the activity of labour court judges, and in Spain the Constitutional Court, that provided the focus for the mobilisation of other actors; in Belgium, it was the pioneering work of our academic collaborator, Eliane Vogel-Polsky, that lit the spark, and in Italy and Germany, too, academic lawyers had a major impact on the reception of EC equality law, including indirect discrimination.[61]

Even if the law on indirect discrimination had been more effectively applied, it was not, in itself, a panacea for workplace inequality. EC law and national law, at least outside the Nordic countries, was based firmly on the premise that equality is an individual right, and the national laws developed within the traditional forms of (usually) civil adjudication for the resolution of individual disputes. The weakness of this approach, in the case of indirect discrimination, is that it is the effect of criteria and practices on groups that must be examined. 'The individual straitjacket inhibits the development of collective or group procedures and remedies.'[62] The European legal systems had not developed the class action that was so important to the growth of anti-discrimination suits in the US. In some European countries, like Britain, an administrative agency or trade union could initiate litigation, but the remedies could do relatively little to change the underlying structures and practices that produce disadvantage. Unlike the US, there was no possibility of court-supervised mandatory injunctions requiring affirmative action.

Another weakness of the law in all these countries was that proof of indirect discrimination depended upon a comparison between representative groups of men and women, and the ECJ rejected the possibility of comparisons with the 'hypothetical' male comparator (how a man would have been treated), so a woman could not improve her position if she worked in a segregated workforce with no relevant male comparator.[63] Moreover, the ECJ also rejected the possibility of comparisons with men employed by different employers in the same industry or service.[64] Above all, the overriding constraint in a market system, as the defence of objective justification illustrates, is that of cost. EC law left it to the national courts to determine whether and to what extent objective factors and 'market forces', other than sex discrimination, justified the adverse impact on women, but the ECJ itself has pulled back from judgments that would have serious financial consequences for employers and occupational pension schemes.[65] The outcome depended on how sympathetic the court was to the business needs of the employer and, in this respect, there appear to have been significant differences in the application of the law on indirect discrimination.[66]

[61] Kilpatrick (2001) 127–28.
[62] Hepple (1996) 254.
[63] Case 43/75 *Defrenne (No2)* [1976] ECR 455, paras 19 and 22.
[64] Case 171/88 *Rinner-Kuhn* [1989] ECR 2743.
[65] Eg Case C-262/88 *Barber* [1990] ECR I-1889, prohibiting discrimination between men and women in benefits under occupational pension schemes, but limiting this to benefits payable only in respect of periods of service subsequent to the date of the judgment (17 May 1990).
[66] Hepple (1996) 250–53.

Something more was needed to achieve substantive equality. What was missing was a legal framework, at both EC and national level, which recognised that discrimination and social disadvantage affect not only individuals but also groups. Only the Nordic countries had moved in this direction.

Positive Action

The notion of 'affirmative action' was first used in the US to describe actions that aim at greater inclusion and participation of women and minorities in the workforce. The term was used in Title VII of the Civil Rights Act 1964 to describe the power given to judges to remedy unlawful discrimination and in Executive Orders made by President Kennedy in 1961 and President Johnson in 1964[67] to define the obligations of a federal government contractor to remedy the under-representation of minorities and women in the workforce.[68] These provisions have had a significant influence in bringing about substantive equality in employment in large corporations in the US, and they were followed in Canada, Australia and some other countries.[69] Several justifications have been put forward for such measures, including compensation for past discrimination, achieving substantive equality and promoting diversity or proportionate representation of all groups in the workforce.

In Europe, the term 'positive action' has been preferred to describe such policies, possibly to avoid any association with 'quotas' or other controversial features of law and policy in the US. McCrudden[70] has identified no less than five different types of action that might fall under the label of 'positive action'. First, there is the eradication of practices that have the effect of disadvantaging a particular group, such as word-of-mouth hiring. This is, in effect, an application of the principle of avoiding indirect discrimination. Secondly, there are policies that seek to increase the proportion of members of a previously excluded or underrepresented group. Thirdly, there are outreach programmes, designed to attract candidates from under-represented groups. Fourthly, there are measures which amount to preferential treatment or 'reverse' discrimination in favour of a particular group (eg women, minorities). Finally, there are attempts to make the criteria for recruitment, promotion and dismissal more objective and job-related so as to reduce the possibilities for subjective discrimination.

Limited use has been made of each of these forms of positive action in European countries. In Northern Ireland, in 1974, a government report proposed that 'affirmative action' should be introduced to improve the representation of the Catholic community in the workforce, and schemes were successfully introduced on a voluntary basis by the largest private employer in the province and in the

---

[67] 41 Code of Federal Regulations (CFR), ss 60–250/s 60/741.
[68] McCrudden (1986) 220–21.
[69] See Hepple et al (2000) 65–67.
[70] McCrudden (1986) 223–25.

civil service. In 1989, the Northern Ireland Fair Employment Act (amended in 1998) imposed positive duties on public employers and private sector employers with more than 10 employees to achieve fair representation of the Roman Catholic and Protestant communities. These employers were required to monitor the composition of their workforces, to undertake periodic reviews (once every three years) and, where fair participation was not evident, to engage in affirmative action. The Fair Employment Commission had residual enforcement powers, and the sanction of denial of government contracts or financial assistance could be used against defaulting employers. A parliamentary report in 1999 found that there was high level of compliance with the law, and that there had been reductions in employment segregation and under-representation of the Catholic community.[71] However, before 2000, other British legislation on sex and race discrimination did not impose positive duties of this kind on employers, and exceptions to the principle of formal equality were allowed only on a restrictive basis, for example measures to encourage potential workers from under-represented groups and to provide training for those groups, but these are inflexible, have been little used and fall short of what is permitted under EC law (see below).[72]

In the Netherlands, a Law on the Promotion of Proportional Labour Participation of Ethnic Minorities, which came into force on 1 July 1994, was aimed at removing obstacles impeding proportional representation in private companies, under the threat of criminal sanctions. Most employers failed to comply, complaining of the administrative burdens, so an agreement was reached by the social partners modifying the legislation to focus on the sector and company level, and by using the civil law.[73] This so-called SAMEN legislation,[74] inspired in part by the Canadian Employment Equity Act 1995, was in force from 1998 to 2004, and then abrogated on the grounds that it had met its objective of raising awareness among employers. The employer was under an obligation to strive for the equal representation of certain target groups, and had to monitor the composition of the workforce and make an annual report. Similarly the Flemish Community/Region of Belgium adopted a Decree on proportionate participation in the employment market of certain target groups by positive action measures, modelled on the Dutch and Canadian legislation. In Germany, some states and cities required positive action. For example, the Hessen Women Equality Act for public administration, adopted in 1993, laid down detailed rules, including binding targets, redefined qualifications by providing that account had to be taken of experience acquired in looking after children or those in care (family work), insofar as they were of importance, and requiring at least as many women as men applicants to be called for interview where women were

[71] House of Commons, Northern Ireland Affairs Committee, Fourth Report (1999), para 48.
[72] Hepple et al (2000) 37–38.
[73] De Schutter (2007) 763.
[74] *Wet Stimulering Arbeidsdeelname Minderheden.*
[75] De Schutter (2007) 770–74.

under-represented.[75] The Hessen Law also required preferential treatment: where the binding targets in a women's advancement plan could not be met otherwise, a woman had to be employed.[76]

A variant on this type of preferential treatment is a provision that allows or requires a member of an under-represented group to be appointed where two or more candidates appear to be equally qualified or deserving. Examples are the Bremen Act on Equal Treatment for Men and Women (1990) and the Nordrhein-Westfalen Law on Civil Servants (1981 amended 1995). The more extreme form of positive action is preferential treatment for members of the under-represented group even though not equally qualified. For example, the Swedish Equality Act 1991 expressly excluded from the scope of unlawful sex discrimination a decision that 'forms part of efforts to promote equality between men and women in the workplace', so permitting preferential treatment. Strict quotas, ie a certain number of positions for members of identified groups, were rare, an example being the Hessen Women Equality Act, which required posts in the academic service to be filled 'with at least the same proportion of women as the proportion of women among the graduates of the discipline in question'.

Positive action measures of this kind risked coming into conflict with EC law. Article 2(4) of the Equal Treatment Directive 76/207/EEC stated that the anti-discrimination provisions were 'without prejudice to measures to promote equal opportunity for men and women in particular by removing existing inequalities which affect women's opportunities' (Article 2). The ECJ, when faced with the tie-break clause in the Bremen Act on Equal Treatment (above) in the *Kalanke* case, held that it went further than was permissible under Article 2(4), construed as an exception to the equal treatment principle.[77] However, two years later, in the *Marschall* case, the ECJ upheld the tie-break provision in the Nordrhein-Westfalen Law (above) on the grounds that there was a savings clause that the rule preferring women applied only where 'reasons specific to another candidate' did not predominate.[78] Provided that there was an element of flexibility in the positive action measure, it was not incompatible with Article 2(4) of the Directive. In 2000, the ECJ also upheld the lawfulness of the provisions of the Hessen Act on Women's Equality (above).[79] By that time, therefore, it was possible for Member States to take positive action in favour of women, provided that the measures were flexible and removed practical obstacles from career paths such as lack of education or childcare, but positive (reverse) discrimination was not allowed.[80] The Treaty of Amsterdam substantially modified Article 119 EC to provide, in the (renumbered) Article 141(4), that

With a view to ensuring full equality in practice between men and women in working

---

[76] Ibid.
[77] Case C-450/93 *Kalanke v Freie Hansestadt Bremen* [1995] ECR I-3051.
[78] Case C-405/95 *Marschall v Land Nordrhein-Westfalen* [1997] ECR I-6363.
[79] Case C-158/97 *Badeck* [2000] ECR I-1875.
[80] Ellis (1998) 260.

life, the principle of equal treatment shall not prevent any Member State from maintaining or adopting measures providing for specific advantages in order to make it
easier for the under-represented sex to pursue a vocational activity or to prevent or
compensate for disadvantages in professional careers.

However, it seems that this amendment has not affected the approach to flexible
positive action favoured by the ECJ.

Positive action also risked falling foul of national constitutional provisions.
For example, the Belgian Constitutional Court (*Cour d'arbitrage*) held that a law
guaranteeing a benefit to women of 60 years of age and above but denying it to
men aged between 60 and 65 was a violation of equality and non-discrimination
clauses in the Constitution, despite the government's plea that the provision was
necessary to erase the disadvantages to which women had been subjected in the
past. The Court laid down very strict criteria for allowing positive action.[81] On
the other hand, the Dutch Equal Treatment Commission (*Commissie Gelijke
Behandeling*) adopted a broader, more flexible approach to the lawfulness of positive action measures, allowing them where they are an answer to a clearly
identified situation of actual disadvantage, are appropriate and necessary to
compensate for that disadvantage, and are transparent.[82]

In practice, positive action has been little used in most countries, particularly
in the private sector. In some states there are ideological objections to positive
action, for example in France, where race-specific training schemes of the kind
permitted in Britain would not be allowed. This stems from the French republican ideal of equality of citizens that regards the recognition of minority groups
within the citizenry as legitimating ethnic separation.[83] There are also prohibitions in France, Denmark and some other countries on collecting or obtaining
data on ethnic origin, or certain other characteristics of employees. This makes it
difficult to implement a targeted and proportionate positive action programme.

The Dawn of Comprehensive and Transformative
Equality? (2000–04)

By the start of the first decade of the twenty-first century, two new ideas were
beginning to be translated into practice in a few European countries. The first
was that laws and practices against discrimination should be comprehensive,
covering all grounds of discrimination—there should be no hierarchy of prohibited grounds. The second idea was that of transformative equality. While
substantive equality affords opportunities to people who have in the past been

---

[81] Case 9/94 *Asztalos v Office national des pensions*, 27 January 1994; De Scutter (2007) 827.
[82] De Schutter (2007) 845.
[83] Bell (2002) 172.

disproportionately excluded without disturbing the underlying social framework that denies them genuine choice, and generates inequitable outcomes, transformative equality is aimed at the dismantling of systemic inequalities and the eradication of poverty and disadvantage.[84] This involves ensuring an 'equality of capabilities',[85] enabling people to have the skills they need to participate in society, to engage in productive activities and to participate in decision-making. The measures needed to achieve this include a positive role for institutions in removing barriers and ensuring that those who need more resources than others get them. Transformative equality implies a strong link between substantive equality and social and economic rights.[86]

Comprehensive Equality

Before 2000, Austria and Greece had no specific legislation against racial discrimination in employment, apart from constitutional provisions.[87] Eight countries had no legislation against disability discrimination in employment, eight had none against discrimination on grounds of sexual orientation and seven had none on job discrimination in respect of religion or belief. Only Finland and Ireland had dealt with age discrimination in employment (see Table 5.2 below). Even where anti-discrimination legislation existed there were significant differences in the level of protection in respect of different grounds of discrimination, and, in many cases, the legislation was partial and there was no effective enforcement mechanism. Only the Netherlands and Ireland had moved towards comprehensive equality law regimes. In the former, the General Equal Treatment Act was adopted in 1994, forbidding direct and indirect discrimination 'between persons on the grounds of religion, belief, political opinion, race, sex, nationality, heterosexual or homosexual orientation, or civil status' (section 1). (Disability and age were added after 2000.) In Ireland, the Employment Equality Act 1998 had forbidden direct and indirect discrimination in all areas of both public and private employment on no less than nine grounds.

The turning point towards comprehensive anti-discrimination regimes was Article 13 of the Treaty of Amsterdam, which came into force on 1 May 1999. This empowered the Council 'to take appropriate action to combat discrimination based on sex, racial or ethnic origin, religion or belief, disability, age or sexual orientation'. The EU's Social Action Programme 1998–2000 saw Article 13 as a means of promoting an inclusive society. It could have remained an 'empty vessel'[88] had it not been for dramatic events in Austria on 3 October 1999. The

---

[84] Albertyn (2007) 257.

[85] Sen (1992).

[86] Fredman (2008) 226–40.

[87] In Case C-187/98 *Commission v Greece* [1999] ECR I-7713 the ECJ held that general constitutional provisions could not constitute sufficient implementation of EC law on equal pay for men and women.

[88] Kenner (2003) 393.

Table 5.2: Anti-discrimination Employment Legislation before Directives 2000/43/EC and 2000/78/EC[a]

Country	Sex	Race[b]	Disability	SO[c]	Religion	Age	Other[d]
Austria	X						
Belgium	X	X	X				X
Britain[e]	X	X	X				
Denmark	X	X	X	X	X		X
Finland	X			X	X	X	X
France	X	X		X	X		
Germany	X	X					
Greece	X				X		
Ireland	X	X	X	X	X	X	X
Italy	X	X	X		X		X
Luxembourg	X	X		X	X		
The Netherlands	X	X			X		X
Portugal	X	X					
Spain	X	X	X	X	X		X
Sweden	X	X	X	X			

[a]Sources: Forbes and Mead (1992){NIRL} 71; Bell *et al* (2007) 83–92; Bell (2002) 145–90; EU Network of Independent Experts on Disability Discrimination (2004).
[b]Variously defined to include such grounds as ethnic origin, national origin and colour.
[c]Sexual orientation.
[d]This category included such strands as nationality, political opinion, civil status, language, social origin and social circumstances.
[e]In Northern Ireland, there was specific Fair Employment legislation covering discrimination on grounds of religion and political opinion (in effect, discrimination between Catholic and Protestant communities).

far-right, anti-immigration Freedom Party won a share of power. Member States, as well as Austria's mainstream political leaders, wanted to be seen to be opposed to the racism and xenophobia associated with the Freedom Party. The European Council meeting at Tampere on 15–16 October 1999 asked the Commission to come forward with proposals to implement Article 13 EC as part of a strategy to promote human rights and fight discrimination. Within months, two far-reaching Directives had been unanimously adopted: Directive 2000/43/EC, prohibiting discrimination on grounds of racial or ethnic origin in the labour market, and Directive 2000/78/EC, covering all the other areas mentioned in Article 13 EC except for sex discrimination, which was to continue along its own path under the enlarged scope of Article 141 (formerly 119) of the EC Treaty. Since 2000 there has been a flood of anti-discrimination legislation in all

Member States implementing the Directives. This process was still ongoing at the time our study ends.[89] There remains a hierarchy of grounds—with sex discrimination, racial discrimination and other grounds each being under separate anti-discrimination packages in several states, so making the law unnecessarily complex and inconsistent.

Transformative Equality

Three examples of transformative policies are gender mainstreaming, measures to overcome institutionalised racism and reasonable accommodation for disabled persons. Such policies, and their legal underpinning through positive duties to promote equality, were only in their infancy at the time our study ends.

According to the European Commission, gender mainstreaming

> involves not restricting efforts to promote equality to the implementation of specific measures to help women, but mobilising all general policies and measures specifically for the purpose of achieving equality by actively and openly taking into account at the planning stage their possible effects on the respective situations of men and women . . . Gender mainstreaming . . . focuses on transforming by questioning the status quo (mainstream) and assuming that a transformation of institutions and/or organisations may be necessary to establish gender equality.[90]

This is not intended to replace traditional gender-related and anti-discrimination policies, such as positive action permitted under Article 141(4) EC (above), but is far broader, requiring impact assessments, benchmarking and active labour market policies. A study by the OECD in 2004 concluded that factors which stimulate female participation include more neutral tax treatment of second earners, tax incentives to share work between spouses, childcare subsidies and paid parental leave, improved female education and vocational training, access to well-functioning labour markets and altering cultural attitudes to working women.[91] In some countries, legal duties were imposed on public authorities to implement gender mainstreaming. This occurred in Denmark in 2000 and in Germany in 2001 and, after the end of our period, in Britain in 2006. In other countries, like Sweden, France, the Netherlands and Luxembourg, gender mainstreaming was formulated as a general policy principle. However, there were large differences in the organisation and implementation of gender mainstreaming and gender equality, the focus in most countries being 'rather narrow and patchy'.[92] There was an emphasis on deregulation and voluntary action by employers that hampered efforts to narrow the pay gap between men and

---

[89] For details see Bell et al (2007); Bell (2002).
[90] European Commission (2008) 5.
[91] OECD (2004) 54.
[92] European Commission (2008) 6–8.
[93] Ibid, 8.

women.[93] Gender mainstreaming was largely absent from 'flexicurity' policies (see chapter 3 above).[94] Moreover, family-friendly measures, such as childcare services, parental leave facilities and flexible working arrangements, were limited outside the Nordic countries, the Netherlands and Britain.

Measures against 'institutional racism' have similarly had limited success in the countries studied. The notion of 'institutional racism was defined by a British inquiry as:

> The collective failure of an organisation to provide an appropriate and professional service to people because of their colour, culture or ethnic origin. It can be seen or detected in processes, attitudes and behaviour which amount to discrimination through unwitting prejudice, ignorance, thoughtlessness and racist stereotyping which disadvantage minority ethnic people.[95]

The interacting processes of institutional racism mean that members of ethnic minorities/immigrant groups do not receive their fair share of benefits and resources from an organisation, are not recruited or offered senior positions to the extent that could reasonably be expected and are excluded from the culture of the organisation. There is a lack of positive action and mainstreaming, little information or consultation with members of ethnic minorities/immigrant groups and inadequate leadership or training to bring about change.[96] As at 2004, Britain was the only Member State to have imposed to positive duty on public authorities to promote racial equality (and in Northern Ireland equality between the Catholic and Protestant communities) and to have taken active steps to eradicate institutional racism.[97]

As far as other Member States are concerned, the Race Directive 43/2000/EC permitted, but did not require, positive action. Article 5 of the Directive provided that 'the principle of equal treatment shall not prevent any Member State from maintaining or adopting specific measures to prevent or compensate for disadvantages linked to racial or ethnic origin'. If the ECJ's case law in respect of positive action for women were applied to the Race Directive, it would put in doubt legislative schemes such as those in the Netherlands giving preference to *allochtonen* (above) and, indeed, the SAMEN legislation was abrogated on 1 January 2004, based on the consideration that its main objective of raising awareness among employers had been fulfilled.[98] Britain had to secure a specific opt-out of the Employment Directive 2000/78/EC to permit, but not require, discrimination on grounds of religion or belief in the Northern Ireland police service and in schools. 'The Race Directive is based on a British model of the

[94] Ibid, 9.
[95] The Stephen Lawrence Inquiry, Cm 4262-I (1999), para 6.34.
[96] Parekh (2000) 74–77.
[97] Race Relations (Amendment) Act 2000; Northern Ireland Act 1975, s 75 (which imposed a similar positive duty in respect of all the other main grounds of discrimination).
[98] De Schutter (2007) 765.

1970s rather than what is required in 21ˢᵗ century Europe in order to achieve racial equality.'[99] Without positive duties to promote racial equality and diversity in both the public and private sectors there is little prospect of overcoming institutional racism, which is still widespread in Europe.[100] A further weakness of the Race Directive is that nationality discrimination was entirely excluded from its scope; it does not cover the access of third-country nationals to employment. There is nothing to prevent Member States from granting more extensive employment rights to non-EU workers, as Italy has done (above), but in many of the legal systems studied there are extensive distinctions between citizens and third-country nationals. Although the Tampere Council (15–16 October 1999) emphasised the need to give third-country nationals who are long-term residents uniform rights that are as near as possible to those of EU citizens, no steps in this direction in the employment field had been taken by 2004. Migrants continued to be seen simply as a means of filling temporary needs in the labour market, with little attention paid to their fundamental human right to equality.[101]

A final example of transformative policies is the legal requirement to provide 'reasonable accommodations' or 'reasonable adjustments' to meet the needs of people with disabilities. In the immediate post-war years schemes were developed for the rehabilitation, resettlement and employment of disabled war veterans. In the period of the welfare state, special measures were taken to compensate and rehabilitate in the vocational sphere those injured in industrial and other accidents (see chapter 6 below). Gradually, employers and others came to recognise the contribution that disabled people could make in the labour market. In the period of economic crisis and deregulation, when disabled people were particularly disadvantaged in the labour market, there was a growth of organisations of disabled people campaigning for disability rights.[102] The majority of the countries studied adopted legal instruments (in some cases, constitutional provisions) that expressly referred to the rights of disabled persons to equal treatment, the exceptions being Britain, Denmark, France, Ireland and Luxembourg. The primary legal tool to assist disabled people in the labour market was a quota system in the public sector. This failed, apart from in Germany, where it appears to have been a relative success.[103] Some countries, such as France, the Netherlands and Greece, extended quota systems to the private sector, but these schemes were, on the whole, incompatible with commercial competitiveness and were usually not enforced in practice.[104]

However, Britain (1995), Ireland (1998) and Sweden (1999) introduced enforceable rights to equal treatment that went beyond traditional models. The problem was how to fit disability into the established framework of

[99] Hepple (2004) 12.
[100] Coussey (2002) 25–39; Rudyer and Spencer (2003) 22–28.
[101] Ibid, 7.
[102] Doyle (1995) 63.
[103] Ibid, 73.
[104] Ibid.

anti-discrimination law. Unlike race, sex or other characteristics that are irrelevant to performance of the job, disability may impair a disabled person from undertaking part of a job in the same way as an able-bodied person. In order to make the principle of equal treatment compatible with substantive equality for disabled persons, it is necessary to require the employer (or other provider) to make reasonable accommodation for the disabled person. As Fredman says, 'instead of requiring disabled people to conform to existing norms, the aim is to develop a concept of equality which requires adaptation and change'.[105] The laws in Britain, Ireland and Sweden adopted this approach, as did the Employment Directive 78/2000/EC. Article 5 of the Directive says that 'reasonable accommodation' means

> that employers shall take appropriate measures, where needed in a particular case, to enable a person with a disability to have access to, participate in, or advance in employment, or to undergo training, unless such measures would impose a disproportionate burden on the employer . . .

In implementing this provision, the countries studied adopted different approaches to the determination of what is 'reasonable'; in other respects, too, the Directive did not produce uniformity, nor did it place disabled persons in a better position than others.[106] Issues of cost and practicability, as well as non-cost justifications, still disbar many disabled people from full participation in the labour market.

Conclusion

The history of laws and practices that seek to promote equality of status at work has several general features. The first is that they have been heavily influenced by international events and human rights movements, including the feminist movement, the civil rights movement in the US, the anti-apartheid struggle, gay liberation and the disability rights movement. They are rooted not so much in labour law as in international human rights law, as proclaimed in the UNDHR and then developed in the field of employment and occupation by the remarkable ILO Conventions No 100 (1951) and No 111 (1958), and elevated into a fundamental principle, in 1998, by the ILO Declaration of Fundamental Principles and Rights at Work. All 15 countries in this study accepted these international obligations, and also the rights to non-discrimination in the ECHR and ESC.

[105] Fredman (2005) 203.
[106] De Schutter (2007) 755–56.

The second feature of equality law and practice is that the interventions of the EU and the ECJ have been of critical importance, notably the implementation and interpretation of Article 119 of the Treaty of Rome and Article 13 of the Treaty of Amsterdam. These interventions were the result of a combination of economic, social and political factors, including the growth of human rights movements mentioned above, the feminisation of the labour force, the attempts to integrate new settled communities of migrants into multicultural societies and the pressures of an ageing population, as well as changed attitudes towards sexuality, disability and other forms of status discrimination.

Thirdly, transplantation of legal ideas and institutions has been the usual method of legal development in this field. Anti-discrimination models were imported from the US into Britain and Ireland, then through dialogues between national courts and the ECJ, and Directives, into EC law and subsequently into national laws and practices. The transplanted laws have developed within the national forms of civil adjudication for the resolution of individual disputes, although sometimes unlawful discrimination is both a civil wrong and a criminal offence. The weakness inherent in this approach is that it has inhibited the development of group or collective procedures and remedies against discrimination. In particular, the European legal systems have not developed the class action which was so important to the growth of anti-discrimination suits in the federal courts in the US and, although the ECJ has insisted that there must be effective enforcement, this is left to applicable national rules, with the result that sanctions are frequently ineffective in practice.[107]

Fourthly, the attempts, since around 1975, to go beyond formal equality or direct discrimination have had only limited success in achieving substantive equality. The prohibition of indirect discrimination does not mean that everyone will have a genuinely equal chance. This requires positive measures, such as active labour market interventions, education and training, and family-friendly employment policies. However, such positive measures have been the exception, rather than the rule, in most countries. One is not supplying genuine equality of opportunity if one applies an unchallenged criterion of 'merit' to people who have been deprived of the opportunity to acquire 'merit'.[108] Moreover, procedural equality, like direct discrimination, suffers from the limitation that consistent treatment can be satisfied by depriving both persons compared of a particular benefit (levelling down) as well as by conferring the benefit on both of them (levelling up). For example, equality of pension ages can be reached either by making women work longer or by letting men work for a shorter period to earn a pension. Towards the end of our period, only a few countries had moved in the direction of imposing positive duties (and then usually only on public authorities) to promote equality at work.

The limitations of formal and procedural equality have led to attempts to

---

[107] Hepple (1996) 253–56.
[108] Hepple (1990) 411.

develop the notion of substantive equality to include some element of redistribution. The post-war social democratic promise in western democracies included an obligation on the state to deliver 'fair shares' and to reduce the inequality between the rich and the poor. However, in the course of the next 60 years the interest in economic equality and the redistribution of incomes all but disappeared in these countries, and the gap between the rich and the poor grew steadily greater both nationally and globally, and for some groups more than others. In part, this loss of interest in redistribution reflects fundamental changes in social structure. Instead of a social structure shaped like a triangle, with a small upper class, a middle class and a large, underprivileged working class, by the start of the twenty-first century European society was shaped more like a diamond, with a small, extremely rich upper class, a large middle class and a small lower class living in relative poverty. Increased social mobility and improved education in most European countries has led to demands for equal opportunities to compete rather than for more welfare benefits. Old social conflicts—notably between class-conscious workers and the bourgeoisie—have been replaced by new individual identities and by conflicts of gender, ethnicity, faith and lifestyle.[109]

This has led to new demands for comprehensive and transformative equality. This issue has been hotly debated by philosophers since the 1970s.[110] Most of them endorse the importance of genuine individual choices; they acknowledge that some people may need more and different resources to enjoy those choices and access to opportunities. They agree that the aim is to narrow gaps in real opportunities, not by reducing the freedoms of some but by increasing the opportunities of those suffering persistent disadvantage. This is not equality of welfare in the sense that social institutions are obliged to distribute the resources over which they have control so as to achieve uniformity. At the same time it is not simply merit-based. It recognises that our opportunities are determined not only by choices but also by circumstances. Some of those circumstances are beyond the control of the individual, such as genetic endowments, gender, ethnicity, disabilities and economic status. Le Grand points out that 'if one individual receives less than another owing to her own choice, then the disparity is not considered inequitable; if it arises for reasons beyond her control, then it is inequitable'.[111] The main criticism of the reliance on choice is that it does not correspond with the real world in which individuals do not have a genuinely free choice, precisely because of differences of wealth, race, gender and economic status.

> The notion that a black woman refused a job can simply move to another job, or choose to improve her educational qualifications, makes some remarkably optimistic assumptions. It ignores the harassment, degradation and humiliation inflicted on black

---

[109] These conclusions draw heavily on Hepple (2008) 1.
[110] Eg Rawls (1971); Sen (1992); Dworkin (2000), Cohen (2000).
[111] Le Grand (1991) 87.

people and women over generations which may reduce their self-esteem and dignity and their motivation to 'improve' their life chances.[112]

The challenge for European countries in the twenty-first century is to develop coherent and comprehensive equality laws, positive duties in both the public and private sectors to promote genuine equality of opportunity, and active labour market policies that mainstream equality. To achieve this they will need effective enforcement mechanisms, active participation by the social partners and specialised bodies for strategic enforcement of the law.

[112] Hepple (2008) 16.

6

Wage Labour and Social Security

ROBERT REBHAHN

Introduction

General

The aim of this chapter is to trace the evolution of wage labour and social security in western Europe between 1945 and 2004. This exploration will focus on six countries which, between them, represent the broad spectrum of European welfare systems.

Social security describes a political arrangement whereby the state provides for or organises benefits in case of basic needs of individuals: sickness, occupational accident and illness, incapacity to work, old age, unemployment, maternity and children, need of personal care, and poverty. As a rule of thumb, one can say that a welfare state exists in a country if the state cares about these social needs. A welfare state is often further characterised by public services and their prominent role in the provision of medical care, education, water and public transport.

In the twentieth century, it was widely held that a full and real exertion of civil and political liberties presupposes a minimum of economic and social security, as well as of education. For this reason, a growing number of states provided systems of 'social security', with individual social rights obliging the state (or an auxiliary) to sustain their citizens in case of poverty or certain needs. However, a hundred years after such systems began to be put in place, there is still a great variety across Europe with regard to their aims, scope and content.

Thus, one needs some guiding questions in order to evaluate their respective merits. First, one has to ascertain to what extent the welfare system enables individuals to uphold a socially acceptable standard of living independently of market participation—that is, without an actual or previous market income. One can speak of decommodification. This leads primarily to the question of whether benefits are means-tested. Benefits in case of poverty (social assistance/income support) are normally means-tested, whereas benefits for other risks normally, in an evolved social system, are not. Only benefits both unrelated to means testing and legally enforceable can be called property rights. One main evolution after 1945 is that social benefits or services are increasingly independent of means testing. The existence of social rights and their shape greatly influence the position of those who have only their labour power to live upon and in consequence depend upon the labour market and labour relations. Their position is the stronger the more they enjoy unqualified social rights without a means test.

Secondly, we must examine the personal scope of protection more closely. A country's system of social benefits may include all people living in the country (residents) and is therefore universal, or it may be restricted to certain groups, such as (former) wage earners or the self-employed. In both cases, it may cover all members of the group or, alternatively, only those who are in a weak market position (modest income) and therefore deemed to need solidarity and collective help, leaving those in a stronger position to rely on the market.

A third question affects the scope of risks covered. Does it cover all risks mentioned above (a comprehensive system) or only some? Many states began with measures aimed at industrial accidents, health insurance and pensions, whereas unemployment benefits and family allowances followed only later, and the need for long-time personal care lagged still further behind, in some cases several decades.

The fourth area to be evaluated relates to the conditions of the benefits, and their amount. The benefit may presuppose a period of adherence to the system, especially contributions during a qualification period. Most cash benefits are of this type, even some that are means tested. The lower the requirement to get the benefit, the higher is the degree of decommodification. Another important factor is the rate of replacement that the benefit secures in relation to the individual's previous market income (secured income). A minimum protection has a replacement ratio below 50%; a rate above 75% protects the living standard. Benefits with a high replacement rate reproduce the results of the markets and therefore also social stratification. The same applies for benefits provided for a certain social group, especially if the system has different rules for different groups. Benefits at a flat rate do not reproduce stratification, but usually contribute less to decommodification. Income-related benefits are usually financed by income-related contributions. Flat-rate benefits are financed either by taxes or by special contributions, which also may be income-related. In both cases, the social benefit has a redistributive effect (if the tax system has one).

Another important question about the structure of the social system is its relation to family structure. The old welfare regimes not only relied on, but also endorsed a specific family model: the traditional gender role model of the male breadwinner. A question of minor social but great political importance concerns the administration of the system: it can be administered by the state itself, by representatives of the potential beneficiaries or by the social partners delegated by the state.

Periodisation

Social security is an expression of solidarity and often leads to redistribution. The extent of solidarity depends on various factors: the community of potential solidarity; the need for and the ability to bestow solidarity; and the willingness to establish such a state of affairs. Right from its infancy, social policy in the European states has been characterised by a predominantly national perspective, an outlook that it still maintains today. European countries, even those which were members of the EU, were, until at least the 1980s, relatively autonomous by today's standards. Their national economies were much more 'closed'. They could avoid cross-border competition much more effectively than today. Currency policy could help to resolve internal problems. Therefore, every state had much more autonomy to decide upon its own social policy. Although these pillars of autonomy faded away with the rise of the EU and globalisation, social policy even today is still a matter for the nation states. The state is the main frame of reference for social benefits and their evolution; no social transfers are paid by the EU, and this is not likely to change in the near future.

The potential for state-organised solidarity depends greatly on the country's relative economic wealth at a given point as well as on the change of economic performance over the course of time. Western Europe witnessed steady economic growth until the 1970s, followed by alternating periods of stagnation and growth. The importance of social security in the six countries we consider in this chapter is shown by the rising proportion of the gross domestic product spent on welfare (Table 6.1). This percentage has risen continuously in all states for many years, albeit on different levels and with occasional exceptions. One could get the impression that there was a nearly uninterrupted growth of welfare. A closer look shows the need for differentiation.

Immediately after 1945 until the early 1950s, there was a phase of economic redress across Europe, when only the most urgent needs were met. Some countries (eg Germany) kept the basic legal features of their system; others (eg

Table 6.1: Welfare state spending as a percentage of GDP[a]

	1950	1970	1980	2001
Britain	10.1	8.6	17.9	21.8
Germany	14.0	15.4	23.0	27.4
France	10.8	17.1	21.1	28.5
The Netherlands	6.7	17.4	26.9	21.8
Sweden	8.3	11.0	28.8	28.9
Italy	8.5	12.4	18.4	24.4
Spain	4.4	8.1	15.9	19.6

[a]Data are from Cousins (2005) 90 *et seq.*

Britain) changed them. The European welfare state was under construction. The 30 years after 1945 were characterised by a constant growth of social rights and benefits, in figures as well as in relation to gross domestic product (GDP). Many states improved the individual's life by collective means.

Several circumstances favoured this expansion of welfare: a great degree of autonomy of the nation state to decide upon its own system; steady economic growth until the 1970s; rising employment rates with a tendency towards lack of unemployment; stable working relations for the employees; a predominance of the male-breadwinner family model accompanied by traditional family relations, which sustained full employment and reduced the need for external help; low demographic problems; a faith in continuing prosperity and growth; and a belief in collective measures. Little consideration was given to the sustainability of the social system in case of an economic crisis or changes in the underlying social patterns. Social policy was seen as a one-way path—always upwards and never back. This expansion ended when the preconditions faded away. By the 1970s, the economic challenge of financing the welfare system began to emerge, particularly after the oil crisis in 1973. Since the 1980s there has been a general feeling of a crisis of the welfare state. It seems appropriate to combine the two phases in one period of construction and consolidation (or expansion). This first period finishes at the end of the 1970s. Many call this period the 'glorious age' of welfare.

There seems to be no consensus on how to explain why most western European states decided to (re)establish welfare, especially for those countries such as Britain, which changed to a more intense welfare system (the Beveridge system). Various explanations are suggested, such as response to the needs of advanced capitalism, the political force of organised labour, and 'a historic compromise' between capital and labour.[1] However, one should also mention other factors, particularly the Second World War.[2] After the war most people—not only the working classes—endured a hard life. Combined with the shared experiences of the war, this led to the common acceptance of collective measures to improve the standard of living. The majority of the population held the state more responsible for the well-being of the citizens than before. The state, they thought, should be a 'social state'. In many countries the improvement of social rights was largely favoured by their extension to the middle class and to farmers, which allowed political coalitions between the labour movement and the parties representing those groups. Last but not least, the expansion of welfare was sustained by the wish to offer a social alternative to the communist countries of eastern Europe.

In the 1970s, the period of steady economic growth ended. However, this did not immediately influence social policy. Many governments, eg those in Britain and Germany, were still attempting to sustain or even improve the 'social net' by deficit spending. It was not until the end of the 1970s that attention turned to the costs of social benefits and their share of public expenses. Governments wished

---

[1] *Cf* eg Pierson (2006) 29–41.
[2] *Cf* Judt (2005) 72–77.

to stabilise or reduce their welfare spending. Many states restructured their systems in the following years by reducing benefits (especially for old age) or adjusting the financing tools. However, Table 6.1 shows that social expenditure in real terms has seldom declined. The changes therefore affected the details of a state's policy rather than its overall expenditure. However, even these small changes affected the structure and the outcomes of social security. Moreover, they were strongly resented by those people who had relied on the previous regulations and now saw their expectations frustrated.

The second period, from 1978 onwards, is one of stabilisation and restructuring of the welfare state: a process that continues into the present day. It started with the Conservatives' rise to power in Britain in 1979. In theory, it is possible to subdivide this period into two phases: one from 1978 to 1989 and the other after 1989, when international competition gained new force. The first 10 years were a period of stagnation and stabilisation, the following years an age of reorientation and restructuring. However, here the two periods will be dealt with together, since stabilisation and restructuring are often closely intertwined.

Changes in Main Preconditions

The changes in social policy in western Europe after 1945 were caused primarily by changes in the socio-economic preconditions of welfare, often accompanied by a change of the political objectives guiding social policy. First, one has to account for the changes in family structure. The traditional social system had benefited from female work outside the formal market economy. It was concentrated on the risks incurred by a male breadwinner. Women's participation in the labour market has steadily grown since the 1950s, and the male-breadwinner model has gradually disintegrated. This has affected the pension system, as well as childcare and personal care. Furthermore, for many people, the dissolution of the traditional family network has reduced the importance of this network as a place of last resort that enables them to sustain a meagre life. Insofar as the possibility to rely on their relations dwindled away for many people, the importance of participation in the labour market grew.

Secondly, the labour market itself has changed. Unemployment has risen since the 1970s in many European countries (see chapter 3 above). This rise can be ascribed inter alia to the extension of labour supply, especially in the first half of this period (female work), later due to a reduced demand for labour. Technological change has rendered many unqualified jobs superfluous whilst others have been 'exported' abroad, where labour is cheaper. Rising unemployment rates have eroded the financial basis of social security everywhere, but especially in the many countries that finance the system by wage-related contributions. Benefits then increase more than contributions. Without unemployment, most social systems would have had fewer difficulties in maintaining the level of welfare. In countries where social security focuses on dependent labour, the rising importance of self-employment and the changes by individuals between dependent and non-dependent work aggravate the difficulties.

A third external change is the constant rise in average life expectancy in most countries. This primarily affects the old age pension, which has become the most significant financial benefit by far. The rise affects the average length of pension payments and alters the ratio between the numbers of working (contributing) people to pensioners. For example, in Germany this ratio fell from 5:1 in 1955, to 4:1 in 1991 and 3:1 in 2006. Longer life expectancy also increases the need for personal care over long periods and the cost of medical care. These costs have also increased due to medical progress.

Last but not least, the willingness to support solidarity measures has declined. The political and ethical ideas guiding social policy have changed, especially after 1989 (see below).

Construction and Consolidation of the Welfare State (1945–78)

National Perspectives—Two Models

After 1945, many European countries, and especially Germany, had to recover from the war. Only those countries that had been less involved in the conflict (eg Sweden) could avoid this disruption of their development. However, by the early 1950s, all countries had consolidated their social system and a typical pattern of welfare emerged. Many countries continued to follow the basic decisions they had taken up until the Second World War, eg Germany and—to a lesser extent—France. Other countries took a new orientation, eg Britain and the Netherlands. For a long time after the war, the political discussion related to social policy focused on two models: the Bismarckian model, developed and upheld in Germany,[3] and the Beveridge model, newly established in Britain. Germany is the prototype of an occupational welfare state, Britain that of a universalistic one.

Post-war Germany mainly adhered to the basic features that originated in the Bismarckian reforms at the end of the nineteenth century; the Nazi Third Reich mainly followed and partly intensified the previous patterns of welfare. In a Bismarckian system, the state organises social insurance primarily for different groups of working people. German social insurance primarily covered only (former) wage earners and their dependents (spouse and children), whose social rights were (and still are) only derivative. Like other countries with a Bismarckian system, Germany established a special regime for public servants, more generous than the general system. Other groups of working people, such as farmers and

---

[3] See Hepple (1986) ch 3.

artists, were only included later in the general system. However, Germany has still not systematically extended the scope of social insurance to all people who earn money by their work. Most self-employed people—even those who are economically dependent—and their dependents are still not covered by the pension insurance. One can hardly attribute this exclusion to the fact that the self-employed are always able to rely on self-help and so the legislator seems to believe that they should look after themselves. Even compulsory health insurance for a long time covered only wage-earners, and it still covers only those people who earn less than a set threshold (now at €50,000 a year).

The different branches of social insurances are administered by representatives of the people concerned, often with employer participation. Benefits are financed by contributions related to earnings (wages). Contributions for employees are divided equally between the employee and his employer. Most cash benefits (eg pensions, unemployment benefits; though not social assistance (*Sozialhilfe*) are linked to the level of the prior earnings of the insured. High replacement rates aim to protect the individual's standard of living. This and the group orientation tend to transfer the social structure into the sphere of social rights. We find an occupational, group-related system of social security implemented by social insurance. The system is based on the model of an employed person—a man—who is in lifelong, full-time employment, and who secures the protection of his spouse and children by derivative benefits, especially a widow's pension.

The Constitution (*Grundgesetz*) of 1949 provides that Germany is a social state (*Sozialstaat*). The most important reform in Germany after 1945 was the Pension Act of 1957. It established the pay-as-you-go (PAYG) principle[4] and dynamic pensions related to gross wages. Another major change regarded social assistance. Until 1954, it was awarded on a discretionary basis; this was altered so that the needy had a legal right to this benefit. At the end of the 1970s, a vast project of codification of social law into a Social Code, then seen as a parallel to the Civil Code, was begun. The codification, which partly was only a compilation, has only recently been completed.

In Britain, the Beveridge report of 1942 recommended a new model of social security: a universalistic and comprehensive system with modest benefits. In 1946 Parliament enacted the National Health Service (NHS), National Insurance and National Assistance Acts. The new social system stood in contrast to the former system in Britain, which was formed mainly by the Liberal reforms of 1906–14. Health care benefits then applied only to the family's breadwinner; the pension scheme was very restrictive and partly means tested. Only unemployment benefits were improved in the 1920s, but these were soon cut back again during the Great Depression. In sharp contrast, the newly established NHS provided medical care to all. The national insurance scheme provided old age benefits for all who had worked for money, not just for a section of the employed. In addition to this,

---

[4] A PAYG system does not save: contributions and/or subsidies (paid out of taxes) in a certain year are used only to finance the benefits of that year.

specific benefits for the employed were established, such as sickness benefits. The national insurance scheme further provided for specific incapacity benefits for those who had worked, as well as a (lower) benefit for all. In addition, benefits in case of unemployment as well as a general system of social assistance were established. The Beveridge model therefore meant that the state organised a social system for all people in need of support (universalistic system), a designation that could potentially apply to the whole population (especially in the case of medical care). Social security was financed through taxes (particularly for the NHS) as well as by relatively low contributions, which were levied on earnings. Cash benefits were therefore modest and often at a flat rate, though mostly not means tested. This applied especially in the case of old age and unemployment benefits. Even old age pensions did not reflect the individual's previous income, but only the length of time for which he or she had been contributing. Benefits in cash therefore were not designed to maintain the previous standard of living.

A Beveridge system inclines to uniform rules and flat-rate benefits, and shows no great internal differentiation. Rules and organisation do not differ according to social structure. In consequence, such a universal system does not tend to reproduce this structure. According to the original intentions of the Beveridge system, social benefits in cash, especially pensions, should not be so generous as to lead people away from additional private savings; to this extent, the concept had a liberal touch. A means-tested social assistance benefit existed, but was not intended to play an important role.

The Beveridge system did not undergo any radical changes until the late 1970s. However, benefits often proved insufficient to live off and did not prevent mass poverty. In consequence, social assistance played a much greater role than originally conceived, especially for old women, who had typically not worked long enough for a sufficient pension. Despite the low payment of benefits to the individual, welfare turned out to be very costly for the state and went beyond the financing basis. In addition, the system was much less redistributive, and reproduced more stratification than had been expected.

The social system of France before 1945 showed parallels to the German one. The new beginning after 1945 followed the same basic features. However, the insurance system was extended to all working people, including the self-employed. The general system covered most employees. Besides this general system, a great variety of special systems were established. This fragmentation remains today. The general regime today covers 75% of the population; all the systems together cover over 95%. Thus, private insurers play a smaller role in the French system than they do in Germany. Nevertheless, for a long time social protection in France focused on people who worked, and did not include all residents. Another main feature of the system was (and still is) that cash benefits are closely related to the contributions paid earlier. This led to a rising deficit in social protection for low- or non-earning people. Until the 1980s, social assistance (*les minima sociaux*) existed only for special groups; there was no universal benefit.

In the Netherlands, social security before 1945 adhered to a German-style system. However, in the ensuing decades, the ideas of Beveridge became equally influential. Until the 1960s, Dutch welfare was at a relatively low level, since the country's Christian tradition still provided assistance to the poor in the form of alms. In the 1960s welfare expanded greatly, and the Netherlands became a leading welfare country. A new structure emerged, the main feature of which was the coexistence of traditional forms of social insurance for the employed (unemployment benefits and sick pay) with newly established insurances covering all citizens (basic old age pension, health and, later, incapacity). Both of these benefits were financed by contributions. It is only more recently that general social assistance has been introduced by the Dutch Parliament.

In Italy, social security before 1945 followed the Bismarckian model. Post-1945, it continued, broadly speaking, along the same path—although the Italian system has certain characteristic features that differentiate it from its German 'parent' in many respects. Notably, the welfare regime—based on developments during the fascist period—was and (albeit to a lesser extent) still is quite particularistic and prone to clientilism. Furthermore, it relied strongly on family structures (familiarism), which favoured a low female employment rate. This might explain the lack of a general social assistance and the low level of unemployment benefits. This seems not to fit well with the Italian Constitution of 1948, which proclaims many social rights. Two major single changes should be mentioned here. Since the pension reform of 1969 pensions are less aligned to prior earnings and more need-designed. In 1978, Parliament established a universalistic Health Service, which is partly tax funded.

The Swedish welfare state is the archetype of the Nordic as well as the social democratic (universalistic) model. There was a constant increase in social benefits and services from the 1930s until the 1990s. The basic pension for all citizens existed as early as the 1930s, together with a functionalistic family policy. This was followed, in the 1950s, by compulsory universal health insurance and the equally universal compulsory additional pension scheme. Sweden, like other Nordic countries, only started to develop its childcare services in kind in the late 1960s, but did so with great vigour in order to enhance the (early) return of mothers to work. Since then, these services have been a characteristic feature of this system. The universalistic and expensive character of the Swedish regime has also made it very egalitarian and redistributive.

In general, the state became more and more important for social affairs after 1950 than it had been in pre-war times. For the Beveridge model this is obvious, but it is also true of Bismarckian systems. Where social insurance is compulsory, it does not leave much place for solidarity procured by voluntary corporations. The increasing influence of the state also meant that, in the Bismarckian systems, the autonomy of the social insurance bodies, run mostly by social partners, declined.

Tendencies in Selected Areas

Coverage of the Insurance Systems

In the late 1940s, most insurance systems only covered dependent workers, not the self-employed or entrepreneurs. Many countries soon extended compulsory insurance further to other working people. Particularly important was the extension to one group of self-employed, the farmers, and their dependents. Farmers were then much more numerous than today and their political support often helped to maintain and develop social security systems for wage labour. Other groups of self-employed were also included in many countries (but not in Germany). However, many countries established or maintained specific insurance schemes for different categories of people. Thus, the social system in many countries reflected the social structure. However, a person was only rarely excluded from the social system or from a benefit (except social assistance) because their earnings exceeded a given threshold.

Sick Pay and Benefits

In circumstances where a wage earner is temporarily unable to work, many countries (eg Germany, Britain) oblige the employer to continue to pay the employee for a certain period; if the illness extends beyond this period, social insurance then takes over the payments. The length of the two periods of payment varies greatly from system to system. Some countries (eg Italy) only impose a duty on the employer, others (eg France) oblige only the social system. However, many systems have changed since 1945, so that it is difficult to establish a general outline. The same applies to the rate of replacement. Nevertheless, one can say that until the 1980s many systems (eg Germany) increased protection, especially for blue-collar workers.

Old Age Benefits

After 1945, all of the western European states decided to follow the PAYG system to support their older citizens. This system relies on an implicit 'generation contract': every generation pays for the pensions of the older generation. There are at least two different regimes. Some countries established a people's rent. For example, this system was established in the Netherlands in 1957, albeit only for a basic pension; today this basic pension is fixed at 70% of the minimum wage after 40 years of residence and contributions. Such a universal pension system can only provide a meagre benefit, and needs supplementing. The second system provides pensions only for those who have worked in a way included in the pensions system for a specified period. This system already existed before 1945 in many states (eg Germany), albeit restricted to blue-collar workers and/or those employees who earned below a certain threshold. After 1945, in many countries the work-related system was extended to other groups. Some countries immediately extended the pension system to all working people, including the self-employed (eg Britain and France in 1945); others restricted the extension to the employed (eg Germany, Spain). The major problem of work-related pensions was that they did not compensate the non-remunerated work of women caring for children and the elderly. Only a few countries provided the same regular pension age for both men and women (eg in France at 60). Many had a higher pension age for men (eg Germany: 65 for men, 60 for women). Until the 1990s, there was a tendency to lower the pension age. Some countries also offered a 'flexible' pension age (eg Germany from 1972 onwards). The second requirement for a pension was a minimum period of adherence to the system. This minimum period varied (and still varies) greatly. For example, Germany required 5 years of work whereas Austria required 15, and Denmark required 3 years of residence (10 for foreigners).

Universal benefits as well as the insurance system usually relate the pension's amount to the period of adherence to the system. A pension under a universal benefit system provides, even in the best cases, only for a basic income (eg Sweden). In work-related insurances, the amount is also profoundly influenced by contributions, although most systems put a cap on the secured income. However, relations between contributions and the amount of the pension varied from country to country. In Germany, the legislator established a very close relation: the whole working life is taken into account. Elsewhere the relation was looser. Some work-related systems aimed at pensions that secured the living standard. Germany and Italy decided to take this path in the 1950s, and pensions could be as high as 80% of the secured income. Other countries provided only for a basic pension. In Britain the universal pension is related to the length of time for which the minimum contribution has been paid, but without regard to the level of income (flat rate); thus the basic pension was (and is) quite low. In France, too, it is not very high.

Another major problem was how to adjust the pensions already paid to inflation and a rising living standard of working people. In the post-war years, the adjustment was typically the subject of an annual political battle. Subsequently, many countries introduced a statutory indexation (revaluation). Some countries linked pensions to the index of prices (France, Italy), others to that of wages (Germany; Italy after 1975) or a combination of both (Sweden). At the time, it was widely held that wages always increase faster than prices.

In those countries where the social pensions were low, the elderly often required a second pension in order to live above the 'poverty line'. Until the 1970s, these problems were not resolved. Even the low pensions were widely seen as an improvement on the previous state of affairs, when the elderly had to rely on private savings and family support. Due to the high average age of retirement combined with the relatively short life expectancy of the period, pensioners often could meet the shortfall with help from their families. Later, many states subsidised or prescribed adherence to a supplementary pension scheme; France began this as early as 1961.

Occupational Accidents and Illnesses

Specific provisions for these risks were the first steps of social security and insurance. Some countries (eg Germany) had established a special branch of social security long before 1945; the rules were well established, and the political battles had been fought long before the war.[5] Thus, after 1945, these countries could simply continue to follow this path. Other countries, such as Britain and France, had previously only enlarged the employers' liability, but not obliged him to insure against liability. The Beveridge-inspired reform introduced a specific social regime that also provided for better benefits than in the case of accidents and illnesses that were not work-related. After 1945, most of the other countries put into place some form of special protection in case of occupational accidents and illnesses, which provided benefits in kind (eg intense health care and rehabilitation) and cash (compensation). Typically, a special branch of social security would administer this protection; Britain integrated it later into the general system. Only in a few countries (eg the Netherlands) were occupational accidents not specifically dealt with and their remedies incorporated into another system. In some countries, occupational insurance was also designed as a substitute for the employer's liability in tort. These features have largely been preserved until today.

The scope of coverage of occupational accidents—'in the course and scope of employment'—has remained mostly unchanged. However, protection was extended in most countries to accidents occurring whilst travelling to or from work. Many countries had (and have) a list of occupational illnesses. Illnesses not included in such lists are only covered if a causal relation can be established between the illness and the specificities of the employee's work. In the course of time, therefore, the relation of a recently diagnosed illness to a previous occupation that may have triggered it was often disputed (eg asbestosis cases). By the 1990s resources were beginning to be concentrated on the more seriously disabled (eg in Britain).

Unemployment Benefits and Social Assistance

The importance of these benefits was great in the first few years after the war. It subsequently diminished, along with the tendency to full employment, and rose again after 1980. Immediately after the war, many countries provided only means-tested social assistance for the jobless (eg Germany). As soon as mass unemployment receded, most countries (re)established a compulsory unemployment insurance system with enforceable rights; France did this later than most countries, in the 1960s. Unemployment insurance is generally restricted to dependent labour. In some cases, the administration of the system was run by the state (eg Britain), in others with the participation of the social partners (eg Germany, France). Some countries (eg Sweden and Belgium) followed the

---

[5] Hepple (1986) 142–46.

Ghent model, with trade unions organising protection. This promoted their membership.

In Bismarckian-oriented countries in particular, the objective of unemployment benefit was to maintain the standard of living, whereas other countries provided only for a minimum allowance. In Germany, the reform of 1957 established the right to unemployment allowance for six months, with a maximum replacement rate of 68%. When this allowance expired, the unemployed individual was entitled to 'unemployment aid', with a lower replacement rate. Britain introduced a flat-rate system in 1945; the rate was remarkably high at the beginning (and much higher than sickness benefits). In Italy, the replacement rate was (until recently) below 20%. In many countries, the decline of unemployment allowed for more generous benefits. In addition, the rules concerning the 'actively seeking work' condition (in particular, which jobs the unemployed could refuse without risking the benefit) became less stringent and more generous. Unemployment came to be perceived more as a social hazard than as the fault of the individual. In consequence, unemployment benefits ceased, in some countries, to be a tool for castigating employees, as had been the case before 1945, where benefits were docked if the unemployed had left work voluntarily, if he or she had been dismissed due to misconduct, or if he or she refused to accept (nearly) any other work. Since the end of the 1960s, many countries (eg Germany in 1969) have adopted a policy of active labour market measures (see chapter 3 above).

Before the Second World War, many, but not all, societies already provided assistance to the most needy according to poor laws, which preceded the welfare state. However, in a welfare state this basic allowance became a social right and not an act of charity. Thus it was a great achievement that after 1945 most, but not all, European states enacted social assistance in the form of a universal, means-tested benefit that was potentially open to all.[6] Benefit payments are typically only granted if the individual is not able to work or is unable to find a job that he or she should accept. In many states, the amount of social assistance rose in real terms between 1950 and the 1970s. With regard to the notion of 'poverty', the then predominant political approach adhered to a rather 'absolute' concept that took account of basic needs, rather than referring to the relationship of the individual's means to a national median income. Only the Netherlands linked the amount of social assistance to the minimum wage. It should be remembered that social assistance also influences the labour market. That this benefit set a reserve wage in those many countries where there was no (general) minimum wage (eg Germany) was particularly important. In Germany, the amount of social assistance had to stay at a level below the lowest minimum wages prescribed by collective agreements.

Social assistance can also be paid to recipients of other social benefits. This complementary function was more important at the start of the first period

---

[6] Some states, eg Italy, have not established any general social assistance; others have established it only recently (eg France).

under review here than at its end. However, in Britain the importance of this double provision has risen over the past half century, since a minimum income for old people with a low pension was secured in Britain (and Germany) only through social assistance, whereas other countries provided a real minimum pension.

Parenthood[7]

In many countries, pre-1945 law already provided for maternity leave for employed women. The leave was mostly unpaid; often the law placed obligations not only on the employer but also on the woman. After 1945, this protection was intensified by lengthening the period and introducing a benefit during the leave. Later some countries introduced a right to a second, optional leave after the end of maternity leave; today it is called parental leave. Only a few countries favoured this leave by a flat-rate benefit. All of these rights were typically restricted to employees.

Alongside maternity leave, various other social benefits relating to children or families have been established in many European countries. France already subsidised larger families before the Second World War.[8] After 1945, other countries followed with different models that must be viewed in their historical context. Until at least the 1950s, the vast majority of people lived in traditional family structures. The female employment rate, which had been high during the wartime, fell back to a low level in the immediate post-war years and only rose again slowly. The birth rate attained an all-time high in the first half of the 1960s. Thus there was no urgent need for political promotion of parenthood. Nevertheless, many states started to introduce family allowances. Often they were employment-related. For instance, Germany (in 1954) and Italy obliged the employer to pay allowances to the father. To begin with, these were often restricted to couples (or even couples with more than one child), and they were often means tested. The Nordic countries and France introduced benefits that were paid to the mother, including cases where the child was born out of wedlock.

Some countries, especially in continental western Europe and Britain, developed public (subsidised) childcare for children over the age of three early on. However, initially, only a small number of places were made available. Since the 1970s, France and Belgium have actively expanded these services in order to enhance the (early) return of parents to work. The Nordic countries only began to develop their childcare service in the late 1960s, but did so then with full vigour. Other countries, especially Germany, left childcare to the private sphere; this favoured the mother's withdrawal from the labour market. In southern Europe, family policy was not important. If any measures were enacted to

---

[7] I am indebted to Ms Niksova for allowing me access to a preparatory paper covering this area.
[8] Hepple (1986) 94–96.

support families, these only benefited the traditional family model and gender roles.

General Remarks

International and European Influences

In 1961, the European Social Charter (ESC) was adopted. It deals with social security primarily in Article 12.[9] According to this Article, every contracting state is obliged to 'establish or maintain a social security system at a satisfactory level at least equal to that required by the ILO Convention No 102' and 'to endeavour to raise progressively the system of social security to a higher level'. The above International Labour Organisation (ILO) convention was signed in 1952, and covers medical care, benefits in case of sickness, unemployment, employment injury, invalidity and old age, as well as family and maternity benefits and survivor benefits. It provides that the standard benefit should amount to a certain proportion of the previous earnings, though the minimum percentages are rather low (unemployment benefit for a couple with two children is set at 45% of previous earnings, old age pension with a spouse set at 40%). However, it accords broad discretion to the states to determine which people should be included in social security. The ILO has since elaborated other conventions,[10] but only a few states have ratified them; and the ESC has not incorporated them.[11]

The European Economic Community (EEC) did not greatly influence social security until the 1990s, with the exception of freedom of movement. Until 1973, there were only six Member States of the Community, and even in 1979 there were only nine. Social policy was seen strictly as a matter for individual states. The EEC did enact Regulation 1408/68, aimed at the coordination of national social security in order to facilitate free movement of workers. The Regulation has (at least partly) achieved this objective, but has not forced the Member States to alter their national systems, nor has it obliged them to make them converge. Nevertheless, it has helped many pensioners to live abroad.

Typologies of Welfare

The last two decades have seen the emergence of a vast body of literature on comparative social policy. A landmark was the 1990 study of Esping-Anderson,

[9] See also Art 13 on social and medical assistance.

[10] Social Security (Minimum Standards) Convention, 1952 (No 102); Employment Injury Benefits Convention, 1964 (No 121); Invalidity, Old-Age and Survivors' Benefits Convention, 1967 (No 128); Medical Care and Sickness Benefits Convention, 1969 (No 130); Employment Promotion and Protection against Unemployment Convention, 1988 (No 168).

[11] For example, Convention no 168 has been ratified by seven states; no 128 by 16 states, eight of them now members of the EU; and no 130 by 15, eight of them members of the EU.

entitled *The Three Worlds of Welfare Capitalism.* It focused on the 1970s and 1980s, the transitional period in our study. He distinguished the liberal, corporatist (or conservative) and social democratic (or universalistic) welfare states. In 1990, he held the archetypal examples of the liberal regime to be outside of Europe (the US and Canada). The characteristics of such systems are means-tested assistance and modest benefits, which should stimulate people to rely greatly on self-help and actively seek work. In Europe, the British regime came (particularly after the Conservative reforms from 1980 onwards) nearest to this type, notwithstanding its universalistic aspects.

The corporatist welfare state is favourable to social rights that loosen the dependence upon the labour market noticeably, but on the other hand are reserved mostly for those who worked before as employees or (if included) as self-employed. In addition, this regime tends towards the preservation of stratification and status differentials. It also aims to preserve the traditional family model; the family is seen as a provider of welfare. Esping-Andersen found this regime in Germany, France and, to a lesser extent, Italy, although there were striking differences between countries (eg in the areas of unemployment benefits and social assistance). The social democratic regime extends social protection to the new middle classes and attempts to promote equality between individuals (not families) by universalistic allowances, which must be of a high enough level to uphold a good standard of living. According to this system, benefits should contribute to reduce the family's contribution to welfare and therefore the individual's dependence on family. Social policy should enhance individual independence. Esping-Anderson attributed this regime to the Nordic countries and the Netherlands. The Nordic model shares strong state intervention with the corporatist model, but the interventionism is more egalitarian.

Esping-Anderson's typology was intensively discussed,[12] particularly in relation to the situation of southern European countries. Some suggested that their welfare regimes were not an undeveloped form of the conservative type but a separate type, characterised inter alia by a stronger concern for the family. Other typologies of welfare were put forward. One, focused on Europe, distinguishes between a Christian centrist and a social democratic group of countries. A third proposal took into account the gender perspective and distinguishes between a general family support model (eg Germany, France), a dual earner support (Nordic countries) and a market-oriented model (eg Britain). However, many social scientists still hold that real systems rarely correspond to ideal types.

---

[12] *Cf* Cousins (2005) 89ff; Pierson (2006) 171–77.

Stabilisation and Restructuring of the Welfare State (1979–2004)

General

Socio-economic Challenges and Changes in Ideas

Since the 1980s, the traditional European welfare systems have come under scrutiny and even attack. The growing scepticism about the welfare state first began in Britain, but other countries followed, sooner or later. The trigger for this new trend was the economic troubles of the 1970s. The slowdown or lack of economic growth coupled with rising unemployment reduced the state's capacity to finance social benefits and public services through public budgets. Competition, both inside the European Community (EC) (enlarged in three steps) and on an international scale, intensified throughout the 1980s, particularly after the establishment of the 'internal market' in 1986 (fully implemented in 1992) and the fall of the communist regimes in eastern Europe after 1989. This reduced the possibility for many enterprises to spend readily the same share of their earnings as before for financing the social system. The problems of welfare after 1989 are often attributed to globalisation (described in chapters 1 and 2 above). This raised expectations regarding the return on capital (often exaggerated), reduced the national possibilities for taxation, and appeared to diminish the share left for wages and social security. However, no consensus has been reached about the impact of globalisation on the welfare state.[13]

Additionally, the social systems that concentrated on (or were designed for) 'legally dependent' workers were challenged by the change in patterns of personal work, and a rising proportion of self-employed persons (see chapter 3 above). They had to decide whether they should include solely economically dependent workers or all self-employed, and how to deal with people who change between dependent and independent work. Perhaps even more important than these economic facts was that the socio-economic preconditions of social security also changed, as noted above. Perhaps the most decisive single factor was the increase in life expectancy. This has produced higher spending by the social system for pensions, particularly since the 1980s. This and the declining birth rate, resulting in fewer young people of working age, make it difficult to continue the 'generation contract'. The rising need for, and willingness of, women to participate in the labour market has had wide-reaching effects on employment, birth rates, preconditions for upbringing of children, and the possibilities for (long-term) personal care for the elderly and disabled by relatives. The widespread dissolution of the traditional family diminished the possibility of the social system relying on it,

---

[13] Cousins (2005) 47ff. A new study claims that the European welfare 'is not doomed' by globalisation: Begg et al (2008).

which had consequences for the situation of women (who could no longer be sure of derived benefits), for the unemployed, for those in need of long-term care and for single mothers, who need financial support. The increasing recognition of female interests and perspectives underpinned all this. Women demanded, and were entitled to, social rights of their own. Today's crucial question is whether social security enhances a specific family model—traditional or otherwise—or tries to be neutral with regard to the individual's choices. The social system greatly influences the possibility of reconciling professional and family life.

Due to the circumstances outlined above, politicians have often claimed that the economy could no longer afford to perpetually increase social rights. It is widely held that social policy has to be sustainable having regard to competition (primarily with the world outside the EC). In many countries, especially France and Britain, social policy therefore became a widely used tool for labour market aims. However, the changes in social security that European countries have witnessed over the past few decades cannot be attributed solely to changes in socio-economic surroundings: there has also been a remarkable change in the prevailing ideas. In the 'glorious age' of welfare (1950–75), the predominant opinion saw security provided by collective measures and solidarity not only as a means, but also as an end in itself. In contrast to this, the liberal school of thought, which has gained force, promotes the market, and social policy is relegated to second place.[14] The proponents of these ideas, both politicians and scholars, stress the dangers attributed to a fully implemented welfare state. They argue that too much safety endangers economic efficiency and undermines personal responsibility, and they criticise the fact that that benefits often reach not those who merit them, but instead those whose political representations are the most influential. Furthermore, many of these proponents doubted the efficiency of public services, and demanded the privatisation of these services. As a result of this, a more functionalistic view of social security developed. Nevertheless, some proponents of the liberal wing conceded that social security could be a positive productive factor and could facilitate the individual's ability to answer the economy's demand for flexibility—but only if social security is designed appropriately. It thus has the function of stabilising the increasingly precarious and unstable life of the individual. The goal of full employment, which guided politics until the 1980s, was not really abandoned, but became less dominant. It is even said that some governments (like that of Thatcher) used unemployment as a means to achieve their policy. The changes in law and attitude can often be seen in new leitmotifs, such as 'there is no such thing as society' (Thatcher), 'making work pay' (Britain under the Conservatives, and France under Sarkozy), 'help to self-help' (Britain under New Labour) and 'empowerment and responsibility' (*Fordern und Fördern*, Germany).

Another change in leading ideas concerns equality among the recipients of social security. In the past special regimes for specific groups, which existed in

---

[14] *Cf* eg Pierson (2006) 40–49.

many countries and mostly procured better benefits than the general system, were widely accepted. Scepticism towards these special regimes grew remarkably, at least since the 1990s, particularly where the benefits differed significantly and both systems needed subsidies paid out of taxes. This led to reforms to bring the special regimes, particularly those for public servants, more in line with the general system (eg Italy, France, less so in Germany). The changes in external facts and in ideas led to manifold changes in the systems of social security across Europe. However, the percentage of GDP spent on social matters mostly stayed at the same level (or even increased), declining in only a few countries (particularly in the Netherlands). In addition, since the 1980s social protection in many countries has even expanded in some areas, especially those of parenthood and long-term personal care.[15] However, many other benefits have been changed, as will be shown later. Even if these changes were small when considered individually, when viewed collectively they have the power to change a system profoundly.

From a structural point of view one has to look at the distribution of risks between individuals (or their employer) and community (social insurance, the taxpayer). A great variety of measures can shift the balance from the community to individuals (privatisation): exclusion of risks from the welfare system; restriction of the persons covered (eg by new or longer qualification periods, or by requiring more to seek or train for work); restriction of the benefits (eg by franchises; calculation of a cash benefit more closely linked to contributions); changes in financing which decrease solidarity and strengthen the correlation to individual risk; and the introduction of a means test.

A universalistic social system financed by taxes may have a greater redistributive effect than a group-oriented system financed by contributions. Contributions usually relate to the income of those insured, but are proportional and not progressive. It seems that many of the countries that include people with higher earnings (as most do) exclude income above a certain threshold from further contributions. This reduces the high redistributive effect of health insurance and of other flat-rate benefits. Contributions for the employee are shared in most countries by the employee and the employer, but the way in which this burden is split between the two parties varies greatly from country to country. In many countries, both parties are obliged to pay half or thereabouts (Germany, Britain); in others, the employer's part is greater (eg in France it is twice that of the employee). The employee's part is rarely greater, though this is the case in the Netherlands. In some countries, the allocation has been altered by shifting the burden onto the employed (eg Germany). Although some attach great importance to this distribution, the employer's share is also, economically speaking, part of the wage.

New ideas about the relationship between economy and social protection led

---

[15] There is also a discussion about 'securisation' of employment rights (eg training, paid holidays), which could improve the situation for employees with short-term employment contracts.

to the new concept of 'workfare regimes' as opposed to welfare regimes.[16] Workfare aims to stimulate innovation and flexibility, and subordinates social policy to the demands of the economy—especially its international competitiveness; cash benefits should be paid only to those able to work who actually work or are in training. In the 1990s, some authors expected that many welfare regimes would soon give way to workfare regimes. However, the implementation of some workfare measures, eg for the unemployed, does not mean that a full workfare regime has been adopted. Such regimes aim at even greater activation and flexibility than a liberal welfare regime. Thus, most say that the welfare state in western European has until now proved resilient. Only Ireland and, to a lesser extent, Denmark have changed to a workfare regime. The other countries retained a welfare system; some stayed in their group of welfare types (mentioned above), others changed between the conservative and the social democratic types.[17]

The Growing Influence of the EC

To date, the EC has not regulated any of the areas of social security, and no social benefits are paid by the EC itself. Social policy is seen as the last refuge of autonomy of the Member States. However, the EC theoretically has the power to legislate upon the 'social security and social protection of workers' (Article 137 EC). Nevertheless, hurdles of unanimity, subsidiarity and the limitation to workers restrict this power. Furthermore, it is doubtful whether the EC's competence would allow the establishment of transnational social benefits and solidarity.

Nevertheless, EC law and politics influence social security in various, increasingly significant, ways. The influence of open borders on economic autonomy and financing social security has already been noted. The Maastricht criteria for the introduction of a common currency, the euro, intensified the budget restrictions and heavily influenced national social policies, specifically in France and Italy. Both factors led to an institutional imbalance between the EC and the individual states with regard to social policy. It is not possible to outline here all the ways the EC influences social security, though some must be mentioned. The freedom of services often requires the social health service of a particular country to pay for services rendered in another country. This opens national systems up to comparison, though even the European Court of Justice (ECJ) does not require that national systems offer the same level of services.[18] But the ECJ increasingly deduces from the freedom of movement and the provisions on Union citizenship that the Member States have to grant social benefits also to people who do not belong to the traditional group of solidarity defined by a

---

[16] Jessup (2002).

[17] Vis (2007) 105.

[18] Case C-372/04 *Watts* [2006] ECR I-04325, paras 90, 100, 131–32; Case C-385/99 *Müller-Fauré and van Riet* [2003] ECR I-04509, para 98.

sufficient relationship to the nation state.[19] The Court thus requires a certain amount of transnational solidarity towards citizens of other Member States, which is seen as critical because it might shift too many financial burdens. Reshuffling the primarily national 'boundaries of welfare' might easily destabilise the basic architecture of the welfare states.[20]

Another important influence exercised by EC law on national social security systems stems from competition law. EC law permits the exclusion of competition in the field of social security only if the state-organised agencies undertake to refrain from competing with private undertakings or among themselves. However, competition law applies if these agencies compete, even in a restricted way. Thus Community law forces the states into either a regime without any competition or a regime that underlies the restrictions of competition law and so impedes intermediate solutions. The Charter on Fundamental Rights will acknowledge the right to social protection and basic assistance (Article 34 EC) as well as that to medical care (Article 35 EC), but only according to Community and national law. Since the late 1990s, the EC has invented a new tool to influence the Member States: the Open Method of Coordination (see chapter 2 above). This 'soft' method also applies to social policy. In 2006, the Social Protection Committee adopted a set of common indicators for the social protection and social inclusion process.[21]

European Social Model?

Politics at the European and national levels often allude to a European social model and claim that this is worth being preserved. Unfortunately, the content of such a model is not too clear.[22] However, one can say that social security is one of the core subjects, and that one cannot identify it with the liberal regime presented by Esping-Andersen. Even if one is sceptical about the typologies of welfare, one could agree that there is a common core of beliefs and provisions that characterises social policy in Europe, at least in those states which were Members before 2004. With this proviso, one may say that the model is characterised by the following points in particular: enforceable social rights in the case of important needs (and not only charity); means-tested social assistance that ensures the means to live in the case of (real) 'poverty' and unemployment; access to charge-free health care in at least severe cases for (most of) the employed, financed by the community or by insurance; and provision for old age benefits which, after a full working life, are above the level of social assistance. However, these features are not even present in all of the pre-2004 Member States.

---

[19] See eg Cases C-209/03 *Bidar* [2005] ECR I-02119, paras 57–60; C-138/02 *Collins* [2004] ECR I-02703, paras 69–72; C-456/02 *Trojani* [2004] I-07573, paras 37ff.

[20] See Ferrera (2005).

[21] Portfolio of overarching indicators; Brussels, 7 June 2006.

[22] Jepsen and Serrano (2006); Kaelble and Schmid (2006).

National Perspectives

In Britain after 1979, the Conservative government changed the welfare system—in at least some aspects, significantly. The conditions for some benefits became more selective and stringent, and the amount of some benefits declined remarkably in relation to the average income. The pension system was particularly affected. In 1981 the revaluation of pensions was tied to changes in prices rather than wages, which caused the basic pension to fall to 15% of average earnings in 1999. The importance of social assistance as a supplementary benefit increased even further. With regard to compulsory additional pensions, the government allowed their substitution by private, capital-oriented pension schemes, which were heavily subsidised. Responsibility for short-term sickness benefits shifted to employers from 1982 onwards. Both factors contributed to an increase in the importance of specialised systems, whilst at the same time the importance of the universalistic system declined. The organisation of hospitals was decentralised and partly privatised; private health insurance was encouraged by tax subsidies. Moreover, in 1979 many council house tenants got the right to buy their lodging, which privatised much public housing. Opponents of the Conservatives warned of the destruction of British welfare. Seen from further away, the changes do not seem to be so drastic; even the relative importance of spending on social policy did not decline. However, the reforms have changed the system profoundly. Inequality was no longer held to be undesirable.

After 1997, the New Labour government in Britain did not restore the old system, but remained committed to the concept of a mixed economy of welfare. However, the possibilities for opting out of the universal regime have been restricted. At the start of the Labour government the focus had been on the NHS and on labour market policy, where the motto of the 'Third Way' was 'welfare to work'. The new way attempted to enforce the relationship between social rights and corresponding duties of the beneficiaries. A big change was to no longer consider the different groups of people without work separately and try to bring them all into work. This has been a success for some groups, such as jobseekers and the young. However, the spending on long-term disability payments has sharply risen. The problem of long-time care remains unresolved. Britain now has one of the highest levels of inequality in the EU, and the highest risk of poverty among the old EU states. It seems that the political differentiation between applicants seen as 'worthy' and those seen as 'unworthy' for a benefit plays a greater role in Britain than in many other countries, although other systems are gradually following suit.

In Germany, cutbacks in the welfare system began to occur from as early as the 1970s. Conversely, there were also important expansions of benefits after 1978, especially with regard to child benefits, and a new insurance for long-term personal care (1995). Although the viability of the German welfare state had been questioned long before 1989, after the reunification, the German social system was extended, unchanged, to the former German Democratic Republic, and subsequently greatly financed by the west German *Länder*.[23] This aggravated the financial problems. After a growing debate throughout the 1990s, the turning point came in 2002 with the 'Agenda 2010' of the Schröder government. The 'Hartz IV' reform altered the system of unemployment benefits significantly. In the same period, Parliament altered the method for calculating pensions, and raised the pension age from 65 to 67 in the long run. These reforms not only changed the content of the social system profoundly, but also affected the way it was perceived by the public. Hitherto politicians had always declared that pensions were safe; subsequently, the public felt otherwise. Poverty amongst the elderly had been almost completely eradicated. However, poverty amongst younger people and, after Hartz IV, poverty of the unemployed has replaced it. Moreover, many now doubt whether the pension system will secure a future income above of the level of social assistance for most beneficiaries. Recently, compulsory health insurance has been extended to all who work and have no other (private) insurance; but pension insurance was extended solely to certain of the self-employed. Thus the specific social costs for dependent labour are high.

France has upheld its fragmented system of social security, although some changes since the 1980s have widened the personal scope of protection. In 1988, a universal minimum benefit to reintegrate people into work was introduced to supplement the fragmented means-tested benefits. The financial problems of welfare led to many discussions on reforms, but only a few materialised. One such reform was the introduction of a special tax for social insurance (*contribution sociale généralisée*), which is also levied on other kinds of income (including capital). The dependency of the insurance systems on paid contributions aggravated the social situation of those who have not worked long enough to get a benefit that allows a decent standard of living to be maintained. One can speak now of a two-tier social system. One answer to this problem was the introduction of contribution-free health 'insurance' for non-working people in 2000, which surprisingly provides for more benefits than the normal health insurance. The general pension system was reformed after 2000; the special regimes were reformed only later, and were fiercely fought over. To promote employment of the less qualified, many low-paid jobs were exempted from social contributions, which undermines the financing of social insurance.

In Italy, social protection, apart from the health service, was restricted to wage earners. Importantly, in the 1990s it was extended to cover economically dependent workers. Since the 1980s, the social system has come under severe financial pressure. The most important reasons for this were the pension system, which was then perhaps the most advantageous in Europe, and a pervasive 'underground' economy (which accounted for least 20% of the total economy). The pensions system, until recently, favoured early retirement (many '*baby-pensionati*'), allowed for many invalidity pensions without disabilities and

---

[23] The *Solidaritätszuschlag* represented only a small part of this redistribution; all social transfers amount to several hundred billion euro.

secured a very high replacement rate. In Italy, pensions took (and still take) a comparatively high percentage of the GNP. Large-scale reforms only began in the 1990s, triggered by the wish to join the euro. Since then there have been several pension reforms, altering most elements of the pension system; but the pension system is still generous in relation to other countries. Other social rights were and still are low in comparison. This applies particularly to social assistance (a general system still does not exist) and unemployment benefits. This may explain the high importance of dismissal protection. Another characteristic feature is an extremely high number of incapacity benefits, especially in the south. However, these benefits are frequently not granted according to need, but according to 'social evaluations' and clientism; they partly substitute unemployment benefits, but give much more than those benefits. The asymmetric and still fragmented structure of welfare makes the Italian regime quite ambiguous.

In the Netherlands, social expenses at the beginning of the 1980s were much higher than in neighbouring countries. In particular, the number of incapacity benefits was incredibly high (a fifth of the potential workforce), and its conditions extremely generous. People used incapacity benefits as a kind of high unemployment benefit. The Netherlands had no active labour market policies for a long time. However, incapacity benefits were radically reformed in 1995. Incapacity was now to be regularly reviewed, and recipients were required to take any acceptable work. Nevertheless, incapacity pensions are still more frequent then elsewhere. Apart from incapacity benefits, many other benefits were cut. The replacement rate was often reduced from 80 to 70%. Since then, the quota of Dutch GDP devoted to welfare has declined remarkably and is now at the west European average. Since 1996, only the employer (and no longer the social insurance system) has to pay in the case of sickness, and statute has shortened the periods of payment. Parliament privatised the risk because social sickness benefits were too widely used. In 1997, the administration of social insurances for the employed was significantly privatised: workers who earn above a relatively low threshold have to take health insurance with a private insurer; today, this affects 30% of all employed. In 1998, incapacity insurance for employed was also 'privatised': employers can choose to stay in the state system or can secure insurance privately. In 1999, the social partners agreed on an intensification of supplementary pensions. However, privatisation is not applied everywhere; even private hospitals must not be profit-oriented. Today, the Dutch system seems better adapted to flexibility of the labour market than other systems, particularly because it does not discriminate against part-time work.

At the start of the 1990s, Sweden was experiencing grave economic problems. Consequently, the replacement rates of pensions, sick pay and unemployment benefits were reduced. With regard to pensions, the contribution burden was partly shifted from the employers to the employees and the state, and the PAYG schemes were supplemented by partial capitalisation. The attention given to gender questions remained high. Sweden seems to be the most gender-friendly welfare system in Europe, and supports intensely the participation of both women and men in the labour market as well as in care work. The accrued importance of earnings-related benefits has somewhat reduced the redistributive character of the regime. The levels of poverty and income inequality are still low, although the latter has risen. Social assistance plays only a minor role.

Tendencies in Selected Areas

Sick Pay and Benefits

There is great variety across the European systems (discussed above) regarding the person obliged to pay these benefits. In the Netherlands, for instance, in 1996 the risk and burden were shifted to the employer. The maximum period of sickness benefits is frequently one year (France, Spain and the Netherlands); in Germany it is up to 79 weeks, and in Sweden there is no time limit. Some countries (eg Austria) reduced the length of sickness benefits; and in Sweden there was fierce discussion about this. Some countries (re)introduced a 'waiting period' of up to three days before sick pay becomes effective (eg in France, Britain, Sweden and Spain), partly to privatise this risk and partly to prevent misuse. However, many countries do not have such a waiting period (eg Germany, Austria). The amount of sick pay varies between 60% (Spain) and 100% (Denmark) of previous earnings; Germany reduced it from 100 to 80% in 1996. In Britain, sick pay consists of a (rather low) flat rate per week. The sickness benefit amounts to 80% in Sweden, 70% in Germany (after a reduction in 1996), the Netherlands and Spain, and about 50% in France, whilst the British lump sum typically works out as lower than these.

Old Age

Since the 1980s the systems of old age pensions[24] have come under financial pressure in all countries. The main challenge stemmed from the rise of the average period of pension payments due to the overall increase of life expectancy. In some countries the problems were also attributable to the rising number of early retirements. In many countries the average age of retirement dropped greatly after 1980, due partly to the generous possibilities for early retirement (especially after a long working life) and partly to the great number of incapacity benefits. After 1980, both means were widely used to absorb unemployment and facilitate the employment of youth, eg in Germany and the Netherlands. In Germany, the average period of payment rose from 10 to 17 years between 1960 and 2004; in other countries, the increase was even greater. However, even after efforts to reform the system, the proportion of working people aged between 55 and 64 still

---

[24] See OECD (2005).

varied greatly between European countries. For example, in 2006, the figure was 22% in Italy and 70% in Sweden.[25]

Another challenge to the pension systems stemmed from the altered role of women. Gender equality and concern over the birth rate increasingly led to demands for women to have entitlements in their own right rather than merely derived pension rights. In work-related pension regimes women who stayed at home to raise children were only covered by a survivor's pension. This basic feature of the system was retained, although it has been moderated. Significantly, some countries (eg Germany, Britain and Austria) now count specific periods of child rearing in the same way as working periods, although a minimum period of paid labour is still necessary for entitlement to a pension.[26] In contrast, countries with a universal system have no major problems in according every partner a pension in her or his own right, because the entitlement is linked solely to length of residence in the country.

Furthermore, the financing of social security has been eroded by unemployment and also, in many countries (eg Germany, but not France), by a decline in the birth rate since 1970, which has reduced the number of young people joining the workforce since the 1990s. These developments have often led to heavy burdens on the budget to finance pensions. Although many states had envisaged a tax-funded subsidy to the pension system, most countries could no longer afford the greater burdens caused by the pensions envisaged in past legislation; thus they tried to make their pension systems affordable and sustainable.

Since the 1980s, there has been a growing tendency amongst European countries to alter the national pension system. However, no western European country has abandoned the basic concept of the PAYG principle and followed the World Bank's advice to switch to capital accumulation and privatise pensions. Nevertheless, some countries, for instance Britain and, more recently, Sweden and Germany, have complemented their traditional system with such systems. Although no system has been radically changed, many have undergone various modifications which together amount to a major reorientation. Some countries made their reforms as early as the 1990s (the first reform in Germany); others followed later (France and Austria in 2003; the second reform in Germany).

One objective of the reforms was to keep people in work for longer. For some years now, the EC has recommended that all people should work until 65. Thus, countries with a low statutory pension age raised it: for example, Italy raised the statutory age from 60 (for men)/55 (for women) to 65/60, Germany raised it first from 60 to 65 then to 67 in 2005 (the female pension age having already been adjusted to 65). However, these changes came under attack in both countries.

[25] In percentages: Sweden 70, US 58, Britain 50, Germany 47, OECD 45, France 40, the Netherlands 39, Austria 27 and Italy 22.5.
[26] Another way to secure pensions benefits for the spouse would be to always split the earner's pension entitlement with the partner; the earner would then get a lower pension than without splitting. However, no country with a group- and earnings-related pension system took this path. Germany applies the splitting solely in the case of a divorce.

Many countries still have different pension ages for men and women, eg Austria (65/60), whereas some countries had a long-established, unified retirement age for both sexes (France, 60; Spain, 65). Alternative tactics for making the pension system more viable included raising the hurdles for incapacity benefits or for early retirement, such as introducing deductions in cases of early retirement (eg Germany, the Netherlands: 2% for each year). Additionally, some countries reduced social contributions for older workers as an incentive for both employers and employees to continue in employment.

A further measure used by some countries to restore the balance of pension systems was the strengthening of the relationship between paid contributions and the pension itself. The period of contributions required for the maximum pension was frequently extended, eg in France to 40 years instead of 37.5. Furthermore, some non-contributing periods that had previously counted towards the pension were abolished (eg university/college attendance). Countries where the pension's amount depended on previous income extended the period of reference for calculating the secured income. In France, it was extended from 10 to 25 years. However, in Germany the whole working life was always taken into consideration. All these measures reduce the replacement rate and strengthen the 'equivalence' between paid contributions and pension, thereby narrowing the gap between a social pension and the principles of private insurance. However, in Germany there have been recent efforts to loosen this relation again by raising low pensions.

Some countries (eg Sweden, Germany) introduced a demographic factor into the pension formula. This was designed to ensure that the average pension declines when life expectancy rises. In addition, the rules related to the revaluation (indexation) of pensions have often been reformed. Germany switched from gross to net wage indexation in 1992. Britain and France changed from a wage to a price index in 1982 and 1987 respectively. Many commentators believed then that this would reduce the increases. In 1995, Italy changed the system for revaluating pensions from a price index to an index related to the GNP. In Germany the wage index, combined with the demographic factor, resulted in the plateauing of pensions over a period of two years, whereas a price index would have led to increases.

In many countries, the various measures of reform have significantly reduced the replacement rate. In 2004, the net replacement of a (male) wage earner with an average income varied greatly, between 100% in Greece and 47% in Britain.[27] The rates for people who earned half or twice the average income are almost equal in some countries, such as Germany and Italy. In other countries, the replacement percentage falls sharply with rising income, as in Britain and France. These reductions could potentially reach a point where the average pension after lifelong work does not much exceed the level of social assistance. This threatens

[27] OECD (2005). In percentages: Austria 93 (before the great reform), Italy 88, Germany 71, France 68, Sweden 68 and Belgium 63. In some countries, the figure relates only to the basic system.

one of the main objectives of the traditional pension scheme: inducing people to work. In Germany, there is already discussion on this matter.

In many countries, survivor's pensions, especially those of widows, had traditionally been generous. Since the 1980s, widowers have had the same rights as widows in almost every country, partly due to EC equality law. However, since the 1990s, many countries have reformed the survivor's pensions, sometimes radically (eg the Netherlands). The replacement rate has often been reduced, and many people have been rendered ineligible on grounds of their own, higher income. Many cuts in the pension schemes affected only the younger generations. Pensioners and people near retirement were often spared the reforms and cuts; a decision which reflects their electoral strength. Future pension policies will have to confront the fact that older people will soon constitute nearly half of the electorate.

In some countries, the 'normal' or basic pension scheme procures only a basic benefit. Countries using this system often established—sometimes already the period 1945–78—a second, compulsory pension system that followed different rules. Since 1960 all Swedish workers have been obliged to adhere to such a scheme; in France (since 1961), Britain and the Netherlands all employed persons are now also included. The complementary schemes initially had mostly defined benefits, although the rules were more insurance-like. In some countries (eg Sweden), this scheme provides higher payments than the basic scheme; in others its importance is much lower (France). The complementary pension in Britain (SERPS; now SSP) was particularly important to the national system. However, the Conservatives allowed employers to avoid adherence to this scheme by opting out and adopting a 'voluntary' pension scheme, which is capital-oriented. Opting out was heavily subsidised by a tax break, which was subsequently reduced by the Labour government. The Dutch system now relies heavily on pensions funds. Sweden has introduced a scheme with defined contributions. Countries such as Germany and Italy, where the standard scheme had long provided a decent replacement rate, did not establish such a second compulsory system.

Optional additional schemes have gained increasing acceptance in recent decades. It was widely held that the social systems could no longer provide a pension sufficient to replace the wage income. Thus many countries (Britain, and later Sweden, Italy and Germany) tried to induce the employers or the employee to adhere by tax relief. The additional scheme typically works through defined contributions and capital accumulation, eg in Germany (*Riester-Rente*, introduced 2001) and Britain. Notwithstanding the complementary and additional schemes, traditional social pensions are still the cornerstone of old age benefits in most European countries.

Occupational Accidents and Illnesses, and Incapacity Benefits

In most European countries the main rules relating to occupational risks have stayed unchanged over recent decades. However, the administrative focus of this branch was increasingly oriented towards prevention rather than benefits. The number of fatal accidents at work has decreased in almost all European countries and all industries compared to the 1970s, although the number is still very high in some countries (eg Spain). New problems arose with the spread of illnesses that may or may not be attributed to an occupation (eg burn-out, depression). The focus on prevention was enforced by EC legislation, notably the Framework Directive 89/391/EEC on health and safety at the workplace. This, and the bulk of special Directives, led to stricter legislation in some countries. The EC also established an Agency for Safety and Health at Work.

The definitions of occupational accidents and risks are still debated, eg with regard to work-induced stress. Recently, in France a stress-induced suicide was recognised as a work accident. However, countries such as Sweden restricted their generous definition of 'covered risk'. Many countries still provide a benefit in the case of permanent incapacity, with a substitution rate above 75%, though these comparatively generous benefits and the possibility of receiving them in conjunction with other benefits have come under criticism. In the Netherlands the reform of incapacity benefits also reduced the occupational accident benefits. In some countries, the issue of employer's liability in the case of an occupational accident is being discussed again, partly because the substitution of this liability by social insurance often disadvantages the injured.

Until 1980, incapacity benefits primarily served to sustain people who were really incapacitated or disabled. After 1980, it seems that they were widely used in some countries to hide unemployment; less frequently, they were also abused by fraudulent claimants. Both strategies were quite prominent in Italy (benefits were a tool for clientilism) and the Netherlands. It was only later, and to a lesser extent, that such tactics became important in Britain and Austria—in the latter case, particularly after the country's restriction of old age pensions. Today, many countries attempt to restrict the access to incapacity benefits in order to keep people in work. A key technique for achieving this goal and for reducing incapacity claimants is a stricter definition of the term 'incapacity'. For instance, in Germany until the 1990s it was sufficient that the person was unable to perform the work he had previously been capable of. Since then, benefits are paid only if the person is unable to do any work available on the labour market; and they will also not be paid if the capacity to work could be restored by retraining. In the Netherlands, a similar retrenchment successfully began in the late 1990s. In Britain, incentives and pressure to get people with incapacity back to work have been increased. In Italy, the reform and curtailment of incapacity benefits has not yet begun. However, it must be borne in mind that people with a partial incapacity often lack the chance to get a suitable job.

Unemployment and Social Assistance

Unemployment rose significantly in many European countries from the 1980s (see chapter 3 above). Nevertheless, the main features of social protection remained untouched, especially that of compulsory insurance, which in most countries covers only dependent workers. In many countries, unemployment led to an increase in social security contributions paid by the rest of the workforce (the percentage was increased); this particularly affected contributions to the unemployment system, but also affected other regimes. However, Germany recently illustrated that the specific contributions can also be reduced. Across Europe the rising unemployment triggered a profound reappraisal of priorities and perspectives. Since the 1970s, the importance of an active labour market policy (eg training) had already increased. The focus then shifted to a labour market policy whose prior aim is to 'activate' the jobless; this shift occurred earlier in the Nordic countries and Britain (1980s) than in continental Europe. The Nordic countries place a high value on such policies. In Sweden, the govern-ment spends as much money on active labour market measures as on benefits. In many countries (eg Germany, the Netherlands), this new orientation led to an immense number of 'tools', which often help to conceal the true rate of unem-ployment. Other measures led to a 'second' labour market, characterised by state-subsidised labour, competing with the 'first' (see chapter 3 above).

Another new aspect was the stricter set of rules for benefits. The waiting period (period of contributions paid before becoming eligible for the benefit) varies greatly between four months (France) and two years (Britain). Long waiting periods disadvantage those who only take up short-term employment. The rules regarding suitable work have become more severe. For instance, since 1995 in Germany, an unemployed person is obliged to accept any kind of job with a salary of at least a certain percentage of the former wage, this percentage decreasing with the length of the payment. There are also stricter obligations to take part in training programmes. In addition, the length of the payment of benefits and their amount vary greatly from country to country. Rising unem-ployment has led to shorter periods of benefits in some countries (eg in Germany from 1995), but other countries have lengthened them. As was the case before the 1980s, unemployment benefits in most countries are wage related; Britain has a flat rate. The rates of replacement are similar in many countries in the case of short-term unemployment (eg 65% of the net earnings in Germany), but national differences are more pronounced in the case of long-term unemploy-ment. The rate has often been reduced (eg in France in 1992 in the case of long-term unemployment), particularly in cases where it had previously been at a remarkably high level (eg Sweden saw a reduction from 100 to 80%). Neverthe-less, benefits are still generous in France and Sweden, as opposed to the situation in Britain. Finally, in Italy, the replacement rate was only 15% until the 1990s; now it is at 40%, with a low ceiling.[28]

Many countries provide a second, special benefit for the unemployed after the 'first' benefit has expired. This benefit is of particular importance in countries where the rate of long-term unemployment is high (eg Germany). Although this

---

[28] For bigger enterprises there exists a special, very generous regime.

second benefit is usually means tested, it can be more favourable than social assistance. It usually pays only over a certain period (eg France, the Netherlands and Sweden). Only Britain and Austria provide a second benefit without a time limit (albeit in Britain often on a much lower level than in Austria). Benefit reforms have also affected these 'second' unemployment benefits; they have been reduced, submitted to a deep ongoing reform (eg Germany in 2003) or even been abolished (eg the Netherlands in 2004).

The most noticeable reforms took place in Denmark, Britain and Germany. In Denmark, where unemployment was high, the reform of 1993 tended to activate the jobless by a policy of 'carrot and stick'. The benefits were, at least for low-paid people, generous and, additionally, paid over a long period of time (initially seven years, later reduced to four): though only if the unemployed person did their utmost to return to employment. Jobless were expected to be active in every dimension (looking for a job, training). In sharp contrast, in Britain the replacement rate of unemployment benefits fell to 25% in the 1990s. The Labour government later adopted new principles: unemployed people must be active jobseekers in order to receive benefits. Their relation to the state is seen more as a contractual one. They get allowances (Jobseeker's Allowance) only if they undertake to fulfil their promises to train and seek a job. The first objective of the new policy was to bring people in to work, especially young people. Another tool is working tax credits, where the state pays a part of the salary. In other countries such measures are controversial, since they may induce employers to reduce wages further.

In Germany, the Hartz IV reform was enacted in 2003. Before this, the 'second' unemployment benefit had been wage related and paid without a time limit. In 2003, it was merged, along with social assistance, into the new benefit *Arbeitslosengeld II* for all those who are able to work. This new benefit is means tested, and has harsh rules regarding suitable work and reliance on savings. Furthermore, the reform drastically reduced the period of the 'first' unemployment benefit from three years to one; after this period, there is now typically only a flat-rate allowance and high pressure to get back into paid work, even if a new job pays less. This change has profoundly affected the German social system. It particularly affects the middle class—at least potentially. According to some, the new 'incentives' reduced unemployment. Nevertheless, in 2007 Parliament repealed a cornerstone of the reform and enlarged the period of *Arbeitslosengeld I* for older people again.

In recent years the European Commission has focused on flexibility of employment and the relationship between dismissal protection and benefits for jobseekers. It argues that intense retraining and favourable benefits combined with a low level of dismissal protection leads to greater efficiency than high protection combined with low benefits. The Danish policy was cited as a model. However, the reforms in Germany and, to a lesser extent, Britain do not fit into this picture. In Germany, dismissal protection has remained unaltered, but benefits have become lower. The policy to make people work also affected other non-working people such as those with disabilities, single mothers and other people potentially able to work. In many countries these groups are being 'asked' more actively to be prepared to work according to stricter rules for—often lower—benefits. This has intensified the disciplinary function of benefits and changed their nature into a reward—not for contributions or citizenship, but for 'effort'. Help presupposes self-help. This emphasises the individual's responsibility for their choices. According to some, this individualisation and the spirit underlying these reforms are at odds with solidarity. However, some say that it represents a new form of solidarity, more oriented towards equality of opportunities than to equality of outcomes.

The rules on social assistance remained largely unchanged after 1980, although some countries (eg Sweden in 1997) reduced the level of payment. However, Italy still has no general scheme, although even the World Bank demands a basic safety net. There is not space here to discuss this at length. However, the French case should be mentioned. In 1988, France introduced a special minimum benefit to reintegrate people into work. Combined with a rather high minimum wage (SMIC), it reduced the incentive to work. Attempts were made to remedy this with a new form of tax credit for poorly paid workers. In consequence, 40% of all workers now earn only up to 130% of the SMIC. Britain introduced similar tax credits. The trend to bring people to work also affected social assistance. Many countries (eg Germany, France, Britain and the Netherlands) qualified this benefit by the willingness to work, including for those people who can work only partially. The unemployed stand to lose the basic cash benefit if this willingness is lacking. Sometimes they are even obliged to accept work that earns less than the unemployment benefit itself.

In some countries (eg Germany), the importance of social assistance also grew for recipients of a 'normal' social benefit, eg a pension or unemployment benefit. If the level of these benefits is lower than that of social assistance, this can negatively affect the willingness of people at the lower end of the labour market to contribute and to work. The cuts of some social benefits brought them nearer to the level of social assistance, eg in Germany and Britain. Where social benefits are linked to contributions, many low-earners may question whether work does indeed pay. This could endanger the obvious function of social security of securing loyalty to state and society. It should also be kept in mind that many people who are entitled to a means-tested benefit do not claim it because they fear social stigma.

Parenthood

The provisions for maternity leave for the employed were further developed after 1980. Directive 92/85/EEC provides for a paid leave of 14 weeks for employees. Some countries, such as Germany, have gone no further, whilst other countries have lengthened the period of paid leave (eg in Italy to 4 months) and some provide for further unpaid leave. With regard to maternity benefits in cash during the leave, in Nordic countries all mothers are entitled to these benefits, whereas other countries restrict the benefit to the insured employees. The benefit's amount for insured mothers is wage related, with a high replacement rate.

Before the 1990s, most countries had already introduced some kind of parental leave regulation. The Framework Directive 96/34/EC introduced a minimum level, but leaves it to the states to determine whether or not the leave is paid. The length varies between six months (Britain) to two or three years or more (Germany, France and Italy). However, some countries (Britain and southern Europe) do not provide for payments during the leave or do so only for a shorter period. Other countries are more generous. In Nordic countries, benefits are often wage related, whereas continental states tend to prefer a flat rate. The details of parental leave reflect prevailing family policy, eg if the father has to take a part of the leave in order to receive (longer) benefits (eg Sweden). France and Italy are more oriented towards the mother's return to work; until recently, the German system was centred on the male-breadwinner model. Similar variation can be observed with regard to the allowance paid to parents (mothers) who stay at home for childcare. The Nordic countries, in particular, have introduced such allowances, while in Germany and Austria they are under discussion.

With regard to child or family allowances, many states have changed over the past few decades from employment-related to universal cash benefits. Only Britain and the southern European countries still have employment-based benefits. Most countries have no further restrictions. However, in southern Europe, benefits are still means tested. In most states, the benefit increases with the second or further child. Benefits are typically paid until the child reaches an age of between 18 and 20, but longer if the child studies. Child benefits are the most generous in France and Belgium, and lowest in southern Europe. The rise in female work participation has increased the importance of childcare provision. In most countries, many children aged between three and six attend institutional childcare. The percentage is higher in France and Sweden than in Germany or southern Europe. In many countries public childcare must still be paid for, albeit often with a means test, whereas higher education may be free (eg Germany). Childcare for children under the age of three has long had a prominent place in France; the Nordic countries followed suit from the 1980s onwards, the Netherlands in the 1990s. However, in many other countries (eg Germany) external care for the youngest children is still much less socially accepted and available.

Conclusion: the Changing Idea of the Welfare State

The welfare state is still alive in western Europe, although it has undergone important changes since its establishment 60 years ago. The continued importance of high public spending on welfare can be seen in most countries. Both the liberal right as well as the far left have long doubted that welfare is compatible with a market economy.[29] The past 60 years in Europe have shown that a high level of welfare can coexist with an economy where the market plays a great role. Moreover, the economic results have not differed much between countries with a liberal approach to welfare and those with a more collectivistic approach. It remains an open question if this will remain the case in the future.

Membership of the EU has not compelled Member States to harmonise their systems. There are still different models of social policy, often with significant differences between national rules at one level or another—though on the surface, the differences appear to have diminished. In any case, the EU increasingly influences the political goals that affect welfare, such as increasing the employment rate and avoiding public deficits. It might also endanger the foundations of solidarity.

Although the total level of social benefits has not decreased, the structure of welfare has changed since 1980. The changes have been implemented mostly step by step, and to a certain extent are 'path-dependent', although a wave of minor changes can alter a system's character. One main factor of change has been the rising importance of benefits for parenthood, unemployment and personal care. Another major change relates to the scope of social security. Since 1945, many states have extended their social protection beyond dependent labour (some to a greater, some a lesser extent), especially with regard to health care, pensions and parenthood. The pre-war tendency towards a universal system at least continued, albeit often not in the way of social insurance but by a tax-funded system.

A third tendency is the gradual demise of the male-breadwinner model in reality and as a paradigm for social policy. In many states an increase in the social rights of women, independent from their spouse, accompanied the rise in female labour market participation. This particularly affected benefits in the cases of parenthood and pensions. Some innovations in social policy were copied in other states, although policies have seldom been genuinely transplanted. An example seems to be the policy of activating labour, which was first introduced in some Nordic states and Britain, and later adopted by other countries.

There are no common European developments that apply to all national systems and all kinds of benefits. However, there seems to be a general tendency with regard to the prevailing ideas. The old paradigm of social security, which lasted until the 1980s, expressed a humanitarian belief combined with a predilection for collective solutions, which also assumed a collective responsibility for most social problems. The 'New Way' of social policy seems to be less collectivistic: the individual is, to a certain extent, held responsible for negative events, or at least for insuring himself against the possibility of such an event occurring. This is not in line with the original concept that the state should help those who cannot help themselves. However, it might be argued that many people today are more able to help themselves than the socially insured were in

---

[29] Pierson (2006) 41–65.

the past. The 'New Way', with its mixed approach of collectivistic and individual protection, accounts for this new mixed form of dependency. Furthermore, a more functionalistic approach has emerged. Social benefits now more frequently require a real need, and some market elements are accepted if this is compatible with the social objective. However, the boundary between social and private insurance becomes opaque if the state subsidises certain private decisions.

Social regimes are often classified according to the degree of universalism, comprehensiveness and decommodification they entail. The comprehensiveness of most European systems has increased, at least because protection has been extended to some needs previously not covered, such as parenthood and care. In no country has the degree of universalism been reduced; in many, it has been increased. Only the extent of decommodification has varied over time. From 1950 to 1980, the extension of social benefits greatly reduced the dependency of the employed on the labour market; after 1980 a gradual but steady recommodification took place in many respects (conditions and replacement rate), which reversed the former tendency. The benefits for jobseekers, the sick, those with disabilities and other recipients of social assistance are now more—and often much more—related to the willingness to work. Only benefits in the case of parenthood are nowadays linked less to work than before, though in any case they are seldom enough to live on.

However, even where benefits have not improved, one should always be aware that social benefits are embedded in the context of the specific country. The differences in the average income between different European countries increased after 1945 and are significant even today.[30] There are big differences in the wealth of nations even in western Europe. This does not merely influence the possibilities to spend, but also the perception of benefits. A standard of living afforded by a benefit may seem generous in relation to the average income in one country, but meagre in another. Moreover, the standard of living affordable by an average German pension in the 1960s may seem to be below the poverty line in present-day Germany—but may still be above the level of pensions in eastern Europe.

Social benefits influence the daily life of an ever-increasing proportion of the European population. To take a single example, in Germany, where social security is still centred on dependent labour, it is estimated that nearly as many people live off social benefits alone as those from their own work. The implications of this for economic efficiency and the political system could be serious.

---

[30] For example, the GNP per person in Portugal today is only at 70% of the EU average.

7

Collective Labour Relations

ANTOINE JACOBS

Introduction

It is well known that structures and institutions in the field of labour relations show considerable tenacity. Once established, they are not prone to change, among other things because they are concerned with power structures in society. They are at the heart of the social fabric. The introduction of new elements is often resisted and more often than not rejected.[1] Changes can, however, be detected if history is analysed over the course of a much more protracted period.

In *The Making of Labour Law in Europe*,[2] I described, on the basis of the Weberian method of 'ideal types',[3] the development of collective labour relations in modern times along the lines of three 'models': repression, toleration and recognition. Broadly speaking, the period between 1790 and 1860 was the period of repression of collective labour relations; the period from 1860 to 1918 was that of their toleration; and the period from 1918 onwards was that of their recognition, although it had to be conceded that 'repression' had returned in the 1920s and 1930s in the dictatorial regimes in Italy, Germany, Spain, Portugal and some other European countries. Ultimately it was the victory of the democratic powers in western Europe at the end of the Second World War that definitively secured toleration and recognition of free collective labour relations in western Europe. However, one had to await the 1970s before this model spread to Spain, Portugal and Greece, and the 1990s before it spread to the countries in central and eastern Europe.

It is the aim of this chapter to explore how collective labour relations have further developed in the democracies of Europe since the end of the Second World War. The chapter will highlight the developments in the constitutions, statutes and judicial decisions, establishing the rules of collective labour relations

---

[1] Fahlbeck (2002) 131.
[2] Jacobs (1986) ch 5.
[3] Weber (1954) 256.

in the various countries. However, as Veneziani has reminded us,[4] the relevance of the written law in this area is secondary compared with the impact of some significant variables of the industrial macrosystem, such as the technological characteristics of an industrial community, market and budgetary constraints, and the locus and distribution of power in the wider, globalised society.

Reconstruction: Building the Pillars of Collective Rights (1945–50)

When arms were laid down across Europe in 1945, the peoples and their governments had to face the rebuilding of their nations. It soon became clear that this reconstruction had to take place along partly old and partly new lines. In western Europe the dictatorial systems had been defeated by the democracies, so obviously the old principles and practices of the liberal democratic states, in force before 1940, could stay in place or be revived. On the other hand, it was widely felt that those principles and practices could not continue or return unmodified. Many believed that a new world had to be built also in the area of labour law and collective labour relations. This ambiguity marked the immediate post-war period in western Europe.

Various countries saw the continued existence or the re-emergence of free trade unions and employers' associations. Notably, on the employers' side the organisational structures that had been formed before the Second World War were continued or revived. Everywhere employers organised themselves along the inherited divisions between big industry, public enterprises, small and medium-sized enterprises and farmers. Sometimes 'social' employers' organisations existed alongside mere 'economic' employers' organisations, and in a number of continental countries there was also a division along ideological lines, notably by Christian employers' associations besides others.[5]

On the trade union side, however, at the end of Second World War there was a strong ideal of uniting the trade union movement, which in several countries had been deeply divided before the war. In the Nordic countries a largely unitary trade union movement re-emerged. In Germany, under pressure of the occupying authorities, unitary, pragmatic and non-ideological trade unions were created. However, in the Benelux countries, France and Italy this ambition, although initially realised,[6] succumbed after only a short spell, notably because the Christians preferred to revive their own unions. Another source of division was the outbreak of the cold war, which caused schisms, notably in France and Italy. In Britain craft, branch and general unions, and the demarcation disputes

---

[4] Veneziani (2004) 162.
[5] Windmuller and Gladstone (1984).
[6] In Italy in the *Patto di Roma*, 1944.

between them, continued to exist because there was no strong unifying centre. Irish unions still were very much divided over the problem of the allegiance of workers to British-based unions. At the global level, the idea of trade union unity was embodied, immediately after the Second World War, in the establishment of the unitary World Federation of Trade Unions (WFTU). However, the outbreak of the cold war in 1948 incited the non-communist trade unions to withdraw from the WFTU. The independent and social democratic unions formed the International Confederation of Free Trade Unions, and the Christian unions the World Confederation of Labour.[7]

During the Second World War in several countries in western Europe politicians of the left and the right, together with employers and trade union leaders, had forged forms of co-operation in the resistance to the Nazi and fascist regimes. When free democratic societies were restored, these experiences were a fertile soil for post-war cooperation, which in some countries even led to agreements between the resurgent organisations of employers and workers in which they recognised each other and showed their willingness to co-operate in the reconstruction of the country: in Belgium, in 1944, the draft agreement of social solidarity[8]; in the Netherlands, in 1945, the establishment of the Foundation of Labour[9]; and in Finland, the agreement of mutual recognition of 1940, renewed in 1944 and 1946.[10] In contrast, in other European countries, such as Italy[11] and Greece, the period immediately after the Second World War was dominated by intensive power struggles between communists and anti-communists, which poisoned industrial relations.

After the Second World War the trade union movement in many European countries quickly gained a large increase in membership, and it was able to maintain that level during three subsequent decades (see Table 7.1). Almost everywhere in western Europe this growth was certainly due to the rapid expansion of both the industrial sector and the public service sector, accompanied by a corresponding decline in agriculture in the 1950s and 1960s. However, the levels of trade union membership varied substantially between countries and, within countries, between one sector and the other.

Trade union law had to be re-established on a democratic basis in Italy and Germany. In these countries trade union freedom was explicitly laid down in the Constitutions of 1948 (Article 39) and 1949 (Article 9III) respectively. In the other democracies trade union freedom was restored to how it had been before 1940. In these countries the rights on organisation in trade unions were traditionally based on constitutional provisions and statutes proclaiming the freedom of association in general positive terms (the Netherlands, Denmark) or on specific laws on trade unions (France, Belgium), or in terms of negative

[7] Vom Beyme (1980) 9–31.
[8] Van Acker (1977) 55.
[9] Windmuller (1969).
[10] Hasselbalch (2002) 21.
[11] Ginsborg (1990) 72–120.

Table 7.1: Trade Union Density in European Countries 1960–2005 (rate of organisation as percentage of the working population)

	1960	1965	1970	1975	1980	1985	1990	1995	2000	2005
Sweden	62	76	78	75	78	81	82	87	80	76
Finland	32	38	51	65	69	69	73	80	75	72
Denmark	57	58	60	69	79	78	75	77	75	72
Belgium	42	40	42	52	54	52	54	56	49	52
Ireland	50	54	59	62	64	60	57	52	41	37
Italy	25	26	37	48	50	43	39	38	35	34
Austria	68	66	63	59	57	52	47	41	37	33
Britain	40	40	45	48	51	46	39	33	30	29
Greece					39	38	38	34	27	23
Netherlands	40	37	37	38	35	28	24	25	23	22
Germany	35	33	32	35	35	35	31	29	25	22
Portugal					62	54	32	25	21	17
Spain					19	10	13	16	17	15
France	20	20	22	22	18	14	10	9	8	9

Source: J Visser, ICTWSS Database, Amsterdam, Institute for Advanced Labour Studies, 2008.

immunities from common law doctrines that had made unions unlawful as in restraint of trade and had prevented them from organising action (Britain, Ireland). In some countries (Denmark, the Netherlands) trade unions and employers associations were treated as normal legal persons, quite similar to other associations, on the basis of the general law of associations. In other countries (Britain, Ireland and France) they were under special statutory regimes, which they accepted, but in a few (Germany, Italy and Belgium) a majority of trade unions refused to register as ordinary associations, so were associations *sui generis*. The rights and obligations of the unions differed from one country to the other.

In many European countries, collective bargaining was already widely practised before the Second World War, but it was only after the war that it became the most common way of fixing working conditions everywhere in non-communist Europe (see Table 7.2). However, in many a country the government wanted to keep a firm grip on the fixing of working conditions. This was the case not only in Germany under the occupation of the allied forces,[12] but also, for instance, in the Netherlands, where after the liberation of 1945 the two Acts on collective agreements of 1927 and 1937 had been restored but encapsulated in a system of wage restraint, laid down in the Extraordinary Decree on Labour

---

[12] Direktive Nr 14 des Kontrollrates von 12.10.1945; text in Blanke et al (1975) 159–60.

Table 7.2: The Coverage of Collective Bargaining in European Countries 1960–2005 (as a percentage of the non-independent working population)

	1960	1965	1970	1975	1980	1985	1990	1995	2000	2005
Austria	95	95	95	95	95	95	99	99	99	99
Belgium	80	80	85	90	97	96	96	96	96	96
France	70	70	70	76	85	90	92	95	95	95
Sweden	70	70	70	70	70	70	88	90	91	92
Finland	63	66	73	77	77	77	81	81	86	90
Netherlands	70	77	76	76	78	79	82	86	86	82
Denmark	67	68	68	70	72	74	69	69	80	80
Spain					68	70	76	78	81	82
Portugal					70	74	79	69	70	70
Greece					70	70	70	70	70	70
Germany	80	80	87	78	78	75	72	68	63	63
Italy	71	70	68	65	65	65	63	61	60	60
Britain	67	67	68	72	70	64	54	36	36	35

Source: J Visser, ICTWSS Database, Amsterdam, Institute for Advanced Labour Studies, 2008.

Relations 1945.[13] In Belgium the government tried more informal controls over wage determination through national labour conferences in 1946 and 1948, where the main lines in the development of wages, taxes and social security schemes were fixed in agreement with labour and management, sometimes underpinned by statutory wage freezes.[14]

France abolished the labour laws of the Vichy regime, but in 1946 adopted a new Act on collective agreements, which had a rather interventionist character to serve the wages policies of the government of the day.[15] In Sweden, the standing practice of central wage negotiations between the central confederations of workers and employers could bring enough order without the need for government intervention. In Italy the government was satisfied by the introduction, in 1945–46, of national intersectoral and sectoral wage agreements, which obliged the parties at enterprise level not to seek improvements on their own account. In Denmark, in 1945, the role of government mediators was re-enforced.[16] Also, in Ireland the government built on the wish for more orderly wage bargaining by developing conciliation and mediation in industrial conflicts by a new Labour Court, established in 1946.[17] In Britain the government, employers and unions

[13] Windmuller (1969) 331–41.
[14] Magrez-Song (1983) 597–612.
[15] Despax (1966) 44–49.
[16] Galenson (1952) 109.
[17] von Prodzynski (1992) 76.

agreed, in 1945, on the continuation of the wartime Order 1305 of 1940, which empowered the government to impose arbitration on the bargaining parties. The reality was, however, that these possibilities were hardly used as the employers and unions, who were closely involved in socio-economic decision-making, conducted themselves in a very orderly manner, and between 1948 and 1950 there was a period of voluntary wage restraint.[18] In Luxembourg the post-war government introduced a system of compulsory conciliation and mediation in wage conflicts, for which purpose the *Office National de Conciliation* was established.

At the legal and political level, a debate arose about more solid anchors for fundamental rights in Europe. As a reaction to the violation of human rights by Nazism and fascism, the idea had emerged that fundamental rights, including freedom of trade union association, the right to collective bargaining and the right to strike, should be better protected in the democratic states than had been the case before the Second World War.

Consequently, this development, which already had its roots before the Second World War in the constitutions of Weimar Germany, the International Labour Organisation (ILO) and the Irish Republic, now became a trend: the inclusion of one or more of these fundamental collective labour relations rights in national constitutions, such as those of France (1946), Italy (1948), Luxembourg (1948) and Germany (1949), at the European level (the European Convention of Human Rights, 1950), and at the global level the Universal Declaration of Human Rights, 1948; the Philadelphia Declaration concerning the Aims and Purposes of the ILO, 1944; and the ILO Conventions Nos 87 and 98, 1948. However, of this trio—the right of trade union association, the right to collective bargaining and the right to strike—one encounters only the right of trade union association in all the documents mentioned above. The right to strike was the least mentioned fundamental right, which reflects the resistance to its recognition in political and social circles and in the judiciary. Europe saw a marked increase in collective conflicts immediately after the Second World War (see Table 7.3) and, although it was recognised that strikes could not be suppressed as fiercely as was done in the Nazi and fascist systems, there was often hesitation to accept their legality. In Belgium, in 1948, the government was empowered to guarantee the provision of essential services during a strike by means of civil requisition.

The recognition of the right of trade union association as a fundamental right certainly contributed to the decline of various forms of anti-trade union behaviour by employers—'yellow dog' contracts, black lists, discrimination against trade unionists, dismissal of trade union militants, and the like. In a number of countries, including the Netherlands, this development happened very quickly and without the intervention of the law after the Second World War, but in other countries anti-trade union behaviour was more persistent, and the legislators and

---

[18] Pelling (1979) 224–9.

Table 7.3: Average Yearly Number of Days Lost Because of Strikes per 1000 Employed Persons 1950–2000

	1950–1959	1960–1969	1970–1979	1980–1989	1990–1999
Netherlands	19.4	16.7	35.7	12.8	19.3
Germany	47.5	12.0	44.7	22.9	10.5
Sweden	49.2	14.7	41.1	167.8	44.3
France	315.5	138.5	167.8	61.7	31.2
Britain	135.9	145.7	521.6	298.8	25.0
Denmark	62.9	129.4	212.4	153.3	151.5
Italy	301.5	730.5	1041.0	433.3	110.6

Source: ETUC, *Transfer* (2002) 592.

the courts had to interfere a number of times to stop such behaviour. This happened in some countries, such as France, on the basis of statutory provisions which predated the Second World War, and in other countries on the basis of freshly enacted laws (Italy, 1970; Spain, 1980; Denmark, 1982).

Germany and Ireland did not make specific laws in this area, but relied on the direct binding effect of their constitutional provisions. In Britain unions relied on their traditional industrial strength rather than the law to protect union rights. In 1946, the Trades Union Congress (TUC) even declined an offer by the Labour government to enact legal protection of the freedom of association, something which they came to regret in the 1980s when the Thatcher government attacked trade union freedom (see below).

In general, one may say that in the decade following the end of the Second World War the basic pillars of collective labour relations acquired the rank of fundamental rights. One of the consequences of this development was the increasing juridification of these pillars. More than in the past, judges took an interest in the precise boundaries of the fundamental rights. This was notably the case in countries where judicial review of statutes or government orders was possible. An early example is the case of *National Union of Railwaymen v Sullivan* in 1946 in Ireland. The Supreme Court of Ireland suspended a large part of the Irish Trade Union Act 1941 because of conflict with the right of trade union freedom, mentioned in the Irish Constitution of 1937.[19]

[19] McCarthy (1977) 171.

The Welfare State: Free Collective Bargaining, Neo-corporatism and Industrial Conflict (1950–72)

Free Collective Bargaining

By 1950 national economic recovery was well under way in all western European countries (see chapter 2 above) and most of the governments believed that they could further relax the heaviest wartime and immediate post-war intervention measures. So the 1950s were characterised by the restoration of a market economy, although it remained very much embedded in state regulation. For the social area this meant that the state was now focusing on establishing comprehensive systems of social security, leaving the fixing of the basic conditions of employment to collective bargaining between both sides of industry. Germany adopted, in 1949, a system of collective bargaining, based on *Tarifautonomie*; France did the same in its law on collective agreements in 1950; and Britain returned, as Kahn Freund coined it, to 'a system of collective laissez-faire'.[20] Also, Italy established a system of free collective bargaining (*autonomia collettiva*), and Belgium did likewise. The recognition of 'collective autonomy' was nothing new to the Nordic countries, where it was already firmly established before 1945 (though in Finland only after 1945). Deviating from the mainstream were the Netherlands, which maintained strong state control on the fixing of wages,[21] and Greece, where the Collective Labour Agreements Act of 1955 maintained a highly centralised and state controlled system of collective labour relations.[22] For the Nordic countries (except Finland) and Britain the long-standing tradition of freedom of the labour market parties meant that in these countries statutory labour law remained in a position secondary to collective bargaining in maintaining collective labour relations and creating individual employment rights. The philosophy was that the self-government of the social partners made statutory labour law superfluous. In countries such as France, however, statutory labour law occupied a dominating position. Other European countries, such as Germany, were in an intermediate position. At the international level, new documents enshrining the collective labour relations rights appeared, notably in the European Social Charter of the Council of Europe (1961) and the United Nations Convention on Economic, Social and Cultural Rights (1966), which recognised the right of association in trade unions, the right to free collective bargaining and the right to strike.

In these years in all the European democracies the sectoral level emerged as the most important level for collective bargaining. The structure of collective bargaining was mainly based on industry-wide (sometimes regional, often

---

[20] Kahn-Freund (1954); Kahn-Freund (1959) *passim*.
[21] Windmuller (1969) *passim*.
[22] Zambarloukou (2006) *passim*.

nationwide) negotiations involving employers' associations and the major trade unions. The social partners had already learnt from the Great Depression that the sectoral level is the most effective to avoid progress being undermined by social dumping.[23] However, the governments pressed for some form of co-ordination at the all-industry level. The wages policies of the Netherlands and Sweden stood out because of their character of solidarity. While in the Netherlands such co-ordination was imposed by the law, in Sweden an equally very centralised bargaining structure was secured by voluntary means as nearly all branch organisations adopted the 1938 Basic Agreement between the national social partners as the basis for their collective agreements. In fact, Sweden became the Nordic country with the least direct government intervention in wage bargaining. In the other European countries co-ordination was more informal and less directed towards solidarity. In Germany an orderly system of collective bargaining was established because German labour relations were strongly dominated by the engineering trade and the IG Metall. Their agreements became the forerunner of most (not all) wage and working conditions negotiations and workplace relations. Also, Austria, Belgium, Ireland and Italy established orderly systems of collective bargaining with only light forms of co-ordination on a voluntary basis. In France and Britain, collective bargaining was less orderly. In France, industrial relations remained highly adversarial, which derived from the revolutionary tradition of an important part of the trade union movement.[24] In Britain, in the 1950s, a conflict between formal industry-wide bargaining and informal shop-steward-led workplace bargaining was already developing.

There was a striking dissymmetry between the European countries with respect to the procedures to conclude collective agreements and their mandatory effects on the contract of employment. In the Nordic countries, the legal capacity to conclude collective agreements was regulated in central agreements between the confederations of trade unions and employers. In France, Belgium, Luxembourg and Ireland this capacity was narrowly regulated by statutes, and in Germany by the courts. In a number of European countries, such as the Netherlands, France and Germany, the mandatory effect of the collective agreement on the individual employment contract was clearly regulated by statutory provisions. In Italy it was construed in legal doctrine and by case law.[25] In Britain collective agreements were presumed to be 'gentlemen's agreements', not legally enforceable between the collective parties, but relevant terms could be expressly or impliedly incorporated into individual contracts; even then, these collectively agreed terms could be overridden (both upwards and downwards) by individual agreement. However, there were a number of statutory supports for collective bargaining in Britain, in particular the Terms and Conditions of Employment Act 1959, replacing wartime measures, that enabled a trade union or employers' association representing a 'substantial proportion' of workers or employers in an

[23] Roberts (1973) 17.
[24] Vigneau and Sobczak (2005) 32.
[25] Veneziani (2004) 171.

industry to report a claim to the government that an employer was not observing the 'recognised [ie collectively bargained] terms and conditions'. The government could refer the matter to the Industrial Court (an arbitration body), which could make an award compelling the employer to observe the terms. The Court's order became an implied term of the individual contracts of the affected workers. Another device was the Fair Wages Resolution of the House of Commons 1946 (extending earlier resolutions going back to 1891), which encouraged government contractors to observe standards established by collective agreements, with the possibility of recourse to the Industrial Court; there were similar provisions in some statutes granting licences or subsidies to private companies.

In Finland statutory law gave sectoral collective agreements automatic binding force upon all firms in a certain trade (the *erga omnes* effect). In France, Germany, and the Benelux countries statutory law provided that the *erga omnes* effect could be effectuated case by case by intervention of the government at the request of the parties to the collective agreement and provided certain conditions were fulfilled. In Italy the Constitution charged the legislator to adopt legislation in this field, but that was never implemented. In 1959 an Act of Parliament gave all existing collective agreements legally binding force *erga omnes*, but a similar Act of 1963 was declared unconstitutional. Italian courts, however, have been very inventive by elaborating auxiliary constructions to give collective agreements a legally binding force *erga omnes*.[26] The law in Denmark and Sweden had no system for extending collective agreements *erga omnes* in the sector, but in Denmark something similar has been created by the courts. In Sweden trade unions could legitimately try to obtain a comparable result by means of strikes, blockades and boycotts, and this practice remained a characteristic of the Swedish system over the years.[27] There were various differences in the enforcement of collective agreements between the contracting parties. This notably was relevant in the field of its effect on the law on strikes, discussed later in this section (see also chapter 9 below).

Neo-corporatism and 'Representativeness'

By the end of the 1950s, collective bargaining in most democratic states of Europe had become a stable practice covering the large majority of salaried workers (see Table 7.2), bringing about increasing spending power to working people, unprecedented in history (see chapter 2 above). Nevertheless, the economic situation was not altogether rosy anywhere in Europe during the first 15 years after the Second World. In this difficult period governments tried to win the support of labour and management for economic governance. They realised that it had become difficult to govern against the stubborn opposition of the employers and trade unions. The areas in which the social partners were engaged

[26] Ibid, 170–72; Giugni (1984) 126–31.
[27] Ahlberg and Bruun (2005).

in socio-economic matters were numerous. Some of these involvements were already present before the Second World War: labour exchanges, the administration of social security, the content of statutory labour law and social security law, participation in tripartite labour courts and tribunals, the fixing of labour conditions in sectors which lacked free collective bargaining procedures, and procedures to extend collective agreements. After the Second World War, these fields rapidly expanded in the wake of the greater involvement of the state in socio-economic life: occupational health protection and general health care, social assistance, social housing, consumer protection, nationalised industries and services of general interest, and regional socio-economic policy making. In some western European countries the social partners became involved in general socio-economic policy making. This last aspect was often effectuated through bodies, which were established by statute, such as the *Sociaal-Economische Raad* in the Netherlands, the *Nationale Arbeidsraad* in Belgium, the *Conseil Economique et Social* in France and in Luxembourg, and the *Consiglio Nazionale dell' Economia e del Lavoro* in Italy.[28] Or it occurred in informal forums such as 'conferences' (Belgium[29] and Ireland) and in the *Stichting van de Arbeid* (the Netherlands). Britain and Germany did not have institutional arrangements of this kind, but trade unions and employers exercised considerable influence over governments through informal means.

The result was that the constitutional systems of various western European nations became clad in a cloak of neo-corporatism,[30] even if that was not clearly expressed in constitutional or other formal texts. In practice, the participation of the social partners in socio-economic governance seldom acquired more than an advisory character as well as participation in the execution of policies. The social partners were only very rarely vested with law making competences. Exceptions were Austria, with its Labour Chambers; the Netherlands, with the Act on the organisation of business, 1950; and the Nordic countries, in the framework of work, safety and environment agencies.[31]

Orwell's saying that 'all are equal but some are more equal than others' could be applied to the treatment of trade unions and employers associations. Certain trade unions were already privileged above others before the Second World War. After the war, the increasing integration of trade unions and employers' associations in socio-economic governance made the distinction between ordinary and 'representative' organisations of workers and employers all the more crucial in countries where these organisations were divided. There were numerous instances in which a selection had to be made, either as regards public law institutions or in labour relations under private law. It appeared to be impossible to treat all trade unions and employers' associations equally. This was recognised and considered as compatible with the fundamental right of trade union freedom

---

[28] Scholten (1968).
[29] Chlepner (1972) 231–32, 326, 393–402.
[30] Crouch (1979a) 123–31,181–96; Vom Beyme (1980) 334–37.
[31] Fahlbeck (2002) 91.

by national courts, by the ILO and by the European Court of Human Rights (EctHR). So, selections could be made—but on what criteria and under what procedures? Since the Second World War most western European states have wrestled with this problem. The exceptions are the Nordic countries, where the organisations are relatively homogeneous and free of internal competition,[32] and Britain, where there is a single trade union centre (the TUC) which has dealt with inter-union conflicts through its own voluntary methods without state intervention. The question of representativeness has its own colour in each country, each with its own unique legal approach. In no country was the problem resolved completely. In the majority of the countries the focus was on the development of criteria for participating in the process of collective bargaining. Only in a few countries was representativeness in areas of public law and administration regulated. In Belgium, the selection was made by the government with a very large margin of discretion.[33] In the Netherlands, the representativeness of organisations within the ambit of Socio-Economic Council and other public law institutions was subjected to criteria developed by the Socio-Economic Council itself. In both countries these criteria privileged the main confederations.

Industrial Conflict

In the 1950s most people accepted the priority of reconstruction of the economy and collective conflicts were not numerous (see Table 7.3), but the trade unions still had an overriding concern to affirm, defend and widen the right to strike and the wider freedom to take collective action. In this period, wartime restrictions on the freedom to strike were removed in Britain[34] and Austria. In these countries, as well as in Belgium, a wide 'freedom' to strike was allowed, although formally no 'right' to strike was recognised. A 'peace obligation' did not exist in Britain; in Belgium it existed on a contractual basis and was only enforceable through indirect mechanisms, not in court. In Germany, in 1955, the Federal Labour Court recognised the freedom to strike albeit with numerous limitations, such as the peace obligation during the term of the collective agreement and a prohibition on striking for conflicts of rights, as distinct from conflicts of interest.[35] The same limitations were regularly applied in the Nordic countries, where special labour courts supervised the use of the weapons of collective conflict. In Italy[36] and France, the right to strike was based on their respective constitutions and was not much limited, not even by the concept of a peace obligation. In France, the courts established that participation in a legal strike could not be treated as a breach of contract as the rights and obligations of the contract

---

[32] See Hasselbalch (2002) 33; Fahlbeck (2002) 117–18.
[33] See De Vos (2003) 51–53.
[34] In 1951 the wartime prohibitions on strikes were repealed: Pelling (1975) 213, 224, 229.
[35] Blanke et al (1975) 236–37.
[36] Veneziani (2004) 169.

of employment are suspended.[37] This development was followed in most European countries, Britain, Denmark and Austria being notable exceptions. The French courts also extended the right to strike (already laid down in the Constitution of 1946) to civil servants (*Dehaene* verdict, 1950) and this development was followed in later years in most European countries in respect of civil servants (other than the police and armed forces), Germany being an exception. In Luxembourg, in 1952, the *Cour Supérieur de Justice* recognised the right to strike, but only as part of the system of obligatory arbitration. In the Netherlands, until the end of the 1960s, the courts remained hostile to the right to strike. A ruling of the Dutch Supreme Court of 1960 confirmed that there was only very little room left for a legal strike.[38] In Britain, in 1964, the House of Lords (the highest court) invented a new tort (threat to break a contract/economic intimidation), outwith statutory immunities from common law liabilities for industrial action that had existed since 1906, in order to hold trade union organisers responsible for strike action to enforce a closed shop, but immunity was quickly restored by an Act of 1965 introduced by a Labour government.[39]

Before the Second World War employers in Europe had not hesitated in exercising their right to try to continue operations during a strike, by using non-striking employees, sub-contractors or newly hired replacements, or the weapon of the lockout. After the Second World War, most European countries saw a large reduction in cases in which employers applied lockouts and the use of 'strike breakers' to replace workers on strike. In some European countries (Germany and the Nordic countries) the lockout was considered to be lawful in principle and continued to be practised. In other countries, such as France and Italy, the lockout was considered to be unlawful in principle and so was generally not used. In a number of European countries it became a common usage for employers to seek compensation for damages caused by an illegal strike. In other European countries the injunction with prohibitory and mandatory orders was by far the most frequently sought remedy for strikes or for aspects of them, such as blockades at the entrance of enterprises. Often the purpose was only to obtain a verdict on the legality of the strike. If the strike was found to be illegal, this decision could influence public opinion, and it gave the employer the guarantee that retaliatory measures (dismissals, lockouts) were allowed.

The number of days lost by strikes increased substantially after 1970 (see Table 7.3), as workers tried to get an increased share of the new wealth generated by economic growth. Many industrial actions occurred spontaneously, outside the responsibility of the unions ('wildcat' or 'unofficial' strikes). Sometimes the organisers of a strike were less interested in peaceful settlements with the employers than in changing government policy, or even in raising the class

[37] *Cour de Cassation*, 20 June 1950; see also Article L 521-1 Labour Code, introduced by the Act of 11 January 1950.
[38] Windmuller (1969).
[39] *Rookes v Barnard* [1964] Appeal Cases 1129.

consciousness of workers to overthrow capitalist society. This and the inconvenience to consumers, or even danger to the public in the case of essential services, caused by the increasing number of strikes prompted questions whether or not the right to strike should be much more limited. Consequently, during this period, in many European countries, legal measures to curtail the freedom of industrial action were discussed publicly from time to time. A number of legal restraints were imposed. In France, the right to strike of civil servants was regulated by an Act of 1963, while the French courts were prepared to contain the mounting number of conflicts by declaring several forms of 'concerted activities' not covered by the constitutional right to strike or by qualifying them as *abus de droit*. In Britain, a Royal Commission (Donovan Commission) in 1968 advised moderate limitations on the existing freedom to strike,[40] but the Conservative government (1970–74) went much further in this respect in their Industrial Relations Act, 1971, emulating some provisions of the Taft–Hartley legislation in the US.[41] In Germany, in 1971, the Federal Labour Court added a further requirement for legal strike action when it introduced the principles that a strike must be the last resort (*ultima ratio*) and must be proportionate, while at the same time limiting the right to lockout. A few years later, the Federal Labour Court was prepared to relax its stringent approach in respect of warning strikes. Likewise, in Denmark courts applied the principle of proportionality to strikes. By way of contrast, in Belgium the courts did almost nothing to contain the collective conflicts that were also surging in that country. As trade unions in Belgium did not have a legal personality, there was in principle no remedy against them in the case of unlawful strikes. Only the loss of agreed advantages or conciliation could mollify them. This legal situation was confirmed by the comprehensive Act on collective agreements and joint industrial committees that was brought onto the Belgian statute book in 1968.[42]

In Britain (until 1958), Luxembourg, Greece and Denmark systems of obligatory arbitration were maintained. In several European states governments were eager to promote all sorts of voluntary procedures of inquiry, conciliation, mediation, arbitration and advice. In Britain, Ireland, Sweden and Finland the statutory but voluntary procedures rendered a substantial contribution to the solution of collective labour conflicts. In France, however, even an impressive pile of statutory provisions on voluntary procedures of conciliation, mediation and arbitration was not helpful in reducing strike activities. France renewed its legal texts in this field in the 1970s and 1980s, but they were as unsuccessful as their predecessors. In Germany, the Netherlands and Italy almost no statutory procedures were established, and conciliation, mediation and arbitration played a minor role in these countries.

---

[40] Royal Commission on Trade Unions and Employers' Associations (1968).
[41] Weekes et al (1975).
[42] De Broeck (1973–74) 284.

Between Wage Restraint and Wage Explosion

By the 1960s, major leaps forward had been made in creating welfare states (see chapter 2 above), and there was an expansion of workers' rights in statutes and collective agreements. France was an exception in this last respect, with collective bargaining stagnating in the years De Gaulle was in power (1959–69). The other western European nations saw the process of collective bargaining proliferate in a number of ways, first in the sections of the working population covered. Collective labour relations were no longer limited to workers in the private sector, and now also covered white-collar workers as well as blue-collar ones, and even sometimes supervisors, independent workers and people on social security benefits. This trend was quickly followed in the semi-public sector (health, education, welfare services) and finally, from the 1960s or 1970s, it also applied in the public sector, where often a separate legal framework for collective bargaining was set up, although in countries like the Netherlands, Italy and Greece this happened only at the end of the twentieth century. Secondly, bargaining was no longer restricted to working conditions but sometimes also included prices, rents, investments, tax matters, profits, additional social security, equal opportunities, personal well-being, and the rights of trade unions and trade unionists and of workers' representation at the enterprise and plant level; later other subjects, such as training and childcare facilities, became important. Thirdly, the participants expanded. The state became heavily involved, and white-collar unions got access to the bargaining tables. Fourthly, the enterprise level became increasingly important compared to the sectoral and central levels. Notably, Britain, Ireland and Italy saw the emergence of substantial company, district or local bargaining to supplement sectoral bargaining. In all countries these new realities caused many conflicts and posed several problems. These problems included the contents of collective bargaining and the determination of the actors at each level, the rules of the game (negotiation procedures) and the problem of co-ordination between the various levels. For example, Italy famously,[43] before 1969, attempted spasmodically to establish a systematic articulation (*contrattazione articolata*) between the various levels of collective bargaining. Also, in Belgium it became increasingly difficult to maintain the co-ordinating function of intersectoral collective bargaining.[44] Only Ireland was successful in bringing about co-ordination between the various levels of bargaining across all industries.[45]

In a number of countries (notably Germany and the Netherlands, and to a lesser extent France) in the 1970s works councils engaged in informal plant-level bargaining, sometimes creating difficulties in the division of labour between them and the trade unions, and moulding the domestic system of industrial

[43] Veneziani (2004) 179.
[44] Mergits (1975).
[45] National Wage Agreements negotiated in the Employer-Labour Conference; see Nevin (1984) 36–52, 164–67; von Prodzynski (1992) 69–87.

relations in a way that differed from those countries in which a single channel of workers' representation prevailed (Britain, the Nordic countries and Italy) (see chapter 8 below). This period also witnessed a global expansion of transnational companies, but the proper trade union response to that, notably by means of transnational collective bargaining, could seldom be realised.[46] Because of all these developments, the character of the outcome of collective bargaining underwent a noticeable metamorphosis, from its initial function as an 'accord-armistice', ending a strike, to a comprehensive charter of rights and obligations for employers and workers. However, this metamorphosis was not universal: it went further in some countries, in some sectors and in some periods than in others.

The boom of the economies in western Europe had created increasing tension in the labour market, which gave the workers significant bargaining power. Employers preferred to give in to demands rather than to lose business, all of which was associated with an unprecedented growth of wealth in the 1960s. The consequences were passed on in prices, resulting in soaring inflation, which led, in turn, to new wage demands. Sometimes the trade unions had to respect peace obligations in collective agreements, while the rank and file claimed compensation for higher prices and were successful in getting wage concessions from the employers ('wage drift'). This tended to undermine the authority of the trade union leaders. Unions then tried to defend their position by negotiating 'opening' clauses or automatic wage compensation clauses in collective agreements. All of this was seldom sufficient to prevent the radicalisation of the rank and file. As well as the many changes in the political area, these developments strongly affected the system of industrial relations and collective labour law in the various countries. In many, the bargaining structures built up in the 1950s fell into a crisis during the 1960s. Sweden and the Netherlands[47] saw their stringent wages policies designed at national all-industry level coming under increased strain. These crises occurred at exactly the same time that governments felt, more than ever before, the need to control economic growth. So in Germany, which was confronted with a wage explosion in the 1960s, the government vainly tried to stem this by setting up co-ordination procedures (*Konzertierte Aktion*). In Britain, wages policies were deployed under both a Labour government (1964–70) and a Conservative one (1970–74)[48] (see chapter 2 above). At this time, Finland became the Nordic country with the greatest extent of direct government intervention in wage bargaining, in the form of tripartite bargaining, resulting in comprehensive incomes policy packages between the government, trade unions and employers' associations.

The economic successes of the 1960s were attended by fast and radical changes in society and culture (see chapter 2 above). In France (May 1968) and in Italy (the hot autumn of 1969) there emerged semi-revolutionary movements that

---

[46] Bendiner (1987).
[47] Windmuller (1969).
[48] Pelling (1979) 261–66.

could only be calmed down by settlements which substantially improved the positions of the workers and the trade unions. In France, the *Accords de Grenelle* between the government, the trade unions and the employers led to improvements in the law on collective agreements (Act of 27 December 1968), notably promoting trade union rights in the enterprise and enterprise-level bargaining.[49] In Italy, the works councils system had not come to fruition. The courts were occasionally prepared to contain the many conflicts by applying old provisions dating back to fascist times, but in other cases they refused to apply these provisions and tolerated a flourishing culture of collective labour conflicts. The stagnation of the 1960s was overtaken by new spontaneous forms of workers' representation, which were protected and guaranteed in the Workers' Statute (*Statuto dei lavoratori*) of 1970. This laid down rules to safeguard the freedom and dignity of workers, and the freedom of trade unions and their activities at the workplace. Other significant laws regulated social security, minimum pay during layoffs and retirement benefits. In many cases these laws were the result of direct bargaining between unions and the government, and were subsequently approved by Parliament and codified by law. In other cases they were based on trilateral agreements between government, unions and employers.

Union Democracy

Most trade unions believe that they are democratic organisations and that they do not need statutory control over their internal affairs. On the other hand, in some countries at this time the media, politicians and courts called for protection of the individual against too much trade union power. The main focus of this protection was the admission and exclusion of members, and the closed shop, which made trade union membership a requirement for obtaining or keeping a job. In Britain, after a number of common law judicial decisions directed at the closed shop, the Conservative government's Industrial Relations Act 1971 attempted to give trade unions a number of statutory rights (eg to recognition and to strike) in return for close legal control over their internal affairs. Most unions boycotted the Act, an easy process because there was a voluntary system of registration, and unregistered unions were not subject to the statutory controls. The Act was repealed by a Labour government in 1974, but some statutory controls remained. In Ireland, Germany and Denmark the rights of individual members were protected by the courts. Democratic procedures in relation to the conclusion of collective agreement were often a reality, but, apart from the British Industrial Relations Act, only in France did they become subject to statutory regulation. A contentious point was the closed shop, which continued to exist after the Second World War, notably in Britain, Ireland and Denmark. From the 1970s, criticism at closed shop arrangements had mounted, and

[49] Ardagh (1982) 95–105.

judgments of the ECtHR threw doubt on their compatibility with the guarantee of freedom of association in the European Convention of human Rights (ECHR), interpreted to include the right not to belong to a trade union.[50] Thereupon the legislators in both Britain and Denmark reduced the legal space for closed shops considerably: by the beginning of the twenty-first century closed shops had become a marginal phenomenon in Europe.

Other hot issues in a number of countries were the financing of trade unions and the relationship between trade unions and political parties. These were subjects of concern in Denmark, but were never regulated there. In Britain, however, the affiliation of trade unions to the Labour Party had led Parliament in 1913 to enact safeguards for individual members, allowing them to contract out of subscriptions and levies for political parties. These controls were tightened under the Industrial Relations Act 1971–4. A final area for concern in several countries has been the possibility that inter-union conflicts might disturb peace in the labour market. Over the years, this has induced legislators in Britain and Ireland, where there were a large number of small unions, to facilitate amalgamations of trade unions. In France, the courts had to interfere many times to solve the legal problems caused by schisms between the trade unions. One of the general trends, in the 1960s, was deconfessionalisation, which gave the Christian trade unions an identity crisis and as a result diminished the gap between these trade unions and social democratic and other unions. When, in the 1960s, the trade unions were in search of closer co-operation at the European level, they were able to profit from a more relaxed atmosphere; on this fertile ground, in 1973, a unitary European Trade Union Confederation (ETUC) was formed, which has since confronted the European organisations of employers: UNICE (recently renamed Business Europe) for big business in the EU, CEEP for public enterprises, UEAPME for small and medium-sized industries, and COPA for agriculture. However, all these associations were stronger in lobbying than in participating in the process of collective bargaining. National employers have tended to be reluctant to give away negotiating powers, so most European employers' associations did not have strong authority. Some were even lacking a mandate to conclude agreements.

All these developments in the national systems of collective labour relations between the end of the 1950s and the middle of the 1970s unleashed a flood of studies and comments on the systems of collective labour relations and the changes in the various countries.[51] Patterns were described as 'centralised' or 'decentralised', strategic models as 'harmonious' or 'conflictual'. As a result of the involvement of governments and social partners, the economic systems had been transformed by 'concertation'[52]; the processes of collective bargaining had

[50] *Young, James and Webster v United Kingdom* [1982] EHRR 38 and *Sigurjonsson v Iceland* [1993] 16 EHRR 422.
[51] Cordova (1985) 333.
[52] Van Acker (1977) 53–54.

become tripartite instead of bipartite,[53] or had developed into 'continuous bargaining'; the militancy of the workers was qualified as 'direct action', or a 'permanent conflict'; and 'the collapse of social democratic consensus' took place. Much discussed among lawyers was the question whether the law was an adequate instrument to regulate labour relations.[54] Looking back from the beginning of the twenty-first century to those days, all these studies and comments appear very dated now. It is still clear, though, that the preparedness of both sides of industry to co-operate with the governments more or less harmoniously, which had determined many national systems of labour relations in Europe between 1945 and 1960, had deteriorated to a large extent.

Responses to Economic Crisis (1973–89)

The economic recession that began in the early 1970s deeply affected the face of industrial relations in Europe (see chapter 2 above). Politicians were initially as much concerned by inflation and rising budget deficits as by increasing unemployment. They tried to fight unemployment initially by state aid to ailing industries and the creation of subsidised jobs, then later by a better distribution of the available work across the working population, for instance by shortening the working week and offering schemes of early retirement (see chapter 3 above). The trade unions were generally slow to change their conceptions of the political economies in which they operated.[55]

In this situation many European countries saw a resurgence of collective bargaining at an all-industry (central/interprofessional) level. Governments, together with the social partners, tried to tackle the various problems by comprehensive agreements ('social pacts') on wages, social security, employment strategies, prices and tax measures. Sometimes these attempts were successful, but more often they failed. When such failures occurred, governments sometimes threatened, or effectively had recourse to legal interventions in wage setting (Denmark, Norway, Sweden, Finland, France, Italy and Belgium). In Sweden, the system of national wage bargaining broke down entirely in 1983. However, in the country with the richest tradition of legal intervention in this field, the Netherlands, statutory wages control was abandoned in the 1980s in the private sector and in the 1990s in the semi-public sector. The government thereafter pinned its hopes on persuasion and tripartite dealings at the all-industry level, modelled after the so-called Wassenaar Agreement of 1982.

The economic recession seriously weakened the position of the trade unions. In a market with a superfluous labour supply, employers were the dominating

---

[53] Adam et al (1972).
[54] Wedderburn (1971) 9, 13, 161.
[55] Martin and Ross (1980) 33–67.

party and the trade unions had difficulty in showing their muscle. Moreover, apart from the Nordic countries and Austria, they had to endure substantial losses in membership (see Table 7.1). This was partly caused by the decline in extracting and manufacturing industries, while the workers in the growing service sector showed themselves less prone to organise. The substitution of a precarious for a permanent labour force also meant shrinking union membership. Although the trade unions saw a strong increase in the membership of women and of migrant workers, both categories could not make up for the losses of male membership. These developments changed the face of trade unionism. The unions of miners and industrial workers gradually lost importance while the trade unions organising the public, semi-public and private services sectors saw their influence grow. White-collar unions sometimes adhered to the traditional confederations and sometimes stood outside them. These developments in a number of European countries led many trade unions to eventually amalgamate into larger entities. On the other hand, in this period there were often national circumstances and motives that caused fresh divisions between the trade unions (for example in the 1980s, in Italy, over the wage indexation system). Apart from the FNV merger in the Netherlands in 1980, the ideologically diverse national trade union orbits in the various European countries did not see formal mergers between confederations, although in Spain the two rival confederations, CCOO and UGT, put political acrimony behind them after 1988. In Greece, some degree of unity was achieved among the major political factions representing in the trade union movement.

Various governments tried to reorganise the system of industrial relations by adopting new legislative measures concerning trade unions, collective bargaining and strikes. Obviously, this was a necessity in countries like Greece, Portugal and Spain, which in the 1970s had switched from dictatorships into democracies. These countries recognised the right to trade union association, to free collective bargaining and to strike in their new democratic constitutions, and adopted new statutes on collective agreements and industrial relations.

In Spain, the Workers' Statute 1980 and the Trade Union Freedom Act 1985 laid down a 'duty to bargain' and contained criteria for representativity for collective bargaining purposes. If the parties to the collective agreement were sufficiently representative, the collective agreement was generally binding *erga omnes*. The statutory rules to sort out some kind of co-ordination between the various levels of bargaining were not successful, but in the following period (below) the interconfederal agreements on collective bargaining in 1992 and 1997 achieved a more systematic articulated collective bargaining structure.[56] In Portugal, the corporatist legislation since 1969 had contained a 'duty to bargain' and this was again included in the 1976 Act, which gave the unions the right to meet with the employer and to exchange views on any aspect of the relationship between employer and employee. However, there was no obligation to reach an

---

[56] Blasco and de Val Tena (2004) 277, 287, 289; Fraile (1999) 269–311.

agreement. The statute allowed the government to extend collective agreements *erga omnes*, if so requested by the parties. A certain co-ordination between the various levels of collective bargaining was brought about by the tripartite agreement on incomes policy of 1987.[57]

In Greece, compulsory arbitration in failed collective negotiations was revived after the end of dictatorship (1974). A new trade union law was passed in 1976, to be replaced in 1982 by a more liberal piece of legislation. In 1983, restrictions on the right to strike were imposed in 'socialised enterprises'. The courts intervened in a number of conflicts within the dominant Greek trade union confederation GSEE.[58] The old system of compulsory contributions of all wage and salary workers was abrogated in 1990, bringing the unions into desperate financial straits.[59] An Act of 1990 replaced the 1955 Act on Collective Agreements by a more liberal legal framework, which did away with mandatory referral to arbitration in case of an impasse in bargaining. The new law introduced a system of mediation and arbitration with optional as well as mildly mandatory elements. Various dialogue-promoting institutions, instruments and mechanisms were also created in these years.[60]

Even some long-standing democracies in Europe adapted their laws on bargaining and strikes in this period.

In Britain, after a miners' strike (1974) had brought down the Conservative government, the Labour government (1974–79) repealed the Industrial Relations Act, which had attempted to bring about a new ordering of industrial relations in one fell swoop (see above). In accordance with a 'social contract' with the TUC, Labour re-established the traditional voluntary approach to industrial relations, underpinning it with new legal supports,[61] including a duty to bargain, and the extension of collectively agreed terms to unorganised employers, as well as a host of new individual rights. Britain also saw statutory provisions to protect and promote trade unions activities (eg time off for trade union representatives).[62] However, after the 'social contract' collapsed in the 'winter of discontent' in 1978–79, the Conservatives, now inspired by neo-liberal ideas under Mrs Thatcher, returned to power and set out on a fresh reform of the British pattern of industrial relations, with the undisguised ambition to reduce the power of the trade unions.[63] They did so this time not by introducing a comprehensive new statute, but by a series of piecemeal amendments in the existing laws inherited from the Labour government. These amendments removed the last remnants of procedures to extend collectively agreed employment conditions, repealed the duty to bargain and abolished the wages councils, which, under different names since 1909, had laid down minimum wages for workers in certain trades.

---

[57] Pinto (1991) 243–64.
[58] Fakiolas (1988) 123–38.
[59] Kritsantonis (1998) 601–28.
[60] Yannakounou (2004).
[61] Trade Union and Labour Relations Acts 1974 and 1976; Employment Protection Act 1975.
[62] Pelling (1979) 285.
[63] Martin (1992).

Through a number of Employment Acts, from 1980 onwards, the rights of individual workers members to sue their trade unions were extended, ballots (with stringent bureaucratic procedures) were required before industrial action could be lawful and the right to strike was severely limited, notably as regards forms of secondary action and picketing.[64] Most telling of all, unions were made legally responsible for strikes initiated by shop stewards, and unions that defied court injunctions to stop industrial action could be, and were, heavily fined for contempt of court, or threatened with sequestration of their assets. Ireland, whose strike law was also built on the British notion of 'immunities' from common law wrongs, did not follow suit, but some of these immunities were more tightly drawn than previously in the Industrial Relations Act of 1990.[65]

In Sweden the right to strike was recognised in the 1974 Constitution and a new statute on collective labour rights was adopted in 1976, the Co-determination Act, which, among other provisions, contained the important innovation of a duty to bargain. A consequence of this legislation was that the balance between collective agreements and legislation was altered, although collective agreements remained the predominant source of norms influencing individual employment contracts. In Denmark, a similar shift in the balance between legislation and collective agreements is attributed to the increase in labour law emanating from the EC.[66]

In France it was the first post-Gaullist left-wing government under Mitterrand that sought to sooth the trade unions with union-friendly reforms in 1982 (*lois Auroux*). The 1968 Act had regulated the capacity to conclude collective agreements in a very generous way, so that even small unions could claim this capacity. Combined with the fact that until 1982 a 'duty to bargain' did not exist, it was difficult to overcome the traditional resistance among French employers to bargain with the unions, and especially with the main communist- and socialist-led unions in France. Therefore the Act of 1982 reduced the possibilities to circumvent the major unions and introduced a 'duty to bargain' at enterprise level.

The level of industrial conflict remained high in this period (see Table 7.3) as employees saw their newly won economic position threatened by rising unemployment, measures of wage restraint and so on. Sweden witnessed all-out industrial warfare in 1980, the Netherlands in 1983, Britain in 1984–85 and Spain in 1988. Various countries also experienced the emergence of industrial action by self-employed workers (doctors, taxi drivers, farmers, etc). Most European countries saw a further proliferation in the variety of forms of industrial action, such as rotation strikes, intermittent strikes, *estafette* strikes (strikes on different days in various factories of the employer), waves of strikes, 'quickie strikes', hourly strikes, partial and successive strikes in different departments of the same plant or in the same department at short intervals, work-to-rule, go slow, go sick,

---

[64] Bercusson and Ryan (2005) 55–56.
[65] von Prodzynski (1992) 185.
[66] Nielsen (2002) 74.

non-cooperation and overtime bans. These forms of action caused a good deal of worry to the courts and scholars, even though in theory the right or the freedom to strike had now been recognised in all European countries (in the Netherlands finally in a landmark Supreme Court case of 1986). In Italy, in 1988, a law was passed to limit the right to strike in essential services. In the 1980s the law on lockouts became more diversified in Germany, Britain and Sweden.

In the meantime, compulsory arbitration had almost completely vanished from the European scene, save in the event of strikes causing major harm to the country (eg Spain). In some countries (Luxembourg, Greece) collective disputes still had to be referred to a conciliation or mediation agency before any strike could be lawfully carried out. Other countries required the written notice of a strike to be delivered some time beforehand to such agents (Finland), which might postpone the strike for a certain time (Sweden) or until the conciliation or mediation attempts had been exhausted (Norway). In order to refine such rules, European countries time and again renewed and renamed the procedures for voluntary inquiry, conciliation, mediation and arbitration, such as France in 1969 and 1982, Britain between 1970 and 1975, and Ireland in 1990.[67]

Governments in all European countries, whatever their political colour, remained convinced that the economic crisis of the 1970s and 1980s could only be overcome by economic growth, which not only had to be attained by more trade and a single currency, but also by wage restraint. To that end, they continued pressing employers and trade unions for some form of central co-ordination and wage restraint. In some countries the government even went so far as to intervene directly in wage setting, but in most countries they limited themselves to supporting voluntary, moderate standard setting by indirect means, such as tax benefits and reforms of labour law and social security. Most politicians, eager to run the economy in concord with the employers and the unions, were prepared to reduce the drive for state regulation and to give way to collective bargaining. In Denmark, in the 1980s, comprehensive technology agreements were negotiated between the national trade union and employers' confederations. The most interesting venture in the interplay of all these developments was Italy, where orderly wage policies had not been possible during the 1970s and 1980s but were finally realised through the conclusion of the Tripartite Agreement of 23 July 1993. It became—as Veneziani describes it[68]—'the cornerstone of Italy's strategy to bring the Italian system up to European standards'. Besides being Italy's first tripartite agreement on incomes policy and employment, labour market strategy and support for the economy, it reshaped the structure of the bargaining system.

---

[67] von Prodzynski (1992) 76–77.
[68] Veneziani (2004) 180.

The Impact of Global Capitalism on Labour Relations (1990–2004)

The socio-economic changes of the 1990s (see chapter 2 above) led legislators, employers and unions to put greater emphasis on the modernisation of labour law and social security law. These developments had many consequences for the labour relations systems in the various countries of Europe.[69] The unions pointed at the weak position of much of the new labour force (precarious jobs) and asked for more job security, but they were often not strong enough to impose their claims. Sometimes, however, in association with left-wing governments, they could make gains, as in France with the 35-hour week. In the *loi Robien* (1996) the French government promised tax reductions in exchange for a shortening of the working week and new hirings. In the Netherlands, in 1997, a compromise was made, called 'flexicurity', that provided more rights for precarious workers in exchange for greater possibilities for employers to enter into precarious employment relationships (regarding these and other labour market policies, see chapter 3 above). In these countries the success of such policies led to a new heyday for collective bargaining.

Generally, however, trade unions were less able to organise the workforce in this 'new' economy than in the old industrial world. They were also less able to formulate uniform claims appealing to the great majority of the workforce, which had become much more fragmented than in the old industrial world. Union density rates kept falling (see Table 7.1). The trade unions were on the defensive. It should be noted that in the 1960s and the 1970s it was the trade unions and the workers themselves who—thanks to their greater bargaining power in those days—pressed for decentralised supplementary bargaining at enterprise level. From the mid-1980s, however, it was the employers who wanted more flexibility and were therefore pressing for more decentralisation in collective bargaining. This was very clear in Sweden,[70] where in the mid-1980s this pressure had caused the downfall of the traditional Swedish system of centralised wage bargaining. In 1990, the employers' confederation finally decided to drop out of the centrally co-ordinated wage negotiations. In information and communication technology and other new sectors there was a tendency for employers not to conclude collective agreements at all. In Britain, by the end of the twentieth century, the same trend had already gone so far that the overwhelming majority of private sector employers had effectively abandoned acting jointly to regulate the terms and conditions of employment in industry-wide collective agreements, limiting themselves to company bargaining; in fact, many of them no longer indulged in any collective bargaining at all. This was despite the fact that in 1998 the new Labour government had given the unions new rights to seek

[69] Ferner and Hyman (1998).
[70] Fahlbeck (2002) 121; Ahlberg and Bruun (2005) 119, 123–24.

recognition for collective bargaining purposes.[71] By the year 2000, there was diminishing interest on the part of employers in collective bargaining in Germany. The German employers' confederation opposed the use of the procedure for the extension *erga omnes* of collective agreements.[72] One of the results of the downfall of collective bargaining in these countries was a widening of the gap between the top and bottom ends of pay distribution. Elsewhere the picture was less bleak. In the Nordic and Benelux countries collective bargaining practices stayed at a high level. In France collective bargaining still covered over 95% of the workers because of the active use of the *erga omnes* procedure. In 2004 a new Act on Collective Agreements was adopted to secure the priority of the bargaining position of the major unions vis-à-vis that of the small unions.

So, when the twentieth century drew to a close, collective bargaining was still the most common way of setting labour standards in most European countries (see Table 7.2). In the 1980s and 1990s much of the laborious development into a multilevel system of collective bargaining had reached a certain level of stability. In a number of countries the system could, by the end of the twentieth century, be characterised as a 'central–decentralised pattern' of labour relations. It was 'decentralised' in the sense that the concrete standard setting was done at the level of the sector or the enterprise, or even on a district or local level. This was a seemingly unfinished process that continually produced new phenomena, such as restructuring deals and wage cuts to enhance the survival of a company (*Bündnis für Arbeit*) in Germany and the 'savings agreements' in Finland. On the other hand, the patterns were still 'central' in the sense that the central organisations of employers and trade unions continued to play a role in bringing about some degree of co-ordination in relation to the activities of the governments and legislators. Examples are the 1993 Joint Advice of the Socio-Economic Council on economic aims and strategies in the Netherlands, the 1997 Industry Agreement in Sweden, the 1997 Confidence Pact between the Government and the Social Partners in Greece, the 1998 Central Agreement on Wage Moderation in Belgium, and new Interconfederal Agreements on stability and collective bargaining in Spain in 1997, 2002 and 2003.

It may be noted here that, by the end of the twentieth century, the organisational landscape on the employers' side had been changed dramatically. Most of the Christian employers' associations had ceased to exist. Traditionally employers were often also organised along two different lines: 'economic' and 'social' organisations. In the course of time this distinction faded away and in various countries, such as the Netherlands, Belgium and the Nordic countries, both types of employers' associations merged. On the trade union side there were also remarkable organisational changes. In Germany, Britain, the Netherlands and Denmark, many trade unions merged to form greater entities that would be better equipped to face the challenges of the modern times. In Italy, France, Spain

---

[71] Bercusson and Ryan (2005) 58–60.
[72] Blanke and Rose (2005) 12–13, 21.

and Portugal, the end of the cold war in 1989 led to a narrowing of the ideological and political gap between the predominantly communist unions and the other unions. This factor also enabled all trade unions in Europe to close their ranks in the ETUC. However, in a number of European countries the traditional landscape of trade unions was disturbed by the rise of 'autonomous' unions.

By the end of the twentieth century, a form of collective bargaining and autonomous rule setting by labour and management at the European level had emerged. Originally their involvement in the operations of the European Economic Community (EEC), established in 1957, was much weaker than in the ILO. They only had a distant advisory role, for instance in the Economic and Social Committee and in the Board of the European Social Fund. However, in the 1980s, when nearly all social law-making in the EEC had ground to a halt due to the opposition of the British government, European Commission President Delors invited the European 'social partners' for informal talks at the Brussels castle of Val Duchesse, which resulted in non-binding statements.

This relative success became the basis for a set of provisions included in the European Community (EC) Treaty (Treaty of Maastricht, 1992), which formalised this so-called European social dialogue. This gave the European social partners the privilege of being consulted before any social measure is taken at European level and enables them to bypass such measures by concluding their own agreements on those issues. Those agreements may then subsequently be implemented by national mechanisms of labour and management, or may be moulded into EC Directives.[73] The Maastricht Treaty became the sanctification of the autonomy of the social partners at the European level. However, by the end of the period studied the European social partners had used this new competence only a handful of times on rather minor issues.[74] It is easy to see why. The employers are reluctant to conclude at the European level agreements with the unions about substantive matters and they know that the unions at this level are too weak to impose such agreements on them.

Other phenomena that could one day become elements of a genuine European system of labour relations, such as cross-border (co-ordination of) collective bargaining[75] and cross-border collective action,[76] were still in their infancy at the end of the period studied.

In the final years of the twentieth century new legal challenges to the system of collective bargaining became apparent. The prevailing winds of priority for the requirements of the market economy had given renewed importance to competition law (see the chapter 2 above). When Dutch companies also claimed this priority over labour market regulations the EuropeanCourt of Justice upheld the immunity of collective labour agreements for European competition law in the *Albany* case of 1998; however, but this was strictly limited to the subject matters

[73] Clauwaert et al (2004) 301–45.
[74] Jacobs (2004b) 347–93.
[75] Blanke and Rose (2005) 9.
[76] Dorssemont et al (2007).

of working conditions and labour market affairs.[77] The autonomy of the social partners, widely heralded in German and Italian doctrine in the 1960s and 1970s, has been weakened. In Sweden[78] and the Netherlands the legislator nullified certain provisions in collective agreements as they were contrary to government policies. The courts also played a role in this field. Collective bargaining partners were obliged to respect the fundamental rights of the individual, such as rights on equal treatment and privacy. This caused the social partners some problems because they often made differentiations and imposed certain forms of solidarity on individual workers. The resurgence of individualism encouraged some workers to refuse to accept the effects on their employment contracts of the choices made by the social partners. In principle, this was not a major problem as, in all countries, clauses in the individual employment contract that are more favourable to the workers prevail over the collective agreement. However, sometimes it may be doubted whether a clause is more favourable. More importantly, in many European countries statutory labour law to an increasing extent contained negotiable elements, which could be replaced *in peius* by collective agreements (see chapters 1 and 4 above).

Sectoral collective agreements have also contributed to decentralisation by using the tool of waivers or opening clauses. This has become widespread practice in Germany.[79] France went the furthest in this respect: the already mentioned Act on Collective Agreements of 2004 authorised company agreements to derogate *in peius* from sectoral agreements on all subjects save on the issue of wages, unless the sectoral agreement expressly prohibited such a derogation.[80] In a number of countries collective bargaining with the unions at company level is especially weak in small and medium-sized firms. In those cases, employers sometimes prefer to deal with the works councils even where the law does not recognise this type of bargaining.

Although at times industrial conflicts have flared up, as in France in 1995, and Denmark and Italy in 1998, since the mid-1980s European countries have seen a dramatic fall in the number of working days lost by collective labour disputes (see Table 7.3). Waging industrial war has become much more complicated than before because of the shift to enterprise bargaining, the change to a services economy, the advent of new technology, increasing globalisation (which makes it relatively easy for companies to shift production), changes in the composition of the workforce and the shrinking membership of trade unions. Against this backdrop of a reduction in the occurrence of strikes, it is clear that in most European countries there was no urgency felt to fundamentally reform the right to strike as it had been stabilised in the 1970s and 1980s. So, during the last 20 years of the period studied, in the majority of the countries of western Europe there were not many major new developments in the right to strike. The courts played their role

---

[77] Bruun and Hellsten (2001).
[78] Ahlberg and Bruun (2005) 118.
[79] Blanke and Rose (2005) 24.
[80] Vigneau and Sobczak (2005) 35.

in balancing the right to strike against other values, notably in the Netherlands, where, departing from a situation of a rather late (1986) recognition of the right to strike, the 1990s were filled with case law to mark out the limits of this right. In Britain, the Conservative government (in power until 1997) finished its programme of step-by-step reduction of the freedom to strike. When Labour returned to power (1997) it did not revive the old pre-Thatcherite strike law, but made only minor amendments to the law inherited from the Conservatives.[81]

In Sweden, in 1998, a State Commission drew up a list of proposals to overhaul the right to strike, but the then social democratic government renounced most of these proposals and tabled only some minor amendments, introducing a mild form of compulsory mediation.[82] In Spain, a 1996 agreement for extrajudicial settlement of conflicts between both sides of industry established mechanisms for mandatory mediation and voluntary arbitration of collective conflicts, as well as minimum services prior to strikes. Only in Italy did there remain a continued drive for legislation restraining strikes, which was finally realised in 1990 to protect the functioning of essential services.[83] In 2000 this law was tightened up by the centre-left government, after industrial action in all public sectors in November 1998 had virtually brought the country to a halt. In Belgium, the general courts have cautiously begun to restrict the right to block an enterprise on the basis of general judicial principles.

Conclusion

Less than two centuries ago, collective labour relations did not exist in Europe. Trade unions, employers' associations and strikes were repressed under criminal law. Collective labour agreements were unheard of. In the century that followed, 'toleration' and 'recognition' of the essential phenomena of modern labour relations—trade unions, collective agreements and strikes—were won in a number of European countries, though not all. And even in the countries where they were won, this was not in a comprehensive way but subject to many limitations. In the period since the Second World War, 'toleration' and 'recognition' of the workers' movement has been secured all over Europe. They were restored and extended in countries where they were lost during dictatorships, such as Germany, Italy, Portugal, Spain and Greece. They have been further strengthened in the countries where they were already present before the Second World War.

The essential collective labour rights, freedom of trade union association, free collective bargaining and the right to strike, have been laid down in national constitutions, in European and international standards (ILO, ECHR, European

[81] Bercusson and Ryan (2005) 55–57.
[82] Ahlberg and Bruun (2005) 120, 128–29.
[83] Veneziani (2004) 186.

Social Charter of the Council of Europe, and the Charter of Nice of the EU), and in national statutes and important case law. For a time, a form of 'repression' was present in compulsory governmental wages policies, but by the end of the period studied these have almost disappeared, save in cases of great economic difficulty. Another form of 'repression', however, was there to stay, namely the various limitations on the right to strike. In the 1960s and 1970s, some scholars went so far as to suggest that the approaches of tolerance and recognition should include most forms of industrial conflict. They regarded industrial conflicts as an often unavoidable incident of labour relations, and considered legal norms and sanctions as blunt instruments in shaping labour–management relations.[84] By 2004, there was little talk about laws against strikes being ineffective or unacceptable. The law has played a significant role in containing industrial action where too much harm to society as a whole was threatened.

However, the concepts of 'toleration' and 'recognition' have proved to be insufficient for a thorough description of the developments in collective labour law in the period since the Second World War.

Therefore, I suggest that the 'ideal types' of repression, toleration and recognition need to be supplemented by two further types: integration and containment. In most western European countries after the Second World War there was more than a mere strengthening of toleration and recognition. That further step deserves the name of 'integration'. The system of collective bargaining has become the main method of standard setting of employment conditions. Labour and management are also involved in the process of creating and enforcing statutory labour law, and are often part of the administration of social security and labour market institutions. They have, in effect, become the co-administrators of the welfare state in many countries. All this can be detected in Germany, France, Italy, the Benelux countries, the Nordic countries, Austria and Ireland, and even, with some major reservations, in Britain. This ideal type also was adopted in Spain, Portugal and Greece after the dictatorships. By the end of the period studied there were many phenomena illustrating that 'integration' was still flourishing in Europe, often under new labels, like the British partnership agreements, the German *Bündnis für Arbeit*, the Dutch *Poldermodel* and the European social dialogue, and with new labels for old tools, such as 'open methods of coordination' and 'flexicurity'. It seems that, with the fall of communism, 'integration' had become a viable concept even in those Mediterranean countries where it had been rejected earlier by large parts of the trade union movements. This is not to say that the systems of labour relations have completely converged on this point. In a number of countries, such as Sweden and the Netherlands, the trade unions and the employers' associations have been prepared to recognise each other's interests, which means that the employers are willing to seriously consider the claims made by the trade unions, while the unions have a positive attitude to

---

[84] Kahn-Freund and Hepple (1972) 60.

technological changes and other measures that may increase productivity. In most other countries the relationship between labour and management has remained much more hostile and marked by suspicion.

From time to time the various forms of 'integration' have been discredited. Critics consider them as 'incorporation'. 'Integration of the trade unions in the state effectuates depoliticising and deprives them of readiness to fight', was already the opinion of the young Kahn-Freund in the Weimar Republic.[85] There continued to be attachment, after the war, to a militant labour movement that is not prepared to be appeased by 'harmony models'. These ideas flourished, notably between 1965 and 1985. Over the years we have seen many occasions at which the trade unions withdrew from formal or informal mechanisms of integration.

However, over a period of six decades, these have been incidental controversies. The long-term trend, since 1945, has been that of an ever-growing involvement of labour and management in the socio-economic governance of the countries of Europe, and also at the level of the EU. As Jacobi put it:

> A stage of bourgeois industrial societies—a capitalist democracy with mixed economy and mixed policy—developed and received its legitimation from the social democraticic Keynesian model of consensus by participation and integration of the working class. It was a model which borrowed considerably from Catholic social doctrine and was not infrequently supported by conservative popular parties and governments.[86]

Since the 1980s, however, one can also distinguish signs of what may be called 'containment'. Neo-liberal economic policies, the emphasis on 'free' deregulated markets, notably implemented by the Thatcher and Major governments (1979–97) in Britain, led to a curtailment of the power of the trade unions in the 1980s and 1990s. In other European countries there were almost no similar developments in statutes and case law. Nevertheless, in these other countries too, the reality was that the trade unions had lost much of their power since the 1980s. There was crumbling membership, caused among other factors, by the growth of individualism and new types of labour, the decline in manufacturing, the rise of flexible work and outsourcing, etc, Europeanisation and globalisation, leading to off-shoring and a downward pressure on labour standards, all of which made it more difficult to organise. It is often said that labour reached the peak of its power in the 1970s, and that since then its influence has gradually declined. As a consequence, the question has risen whether in the twenty-first century collective bargaining will remain as important as it was been between 1945 and 2004. Although politicians continue to pay lip service to it, it enjoys less support from employers and economists, is threatened by the trends of globalisation and individualism, by falling union membership, and by

[85] Kahn-Freund (1966) 149–210.
[86] Jacobi (1988) 193.

the fact that it has not yet become geared to the labour market of modern service industries.

In conclusion: although we must trust that in Europe the days of repression of collective labour relations are now definitively gone and that at least 'toleration' and 'recognition' will be the permanent attitudes of society towards collective labour relations, it is uncertain whether integration will prevail now that we are seeing increasing symptoms of containment.

8

Workers' Representation at the Plant and Enterprise Level

ULRICH MÜCKENBERGER

Continuity and Change in Workers' Representation

Workers' representation at the plant level has experienced a dramatic upheaval over the last six decades. This was triggered first by the post-war economic boom, leading to a period of rapid expansion and consolidation, culminating in the 'golden age' of the 1960s and 1970s. Since then it has undergone a process of restructuring in response to Europeanisation and globalisation, and the decentralisation and fragmentation of work and the workforce. Many of the legal developments concerning workers' representation in the post-war period can only be understood in light of the anti-war and anti-fascist efforts of that period. The developments towards industrial democracy and workers' participation in the late 1960s and early 1970s are connected with both the deep restructuring of the Fordist system of production and the mass demonstrations of workers and students against authoritarian political and industrial regimes. The early twenty-first-century crisis of collective representation has to be assessed against the background of a work pattern of flexible specialisation and a socio-cultural pattern of individualisation. It is under the impact of what James Rosenau calls 'fragmegration': worldwide integration and ubiquitous fragmentation of an increasingly electronically connected economy and sphere of work.[1]

The changes we face in the industrial and service regimes and their systems of workers' representation are closely embedded in fundamental changes in groups of societies (like the EU, the North American Free Trade Agreement and Mercosur), or even the global networks of societies. Globalisation—as denationalisation not only of transfer of goods and services, but also of direct investment and finance capital, supported and speeded up by information

---

[1] Rosenau (2003).

technology[2]—has linked workplaces in different corners of the world closer together than ever before, and is therefore an unprecedented challenge to any form of workplace representation. This is why workplace representation is also undergoing a hitherto unknown—albeit slow—process of denationalisation: be it Europeanisation, in the sense of the European works councils or workers' representation within the European company; or transnationalisation, in the sense of world works councils, global codes of conduct, the United Nation's (UN) Global Compact, worldwide trade union network-building and institutionalisation.[3]

This analysis will compare different European structures of shop-floor representation and functions of shop-floor representatives.[4] The diversity of workers' representation systems in Europe has shown a remarkable continuity (in modern legal–economic terms, 'path dependence')[5] in spite of the aforementioned upheaval. With regard to structures of shop-floor representation, we can distinguish separate (employee-only representation) and joint bodies (employee and management representation). Within the former category, systems differ in the manner in which trade union representation and non-union representatives interact. There seem to be three main types. In single-channel systems, workers' representatives receive their legitimation via trade union designation or election, as is the case in Britain, Denmark, Italy, Sweden and Ireland. In dual/plural-channel systems trade union bodies exist alongside non-union representation, either with exclusive functions and prerogatives of trade unions, as in France, Spain, Portugal and Belgium, or with trade union functions shared with elected institutions in a complementary way, as in Germany, Austria, the Netherlands and Greece. There are overlaps to systems of unitary bodies within a dual-channel environment. They have 'unitary' bodies, elected by unionised and non-unionised workers, with a wide representative function, and are relatively independent from trade unions. Some of these bodies are highly institutionalised and 'juridified',[6] for instance in Germany, Austria, France (with the *comité d'entreprise* alongside *délégués du personnel*), Spain, Portugal, Greece, the Netherlands and Belgium. Unitary systems sometimes have additional joint bodies with an ancillary or specialised role (France, Belgium, Denmark, Britain, Italy). Other systems are less institutionalized, and are instead governed by collective bargaining rather than by statutory law (Ireland).

We distinguish five categories of functions of workers' representation. The first four are establishment-related, the last is enterprise-related. In nearly all countries, representatives have a communicative role within the workforce and therefore enjoy a protected legal status. Management–labour–related rights of participation range from the right to receive information (mandatory under the

[2] Castells (2000); Sassen (2006).
[3] Cf Hepple (2005); Moreau (2006); Craig and Lynk (2006).
[4] This systematisation follows current debate: Biagi (1990); Summers (1998); Szell (2001); Visser (2004).
[5] Roe (1996).
[6] Mückenberger (1988).

Directive 2002/14/EC, which will be dealt with later), the right to be heard ('voice'), the right to consultation and deliberation, veto rights of employees' representatives and, finally, the right to decide jointly, like the German and Austrian *Mitbestimmung* model, with equivalents in the Dutch, Greek, French and, albeit on the basis of collective agreement, Swedish models. There are specialised forms of participation on matters such as health and safety at work (see below); job classification; and conflict-solving conciliation and arbitration machinery and procedures (see chapter 9 below).

The greatest diversity of functions lies at the enterprise level. Enterprise-level co-determination (*Mitbestimmung*) used to be unique to the German system, although other countries, like the Netherlands and Denmark, attempted their own brands of this. However, with the European company (*Societas Europea*), this form of participation has been open to adoption by other Member States, to varying degrees, and with certain modifications and mixes.[7] In this respect, it is necessary to distinguish between the two forms of European companies: those within the monistic system (board) and those with a dual system (a supervisory board—*Aufsichtsrat*—and an executive committee—*Vorstand*). On this basis, the negotiated type of participation of workers in the European company can be identified and compared.

There are already some comparative descriptions of the legal forms of employee representation.[8] Some of them have a certain historical perspective.[9] There are also several cross-national studies of workplace representation that try to draw on other legal systems in a kind of a cross-country transfer of know-how (*Lernprozess*).[10] Most of these studies are either outdated or focus exclusively on the comparative angle, failing to take into account historical developments and the socio-economic context. In the following, we endeavour to address this deficit by concentrating on a socio-economic account of the important features of the post-1945 development of workers' representation law.

Reconstruction (1945–50)

The history of plant labour relations in Europe after the Second World War cannot be understood and interpreted outside of the context of the war experience and the way in which the need for political, economic and social reconstruction was felt by governments, social partners and citizens. It is well

---

[7] Directive 2001/86/EC supplementing the Statute for a European company Regulation 2157/2001/EC with regard to the involvement of employees.

[8] Eg Kahn-Freund (1976b); Paton (1977); Aaron and Farwell (1982); Hanami and Monat (1987); Biagi (1993); Rogers and Streeck (1995).

[9] Eg Bonell (1983); Slomp (1990); Blanpain (1994).

[10] Eg Williams (1988); Wedderburn (1991); Rogers (1995).

known, and needs no explication here, that the overwhelming desire for peace shaped all activities—be it at the plant, societal or institutional level.

Workers' representatives were regarded as 'men of the first hour' who took over many responsibilities in the rebuilding of factories and gained at least de facto power. The political power of the councillors' movement was not comparable with the period following the First World War.[11] On the continent, strong divisions emerged between plant representatives and trade unions within the occupied countries. After the schism between the Soviet Union and the three western allies, the labour movement and labour law in western Europe were largely de-politicised, and workers' representation became more 'order-oriented': unions were predominantly economically oriented, while shop-floor representation was productivity-oriented.

Economic and social restructuring after 1945 showed a variety of forms, actors and strategies.[12] What is particularly interesting in the context of this chapter is first, to what extent these strategies contributed to the introduction of new forms of labour law at plant level; and secondly, whether or not these newly invented forms were capable of successfully meeting the need for sustainable economic and social restructuring. These issues would go on to affect the future of labour relations.

Eichengreen[13] emphasises the different paths towards co-operation between capital and labour that were taken in the immediate post-war period, some of which had a direct impact on the post-war plant-representation systems. Institutions allowed the parties to monitor one another's compliance with the terms of their (explicit or implicit) agreement (examples from Germany, Austria, the Netherlands and Sweden will be given in the next section). Rewards and penalties encouraged co-operation (conditioned subsidies and tax advantages, eg in Austria, Sweden and Germany). Public programmes bonded labour to individual firms (social insurance and labour standards advantages in return for wage restraint in Belgium, Norway, the Netherlands, Sweden, Denmark, Germany, Austria and Italy). Wage bargains were co-ordinated across firms and sectors (the German and Swedish arrangements were prototypical). These strategies were embedded in currency policies and external financial assistance (above all, the Marshall plan); and the establishment of European agencies allowed investment planning, free trade and innovative cooperation (like the European Coal and Steel Community as a predecessor of the European Economic Community (EEC)).

The strategy of mutual monitoring of compliance—itself shaped by other labour and social strategies—was paramount. What shop-floor institutions were newly invented in the post-war period, and to what extent were they able to contribute to the economic and social restructuring that was needed after the

---

[11] Ramm (1986) 243–60.

[12] From a political point of view, see Judt (2005); from an economic one, Eichengreen (2007); from a social one Kaelble (2007); and from a global point of view, Frieden (2006).

[13] Eichengreen (2007).

experience of the war? We shall see that these 'inventions' were not conjured from scratch but rather built on a certain diversity of heritage from the pre-1945 era. It is at this point, therefore, that we shall begin our investigation.

Corporatist Heritages: Pre-1945 Conditions

The successful growth of the European economies after 1945 paradoxically drew on the existence of more or less 'corporatist' institutions and practices that had existed before the end of the war. In the pre-1945 phase, different forms of corporatism in Europe ranged from authoritarian Nazi forms, whether due to a fascist government in the country itself, like in Italy and Germany, or due to Nazi occupation, as in Austria, France, and the Netherlands, to self-governed liberal and social forms (such as Sweden). In spite of this diversity, the manifestations of corporatist heritage had in common both a highly centralised decision-making process, regardless of whether or not collective bargaining was still permitted, and a developed, establishment-level labour representation. However, the latter was restricted to implementing centrally set labour standards, thereby ordering and pacifying class conflict. The post-1945 developments built on this heritage in a way that helped to integrate labour relations into the newly emerging economic growth, both by newly centralising collective negotiations, albeit now mainly on a voluntary level, and by strengthening the authority of the outcome of negotiations at the plant level. Thus, even a cursory examination reveals that the foundations of post-war workers' representation were already in place.

A good example of this heritage is Sweden. The industry-wide unions gained ground early on vis-à-vis plant or enterprise unions, and were all affiliated to the Swedish Trade Union Confederation (*Landsorganisationen i Sverige* (LO)). An Act on collective agreements adopted in 1928 was followed by the Basic Agreement in 1938. The philosophy was self-government of social partners making legislation superfluous. Nearly all branch organisations adopted the Basic Agreement. This was followed by 'collaboration agreements'. Among these were the works councils agreements of 1946 and 1966, which were implemented by collective agreements, not by legislation (see below). This interaction between centralised and decentralised industrial relations became significant. After the Second World War, central wage negotiations between the Swedish Employers' Confederation (Svenska Arbetsgivareföreningen (SAF)) and the LO became a pattern of behaviour until 1983; and this centralised, peaceful non-state model provided, equally at the plant level, a model for orderly industrial relations.

Let us take the Netherlands as a further example. The role of government in labour relations had already been strengthened following the First World War. Building on this, the government began to encourage the establishment of bipartite bodies at the sectoral and national inter-sectoral levels. Based on this heritage after the Second World War, the government could maintain tight control of wages and prices until well into the 1960s and follow a Keynesian pattern of economic policy—'[a] sort of tripartite social economic government'.[14] From this stemmed a well-developed practice of institutionalised consultation and co-operation at the all-industry level, as embodied in the Foundation of Labour in 1945 and the Social and Economic Council in 1950, both of which were corporatist organisations of business, with joint industrial boards for each sector and commodity boards for each chain of products. In the framework of this very centralised wages policy, equally peaceful works constitutions could develop. This works constitution was based on a bipartite, not a monistic, structure until 1979.

The corporatist heritage for a peaceful plant relationship can be reconstructed in a similar way for both Germany and Austria. The German Trade Union Confederation (*Deutscher Gewerkschaftsbund*) had gained recognition, by both employers and the state, during the First World War. This recognition went along with the completion of a legal workers' plant representation in 1919, which had powers to implement labour standards. The experience of Nazism and war affirmed the tendency toward 'unity' and 'community' (*Gemeinschaft*) as principles of both trade unionism and plant relationship. Had it not been for the Allied occupation forces, unitary general trade unions would have prevailed in post-war Germany, rather than the branch union system, which then continuously developed. Labour Chambers were the most prominent feature of the pre-1945 corporatist heritage in Austria. They emerged after the First World War, building a statutory representation of employees that grew to be especially influential. They were destroyed by Nazism but were restored after 1945, accompanied by works councils.

Britain and France did not have a corporatist heritage on which to build post-war economic reconstruction and the corresponding order of plant relations. Britain had not suffered German occupation. Workplace representation in Britain had its origins in voluntary shop stewards in the engineering and shipbuilding industries, with whom employers had been willing to negotiate during the First World War.[15] This declined in the inter-war years, but joint production committees with shop stewards flourished during the Second World War. By way of contrast, France[16] had the unfortunate experience of the Vichy Charter of Labour of 1941, which brought a corporatist spirit into labour relations, contrary to French tradition since 1791. However, this corporatist experience never attained the status of a 'heritage' to be upheld in the post-war phase. On the contrary, the Vichy regime was regarded as a betrayal that had to be overcome as soon as possible. French labour relations were re-established on a politically and religiously divided structure. At the plant level, this meant a militant multitude of union-controlled bodies seeking recognition and bargaining power. This structure provided no equivalent to the orderly shop-floor systems mentioned above. Italy, on the other hand, had a much stronger corporatist tradition during the

---

[14] Jacobs (2004a).
[15] Ramm (1986) 249.
[16] Le Crom (1998a, b).

fascist period. However, this was eliminated as early as 1948 in the post-war anti-fascist climate, which also led to the trade union split. Here, too, there were no preconditions for a centrally ordered and co-managed system of legal workers' representation.

The respective existence or non-existence of corporatist traditions hence had an indisputable impact on the structuring of the post-war workers' representation in various countries and, indirectly, their appropriateness for the 'golden age' of economic growth in Europe.

Trust-building Workplace Relations

The immediate post-war strategies—legal or otherwise—had, besides keeping wage developments under control, the further goal of creating an everyday plant relationship that allowed for co-operation as well as innovation. 'Trust' was a precondition of both objectives since both contained an implicit contract—that current wage restriction would be rewarded, in the near future, by increased wages and that peaceful co-operation at the plant level would be rewarded by common progress and secure jobs. In Germany, two structures played a key role within this context. 'Enterprise co-determination' (*Unternehmens-Mitbestimmung*) was implemented at the board of directors and supervisory board levels; the 'works constitution' (*Betriebsverfassung*) was implemented by works councils on a plant or establishment level. They were to integrate workers' interests, and potential unrest, into the context of the firm's interests as a whole, and the interests of the entire economy. However, in a reciprocal relationship between capital and labour, they also committed management to deal responsibly and transparently with the legitimate interests of the workers. There was an implicit contract requiring guidelines for both faithful co-operation and mutual rights (on transparency, legal behaviour and loyalty) capable of being enforced in cases of conflict or against free-riders.

In the quest to achieve everyday trust at the plant level, the post-1945 works councils' regulations in Germany (statutory) and in Sweden (collective bargaining) were paradigmatic. In Germany, the 1951 Coal and Steel Co-Determination Act was passed in response to the threat of socialisation. It provided for full parity between employees and shareholders in the supervisory board and a workers' director accepted by the unions on the board of directors. In addition to this enterprise-level co-determination, provision for establishment/plant-level participation was promulgated in 1952. The Works Councils Act built directly on the 1919 Weimar Act.[17] The Allied Control Council allowed the establishment of works councils as early as March 1946. Day-to-day practice continued as harmoniously and with as much determination as it had done before the intervention of Nazism and the 'leader principle' (*Führerprinzip*), laid down in the 1934 Act to

---

[17] Ramm (1986) 251–54.

Order National Labour, if not more so because of the memory of fascism and war, and of the immediate need to reconstruct the economy. There was a dispute between trade unions and the Adenauer administration about the weak role of unions within the works constitution, but the basic features of the Act were not contested. Establishment-level co-operation should be based on trust not challenged by open conflict. Works councillors' activity had to take place within the framework of labour standards set outside the plant, by collective agreements or by law. Within this framework, councils had legally enforceable rights to information and consultation in most firm matters, and to co-determination in the bulk of 'social' matters', thereby limiting managerial prerogative, but they had no right to strike. The state of affairs in Austria was substantially similar; when the Labour Chambers were restored after 1945 (Workers' Chambers Act 1954), works councils were set up, although with fewer co-determination rights than in Germany.

The case of Sweden differs formally from the German one, but has functional similarity. There was no works council legislation at all. In Finland a weak Act on Production Committees was passed in 1949, ending the development of radical anti-war shop-floor control. The Swedish 1938 Basic Agreement between the LO and the SAF (the Saltsjöbaden Agreement) was followed by 'collaboration agreements', among which were the works councils agreements of 1946 and 1966. These works council agreements were a product of, and in fact reproduced, trade union power. They consisted of information and joint consultation, not formal co-determination, in the areas of production, economy and personnel. Local bargaining took place within the framework of, and under the authority of, central negotiations between the SAF and the LO. The result was '[a] sort of model for orderly industrial relations'.[18] The system at that time was still bipartite in composition, bringing workers' representatives and management directly together, but it lacked strength for workers, who had developed increasing participation demands in the late 1960s. However, within the next two decades, it was complemented by the establishment of a coherent social insurance system, which had a practical impact similar to that in Germany. There, too, only a small minority of rights had to be legally enforced: the great majority of cases were solved with 'common sense', practical solutions, without appealing to the law and its institutions. This may be a manifestation of the 'small countries' effect: smaller countries provide for better preconditions of trust than bigger ones do, not only in the macrostructures of society, but also at the microlevel of plants, departments and work groups.

This 'small country' effect is also evident in the Netherlands and Belgium. Dutch works councils had a statutory basis, the 1950 Work Councils Act. However, this was a weak piece of legislation according few rights to workers' representatives. An effective extension of the legal rights of works councils took place only in the 1970s. But here, too, as in the Swedish case, the existing 'trust

---

[18] Adlercreutz (1998) 44.

culture' in industrial relations did not require legal regulation—in fact, it functioned better without it. The practical outcomes do not differ greatly from the German case. In Belgium, there was a national agreement on union committees in 1947 and Acts on works councils and health at work in 1952. However, soon collective bargaining prevailed again.

Counter-examples to this are Britain, France and Italy, none of which developed a coherent system of plant-level co-operation. In Britain, no need for practical change was felt in the labour policy. The 'collective laissez-faire' style in industrial relations, including multi-unionism, voluntary shop-steward structures, demarcation policies and closed shop agreements, remained untouched (see chapter 7 above). The need for a legally structured labour policy was seen only in the early 1960s, when the demands for effective state wage and income policies necessitated, as a precondition for their implementation, more orderly and accountable workplace relations.

France, with the Ordonnance of 22 February 1945, aimed at reforming the structures of the enterprise for the first time. Legislation remained limited to private firms. Extensive rights of representatives of workers existed only in the nationalised sector. The reason for this hesitant development of shop-floor relations was the post-war schism of unionism along political and confessional lines, which equally affected plant relations. A spirit of co-operation was not universally shared. Even if it existed in certain national unions, local antagonism and competitiveness prevented the integration of workers' interests into a community of production, as was observed in Germany and the Nordic countries.

Meanwhile Italy eliminated the corporatist heritage during the late 1940s. At the same time, trade union unity was achieved immediately after the Second World War, with the *Confederazione Generale Italiana del Lavoro* (Italian General Confederation of Labour), which organised the more than six million workers who were suffering from the political split of the Catholic Christian democratic and social democratic factions. This resulted in diffidence towards any workers' involvement in private firm decision-making or in other forms of bilateral institutions. Therefore no such legislation was passed in the post-war period. Plant commissions, abolished by fascism, were re-established in 1943 only through collective agreements, whilst joint committees appeared within the public sector.

Economic Growth and the Welfare State (1950–73)

During the 1950s a collective labour law emerged that was both integrated into the market and channelled by it. This new legal framework boasted a workers' representation system that both channelled shop-floor conflict and kept managerial prerogative free from other social or political intervention. The economically successful outcome of this model made it socially acceptable in spite of extensive national diversities. However, the 1960s introduced tensions. Trade unions were jaded and forced into macro-economic arrangements of anti-inflation policies, sometimes against their membership. Decentralised protest movements began to emerge, bringing together workers and students, and resulting in substantial progress in workers' participation rights (France, Italy, Germany). In workers' representation law this was a step towards 'countervailing power' instead of a 'partnership' system. Both systems of workplace representation—the adversarial one and the co-operative one—continued to co-exist, but the tensions between different national concepts and strategies (*autogestion* versus *Mitbestimmung*, *statuto dei lavoratori* versus 'co-management' and 'industrial democracy') rose.

The Golden Age

Workplace relations did not change substantially during the 1950s and early 1960s. The main shift had already taken place between 1945 and 1950. Everyday work relationships developed according to the modes of laissez-faire and collective bargaining rather than statutory intervention. Everyday workplace relations were shaped by economic and socio-cultural factors rather than by legal ones. However, these everyday plant customs and practices informally anticipated that which, in the late 1960s and the 1970s, would become legally institutionalised.

Economic and social progress clearly went hand in hand with co-operative shop-floor regulation. Rapid growth took place in all western European countries with co-operative or corporatist work cultures. Co-operative plant relationships had an enormous impact on economic success. There were two main reasons for this. First, viewed from a purely 'industrial' point of view, Europe's productive capital stock was roughly the same in 1947 as it had been 10 years earlier; indeed, in Germany it was even higher, due to wartime investment. At the conclusion of hostilities, industrial production was at barely 40% of pre-war levels in Belgium, France and the Netherlands and less than 20% in Germany and Italy; however, output was quickly boosted by putting people back to work. Hence economic reconstruction did not begin from scratch but rather involved the reinstatement and modernisation of only partially destroyed primary goods (coal and steel, chemical agents, etc) and the manufacturing industry. Secondly, under these circumstances, incremental rather than radical innovation was required.[19] It was not changes in system parameters of production that were required, but rather refinement and development within the existing parameters. The necessary ingredients for incremental performance are plant-based work organisation and plant-dominated industrial relations. The trust relationships to which the post-war period owed its economic success were, from a production-centred point of view, deeply rooted in a predominantly plant culture.

---

[19] Hall and Soskice (2001) 38–39.

This factor is significant in the comparison of German and British workplace relations. During the post-war period in Germany, workplace relations were dominated by the engineering trade and the German Industrial Union of Metalworkers, *Industriegewerkschaft Metall* (IG Metall). Despite the fact that an increasing number of unskilled workers were entering the industry and the union, IG Metall was still dominated by male skilled workers, frequently toolmakers, products of the German system of vocational training. They dominated works councils, and local and regional, as well as national, trade union structures. Plant culture trickled down into the non-plant constituency and thus became predominant, although male skilled workers were a minority in the overall membership. The 1950s slogan 'One plant—one union' (*Ein Betrieb— eine Gewerkschaft*) meant unity under the leadership of skilled male labour.

British workplace relations differed greatly due to multi-unionism, the co-existence of plant, branch and general unions, and the various demarcation strategies and conflicts between them. Additionally, the vocational training system differed from that in Germany. British unions regarded access to and length of vocational training from the perspective of control of the local labour market whereas German unions regarded them from the point of view of efficiency and performance in production. In Britain, separate organisations of skilled workers existed in each sector, such as engineering or printing industries, and thus did not provide overarching unity. Demarcation excluded the trickling-down process leading to the hegemonic unity as described for the German system.

Meanwhile, 1950s France was practising a form of neo-liberalism.[20] Collective bargaining played a much greater role than statutory regulation. In the Nordic countries, statutory regulation of workplace relations was found only in the immediate post-war years and then again in the late 1960s and 1970s.[21] Most workplace relation issues was resolved by custom, practice and collective bargaining. Finally, many countries, such as Sweden, Germany and the Netherlands, shifted their statutory activity to social and social security law.

Around May 1968

The culmination of the golden age was marked by a Europe-wide protest movement of students and workers, which had a significant impact on workers' representation (see chapter 2 above). The post-1968 period was dominated by social democratic governments and led to institutional changes, all of which enhanced workplace labour power. Thus the existing gulf between legalised, institutionalised forms of participation and less legalised, trade union-oriented forms of workers' solidarity widened still further.

The Nordic countries made early progress with institutional changes, mostly

[20] Pélissier et al (2000) 17.
[21] Hasselbalch (2002); Edström (2002).

on a voluntary basis. In Denmark, a series of agreements on works councils started as early as 1965. In 1970 an agreement between the Confederation of Danish Employers, *Dansk Arbejdsgiverforening* (DA) and the Danish Confederation of Trade Unions, *Landsorganisationen i Danmark* (LO) led to the stronger involvement of workers in companies. The important Co-operation Agreement, concluded in 1986 between the DA and the LO, provided for information, consultation and grievance rights and procedures, with the aims both to protect workers and to enhance productivity of the firm. In Sweden, as already noted, the Basic Agreement was followed by collaboration agreements (see above). Finland started taking steps towards industrial democracy later, in 1977, and on the basis of the Swedish concepts. The Swedish bipartite works councils were strongly influenced by trade unions. The agreement provided for extended information and joint consultation in the areas of production, economy and personnel. A period of industrial unrest was followed by a public investigation in 1971. In 1975 an agreement between the LO, the SAF and the Negotiation Cartel for Salaried Employees in the Private Business Sector, *Privattjänstemannakartellen* (PTK) was concluded on economic committees and workers' consultants. In 1976, after heated debate, the Act on Co-Determination in Working Life was passed. Contrary to the voluntarist Nordic tradition, a new pattern of interplay between collective agreement and statute emerged. From 1970 onwards there was a stronger statutory impact on plant representation.

The Swedish measures differed from other European examples. The Co-Determination Act 'aims to give employees, through their unions, co-determination in the conduct of affairs in enterprises and public authorities; it aims at democratising working life'.[22] The implementation of this Act by agreements took until 1978 in the public sector and 1982 in the private. A preceding Act on the Position of a Trade Union Representatives at the Work Place of 1974 was amended in 1975, 1976 and 1982, granting time off and non-discrimination rights for trade union representatives. The Co-Determination Act contained a right of negotiation, on important alterations of the employer's business, between an organisation of workers and the employer; a right to information; a right to collective agreements; and a peace obligation when bound by a collective agreement. For cases of industrial disputes, it provided for mediation between the two sides, damages and legal proceedings before a court. The significant points here are first, that the statutory regulation promoted implementation via collective agreement, and secondly, that it implies trade union rights and obligations. The balance once more tipped in favour of collective bargaining with the 1982 Agreement on Efficiency and Participation between the SAF, the LO and the PTK, based on the Co-determination Act.

It contained common values and, besides covering the development of work organisation, technical development, and the financial and economic situation of the company and its resources, also stated that 'co-operation in the spirit of trust

---

[22] Adlercreutz (1998) 46.

between the workers' trade union representatives and the employer's representatives is critical for the successful development of jobs and participation'. Faithful co-operation and workplace participation are strongly emphasised. Another example of a statutory intervention can be seen in the 1976 Act Concerning Board Representation for the Privately Employed (replaced by a new Act in 1987). This provided that, in companies of at least 25 employees, two (and for those with more than 1000, three) representatives could be sent to the board of directors. The feature that is specific to the Swedish system and its tradition of autonomy is that these representatives are appointed by the firm or the local trade union.

In France and Italy, a politicised, state-oriented attitude can be identified within this period of unrest and protest, but it was equally union-oriented in the legal reform of workplace representation. In 1968, France was at the centre of the working class movement and revolt. There were obviously connections all over Europe—to Italy, Poland, and intellectual groups in Germany, Britain, Spain, Portugal and elsewhere. One of the first outcomes in the field of workers' representation was the Act on Trade Union Rights in the Enterprise of 27 December 1968, prefigured by the famous *Protocole de Grenelle* of 27 May 1968.[23] Prior to May 1968, employers and politicians were reluctant to allow unions to exercise their duties within the firm. The Grenelle protocol facilitated the shift in their attitudes. The French Minister of Social Affairs, Maurice Schumann, stated frankly: 'If one says to me that the May events have provoked this new step of social progress, I would reply that they undoubtedly have accelerated it and that I am happy about that.'[24] Long after the recognition of the personnel delegates in 1936[25] and the enterprise committees in 1945, the Act recognised trade unions in the internal world of the enterprise. The legal implications of this were threefold: representative trade unions acquired the right to free expression and action within the firm; an exclusively union-elected union delegate emerged alongside elected representatives (personnel delegates, enterprise committees); and the enterprise became a unit of collective bargaining. A parallel effort to increase participation of workers in the decision-making or management of the enterprise was postponed *sine die* after the defeat of General de Gaulle and his subsequent resignation.[26] The regulation of workers' representation here was not abstentionist, like in the Nordic and British cases, but instead state-oriented and interventionist. But workplace representation remained militant and non-co-operative. It avoided co-management as prevailing in the Nordic countries and still more so in Germany: workers and their representatives were taking over responsibility for the enterprise.

[23] Borenfreund (1998).
[24] 'Si l'on me dit que ce sont les événements de mai qui ont provoqué cette nouvelle étape du progrès social, je répondrai qu'ils l'ont sans doute accéléré et que je m'en réjouis' (JO, Débats Ass nat, 5 décembre 1968, 5049).
[25] Ramm (1986) 250.
[26] Pélissier et al (2000) 18.

Similarly, Italy also chose not to follow the path of co-determination or institutionalised participation at the shop-floor level in the post-1968 period. The Workers' Statute (*Statuto dei Lavoratori*) of 20 March 1970[27] clearly had links with the protest movement, but it focused on 'rules to safeguard the freedom and dignity of workers and the freedom of trade unions and of their activity at the workplace'. The Act followed an integrated approach, linking individual rights of workers (Title 1) with individual trade union rights of workers (Title 2) and collective trade unions rights (Title 3) for the first time. In this manner, workplace representation was meant to unite freedom of expression (Article 1), data and personality protection (Articles 4 and 6) and health and safety rights of workers (Article 9) with their right to establish and belong to unions and to exert union activities at the workplace (Article 14), and with trade union rights to act (Article 19), to assemble (Article 20), to collect membership fees and to conduct ballots at the workplace (Articles 21 and 26). Rather than leading to an internal participatory organisation of the firm, the Act was meant to 'constitutionalise' the sphere of work—ie to establish a power equilibrium of workers vis-à-vis employers in the establishment and in the wider civil society.[28] It extended the voice of unions to the spheres within and outside the enterprise; in this way, workers' individual rights strengthened trade unions as countervailing powers within the enterprise. The Act was to be the basis of an 'activity of self-protection with effectiveness within the establishment'.[29] Neither shared responsibilities nor co-involvement in economic affairs of the firm were intended with this Act. This implied an increase in workers' representation—but as an antagonist rather than as a partner.

Germany took the opposite direction. Despite cross-border contacts and interactions between trade unions and union-oriented intellectuals all over western Europe, there was a sharp division between co-operative or community-oriented and adversarial or class-oriented strategies of workplace representation. Germany and Austria were relatively isolated in taking (or, rather, maintaining and extending) the former approach. In 1972, the German Works Councils Act was amended, and the Enterprise Co-Determination Act was passed in 1976. The motivation for the reforms was wildcat strikes in 1967—Germany's first experiences of crisis—were the students' movement of 1968, the breakdown of the Adenauer/Kiesinger administration and the emergence of the Brandt/Genscher regime. The revised Works Councils Act retained the fundamental principles of the 1952 Act. Greater co-determination rights in regulation of hours and wages were granted. Works councils acquired rights and opportunities to influence personnel policies and the ergonomics of the workplace. The competence of arbitration boards (*Einigungsstelle*) for settling collective disputes on a

---

[27] Treu et al (2000) 23; for the historical origins of the Statute, the *commissiones internas* and their re-establishment in 1943, by the accordo Buozzi-Mazzini, see Giugni (1976); see too, Wedderburn (1991).

[28] Ghera (2000) 22.

[29] Giugni (1992) 21.

plant level was considerably increased and juridically sharpened. On the economic level, as distinguished from the social and personnel ones, the 1972 reform only extended information and consultation rights. Compared with other systems of workplace participation (eg Sweden) the German system was highly juridified: it had a purely statutory basis, and all rights were legally enforceable. That this did not lead to an end of social partnership and an increase in workplace litigation is due the mechanism 'bargaining in the shadow of the law'. The bargaining power of works councils grew as a result of the potential recourse to formal rights and court proceedings: in most cases this did not hinder, but rather encouraged, consensus between the parties. The 1976 Co-Determination Act, covering firms with more than 2000 employees, broadly followed the trade union demands for parity of management and labour. A parity of seats (and votes) in the firm's supervisory board were reserved for workers' representatives. However, management staff representatives were counted as workers, and the casting vote in case of lack of consensus remained with employers' representatives. In the firms covered by this Act, workers' directors (within the board of directors) were usually appointed on the proposal of unions. This was a new approach to *Mitbestimmung* in Germany that complemented co-determination in the coal, iron and steel industries, dating from 1951 (with full parity), and co-determination in other joint-stock companies (with one-third of the seats on the supervisory board reserved for workers). Despite the efforts of employers and employers' federations to legally challenge these new Acts, or to circumvent them in practice, the highest labour and constitutional courts upheld and secured them. For a practical assessment of this juridified mode of decision-making, it is important to know that the vast majority of the decisions of a supervisory board are taken by unanimous vote.

Workers' representation in Austria was regulated by the 1974 Collective Employment Regulation Act. This increased the influence of works councils in both personnel and social matters. Amendments in 1986 and 1990 brought new rights of participation, particularly concerning the extension of works councils' rights in company groups. The presence of trade unions in establishments remained low. The 1974 Act introduced a one-third employee participation, appointed by the central works council, in the internal controlling body of certain large undertakings. However, no other participatory power was present at the undertaking level: this remained managerial prerogative. Undertakings with fewer than five workers were not covered. The similarities with Germany are conspicuous. The works council was a workers-only body. It had general participation rights and co-determination, above all in social affairs. In cases of regulatory disputes, particularly disputes over co-determination rights, the arbitration board was allowed to make an award.

The situation in the Netherlands was as follows. The year 1970 witnessed a growing trend towards shop-floor democracy, with four Acts introduced in the same year: on the annual accounts of the company; on company inquiries; on management structure of major enterprises; and a new Works Councils Act.

There was no strong influence of works councils or unions on the composition of top-level management. It is only since 1979 that the works council has been composed only of workers. Prior to this, the company's chief executive officer presided over it. In 1994, the Works Councils Act was extended to cover the public sector. By the beginning of the twenty-first century, there was a duty to establish a works council when at least 50 workers were employed, and an optional representation in plants with more than 10. The Dutch type of plant representation remained less extensive than the German one. In undertakings with at least 100 persons, or 35 persons employed for more than one-third of normal working time, the employer was obliged, 'in the interest of the satisfactory performance of all the undertaking's functions, to establish a works council for consultation with and the representation of the persons employed in the undertaking' (section 2, paragraph 1). Between three and 25 members were to be elected by the persons employed in an undertaking from among their own number (section 6). Consultation with the works council was mandatory (section 23). Special powers of works councils were granted in respect of a list of issues, like fundamental changes in the plant (in such cases, a very detailed consultation procedure had to take place with no co-determination rights). In certain social issues, the approval of the works council was necessary; if this was not granted, 'the employer may request the industrial committee[30] to approve it' (section 27, paragraph 4). The precedence of collective agreements over agreements between employers and works councils was legally guaranteed. In a comparison of the Dutch system with that of Germany, Jacobs concludes:

> There is a dual system of workers' representatives (unions and works councils) like in Germany. However, no direct representation of the workers in supervisory councils of big enterprises as in Germany takes place. Collective bargaining on a national inter-sectoral level is much more important than in Germany; collective bargaining at enterprise level is less developed than in Germany.[31]

Contrary to the continental and the Nordic countries described above, Britain continued the scepticism about institutionalised workers' involvement at both the establishment and enterprise levels. Prior to 1974, there was no significant attempt to establish forms of worker participation besides collective bargaining in the private sector. The maintenance of voluntary collective bargaining remained the rallying point around which the protest movements against the 1971 Industrial Relations Act were mounted (see chapters 2 and 7 above). During the 1970s, tendencies towards industrial democracy gained momentum—for instance in the 1977 Bullock report, which (by a majority) recommended equality of representation of employer and workers with a smaller number of

[30] A paritarian government established body set up for each sector: Jacobs (2004a) 185.
[31] Jacobs (2004a).

independent members on boards of directors.[32] The Labour government, bowing to pressure from the Confederation of British Industries, was not willing to go beyond minority workers' representation on the board, and this was to be made compulsory only as a last resort when agreement could not be reached.[33] However, even this watered-down proposal was never implemented either statutorily or by collective bargaining. The Conservative Thatcher regime during the 1980s put an end to aspirations of workers' participation. Nevertheless, from the late 1970s onward, certain customs and practices of 'joint committees' came to the fore, for instance in the machine-tool and printing sectors.[34] These informal changes to some extent prepared the ground for post-1980s developments towards workplace information and consultation under European guidance, analogous to the informal workplace practices of the 1950s on the continent that anticipated their juridification in the 1960s and 1970s.

The developments towards greater workers' participation (in the form of collective information and consultation procedures) had some international backing foreshadowing the supranational European developments both before and after the turn of the century.[35] The 1977 International Labour Organisation (ILO) Tripartite Declaration provided for 'regular consultation on matters of mutual concern'.[36] The 1976 Organisation for Economic Co-operation and Development's Guidelines for Multinational Enterprises required employers to 'provide to representatives of employees information which is needed for meaningful negotiations on conditions of employment' and 'provide to representatives of employees … information which enables them to obtain a true and fair view of the performance of the entity or, where appropriate, the enterprise as a whole'.[37] Simultaneously, the EEC, following the first social action programme of 1974, launched Directives containing information and consultation rights for workers representatives[38] and undertook the first steps towards co-determination within the European company, although these were not achieved for another 30 years.

All in all, the development of workplace participation showed a dual face. After experiences of crisis and industrial unrest emerged, participation instruments under the prevailing impact of social democratic governments were substantially extended. Eichengreen sees this as a paradox: certain institutions of social integration and cohesion within the immediate post-war period and the

---

[32] Report of the Committee on Industrial Democracy (Chairman: Lord Bullock), Cmnd 6706 (1977).

[33] Industrial Democracy, Cmnd 7231 (1978).

[34] See Brown (1981); Daniel and Millward (1983); for a German–British comparison, see Marsh et al (1981); Mückenberger and Duhm (1983); Mückenberger (1988).

[35] Directives of 1994 (94/45/EC), 1997 (97/74/EC), 2001 (2001/86/EC) and 2002 (2002/14/EC).

[36] Para 56.

[37] Sections on Employment and Industrial Relations nos 2 and 3: Blanpain (1994) 8.

[38] Directives on collective dismissals (75/129/EEC, Art 2) and on transfers of undertakings (77/87/EEC, Art 6).

golden age (which we can associate with works councils) had helped to reconstruct capitalist growth and expansion. He observes:

> Toward the end of the 1960s, output and productivity growth began to slow, and macroeconomic instability reared its ugly head . . . At this point, the same institutions that had played such a positive role in the preceding years became obstacles to growth.[39]

This harsh assessment will be scrutinised later in this chapter.

Excursus: Health and Safety Representatives (1968–89)

Human integrity and well-being requires the possibility of self-determination and self-defence at the place of origin of the risks that challenge this integrity and well-being. This is why workers' representatives actively take up the work-related risks and try to cope with them through prevention of occupational accidents, and more effective forms of treatment and compensation. Remarkable shifts can be observed within the post-war period. These can be roughly characterised by two mutually enforcing trends: one is factual, the other normative in kind.

At the factual level, the modern world of work has radically altered the types of accidents and illnesses from which working people suffer. In industrial society (mines, maritime or road transport, mechanical engineering, chemical processing, etc) a specific risk can usually be identified as the cause of a death or personal injury. Thus, in the case of traumatic injury, both legal responsibilities and remedies are relatively easy to identify. In contrast to this, workers in the service sector are more likely to be confronted with chronic conditions. These are not due to a single traumatic event but are instead caused by long-term exposure to harmful conditions. The spectrum of symptoms varies widely: from personal injury (cardio-circulation, musculoskeletal disorder, metabolism, back dysfunction, etc), to prolonged exposure to harmful substances (leading to cancer or allergies), to purely psychological damage (stress, depression, impairment of one's well-being in the context of harassment or bullying at work) that (psychosomatically) manifests itself in physical form. The range of remedies is equally broad: no single cause can be identified and eliminated; the 'setting' of everyday working life has to be rearranged in its entirety.

At the same time, the normative understanding of disease has fundamentally changed over the last 60 years. The earliest and clearest legal evidence of this shift can be seen in the constitution of the World Health Organisation (WHO), which in 1946 established, as a first and supreme principle, that: 'Health is a state of complete physical, mental and social wellbeing and not merely the absence of disease or infirmity.' From the moment of its publication, this dynamic and

---

[39] Eichengreen (2007) 47–48.

revolutionary definition has challenged the 'blinkered' minds not only of labour and social security lawyers, but also of doctors, judges and politicians. This understanding is both modern and visionary in that it focused, as early as 1946, on the interferences of everyday life into the well-being of workers, and calls for legal remedies that, instead of treating working people as objects, involve them individually and collectively in the improvement of their overall well-being.

It is against this background that we can understand the development of workers' participation that has taken place. The ways in which different European countries have dealt with work accidents and occupational illnesses have been many and varied.[40] After 1968 all of the countries analysed here made a paradigmatic legal shift with regard to health and safety in the workplace. Plant health and safety officers and workers' representatives, on a specialised and highly skilled level, have improved the ability to cope with work risks at the place of their origin. The most advanced countries developed an approach combining social insurance (on which see chapter 6 above) and public labour inspection with systematic interactive and preventive risk-management at the plant and branch level.

A virtually synchronous qualitative step forward took place in the early 1970s in nearly all the countries studied. Interestingly, this phase emphasised above all the in-plant levers of labour protection, namely health and safety specialists and workers' representatives. It opened the door to a systematic and prevention-oriented risk-management, bringing together in-plant actors with labour inspectors and social insurance representatives, rather than merely compensating injuries that had already occurred. Instruments differed from country to country. For instance, Finland used the collective agreement: on the basis of the 1946 basic agreement, an agreement on occupational safety was concluded in 1968 that also provided for wider involvement of workers and their representatives in monitoring labour conditions. An important statutory instrument was the Italian Workers' Statute of 1970, which provided, in Article 9, for the workers' and their representatives' right to monitor the occupational accident and disease-related rules. It did not, however, grant clear bargaining rights. Austria promulgated the 1972 Workers' Protection Act, which, in its section 2, was clearly plant- and participation-oriented. In Germany, the 1972 reform of the Works Councils Act and several Acts of the 1970s concerning plant doctors, safety experts, workplace conditions and dangerous agents at work were embedded in an overall strategy of 'humanisation of work' (*Humanisierung der Arbeit*). This strategy combined instruments and competencies of worker representatives, social partners, state agencies and health experts in an interactive and participatory way. In Britain, the 1972 Robens Report criticised the scattered British health and safety system for not covering some 5 million workers. Consequently, the comprehensive 1974 Health and Safety at Work etc Act strengthened the monitoring power of safety

---

[40] For the period before 1945, see Hepple (1986) 142–46; and for social security post-1956, see chapter 6 above.

representatives and committees, though with weak negotiating competence. New institutions were set up, such as the Health and Safety Commission and Executive in Britain in 1974, the Agency for the improvement of working conditions in France in 1973, the National Institute for Work (*Arbetslivinstitutet*) in Sweden in 1973, and the European Foundation for the Improvement of Living and Working Conditions in 1975. In the Danish system, health and safety at work had long been under the regime of separate voluntary agreements (industry, agriculture, forestry etc). However, the 1977 Act on the Working Environment replaced these agreements by a comprehensive legal framework establishing a local safety organisation, composed of the social partners and factory inspectorate, within which representatives of wage earners and management were to play an important role. Similarly important were the 1977 Acts on working environment in Sweden and Norway.

A later incentive to develop occupational health and safety law was the 1986 Single European Act, which (under Article 118a of the amended Treaty) had transferred competencies to the EEC with regard to legally shaping the working environment. This gave rise to the important health and safety Framework Directive 89/391/EEC, which linked the preference for prevention against occupational injuries (Articles 1, 5–7 and 14) with a hitherto seldom emphasised involvement of workers and their representatives (Articles 10–12) and an interaction with external health and safety experts and associated agencies with regard to information, education and co-operation. The 1989 Directive is a cornerstone of the approach to occupational health and safety that we earlier termed 'systematic'. The Framework Directive was followed by a flood of particular Directives applying the general principles to particular groups of persons, agents, branches and risk.[41] The health and safety issue seems, along with the anti-discrimination issue, to be one of the only fields of European labour-related policies that has remained vigorous and effective, and has survived the deregulation, non-regulation or soft-regulation trends.

What we can conclude as far as workers' participation in the occupational injuries issue is concerned is that, besides long periods of incremental progress, the legal development saw radical innovation in the early 1970s. This took place at the end of the industrially dominated age in Europe and its entry into a service and knowledge-based society, a development that was accompanied by protest movements. Under these conditions the new attitudes towards occupational disease in its two forms (as outlined above)—the epidemiological as well as the normative—installed itself within the legal system as a modernised, integrated

[41] Among the most important directives are: 89/654/EEC workplace; 89/655/EEC work equipment; 89/656/EEC personal protective equipment; 90/269/EEC manual handling of loads; 90/270/EEC display screen equipment; 90/394/EEC exposure to carcinogens at work; 90/679/EEC biological agents at work; 92/57/EEC temporary or mobile construction sites; 92/58/EEC safety or health signs at work; 92/85/EEC pregnant and breastfeeding workers; 92/91/EEC mineral-extracting industries—drilling; 92/104/EEC mineral-extracting industries; 93/193/EEC board fishing vessels; 98/24/EC chemical agents at work; 1999/92/EC risk from explosive atmosphere; 2000/54/EC exposure to biological agents.

system of diversified social actors and agencies whose co-operation was necessary to cope with the problem of illness and injury at work. The modernised system, however, requires the involvement of workers and workers' representatives in health and safety at work.

This progress, like all the progress we will review in the rest of this chapter, is ambivalent. The quest for health in our knowledge-based society and its legal framework has lost its innocence. It is no longer just the 'complete physical, mental and social wellbeing' (as the WHO termed it) transferred to the world of labour as the 'humanisation of work'; instead, it is an ever more important element of the global quest for competitiveness. If Europe is to be the world's leading knowledge-based economy with the highest innovative productivity (instead of the lowest cost of labour), as the Lisbon summit postulated, the complete physical, mental and social well-being of workers will become a neces- sary ingredient of any comparative advantage of European enterprises and the European economy. This ingredient has to be carefully protected, not only against selfish employers, but also against the workers themselves.

Economic Crisis (1973–79)

The period of 1973–79 was marked by a paradox.[42] While the oil shocks marked the beginning of a downward economic cycle of stagnation and unemployment, the political and social cycle implied the golden age of industrial democracy (see chapter 2 above). For example, in Germany, Chancellor Willi Brandt's slogan 'To dare to be more democratic' (*Mehr Demokratie wagen*) brought the industry- wide breakthrough of enterprise-level *Mitbestimmung*. In Sweden the 1976 Co-Determination Act (above) was passed. The Dutch socialists made steps forward in workers' participation in the mid-1970s, in the shape of capital forma- tion for employees and land reform. Frieden sums up the paradox that, as the recession continued, governments everywhere faced insistent demands for greater industrial democracy. The other side of the coin was that 'stagnant business conditions and continuing inflation saddled the Western world with stagflation, an ugly word for an unpleasant reality'.[43] In fact, 'stagflation' was the outcome of the contradiction between the economic and the socio-political cycles.

The 1973 'oil crisis' marked only a superficial indicator of a turn in labour relations and workplace representation that was of a much deeper and more fundamental nature, and brings us back to the considerations raised by Eichengreen (above). The economic troubles of the 1970s spawned crises in both the normal employment relationship and representation. A remarkable shift in employment sectors had started, with manufacturing being replaced by tertiary

---

[42] Frieden (2007) 364ff.
[43] Ibid, 368.

or service work. During the 1950s and 1960s the industrial and service sectors had grown in parallel, accompanied by a corresponding decline of agriculture. In the 1970s the service sector continued to grow, whereas the industrial sector all over Europe began to stagnate and go into decline, such that

> by the end of the 1970s, a clear majority of the employed populations of Britain, Germany, France, the Benelux countries, Scandinavia and the Alpine countries worked in the service sector—communications, transport, banking, public administrations and the like. Italy, Spain and Ireland were close behind.[44]

Along with tertiarisation went an increase in female employment (see chapter 5 above) and an increasing destandardisation in labour relations (fixed term, agency work, etc; see chapter 3 above).[45] We recognise a paradoxical extension of workers' representation rights, although not in the same way in different states. The real effects of tertiarisation and individualisation followed only in the 1980s, whereas the 1970s showed a counterfactual collectivisation of shop-floor representation.

In Britain, under the Labour government of 1974–79, the 'social contract' resulted in new collective bargaining rights but no formal extensions of workplace representation rights. The EEC encouraged visions of industrial democracy that had been unthinkable in Britain before it became a Member State in 1973. In a document of 1973, the Trades Union Congress took a positive stance vis-à-vis social partnership agreements (despite certain scepticism towards the German system of statutory works councils) and the EEC's initiative towards European works councils and the European company with workers' representatives on the supervisory board.[46] The British Labour Party and trade unions were beginning to go over from an anti- to a pro-EEC orientation. Nevertheless, despite proposals for some form of board-level representation of workers, no practical step towards shop-floor representation resulted (see above). The Netherlands remained even more sceptical about workers' representation in the supervisory board. In these years of expansion of workers' participation, they continued to put their trust in trade union autonomy and compromise rather than in statutory representation in the enterprise bodies.

At the same time, the 'participation wave' engulfed continental Europe, covering nearly all European countries, although in extremely different forms and often involving political controversy between governments and social partners. The participatory approach went hand in hand with stricter income policies, austerity programmes and curbs in social security standards, often under social-democratic governments (see chapter 2 above). Some scholars even argued[47] that there was a sort of 'exchange mechanism' between social

---

[44] Judt (2005) 327–28.
[45] Kaelble (2007) 73ff.
[46] TUC (1973).
[47] Crouch (1979b).

democratic governments and organised labour. The former granted participation rights in decision-making at the enterprise level in exchange for restrictions on wages and social security.

Jacobs[48] claims that all these participatory developments mark an already counterfactual effervescence of industrial democracy before its implosion under neo-liberalism. This correctly hints at the inversion of the social democratic reforms of the late 1960s until the early 1980s. It is true that there was a radical change in workers' representation, but this change did not imply abolishing workers' participation. It only stopped tendencies towards countervailing power or workers' self-management (*autogestion*), which had dominated, for instance, Italian and French shop-floor representation during the 1960s. Additionally, this change brought forth a trend towards 'co-management' as a new form of workers' representation. Information and consultation rights of workers had always had two functions: they expressed the desire of workers for recognition and social justice, and the need of management for control, transparency and involvement.[49] The suggestion of abolition of participation rights therefore is wrong—there was only a functional change in the ensuing periods.

Restructuring and Deregulation (1980–96)

After the end of social democratic pre-eminence in Europe and the decline and eventual implosion of the Soviet Union, the twin crises of the economy and of political representation provoked a fundamental change in workplace relations, both empirically and within the dominant discourse (individualisation, pluralisation, etc). Structures and functions of workplace representation within this period developed differently, according to the country-specific 'varieties of capitalism'[50] (see chapters 1 and 2 above). However, new forms of workplace representation emerged everywhere at the cost of trade union and unitary shop-floor representation powers. They consisted in informal, direct representation, particularly for white-collar workers, such as the Italian rank-and-file committees in the public and service sectors that emerged from 1987 (*comitati di basi-cobas*). Individualisation became crucial for the legal structure of workplace representation. There was an increase in individual workers' rights as opposed to collective rights. Individual rights were to be found in the German works councils' reform 1972. In France, the *lois Auroux* of 4 August and 28 October 1982 concerned the *droit d'expression* and representation of employees. The first of these laws, in particular, challenged collective representation in the traditional

---

[48] Jacobs (2006).

[49] See the seminal analysis of the American economist Smith (1991); *cf* the accounts of Rogers (1995); Freeman and Lazear (1995); FitzRoy and Kraft (2005).

[50] Hall and Soskice (2001).

sense—'shop rules and the right of the employees to express themselves directly'.[51] The question was raised whether individuals 'need' collective representation or whether they can better express themselves directly. Fragmentation and social exclusion were the inevitable corollaries of individualisation. From the early 1980s onwards, the crisis of the standard employment relationship and the increase in atypical employment gained empirical importance and attention among scholars (see chapter 3 above).[52] The rise in atypical employment affected representation in numerous ways. The formalised system of shop-floor representation translated some interests more powerfully than others. Workplace representation was mostly dominated by 'normal', 'typical' or 'standard' workers, thus more or less excluding atypical and non-standard workers, often at the expense of female workers. Thus the crisis of the standard employment relationship caused a crisis of the 'representativeness' of workplace representation. New forms of representation emerged which were not universal, but fragmented— separate representation bodies for hitherto unrepresented or under-represented groups of workers, or the mandatory integration of these groups of employees into the existing representation bodies, through quotas, non-discrimination principles and special procedures.

An example of separate representation bodies is the 1988 German Act for the establishment of plant committees for senior white-collar workers (*leitende Angestellte*). Whereas the distinction between blue- and white-collar workers had been losing ground in German workplace representation law (the 'group' division between blue and white collar was abolished in the 2001 reform), the distinction between senior white-collar employees and the rest of the workers has been strengthened. The 1972 Works Councils Act excluded them from coverage. The 1976 Co-Determination Act guaranteed seats in the supervisory board to senior white collars in correspondence to their numerical relation to the workforce— allocating them, however, to the workers' bench of the board. The 1988 Act granted them a separate plant representation with information and consultation rights, but no rights of co-determination.

Examples of mandatory integration into existing representation bodies can be found in the anti-discrimination provisions of the workplace representation laws of the EU Member States, most of them following the equality-oriented European guidelines and Directives. The European legislation on gender equality (Article 119 EC) here clearly took the lead (see chapters 3 and 5 above). Correspondingly, the 2001 reform of the German Works Councils Act introduced a mandatory quota of seats for the under-represented sex, corresponding to their share of the workforce. Other examples of this strategy affect the regulation of non-standard forms of employment. This can be seen in collective agreements; for instance, in Denmark, a duty was placed on the employer to ask the works councils for permission in case of introduction of part-time work. In Germany,

[51] Despax and Rojot (1987) 36.
[52] See Mückenberger and Deakin (1989); for an international account, see Tálos (1999).

a statutory duty—but only to inform the works council about part-time and fixed-term work—was established in the 2000 Part-Time and Fixed Term Contracts Act. German developments may also be cited concerning the representation of fragmented parts of the workforce. The German Federal Labour Court ruled that self-employed taxi drivers, working under a common time schedule, although without employees, should be allowed to form a works council. Similarly, in Spain temporary workers have been represented by the workers' representatives of the user firm since 1994 (Article 17 Temporary Work Agencies Act). In plants where several firms work together, all of them have to nominate coordinators for health and safety prevention (Article 13, Royal Decree 171/2004). The German 2001 works councils reform also changed the representation of agency workers. According to German law, these workers have a contract of employment with the provider firm and are represented by the provider firm's works council. After the reform, they were allowed, as in Spain, to enjoy certain services of the user firm's works council and to take part in the user firm's works council elections if they had worked for at least three months in the user firm. All these examples show that it is possible to draw a legal bond of 'representation' within a firm even if there is no legal bond of 'employment' to the firm.

The law thus operates with two representation strategies with regard to fragmentation of the workforce: one is the legalisation of separate forms of representation; the other is mandating equality in existing representation bodies. This dual approach is not contradictory. The law takes into account the increasing diversity within the ranks of workers by granting a (hopefully corresponding) diversity of representation. However, the law does not accept that diversity ends up in disparity. Where fragmentation leads to social exclusion (here in the sense of non-representation), the law therefore prefers mandatory equality-oriented integration of interests into the existing forms of collective representation.

Another development going hand in hand with deregulation and restructuring objectives in the dominant discourse in the late 1990s was a redefinition of the objectives of the enterprise. 'Corporate social responsibility' (CSR), 'corporate identity' and 'corporate governance' became labels in the discourse first for big companies, then for enterprises in general. CSR regards the company no longer as independent from society and the externalities it imposes upon society, but as 'embedded' in society. According to Sainsaulieu,[53] the enterprise is a societal affair ('*L'entreprise—une affaire de société*') and responsible to its stakeholders (including workers, but also the environment, culture, etc). There are three main components of CSR: that the enterprise has a commitment towards positive externalities for society; that this commitment goes beyond the legal obligations of the enterprise; and that this commitment is voluntary. Companies frequently express their CSR in 'codes of conduct' or other, unilaterally established, informal rules of behaviour—often extending beyond borders in

[53] Sainsaulieu (1992).

global supply chains.[54] Sometimes CSR has implications for workers' representation; however, such implications are typically ambivalent ones. Workers' promotion in CSR is often regarded as individual promotion rather than collective protection—it thus contributes to the crisis of representation discussed below. Due to its voluntary nature, CSR leads to a distinction, in Banerjee's words, between the 'good, the bad, and the ugly: some enterprises take societal responsibility seriously, some subordinate it to capital accumulation, and some pretend they take society seriously in order make better profit'.[55]

Globalisation: the European Response (1997–2004)

Besides—and along with—tertiarisation and individualisation, workplace representation has increasingly been influenced by the 'blurring boundaries' of production and services.[56] Globalisation here means 'denationalisation', not only of commodity exchange and free movement of labour, but also of investment, financial flows and worldwide electronic flows of knowledge and data.[57] Denationalisation has increasingly been a challenge for workplace representation due to two of its consequences: economic decision-making is systematically decoupled from the national sphere, thereby rendering national legislators increasingly less able to cope with the regulatory problem caused by these blurring boundaries ('regulatory void'). These trends are confirmed by Europeanisation in the social policy and employment field expressed in the social protocol of the Maastricht Treaty (1991), the social policy and employment chapters in the Amsterdam Treaty (1997–99), the ambitious programme of the Lisbon summit (2000) and, accompanying all these developments, the increased importance of the social dialogue (see chapter 7 above).[58]

The Community has played an important role in the law of workplace representation in the Member States. The influence of these bodies brought about not only consolidation and harmonisation, but also recognition of participatory modes of information and consultation by workers' representatives throughout Europe. The idea of 'works councils' has increasingly gained ground, even in those countries in which the institution of statutory, non-union workers' representatives was an alien concept. The Europeanisation of workplace representation took place in three historically successive, although co-existing, modes: (i) the Community method after the first Social Action Programme 1974; (ii) works councils' legislation, from the Maastricht social agreement (1992) to the Directive

---

[54] Hepple (2005) 72–76.
[55] Banerjee (2008).
[56] Barnard et al (2004); Hepple (2005); Moreau (2006); Craig and Lynk (2006); Blanpain et al (2007).
[57] Castells (2000); Sassen (2006); Mückenberger (2007).
[58] Mückenberger (2004); Degryse (2006); Dufresne et al (2006).

on a general framework for improving information and consultation rights of employees (2002/14/EC); and (iii) the 'new' mode of social policy (social dialogue, open method of co-ordination (OMC)). The regulatory steps since the 1974 action programme have created a patchwork of Community-wide workplace participation. The works councils' legislation from the early 1990s onwards created what may be termed a 'European collective labour law'. This became—with a unique interplay between states and social partners (*legislation négociée*)—an historical climax in European workplace representation-oriented labour law. The invention, at the Lisbon Council of 2000, of the OMC as a new mode of social policy led to a new form of voluntarism. We cannot yet clearly assess whether this is a general 'watering down' of Social Europe or a kind of transition step towards a cosmopolitan procedural self-regulatory system of collective workplace relations.

Community Method

The Europeanisation of workplace representation started in a piecemeal fashion. It emerged with the birth of Social Europe in the 1974 Action Programme. It has been mentioned earlier in this chapter that information and consultation rights for workers' representatives, at the European level, started in the fields of collective dismissals (Directive 75/129/EEC) and transfers of undertakings (Directive 77/87/EEC). At that time, the first steps towards co-determination within the European company were being planned, albeit without success. Much of the regulation that followed, such as the youth employment and working time Directives, provided certain information and consultation rights, but these were frequently only in order to provide derogation opportunities from substantive labour standards (see chapter 7 above).

This first wave of Europeanisation had three important effects. First, it demonstrated that Europe could bring about a social dimension that went beyond the national social compromises. This created a pull factor for those in the Member States who were sceptical about European integration, notably Britain and, later on, the Nordic countries. The ensuing pro-European shifts in these countries may have resulted from this social dimension. Secondly, the patchwork of information and consultation rights—despite not addressing a specific kind of workplace representation or 'works councils'—implicitly required national mechanisms of a legally enforceable and sustainable information and consultation procedure. These thus paved the ground for national enactments of Community-wide information and consultation requirements, as is provided for in the 2002 Directive on information and consultation rights. Thirdly, these steps subtly encouraged the idea that Europe is not just a competition-oriented economic market but is equally a social, solidarity-oriented community, on the path towards the establishment of a sort of 'European social model', which was to develop during the decades to come. The failure of initiatives in the 1970s indicated that a 'top-down' approach to Social Europe was, at the time, premature. The piecemeal method of legislation was more appropriate to this period.

Works Councils: a Success Story?

The breakthrough toward a European institutionalisation of workplace representation in the mid-1990s was a highlight in European labour law history. Collective representation played a double role in this game. On the one hand, within a short time span, the Val Duchesse talks, inspired by the Commission President, led to both the EC Social Policy Protocol (1991), providing for European competence for information and consultation legislation, and to the 1994 European Works Council Directive.[59] This, in turn, facilitated the end of a 30-year dispute over the European company and its enactment, through an (albeit flexible) mode of participation of workers. It equally allowed the first Community-wide generalisation of information and consultation rights to emerge, without the need for the establishment or enterprise to have a Community-wide activity. This European legislation showed a successful interplay between the legislative process and the social partners. Both the 1991 social policy agreement and the 1994 Directive were drafted by the European social partners. The agreement had provided for a double consultation procedure and the social dialogue competency now contained in Article 138 EC. Both measures were enacted by Community legislation. They thus had a Community-wide effect, which could not have been achieved by the social partners alone. This *legislation négociée* brought about both legitimacy and effectiveness.

It would be interesting to cross-evaluate both the processes of transposition of the European Works Council Directive into national law[60] and the transnational impacts and interdependencies resulting from the activities of the councils. Because of the pre-existing types of works councils in Germany and the Netherlands, their Acts on European Works Councils, passed in 1996 and 1997, respectively, were both very close to the Directive, with a few extensions and modifications. More interesting is the case of Sweden, which normally exceeds the minimum requirements of the *acquis communitaire*. The main novelty of the Swedish Act on European Works Councils is that the European Works Council is composed only of workers' representatives and is no longer bipartite. Further novelties arise due to the fact that European Works Council is not a trade union body, but a legal person independent from the union. Agreements concerning European Works Councils are not collective agreements in the Swedish sense, but are based on parity between management and labour.

The most interesting case, with respect to the European workplace representation legislation, is Britain. The 1997 extension of the European Works Council

---

[59] Rhodes (2005); Blanpain (1998); Weiss (1996, 2004).
[60] Blanpain (2004).

Directive to Britain ended the two-speed system of European labour law allowed by the Maastricht social protocol. The 2002 Directive on information and consultation rights challenged every aspect of work culture. In its aftermath, Britain experienced, at least from a legal point of view, a new dimension of collective workplace relations. The outcome was a juridification of British workplace representation.[61] However, it should not be forgotten that the basic change concerns the legal, though not necessarily the factual, everyday-life workplace level.

Two observations regarding the European Works Councils should be stressed. First, nearly half of the enterprises falling under the coverage of the Directive have a European Works Council. Out of these approximately 500 enterprises, the overwhelming majority concluded agreements in 1996 (continent) and 1999 (Britain).[62] Most of them were made under Article 13 of the Directive, opting out of the provisions of the Directive and indefinitely renewable by the social partners at the establishment/enterprise level. The rest of the cases ended up in long disputes, finally leading to the application of the minimum standards laid down in the appendix to the Directive. In practical terms, this means that the legal provisions of the Directive played a minor role in workplace relations. Far more significant was the mere existence of the Directive. This served as an incentive to conclude agreements at the plant level, thereby avoiding the provisions of the Directive. This already expresses a step toward 'soft' regulation. The legal provisions serve less directly, and are not mandatory in the manner of the Community method; rather, they serve as a 'lever' for an extra-legal consensus or 'bargaining in the shadow of the law'.

The second observation to be made about the British change is that, from the point of view of the contents of the legal provisions, they fall short of the co-determination or co-decision modes of participation provided in the German, Austrian and (although with minor differences) Swedish models. Information and consultation provide for a more extended transparency and communication in plant relations—they do not change the power relationship. What we know from the reality of European Works Councils agreements is that, in practice, they have brought about denser transnational communication between works councils and a better ability to cope with 'difference' (different plant and union organisation, different legal frameworks, different language and culture). For a German scholar, this does not seem to be very much, but from the point of view of a European culture of co-operation, it may be regarded as important progress towards transnational cosmopolitan solidarity.

New Methods of European Governance: Progress or Nightmare?

At the dawn of the twenty-first century, European policy had not totally

---

[61] *Cf* the British–German comparison, at an earlier stage, in Mückenberger (1988).
[62] Kerckhofs (2006).

abandoned the path of the Community method[63] (see, for example, the anti-discrimination Directives, chapter 5 above). However, Commission and Council are increasingly using 'soft' tools rather than legislation (see chapter 1 above). One of these is the social dialogue, discussed in chapter 7, above. The other is the OMC (see chapter 1 above). This will, in all probability, play a role in the further development of the European participation models. However if we look at the modest results of OMC within the European Employment Strategy (EES), we do not have strong grounds for optimism with regard to workers' participation. Will OMC lead to 'window dressing', like most of the examples produced so far by the EES? Will it lead to a downward spiral, regarding co-deter-mination as an obstacle to competition, hence as alien to the common market?

By 2004, workplace representation had become increasingly linked to national interests, at the cost of transnational solidarity. However, certain cases of transna-tional works councils' co-operation (via European Works Councils) have successfully taken place. Moreau[64] points out that in some cases the councils have implemented the ILO core conventions (see chapter 1 above) through their regu-latory practice (such as certain codes of conduct of enterprises). However, protectionist tendencies vis-à-vis the less developed world are also discernible.[65] Will the new code of conduct movements, the UN's Global Compact and the efforts to render ILO policy more effective contribute to a new type of cosmopol-itan-oriented shop-floor representation, fettering and 'civilising' economic globalisation?[66] The question whether, under the impact of globalisation, shop-floor representation will undergo or contribute to a 'race to the bottom' or a 'race to the top' is still unanswered.[67]

---

[63] See Directives 2000/43/EC, 2000/78/EC, 2002/73/EC, 2004/13/EC, 2006/78/EC. *Cf* the recent account by Schiek et al (2007).

[64] Moreau (2006).

[65] Craig and Lynk (2006).

[66] Arthurs (2006); Burkett (2006).

[67] Hepple (2005).

9

Enforcement of Labour Law

JONAS MALMBERG

Introduction: the Pre-war Heritage

Labour law consists to a large extent of substantive rules on how employers, employees and workers' representatives are allowed to act. This chapter deals with procedural rules and institutional arrangements aimed at enforcing these substantive rules in the workplace.

It is possible to distinguish between three different kinds of enforcement processes. In the first, supervision and enforcement is a task for public authorities, such as labour inspectors or equality bodies (*the administrative process*). In the second, the supervision and enforcement of rules is entrusted to trade unions, works councils or other workers' representatives (*the industrial relations process*). National laws contain extensive regulations on the role of trade unions and other workers' representatives in the enforcement of labour law. In the period covered by this book, it came to be commonly accepted that workplace representatives have an indispensable role to play in the enforcement of labour law. Where there are suspicions that a certain norm of labour law has been violated, information, consultation and negotiation will be used to assess the facts, and to discuss whether a rule has actually been violated and, if so, how this should be remedied. Rules on information, consultations and negotiation aim to underpin industrial relation processes as a means of enforcing substantive rules of labour law. Such rules strengthen the opportunities for workers' representatives to influence projected managerial decisions (eg on collective redundancies), and to control how substantive rules have been applied in the workplace.[1] The third kind of process is *the judicial process*, where the enforcement of rules is carried out through judicial procedures in courts or tribunals. A judicial process may be initiated by individual employees (individual judicial processes), by their representatives (collective judicial processes) or by inspectors or other official agencies, or even, in some countries, by non-governmental organisations. The judicial

---

[1] Van Peijpe (2003); see also chapter 8 above.

processes in labour law contain several special features that distinguish them from the ordinary courts and tribunals.

One aim of this chapter is to analyse the evolution of these three kinds of process and the interrelationships between them. The function of these processes could be said to create an effective enforcement of labour standards. It is, however, possible to distinguish between two different views on 'effectiveness'. One view stresses the possibility for individuals—either on their own or with the help, for example, of trade unions or an equality agency—to enforce their rights. In this view, the enforcement mechanism is more effective the more accessible it actually is, for example for a woman to claim her right to equal pay for work of equal value. This view might be described as entailing a micro-perspective on enforcement. The other view focuses more on how rules manifest in society as a whole than on the possibility for individuals to pursue their claims. In this latter view, for example, enforcement is more effective the higher the proportion of women who receive equal pay for work of equal value. This can be regarded as entailing a macro-perspective on enforcement. Further, it should be kept in mind that the impact of dispute resolution is not limited to the actual disputes in question. Judicial processes in particular have the potential of being formative for the content of the law (*lex lata*). The evolution of the enforcement processes is to a large extent determined by the aspiration of the social partners to control the outcome. Thus, the trust and confidence of the social partners in the courts and judges is an essential component in the history of enforcement of labour law.

The chapter concerns mainly the handling of 'disputes of rights', as opposed to 'disputes of interests'. The distinction between the two kinds of disputes is common in labour law in most countries.[2] Disputes of interests concern conflicts regarding the establishment of new or modified condition of employment, mainly through collective agreements. Such conflicts involve non-justiciable issues. Under the heading of disputes of interest are usually found discussions on the laws of strikes, and the handling of industrial conflicts through conciliation, mediation and arbitration (see further chapter 7 above). Disputes of rights, on the other hand, concern alleged violations or non-application of an existing legal norm, such as a statutory provision, a clause in a collective agreement or a provision in an individual employment contract. In some countries, such as Denmark, Germany and Sweden, the distinction is linked to the idea that disputes of rights should be resolved by a court, not by industrial actions.[3] The distinction is far from clear. On the one hand, industrial actions may be used as a mean to enforce an existing legal norm. In Sweden, for instance, industrial action is an accepted means for the employee side to recover outstanding pay from the employer (*indrivningsblockad*). On the other hand, judicial processes are often used in a strategic manner in order to change the content of law. This is especially obvious concerning cases before the European Court of Justice (ECJ) and the European

---

[2] Eg Aaron (1985) 3.

[3] Compare Art 6 of the European Social Charter (1961), which protects the right to collective action in cases of conflicts of interest.

Court of Human Rights (ECtHR). It seems that the question whether a dispute is regarded as a dispute of rights or of interest does not so much depend on the conflicting demands or claims of the parties as on how the parties argue the case. If workers are dissatisfied with the existing wage level, they may demand a change in the collective agreement, but they may also claim that the existing collective agreement is invalid (for example, as contrary to discrimination legislation).

Reconstruction and the Autonomy of Labour Law (1945–70)

Administrative Procedures

The early creation of an administrative body in charge of controlling the correct application of labour law by the employer can be regarded as an important feature of work-related legislation.[4] The first labour laws passed in the European countries concerned working time and health and safety at work, and it turned out that such legislation could not be effectively enforced without a specific state organ in charge of its application. Differing from general contract law, the enforcement of labour law has not been left to the parties themselves. Administrative authorities intervene, under different modalities and in different areas according to country, to counteract the weakness of the main interested party, namely the worker. British legislation offers an early example of provision for independent labour inspectors. In France and the Netherlands, labour inspectors were created at the end of the nineteenth century precisely for the purpose of controlling the correct application of the new statutes on working time. In the Nordic countries, the first laws on occupational safety were introduced at roughly the same time, and it was the duty of the administrative authorities to supervise the law. In the British model, factory inspectors were introduced for this reason, although the resources available to them were very modest.[5]

All legal systems under review had developed some type of non-judicial control through administrative organs before 1945. However, these administrative organs differed considerably from one state to another. They included state organs, like labour inspectors and other public authorities, at a centralised or decentralised level, that play some role in the application of labour law. In some countries, labour inspectors have been entrusted with powers relating to a wide range of topics, such as product safety and market surveillance (eg Germany), calculation of redundancy payments, assisting workers with letters of resignation

---

[4] Hepple (1986) 77–88.
[5] Bruun et al (1992).

and on-the-job training (eg France).[6] In other countries, such as the Netherlands, the labour inspectorate was entrusted with more limited tasks, especially in the fields of health and safety, working time, child labour and migrant labour.

Judicial and Industrial Relations Procedures

Pre-war Heritages

Special bi- or tripartite labour courts had already been established in many countries before the Second World War. The first labour courts were established in France through the *conseils de prud'hommes*, which were developed in the early nineteenth century.[7] Following reforms in 1905 and 1907, these tribunals were accepted by both sides of the labour market. The legislation was more or less intact until the so-called Boulin reform in 1979.[8] In Denmark a tripartite dispute-resolution body for collective disputes was established by law in 1910. The German labour courts were introduced in 1926, although with predecessors stemming from the nineteenth century. In Sweden a single labour court was set up in 1928, inspired mainly by the Danish example. The establishment of both the German and Sweden courts were subject to intense political debate.[9] They were, and still are, tripartite. The German labour courts, which lost their independence during the Nazi period, were re-established after the war in the different states (*Länder*). With the foundation of the Federal Republic of Germany, and the Constitution in 1949, there was a basis for a unified labour law. The Constitution required the establishment of a Supreme Labour Court (*Bundesarbeitsgericht*). This constitutional assignment was implemented through the 1953 Labour Court Act (*Arbeitsgerichtgesetz*). The German labour courts received much of its present foundation through this Act.

In Austria, tripartite labour courts were also re-established in 1946. There was, in addition, a special tripartite Board (*Einigungsamt*) competent for dismissal protection and collective disputes. The Board was first established in 1920 and re-established after the Second World War. In Finland and Ireland, tripartite labour courts were established in 1946. In Spain, tripartite industrial tribunals were first established in 1908. Their competences were modified in 1922, and they were complemented by joint juries (*Jurados Mixtos*), which handled industrial conflicts. Both these bodies were abolished during the Franco dictatorship and were replaced, in 1940, by labour courts (*Magistraturas de Trabajo*), composed of a single professional judge. During the authoritarian regime, which denied even minimum collective rights, the function of these labour courts differed considerably compared to other western European labour courts. In Britain and the Netherlands, on the other hand, no specialist labour courts were

[6] See further, Report III (Part 1B), International Labour Conference, 95th Session, 2006.
[7] Ramm (1986) 270; Blanc-Jouvan (1971) 15ff.
[8] Blanc-Jouvan (1971); Supiot (1987).
[9] As regards Sweden, see Kumlien (2004) 268ff.

established at that time. In Italy, special labour courts (*Collegi dei Probiviri*) had been established in 1893, but were abolished during the fascist regime in 1928.[10] After the Second World War, labour disputes were handed by ordinary courts.

An important argument for setting up labour courts was to achieve a more accessible, informal and speedy procedure than in the ordinary courts. It seems that the procedure in the labour courts from time to time has been the forerunner of changes in procedure in the ordinary courts. In Sweden, the procedure in the labour court adopted in 1928, based on a rather informal procedure with oral presentations and limitations of time, served to some extent as a role model for the reform of the general Code of Procedure in 1942. In Germany a preliminary conciliation hearing before the chair of the panel, which has been the practice in the labour courts, was extended to the civil jurisdiction in 2002. However, in many countries over time there has been criticism of 'legalism' in the procedures of the labour courts. Hepple concludes that, although the establishment of labour courts may provide for improvement of the judicial proceedings, there is nothing inherent in the specialisation that leads to this improvement.[11] Nor are there any significant differences between labour courts and ordinary courts when it comes to the methods of solving disputes. In general, labour courts in Europe, just like ordinary courts, tend to apply strict principles of law when deciding the case. Adjudication in labour courts is not a matter of finding a compromise, as in conciliation or some forms of arbitration.[12]

What primarily distinguish labour courts from the ordinary courts are their specialist jurisdiction and their composition. A central feature in the early evolution of labour law was distrust of the ability of ordinary courts (the courts with general competence in civil matters in a particular legal system) to handle labour disputes. Legislation and jurisprudence were unsure as to how to deal with growing trade unionism, strikes and collective agreements. The legal effects of collective agreements were unclear. The concepts and principles of the private or common law usually applied by the ordinary courts were based on ideas of individualism and freedom of contract, whilst the trade unions advocated collectivism and solidarity within the working class. In many countries, the ordinary courts were also accused of being 'class-biased' and to disfavour trade unionism. Thus there was a wish to create or maintain a labour law autonomous from civil or common law principles as well as independent of the ordinary courts. One way of doing this was to take labour disputes out of the ordinary courts. Further, it was often argued that the judges of the ordinary courts lacked the first-hand knowledge of industrial practice. The bi- or tripartite composition is usually viewed as a means to preserve the autonomy of labour law, and to provide the expertise of industrial practices, such as wage systems.[13] The assumption is that the lay judges of a specialist court, because of their background and

---

[10] Giugni (1971) 249ff.
[11] Hepple (1988).
[12] Hepple (1988).
[13] Cf Wedderburn (1987).

expertise in the subject, are more likely to demonstrate the sensitivity required when dealing with labour disputes.[14] In this way, the trust and legitimacy of the courts is expected to increase as a result of the institutionalised participation of the social partners.

The role of the lay members in the labour courts is commonly not to represent particular interests but to contribute industrial relations expertise and knowledge and act as equal judges with the legal member.

Continental Models—Primacy of Individual Judicial Processes

The main mechanism for handling disputes of rights that developed in many continental states like France and Germany was through special labour courts. The French *conseils de prud'hommes* had a bipartite composition. Their members were elected representatives of employers and workers. Elsewhere, for example in Austria, Belgium and Germany, tripartite tribunals were more common.

In Germany, three instances were established (*Arbeitsgerichte, Landesarbeits-gerichte* and *Bundesarbeitsgerichte*). In Belgium, the first instance is the Labour Court (*Tribunal du Travail*), whose decisions are appealed to the Labour Court of Appeal. The last instance is the Supreme Court (*Cour de Cassation*), which is not a specialised labour court. In France, the first instance is the local labour court. In contrast, the Austrian labour courts of first instance are normally a special chamber of the ordinary district courts, and the professional judges will often switch between the general chambers and the special labour or social chamber. Only Vienna has a specialised labour court of first instance. In both France and Austria appeal is made to the ordinary civil courts (regional courts and the Supreme Court). These courts set up special chambers for this purpose.

The German labour courts were given general jurisdiction in all (civil) labour disputes, whether individual or collective and are regarded as specialised civil courts, separate from the ordinary civil courts, just like the German administrative law courts or social security courts. The competence of the French *conseils de prud'hommes*, on the other hand, is limited to individual disputes, while the collective disputes are dealt with by the ordinary courts. The dividing line between individual and collective disputes in France is rather unclear. In principle, a dispute is regarded as individual if its object concerns only one employer and one employee. A conflict does not lose its character of being individual if several employees, all in dispute with the same employer, present similar claims to the tribunal. On the other hand, a dispute is considered to be collective if a collective interest is at stake (for instance, the exercise of staff representatives' prerogatives), even if all the employees objectively involved are not engaged in the confrontation. In practice, characterisation of disputes as individual or collective may depend on the legal choices made by those involved. The *conseils de prud'hommes* do not have competence in disputes regarding the employment

[14] Vranken (1987–88).

relations of public employees (*fonctionnaires*). These disputes are dealt with in administrative courts. The Belgian labour courts are competent in matters of individual labour law and social security law, but not in matters of collective labour law.

No special labour courts were created in the Netherlands and Italy. Instead, the ordinary courts play a prominent rule in the resolution of rights disputes. In the Netherlands, the disputes are adjudicated in first instance by *kantonrechters*. The *kantonrechters* were separate courts until 2002, when they were incorporated in the district courts as special chambers for small claims, family cases and cases related to employment contracts. In appeal the disputes are adjudicated by *gerechtshoven*, and in cassation by the *Hoge Raad*. Due to the high respect for the judges' competence and their considerable degree of 'social sensitivity', no pressure for establishing special labour courts has been exerted. The question has been how to make the process accessible, speedy and cheap. In the procedure before the *kantonrechter*, no lawyer is needed. The workers may handle their own case or bring non-lawyers as counsel, for instance trade union representatives. The fees have been rather modest. It has also been possible for the trade unions to engage in the case if collective agreement issues are involved. Over the years this system has not been questioned by employers, trade unions, lawyers or labour law scholars.

In Italy, the Constitution of 1948 contained a prohibition of special courts, such as labour courts. The prohibition was a reaction to the abuse of special courts during the fascist regime. Thus, labour disputes fell under the ordinary jurisdiction of civil courts and, until 1973, in principle they followed the 'ordinary' procedures. Before the 1973 reform (see below) criticisms of the court procedures were made and voices were raised for the establishment of special procedures for labour disputes.[15]

The continental models described here were based primarily on individual judicial enforcement procedures. Irrespective of whether disputes were judged by a specialised labour court or by ordinary courts, the judicial procedures were mainly initiated by individual employees, possibly with support by the workers' representatives. Works councils and trade unions normally had the right to stand in court for the defence of their own rights. However, the possibility for workers' representatives to litigate disputes over the rights of individual workers varies between countries.[16]

The British Model—Primacy of Industrial Relations Processes

The idea of establishing specialised bi- or tripartite labour courts did not gain foothold in Britain until 1968, when the Donovan Royal Commission on Trade Unions and Employers' Associations, concerned about the relatively high level of wildcat (unofficial) strikes over issues such as disciplinary action, proposed a

---

[15] Giugni (1971).
[16] Van Peijpe (2003) 153ff.

system of labour courts (see below). Until then, concern for preserving the autonomy of labour law had taken another direction. In 1959, Otto Kahn-Freund described the industrial relations system in Britain as one of 'collective laissez-faire'. Industrial relations had developed as a voluntaristic system and both employers and trade unions wanted it to be kept as autonomous from state control as possible. Most employment conditions (like working time, pay, holidays and dismissal) were established through collective agreements, which were not regarded as intended to create legally enforceable obligations between the collective parties. Since the mid-nineteenth century the courts had recognised the normative effects of collective agreements as legally binding custom and practice, but it was extremely rare for individual workers or employers to enforce them through individual contracts. Also, grievances and dispute procedures were kept out of the realm of the courts. In practice, enforcement was organised through complex and rather informal mechanisms. The practice was described in the following way by Wedderburn and Davies in 1969:

> Grievances, however, are rarely pursued by use of legal machinery. Aggrieved workers seek their shop steward rather than a solicitor; and their cases will inevitably be processed not by way of writs and lawyers but through the maze of varied voluntary 'procedures' established by collective agreements, which serve for their solution in different ways in different industries.[17]

In this system, no sharp distinction was drawn between conflicts of right and conflicts of interest. The social partners resolved conflicts by means of negotiation, by utilisation of established procedures or, though this was generally a last resort, by industrial actions such as strikes and lock-outs, irrespectively of whether the dispute concerned the establishment of a new substantive rule or the application of already existing ones. By the 1960s, such procedures covered the majority of employees, although a large proportion of workers—mostly women—were still left without any social or legal means to pursue grievances.[18] The disputes mainly concerned wage issues, though grievance procedures concerning discipline and dismissals were also common. Wedderburn and Davies state that the outcome of these procedures was almost invariably accepted, even though they included reinstatement, a remedy that was not available in the courts. These procedures were generally open only for union members.[19]

The Nordic Model—Primacy of Collective Judicial Processes

The point of departure in Denmark, Sweden and Finland differed from both the continental models and the British model. In these Nordic countries the enforcement procedures were—just as in Britain—primarily focused around an

---

[17] Wedderburn and Davies (1969) 2.
[18] Kilpatrick (2002).
[19] Wedderburn and Davies (1969) 137.

industrial relations approach, but were combined with a (collective) judicial approach. In all three countries there were tripartite labour courts (established in Denmark in 1910, in Sweden in 1928 and in Finland in 1946), with jurisdiction mainly in collective disputes (ie industrial action and collective agreements). Further, there was only a single labour court, covering all disputes in the respective country. No appeal was available against the Labour Court's decisions.

The social partners in Denmark have a long-standing tradition of cooperation and trust. In 1899 the two dominant organisations on the labour market, the employers' organisation DA and the national trade union LO, concluded the September Compromise (*Septemberforliget*).[20] The September Compromise was based on a mutual understanding that negotiations and agreements between organisations on a central level were the future system of labour relations. Further, a tripartite dispute-resolving body for collective disputes was established by the social partners. In 1910, this Permanent Court of Arbitration (*den faste voldgift*) was established for handling of legal conflicts, especially sanctioning of breaches of collective agreements. The court was renamed the Labour Court (*Arbejdsretten*) in 1964. Furthermore, in 1908, the main organisations had agreed upon a system of conciliation in all kinds of local conflicts and arbitration in legal conflicts as far as interpretation of collective agreements was concerned. The primary goal of both the legislation and the agreement is peaceful settlements in all kinds of disputes on the labour market. This system still forms the basis of dispute resolution. Disputes concerning collective agreements—which at the time were almost the totally dominant form of regulation—were settled via the 'industrial system' (the *fagretlige* system), ie through lengthy negotiation procedures and, ultimately, by the Labour Court or an industrial arbitration tribunal. Only the organisations—and not the individuals—were allowed *locus standi* before these institutions. This gives trade unions a strong position in the enforcement process, which (in Norway) is described as a monopoly in litigation. Disputes over interpretation of statute law, on the other hand, were and still are dealt with by the ordinary courts, without any need to pass through preliminary negotiation procedures. Except for the White Collar Workers Act of 1938, there was almost no labour legislation in Denmark before the 1970s.

The Swedish Labour Court (*Arbetsdomstolen*) was established in 1928, with a view to resolving conflicts deriving from collective agreements. Besides providing for tripartite composition, the 1928 Labour Court Act contained two elements, intended to strengthen the power of social partners in the enforcement process: *locus standi* for organisations and compulsory grievance negotiations (*tvisteförhandlingar*). According to the Act, organisations representing either the employer or the employee had a right to engage in a court action on behalf of any of its members without any formal power of authorisation. However, in contrast with Denmark, a member of an organisation had a subsidiary right to engage in a court action. If the organisation did not bring a dispute before the Labour Court,

---

[20] For text, see Hepple (1986) 383.

the individual member could choose to start a procedure on his own account. Further, it was a procedural prerequisite that grievance negotiations had taken place between the parties of the collective agreement before a dispute is brought before the Labour Court. The jurisdiction of the labour court was limited to disputes concerning industrial actions and collective agreement. Before the 1970s, labour legislation was rare. When labour law statutes (of a private law character) were occasionally adopted, the Labour Court was given jurisdiction regarding these Acts (for instance, the 1963 Holiday Act). Labour disputes raised by individual employees not related to collective agreements or any particular labour legislation were brought before the ordinary courts.

Together with the 1946 Collective Agreements Act, the establishment of the Finnish Labour Court in 1946 was a part of the reform of industrial relations in Finland. Prior to the Second World War, the number of collective agreements was small and their impact was rather insignificant. The composition and jurisdiction of the Labour Court were rather similar to the Swedish Labour Court at the time.

Comparative Notes

In the continental models, the individual judicial procedure was the most important process. Trade unions and/or works council's representatives could assist the employee when going to court, but they did not 'own the dispute'. In Britain and the Nordic countries, the focus was almost totally on creating effective enforcement from a macro-perspective: in Britain, by the almost total dominance of industrial relations processes; in the Nordic countries, by adopting a mixture of industrial relations processes and collective judicial processes. These policies seem to have been based on the idea that the power of organised labour is an indispensable instrument to support the effectiveness of labour law. As Kahn-Freund put it in 1972:

> As a power countervailing management the trade unions are much more effective than the law has ever been or ever can be . . . Everywhere the effectiveness of the law depends on the unions far more than the unions depend on the effectiveness of the law.[21]

The other side of the coin is that individuals in such systems have a subordinate position. This can be illustrated by a Swedish example. The first employment protection regulation for blue-collar workers was introduced through the 1964 basic agreement. According to this collective agreement, disputes concerning unfair dismissals were handled by an arbitration board, established for this purpose. However, only the social partners—and not individual employees—had *locus standi* before the board. Nor were the individuals entitled to pursue a claim according to the basic agreement in court. In this sense, employment protection was afforded by the basic agreement fully administrated by the social partners

---

[21] Kahn-Freund (1972) 12.

and not as an individual entitlement. In such a system, almost no weight is put on enforcement from a micro-perspective.

Juridification (1970–90)

Introduction

The 1970s was a period of intense legislative activities in the field of labour law in many countries and also at the European level. This juridification of employment and industrial relations put pressure on the enforcement processes.[22] The juridification might in part be ascribed to the changes in attitude towards authorities that appeared in the aftermath of the radicalisation during the late 1960s. It has been argued that the exercise of power both in the public sphere and in the family went into crisis, leading to a transformation in how legal power was exercised. According to Supiot, one change was the loss of importance of discretionary power as compared with functional power, manifested through a greater control of the exercise of power—a priori as a duty to motivate decisions (eg through information and consultation procedures) and a posteriori as an enhanced role of the courts.[23] The evolution of labour law seems to fit well with this hypothesis, in relation to both the employers' prerogatives and to the power exercised by trade unions in relation to their members.[24] When it comes to enforcement of labour law, these tendencies contributed to the increased importance of individual judicial processes at the expense of industrial relations processes.

The Continental Models

The pressure for change in the continental models seems to have been moderate. A juridification of the substantive law created an increase in the number of court cases. In Germany, the number of cases in the labour courts grew in the 1970s as a consequence of new statutes, especially concerning collective labour law (the new Works Constitution Act, *Betriebsverfassunggestez*, 1972, and the Co-Determination Act, *Mitbestimmunggestetz*, 1976). Due to this increase in cases before the courts, the Labour Court Act was revised in 1979 in order to speed up the proceedings in labour court disputes. The faster procedures were to be achieved through different measures, including an accelerated procedure in dismissal disputes. In 1973 a special system of court proceedings in individual labour

---

[22] On the concept of juridification, see eg Teubner (1987).
[23] Supiot (1999a).
[24] Compare Simitis (1994).

disputes was introduced in Italy. The aim of the reform was to establish a procedure with greater speed, immediacy and emphasis on oral evidence, although disputes continued to be handled by a single judge (*pretore*) in the first instance. Such changes were also made in France (1979 and 1982).

Further, during this period there was a tendency towards juridification of enforcement processes. The lay judges in the French *conseils de prud'hommes* had traditionally not been legally trained. The judges chosen by the employers were often heads of small or medium-sized companies, whereas the judges chosen by the employees were usually ordinary workers, not, for instance, trade union officials. Dispute resolution in the tribunals was to a large extent based on industrial customs and compromises between both sides. However, since the 1950s a core of specialised labour lawyers has become important as legal advisers in processes before the tribunals. It is reported that, according to members of tribunals, the influence of the trained lawyers leads to the juridification of a conflict and impedes an informal settlement.[25] In Germany, the early professional judges were not necessarily trained lawyers; since 1961, however, professional judges have had to have the same qualifications as the judges in ordinary courts.[26]

Another aspect of the autonomy of labour law is the efforts of the social partners to acquire and maintain influence on the appointment of judges in the labour courts. In Germany, this had been one reason why the labour courts were under the jurisdiction of the Minister of Labour rather than under the Ministry of Justice. In 1971, Ramm argued that any attempt to transfer the administration of the affairs of the labour courts to the Ministry of Justice would meet with stiff opposition from the social partners, which still mistrusted adjudication by the ordinary courts due to their previous manifest class justice.[27] In 1990, an amendment to the Labour Court Act made it possible for the states (*Länder*) to make such a transfer, which has been done. According to the Labour Court Act, the Supreme Labour Court is still under the Minister of Labour.

After the democratisation in Portugal and Spain, the function of the labour courts was transformed. In Portugal, following the adoption of the 1976 Constitution, the labour courts were brought within the system of ordinary courts, as a special division. In Spain, the labour courts were integrated in the judiciary in the form of the social courts and retained much of their operational identity, using, for example, rapid verbal procedures. There are also examples of attempts to reinforce the role of the workers' representatives in the enforcement processes. In Italy a new interim procedure concerning anti-union conduct (*condotta antisindicale*) was introduced in Article 28 of the 1970 Workers' Statute. Anti-union conduct was given a broad definition and is extended still further in case law. After a summary procedure, the judge may order the employer to stop the conduct with extremely strong remedies. However, Article 28 of the Worker's Statute does not allow the union to bring individual cases before the court, even

---

[25] Supiot (1987).
[26] Ramm (1971).
[27] Ibid, 147.

if the worker's demand is based on a collective agreement. The Article only allows the unions to protect 'their' rights and interests as organisations. The Article, which Wedderburn has described as one of the most remarkable in modern European labour law, is regarded as a pillar of the Italian labour law system.[28] A similar procedure was introduced in Britain in 1976, but was rarely used in practice. In 1986, Austrian labour courts were fundamentally reorganised and their jurisdictions extended. Before 1987, only the person directly concerned had *locus standi* before the labour courts; since then, it has been possible for works councils and trade unions to bring cases before the courts, but only for 'abstract' claims. They may approach the Supreme Court for a kind of preliminary ruling in order to clarify the interpretation of law. The ruling is based on the facts presented in the claim without hearing evidence. The ruling is binding as to the interpretations of the law, but not as regards the facts. In Portugal, the right of trade unions to appear before court representing or acting as a substitute for employees has been extended.

The British Model—Development in the Direction of Individual Judicial Processes

If the changes of the continental models were rather moderate, the transformation of the British enforcement system was more profound. The late 1960s and the early 1970s in Britain have been described as a watershed when 'collective laissez-faire' collapsed.[29] Already in the early 1960s the significance of industrial relations processes for enforcement started to diminish.[30] In some sectors, industrial action became the first rather than a last resort in reaction to dismissals. Such 'wildcat' strikes, which were not in line with procedures in the industries in question, became a problem. There was a concern that 'informal' industrial relations were escaping the control of the 'formal' system. The Donovan Commission in 1968 recommended the introduction of a statutory right not to be unfairly dismissed, partly in the belief that this would stem the incidence of wildcat strikes.[31] Such a statutory right was introduced in the Industrial Relations Act 1971. The jurisdiction in disputes over unfair dismissal was given to the industrial tribunals. The Donovan Commission was much influenced in this respect by Kahn-Freund, a member of the Commission and one of the academic founders of labour law in Britain, who had been a judge of the labour courts in pre-Nazi Germany.[32]

The industrial tribunals, which in 1996 were renamed employment tribunals, were first established in 1964 but (contrary to Kahn-Freund's advice) were not

---

[28] Wedderburn (1990) 159.
[29] Davies and Freedland (1993) 640.
[30] For the following, see Wedderburn and Davies (1969) and Kilpatrick (2002).
[31] Royal Commission on Trade Unions and Employers' Associations (1968).
[32] About Kahn-Freund see, eg Freedland (2004) 299–323.

given general competence in labour disputes; they could only exercise the jurisdictions conferred upon them by statute. At the beginning, the jurisdiction of the
tribunals was rather limited (such as disputes concerning the 1965 Redundancy
Payment Act). In pace with the growth of statutory individual employment
rights, the competence of the tribunals has gradually expanded, so that by the
beginning of the twenty-first century, employment tribunals had powers to
determine over 70 different types of complaint, including complaints of unfair
dismissal, race, sex and disability discrimination, unauthorised deduction of
wages and redundancy pay. Some breach of contract disputes can be brought to
tribunals, but most go to the ordinary courts, which also have sole jurisdiction in
respect of torts (for example arising from industrial action).The tribunals are
tripartite judicial bodies. Decisions from the tribunals may be appealed to the
Employment Appeal Tribunal (also tripartite), the Court of Appeal and the
House of Lords, on the grounds of 'error of law'. The British development indicates a sharp turn from industrial relations processes to individual judicial
processes.

The Nordic Countries—Development in the Direction of Individual Judicial Processes

Sweden also experienced a wave of labour legislation during the 1970s, with the
1974 Employment Protection Act and the 1977 Co-Determination Act being the
most prominent examples. In 1974 a new Labour Dispute Act was adopted, regulating the procedures in the Labour Court. Through this Act, which is still in
force, the dual system with collective disputes handled by the Labour Court and
individual by the ordinary courts was repealed. The Labour Court obtained
general jurisdiction for the resolution of all disputes of rights between employers
and workers, either as a first and last instance or after appeal from an ordinary
district court (*tingsrätt*). The process in the Labour Court remains linked to the
unions and to collective agreements in several ways. The Labour Court handles
cases as first and last instance where a union or employers' association is bringing
an action, in its own right or on behalf of one of its members, concerning an
employment relationship regulated by collective agreement. It does not matter if
the case concerns a collective agreement, a statute or an individual employment
contract. It is still a procedural prerequisite that grievance negotiations have
taken place between the parties of the collective agreement before a dispute is
brought before the Labour Court (as first instance). For other disputes, the case is
first heard by a district court. Nevertheless, the reform was, together with new
legislation, especially the 1974 Employment Protection Act, a clear step away
from a labour law systems dominated by collectivism.

In Finland a new Labour Court Act was adopted in 1974. In contrast to
Sweden, the dual system, with collective disputes handled by the Labour Court
and individual disputes handled by the ordinary courts, was kept unchanged. In

Denmark, no 'explosion of labour law legislation' took place. Through the successive transposition of EC Directives, however, some statutes were adopted. Nevertheless, the system of enforcement through industrial relations and collective judicial processes remains the dominant one.

Extensions of the Tasks of Labour Inspections

The traditional understanding of the tasks of labour inspection has changed during recent decades, partly because of changes in the world of work, such as fragmentation of the labour market, a growth in foreign and migrant workers, new forms of subcontracting or outsourcing, the increase in atypical working arrangements and relationships, and the increased participation of women in the labour market. These factors, and others, have had a considerable impact on the traditional concept of labour protection.

Since the 1970s there has been shift in the regulatory technique in the area of health and safety. Emphasis had gradually shifted from traditional models of giving substantive protective regulation to provisions prescribing procedures for risk assessment at the workplace. This shift bas been further promoted by the 1989 EC Framework Directive on Health and Safety.[33] The functions entrusted to labour inspection are essentially the enforcement of the legal provisions relating to conditions of work and the protection of workers while they are engaged in their work. Nevertheless, the manner in which these functions are discharged varies greatly between countries. The differences lie in the amount of time devoted to the various inspection functions, including prevention and control and inspections at the initiative of the inspection services on the one hand, compared with those undertaken in reaction to complaints, functions relating to occupational safety and health and those relating to compliance with other conditions of employment on the other. In certain countries, priority is given by governments to combating clandestine work or illegal employment, which is increasingly linked to enforcing immigration law (Belgium, Italy and Spain).

Extension of Administrative Enforcement to the Field of Discrimination[34]

From the 1970s onwards, different forms of administrative enforcement of equality and discrimination legislation were developed. Alongside the growth of discrimination and equality legislation, it was also recognised that statutory provisions alone were not sufficient to combat discrimination (se chapter 5

---

[33] Council Directive 89/391/EEC of 12 June 1989 on the introduction of measures to encourage improvements in the safety and health of workers at work. See further Walters (2002).

[34] For the following, see Moon in Schiek et al (2007) ch 8; McCrudden (1993) and Laulom (2003)124ff.

above). Several states designed public equality bodies in order to move beyond
the letter of the law. These are called agencies, commissions or ombud (or
ombudsmen).[35] The first equality body was set up in Britain in the 1960s (the
Race Relations Board). The tendency was for separate bodies to be created for
different grounds of discrimination. In Britain, two equality bodies were founded
in the 1970s: the Equal Opportunities Commission was set up under the Sex
Discrimination Act 1975 and the Commission for Racial Equality was set up
under the Race Relations Act of 1976. A Disability Rights Commission was
created under the Disability Discrimination Acts of 1995 and 1999. In Sweden,
the Equal Opportunities Ombudsman was established in 1980, followed by the
Ombudsman against Ethnic Discrimination (established 1986), the Ombudsman
against Discrimination on grounds of Sexual Orientation and the Disability
Ombudsman (both established in 1999). In Finland, the Ombudsman for
Equality was set up in 1986 and the Ombudsman for Minorities in 2001. The
Austrian Equal Opportunities Ombud (established 1991) was limited to equality
between men and women.

In countries where equality bodies were established later, these generally
covered every form of discrimination prohibited by law. This was the case, for
instance, with the Belgian Centre for Equal Opportunities and Opposition to
Racism (1993) and the Greek Ombudsman (1998). The Dutch Equal Treatment
Commission (1994) was preceded by a commission for sex discrimination only.
There seems also to be a tendency towards mergers of specialised employment
bodies. In Northern Ireland, the three existing equality bodies were merged in
1999 to form a single Equality Commission for Northern Ireland.[36]

In France, labour inspectors were charged with control of the application of
the equality principle, and no explicit enforcement role was given to any body
other than the Labour Inspectorate. However, in 2004 the High Authority against
Discrimination and for Equality was established. The Authority has the task of
controlling all forms of discrimination prohibited by law or by an international
agreement to which France is party. In Germany, no equality body had been
established at federal level by 2004.[37] Neither was any equality body set up in
Spain.

The equality bodies take different forms and perform different functions. One
primary function is usually to provide legal assistance to victims of discrimination. Some bodies support individuals who wish to take legal action, either by
representing them in court or by giving legal aid. Some bodies can investigate
claims and issue opinions. These may or may not be legally binding. If the find-
ings are not legally binding, the victims may themselves take the case to court.
This is the case in the Netherlands. A common problem for equality bodies in

[35] The term 'ombudsman' is the only Swedish legal term that has reached the international legal
language.
[36] Since 2007 three separate commissions in Britain have merged into the Equality and Human
Rights Commission (EHRC). The Swedish ombudsmen will be merged in 2009.
[37] Though a Federal Anti-Discrimination Agency was set up in 2006.

assisting individuals is the lack of resources. The different bodies have tried to develop strategic approaches in order to maximise their effectiveness. Such strategies may involve assistance in litigation. For instance, the British Equal Opportunities Commission supported test cases that resulted in some of the most significant judgements of the ECJ on sex equality issues.[38] The bodies often seek alternative methods for promoting equality, like using mediation and conciliation as a tool for individual dispute solving, or by more generally trying to promote alternative behaviours on the labour market through information and recommendations (in some cases, legally binding), and by conducting independent inquiries.

Alternative Dispute Resolution and Europeanisation (1990–2004)

Alternative Dispute Resolution

The growing body of statutes on individual labour rights introduced especially since the 1970s put considerable pressure on individual judicial procedures. The number of cases before labour courts and tribunals has increased. At the turn of the century, the British employment tribunals registered over 130,000 claims per year. In 2004, around 600,000 cases were brought before the German labour courts. In Italy, more than 300,000 labour disputes were pending before the first instance courts and almost 60% of the civil cases arriving at the Italian Supreme Court (*Corte di Cassazione*) are labour cases.

These developments have triggered an intense debate on alternative dispute resolution (ADR) in labour disputes. In this debate the focal point is how to reach speedy and cheap resolution of individual disputes. The question of how labour rights are to be effectively enforced is less pronounced. The centre point of this debate is on techniques for individual dispute resolution in the workplace or before a final court proceeding, through different forms of mediation or conciliation. For example, in Britain ADR became a major theme under the New Labour government from 1997. The Employment Rights (Dispute Resolution) Act 1998 set up a private 'arbitration alternative' to employment tribunals in unfair dismissal cases, but in practice this did not prove attractive to either employers or workers, and was rarely used.[39] To some extent, the promotion of ADR, while providing for better access to these procedures, has also made it harder to use judicial procedures. The British Employment Rights Act 2002 introduced complex procedural limits on workers' access to employment tribunals.

---

[38] See, eg Case 152/84 *Marshall* [1986] ECR 723 and Case C-262/88 *Barber* [1990] ECR 1889. See further Kilpatrick (2001), and chapter 5 above.

[39] Hepple (2002) 248–49.

Commenting on policies of British New Labour in the late 1990s, Davies and Freedland have argued that

> it is hard to avoid the conclusion that [the New Labour Government] proposal quite extensively crossed the line which separates measures to facilitate the settlement of disputes from measures to stifle the assertion of rights which might give rise to disputes.[40]

Similarly, during the 1990s various changes were adopted in Dutch procedural law affecting labour disputes, making the procedure less favourable to the workers, for instance by higher fees. However, this has given rise to very little discussion. In the Nordic countries, where industrial relations procedures have remained strong, the debate on ADR has been less pronounced.

International Procedures and the Autonomy of National Labour Law

During the 1990s, it became increasingly clear that judicial processes in international fora might be used as a tool for changes of national labour law. These possibilities limit the autonomy of national labour law. The final decision-making authority and control no longer reside at national level. Ultimately, international bodies may decide what is feasible and permitted in national systems.

The evolution of EU law has given rise to new possibilities for national actors to question national labour law in national courts. According to the Treaty of Rome, it was primarily a task for the European Commission to check that Member States fulfil their obligation to transpose directives into national law. This is often described as the public enforcement model. However, it is also possible to talk about a private enforcement model.[41] This model is based on the preliminary reference procedure prescribed in the Treaty. According to Article 234 EC, national courts may make references for a preliminary ruling on, inter alia, the interpretation of the Treaty and of secondary EC law (Directives, for example). Through the system of preliminary rulings it is possible for private parties to challenge national law through procedures in national courts. Over the years, the ECJ has developed several measures designed to enable private parties to benefit from EC law even when Member States have failed to fulfil their duties according to the Treaty and secondary legislation. There are four principal measures that have been created by the ECJ. First, the Court has declared that every national court must, in a case within its jurisdiction, set aside national law that conflicts with provisions of the Treaty or directly applicable secondary EU law (the doctrine of supremacy). Secondly, the Court has introduced the principle of direct effect. This principle means that, under certain conditions,

[40] Davies and Freedland (2006) 65. See also Hepple (2002) 246ff.
[41] Kilpatrick (2000).

individuals are entitled to rely on Community provisions directly before any national court. Thirdly, the Court has established that the authorities of the Member States, including the courts applying national law, are required to interpret national law in the light of the wording and the purpose of Directives (indirect effect or consistent interpretation). Finally, the Court has held it as a principle of Community law that Member States are obliged to make good loss and damage caused to individuals due to breaches of Community law for which any Member State can be held responsible. The principle of state liability is applicable to any case in which a Member State breaches Community law, whatever the organ of the state whose act or omission was responsible for the breach.

The private enforcement model has in practice been used by social partners, non-governmental organisations, academic lawyers and practitioners. In fact, many of the cases in which the ECJ has developed the private enforcement model have concerned labour law disputes. In those cases the question has often been whether the national regulation is sufficient to fulfil the demands of EC social policy, especially in respect of the principle of equality between men and women. The relative success these efforts have met with before the ECJ might be seen as a consequence of the coincidence of the ambition of (usually) women to achieve equality with the pro-integration attitude of the Court (see chapter 5 above). On the other hand, the same procedural instruments have also been used to question whether national labour laws or industrial relations practices have been in line with EC economic policies. Even such approaches have from time to time been successful (see chapter 2 above).

Judicial review of national labour laws and industrial relations practices might also take the form of complaints before the ECtHR. The Court has delivered important decisions concerning the negative freedom of association,[42] employee privacy[43] and freedom of speech.[44] The European Social Charter (1961, revised 1996) includes fundamental rights in the field of social policy generally and specifically in the fields of employment and industrial relations. Due to poor enforcement procedures, the Social Charter was earlier described as 'little known, rarely referred to and often ignored in practice'.[45] However, in 1995 a new collective complaints procedure was introduced that made it possible for the trade unions, employers' organisations and non-government organisations to bring cases before a committee of independent experts (European Committee of Social Rights).[46]

The complaints procedure before the International Labour Organisation (ILO) Committee on Freedom of Association should also be mentioned.

[42] *Young, James and Webster v the United Kingdom* (appl nos 7601/76, 7806/77, Judgment of 1981–08–13); *Sibson v UK* (appl no 14327/88, Judgment 1993–04–20); *Gustafsson v Sweden* (appl no 15573/89, Judgment 1996–04–25).

[43] *Madsen v Denmark* (appl no 58341/00, decision 2002–11–07) and *Wretlund v Sweden* (appl no 46210/99, decision 2004–03–09).

[44] *Fuentes Bobo v Spain* (appl no 39293/98, judgment 2000–02–29).

[45] Hepple; see reference in Kilpatrick (2000) 244.

[46] Harris and Darcy (2001).

According to this procedure, national trade unions and employers' organisations are allowed to submit complaints concerning violations of trade union rights to the Committee on Freedom of Association. Complaints can be made even against governments that have not ratified the relevant conventions. The Committee is a tripartite body with an independent chairman. After a preliminary study, the committee may, if an infringement has been established, recommend that the Governing Body make the concerned government aware of the problems and invite the government to solve it.

This multiplicity of international fora for judicial review opens up the possibility for conflicts not only between national and international laws, but also between different international bodies. For example, in the GCHQ dispute—which concerned the freedom of association for civil servants in Britain—the European Human Rights Commission denied that there had been a violation of Article 11 of the European Convention on Human Rights (ECHR), while the Committee on Freedom of Association was of the opinion that the UK had breached Article 2 of ILO Convention No 87.[47]

European Court of Human Rights Influences on National Procedures

Both the ECHR and the EC have influenced judicial procedures in labour disputes. Article 6 of the ECHR provides the right to a fair and public hearing within a reasonable time by an independent and impartial tribunal established by law, inter alia with regard to the determination of civil rights and obligations. The case law of the ECtHR implies that individuals whose civil rights are to be determined have *locus standi* before a court of some kind. In Denmark it was for a long time unclear whether a member of a trade union could pursue a claim on the basis of a collective agreement. A 1997 change in the law made it clear that individual trade union members may pursue a claim if the trade union refrains from getting involved in the dispute. In that case, the claim will be pursued before the normal courts. The change in the law was claimed to be necessary in order to comply with Article 6 of the ECHR. Already, in 1994, a judgment from the Danish Supreme Court, referring to the European Convention, had established that such a subsidiary right existed. However, the ordinary court may not award punitive damages, which is the normal sanction for breach of collective agreement in the 'industrial system'. Thus, in Denmark, the sanction available for the employee is less effective than the one available for the trade union.

Further, the independence and impartiality of tripartite Labour Courts has been addressed. In Sweden, there has been repeated discussion of the question whether the composition of the Labour Court is in conformity with the ECHR. The discussion was triggered by the *Langborger* case in 1989, which concerned

[47] O'Higgins (2002) 64.

the Swedish Housing and Tenancy Court.[48] In the *Kellerman* case, a non-organised employer claimed that the Swedish Labour Court was not impartial because of its composition with the lay judges nominated by the trade unions and employers' organisations. The ECtHR observed that the lay judges sitting on the Labour Court have special knowledge and experience of the labour market. They therefore contribute to the court's understanding of issues relating to the labour market and appear in principle to be highly qualified to participate in the adjudication of labour disputes. The ECtHR also noted that the inclusion of lay assessors as members of various specialised courts is a common feature in many countries. Nevertheless, their independence and impartiality may still be open to doubt in a particular case. This could be the case if the lay judge has a real or apparent conflict of interest with one or both of the parties. The ECtHR held by five votes to two that there had been no violation of the Convention.[49] In Denmark, similar criticisms have led to an amendment of the law concerning the Labour Court. The 1997 amendment of the Labour Court Act allows for a session of the presidency without lay judges if one of the parties (for example, a non-organised employer) so requests. In the Netherlands, the composition of and procedures before the courts and quasi-courts in matters of labour law and social security have been questioned in relation to the right to a fair trial under Article 6 of the ECHR. This has resulted in a number of adaptations in the statutory arrangements. In Britain, it has long been established that members of an employment tribunal cannot sit in any case in which they have a conflict of interest, eg where they are members of the same union as one of the contesting parties, or know a witness in the case. The Employment Appeal Tribunal has gone further and held that an employment tribunal cannot be impartial in a case involving adjudication upon cases against a government department that both administers a statutory benefit and nominates members of the tribunal.[50]

The Influence of the Principle of Effective Enforcement

The bulk of EU labour law consists of Directives, which are binding upon the Member States as to the result that must be achieved, but leave it to the national authorities to choose the form and method (Article 249 EC). One characteristic feature of EU directives is that they usually only state which conduct is accepted or not, or which situations are to be protected; they do not normally say anything about the means by which the rights and obligations prescribed shall take effect in a national context. The assumption is that, in the absence of European rules on remedies and procedures, domestic procedures are to be applied.[51]

---

[48] *Langborger v Sweden* (appl no 11179/84, 1989–06–22).
[49] *Kellerman v Sweden* (appl no 41579/98, judgment 2004–10–24).
[50] *Scanfuture UK Ltd v Secretary of State for Trade and Industry* [2001] IRLR 416 (EAT). The ECHR is now incorporated into UK law through the Human Rights Act 1998.
[51] For the following, see Malmberg (2003).

Although rules on procedures and remedies are primarily a matter for the Member States, Community law may still affect such rules, since the principle of subsidiarity does not give Member States full autonomy in deciding the rules that should be applied. The ECJ has developed in its case law two principles as to how Community rules shall be protected in the Member States. According to the first principle, Community rules are not to be discriminated against by providing less favourable conditions for enforcement in comparison with domestic rules of a similar nature (*the principle of equivalence*). The second principle concerns the effectiveness of enforcement methods (*the principle of sufficient effectiveness*). Sometimes, the Court has stated that national rules may not render the exercise of (rights conferred by) Community law virtually impossible or excessively difficult. In later case law, especially concerning remedies, the Court has indicated more intrusive control, stating that enforcement rules shall guarantee real and effective judicial protection.[52] The two principles are cumulative, and are here referred to as *the principle of effective enforcement*. This principle (ie the principles of equivalence and sufficient effectiveness in tandem) has developed on a case-by-case basis. It is commonly said that in the 1980s and the early 1990s the ECJ pursued an interventionist approach towards effective judicial protection. Since the mid-1990s the Court seems to have been more inclined to protect national procedural autonomy from the 'assaults' of effectiveness. The case law of the ECJ on effective enforcement has been 'codified' in later EU Directives—sometimes by reproducing within the legislative text the precise wording previously used by the Court.[53]

The case law of the ECJ concerning effective enforcement of EU labour law deals almost exclusively with judicial procedures. There is extensive case law regarding questions such as access to judicial protection for individuals, sound rules of procedure (time limits, burden of proof and the *ex officio* application of Community law) and adequate reparation for the infringement of rights. Through this case law a principle of judicial protection has been developed. The core of this principle is that Member States must ensure that individuals may effectively rely upon the rights conferred by EU law before national courts. Thus, the principle enshrines a micro-perspective on enforcement, and indicates a rather narrow understanding of enforcement as limited to judicial processes. Until recently, administrative and industrial relations procedures have received only scant attention at the EU level. Such a difference in focus between the EU and national levels is clearly illustrated by the rules on *locus standi*. According to the case law of the ECJ, all persons have the right of access to a competent court to dispute measures they consider to be contrary to the rights conferred on them by EU law.[54] This is usually explicitly regulated in labour law

---

[52] Case 14/83 *von Colson* [1984] ECR 19891, para 23.
[53] Eg Art 8.2 of Directive 2002/14/EC establishing a general framework for informing and consulting employees in the European Community. See also Malmberg (2003) 34.
[54] Eg Case 222/86 *Heylens* [1987] ECR 4097.

Directives.[55] However, these Directives have traditionally not contained any rules providing trade unions or other workers' representatives with *locus standi* in national courts. Nor has the case law of the ECJ so far provided any explicit support in that direction. By contrast, national laws to a large extent give trade unions and other collective interest representatives a standing in disputes concerning individual members of their organisation. The labour law Directives adopted in recent years have marked a new direction in this area. The Employment Directive, 2000/78/EC (see chapter 5 above), expresses a new awareness of the need to take both micro- and macro-perspectives on enforcement into account. The Directive not only regulates individual judicial processes, but also explicitly deals with the industrial relations process as a means of enforcement (Article 13).

In the last decade the role of equality bodies has also been recognised at EU level. According to the Race Equality Directive, 2000/43/EC, the Member States must designate a body or bodies for the promotion of equal treatment of all persons without discrimination on the grounds of racial or ethnic origin. These bodies must provide independent assistance to victims of discrimination, conduct independent surveys concerning discrimination, publish independent reports and make recommendations (Article 13). Similar provisions are found in the Equal Treatment Directive, 2002/73/EC. When these Directives were adopted, most of the Member States had already set up various kinds of equality body (see above).

Conclusion

The evolution of enforcement of labour law after the Second World War was largely shaped by the pre-war heritage. The institutional setting for different enforcement procedures were in most of the countries covered in this study, already in place by the end of the war. In all countries there was some form of control of health and safety issues through public administration. In most of the countries, bi- or tripartite labour courts already existed, or were created or re-established at the end of the war. Nevertheless, the institutional design of the enforcement processes differed.

The different institutional choices made in the formative phase might be viewed as the outcome of diverging regimes for industrial relations and production. In some countries, such as Denmark, Germany and Sweden, the state supported a cooperative form of industrial relations by providing the tripartite labour courts during the first decades of the twentieth century. The labour courts were—at least after the war—promoted by trade unions and accepted by

---

[55] See, eg Art 9 of the Transfer of Undertakings Directive and Art 6 of the Equal Treatment Directive.

employers' organisations. The relatively early establishment of these courts might partly be explained by the fact that industrial relations were based on a relatively high degree of cooperation and trust. And when the courts were established, trade union leaders and employers worked together in the courts to enhance this basic attitude. British industrial relations were more polarised, and both employers and trade unions were more suspicious of state intervention.[56] The traditional attitude was to keep industrial relations and labour out of the courts.

In the continental models, the individual judicial procedure was the most important process before the 1970s. In Britain and the Nordic countries, the focus at that time was almost totally on creating effective enforcement from a macro-perspective: in Britain, by the almost total dominance of industrial relations processes; in the Nordic countries, by adopting a mixture of industrial relations processes and collective judicial processes. The rules on procedures and remedies are dependent on the evolution of the content of the substantive parts of labour law. When labour law consisted mainly of health and safety regulations, administrative procedures were predominant. In periods and countries where employment conditions were more or less exclusively regulated by collective agreements, the industrial relations processes were the principal enforcement mechanism.

The expansion of labour law statutes since the 1970s has led to more emphasis on individual judicial processes. In the continental models, in which enforcement has been organised mainly around individual judicial processes, the pressure for change has been moderate. In Britain, on the other hand, there was a sharp turn from industrial relations processes towards individual judicial processes. In the Nordic countries, too, individual judicial processes have become more important, although the enforcement through industrial relations and collective judicial processes has remained dominant. In this way, the evolution of enforcement procedures has strengthened the trend towards individualisation of labour law and labour disputes.

In many countries, these developments have put considerable pressure on individual judicial procedures by raising the quantity of litigation and have thus triggered an intense debate on ADR in labour disputes. Alongside the growth of discrimination and equality legislation from the 1970s, it was also recognised that statutory provisions were not alone sufficient for combating discrimination. Thus, most countries have established some kind of administrative enforcement by agencies, commissions or ombud (or ombudsmen) in the field of discrimination.

One important historical reason for establishing bi- or tripartite labour courts or industrial relations processes was to increase the trust and belief in these processes by the social partners, especially the trade unions. During the 1990s, it became increasingly clear that final decision-making authority and control of labour law no longer resided at the national level. Ultimately, it is to a large extent

---

[56] Blankenburg and Rogowski (1986).

supranational courts—the ECJ and the ECtHR—and other international supervisory bodies –such as the ILO Committee on Freedom of Association and the
European Social Rights Committee—that decide what is feasible and permitted
within national industrial relations systems. This does not mean, of course, that
all authority has been transferred to these courts and supervisory bodies; there is
still a significant degree of influence left at the domestic level. What has changed
is that the social partners, national courts and ultimately the legislature are no
longer able, on their own, to control the game plan close to home. Control takes
place within the framework of a complicated system of influence and interaction
between numerous national, foreign and supranational decision-makers and
other actors, in which none alone possesses sovereign authority to make the final
and more overarching decisions. In this sense, the autonomy of national labour
law has decreased.

Appendix I

The Countries: A Short Guide

Austria

Territory and Population

Austria has a land area of 83,871 km^2, and a fairly stable homogeneous population. By 2004, this was 8.1 million. Foreign workers make up about 10% of the labour force. By 2005, life expectancy was 76 (men) and 82 years (women). Gross national income (GNI) per capita was €27,700.

Constitutional Development

After annexation by Germany in 1938 and the Allied occupation at the end of the Second World War, Austria's State Treaty 1955 declared the country 'permanently neutral'. Austria has been a Member State of the EU since 1995. It is a republic organised as a federation of states. Labour law falls within the Federal government's area of competence. The Basic Law on the General Rights of Citizens (StGG) and the European Convention on Human Rights (ECHR), incorporated into Austrian law, guarantee fundamental rights, including freedom of association (but not the right to strike), property, privacy and the right to earn a living. The equality of all citizens is also of fundamental importance.

The competence to legislate rests primarily at the federal level, but the *Länder* have important administrative responsibilities. The National Council (*Nationalrat*) is the legislative body and passes ordinary legislation by simple majority. Constitutional legislation requires a two-thirds majority for passage with a quorum of at least half of its elected members. The Constitutional Court can overrule unconstitutional legislation and executive acts. A unique feature of the Austrian system, re-established after the Second World War, is the Chambers of Labour, with each *Land* having its own regional chamber and all nine regional chambers forming the Federal Chamber of Labour (*Bundesarbeitskammer*). All workers, subject to certain exceptions, are compulsory members of the chambers, which have several functions. These include the promotion of the social, economic, professional and cultural interests of workers, the unemployed and pensioners. Since 1992, they have been responsible also for advising individual workers in labour and social matters and providing legal representation. However, in practice the chambers do not exercise their right to conclude collective agreements because of the statutory principle of the primacy of voluntary trade associations. This means that if a voluntary association concludes a collective agreement (see below), the chamber loses its power to do so.

Labour Law

Nearly all labour legislation was prepared by the social partners, or at least enacted with their consent, with the result that changes of government did not lead to changes in legislation. There is no comprehensive labour code, but only a multiplicity of statutes and some partial codifications. In 1947, the Collective Agreements Act (*Kollektivvertragsgesetz*), governing collective agreements, and the Works Councils Act (*Betriebsrätegesetz*), dealing with works councils, the conclusion of plant agreements and dismissal protection, reintroduced and improved the system of collective bargaining and the industrial constitution that was already in force before the Second World War. The rules on collective bargaining, workplace representation and dismissal protection were codified in the Labour Regulation Act (ArbVG) of 1974. The post-war legislation continued the tradition before 1934, of applying separate employment rules to blue-collar workers (*Arbeiter*) and white-collar workers (*Angestellte*). In 1974, the rights of the two groups to sick pay were approximated but not equalised and in 1976 holiday entitlements were harmonised, as were the rules on severance pay in 2003. Continuing differences between the *Arbeiter* and the *Angestellte* pertain mainly to the periods of termination, the causes of dismissal and continued remuneration periods in the case of sickness.

There is a hierarchical structure of labour law. The hierarchy is as follows: (i) EU law, and constitutional law; (ii) binding acts/statutes of Parliament; (iii) ordinances (only of minor importance); (iv) collective agreements; (v) company agreements; (vi) contracts of employment; (vii) non-mandatory statutes (or collective agreement); and (viii) employers' instructions. Special agreements (eg company agreements or contracts of employment) are valid only if they are more favourable for employees than the 'higher' regulation, or deal with matters not regulated there. However, the collective agreement could (but seldom does) rule out this possibility. Collective agreements are very important. The principal function of these agreements is setting wages (there is no state minimum wage), but they also cover other labour standards, such as hours, vacation allowances, notice and expenses, among others. In the past the legislator sometimes took over regulations previously enacted in collective agreements. Only bodies with a statutory mandate can conclude collective agreements, and these bodies are usually statutory employer organisations and the ÖGB (below).

Most legal disputes concerning the individual employment relationship are dealt with by special labour courts, consisting of a professional judge, one associate judge with employer status and one with employee status. In most regions they are specialised chambers of a higher ordinary civil court. The proceedings of labour courts were fundamentally reorganised in 1986, and their jurisdiction expanded. Appeals go to special chambers (including one employer and one employee judge) of one of the four *Oberlandsgerichte*, and from these to a special chamber of the highest court, the *Oberster Gerichtshof.*

Political Parties

The major political parties are the Socialist Party (*Sozialistiche Partei*) and the Austrian People's Party (*Volkspartei*). There are also the Freedom Party (*Freiheitliche Partei*), which was very strong at one time, and the Green Party. The Socialist and People's Parties shared a coalition from 1948 until 1966, and this led to criticisms of compromised legislation. After 1966, the two parties exchanged power until they once again came together in a coalition in 1986. The People's Party entered a coalition with the right-wing Freedom Party causing strained relations within the EU. The Freedom Party split up in 2005.

Trade Unions

Austria has a unitary trade union movement in the form of the *Österreichischer Gewerksehaftsbund* (ÖGB), to which about 40% of employees belong (in the 1970s nearly two-thirds were members The ÖGB is a non-partisan body which was a significant economic and social force.[1] It enjoys a de facto monopoly in collective bargaining (not by virtue of statute). Its leading posts are often filled by persons from the political parties and members of parliament. No form of employee participation can be validly agreed between employers and employees if not allowed for in the Collective Employment Regulation Act (ArbVG). There is close interaction between the ÖGB and works councils in companies. The employers generally have to join the Chamber of Commerce (*Bundeskammer der Gewerblichen Wirtschaft*).

Although the member unions of the ÖGB, which are legally solely parts of the ÖGB, conclude collective agreements themselves, there was great coordination between them, so that the member unions acted more than agents of the ÖGB. In the past, many union leaders were also members of Parliament, and until 2000 the Federal Minister of Social Administration was usually a high-ranking ÖGB member. In the past the ÖGB had easy access to the government, so it could assess whether statute or collective bargaining would better

---

[1] In the first half of 2006 the ÖGB was endangered by a financial scandal in a bank that it owns, and apparently lost its whole fortune (including strike-funds).

promote its political objectives. This has changed in the 1990s. At the enterprise level, the ArbVG empowers employees to elect leaders for their workplace, and the statutory-based works councils allow employees to participate to some extent in enterprise operations. By statute, the ÖGB and Labour chambers are required to support the efforts of the works councils. Because works council members are very often union members as well, conflicts of opinion and agenda are rare between these two structures. As a result, strikes are not common, and industrial action usually stems from independent bodies representing employee interests.

Belgium

Territory and Population

Belgium has an area of 30,258 km^2, and by 2004 a population of 10.3 million, made up of Flemish (Dutch-speaking) and Walloon (French-speaking) communities, as well as a small German community. Foreign workers make up 8–9% of the labour force. In 2004 the GNI per capita was €26,350.

Constitutional Development

Belgium is a constitutional monarchy. Increasing friction between the Flemish and Walloon communities led to a push by both groups toward regional autonomy, which began in 1971. Negotiations between the main French and Flemish political parties in the 1980s led to separate Flemish- and French-speaking areas of the Belgian union and an agreement to enact constitutional amendments. A separate government for the German-speaking communities has been established as well. The latest incarnation of the constitution materialised in 1994, delegating most powers to the regions. While Brussels is the national capital, it does not have the same amount of regional power as that given to Wallonia and Flanders and therefore cannot influence power relations between the other two regions. However, conflicts in jurisdiction do occur between the regional and national levels. Notwithstanding the regional structure, Belgium remains a single economic and monetary union. Legislative power consists of the King and Parliament. Executive power is delegated to the King and Ministers, while courts and tribunals undertake the country's judicial functions. Regional governments decide on 40% of the budget, but the distribution of funds relies on revenue sharing with the federal government in many cases. At the regional and community levels, governments have control over functions such as cultural decisions, education, employment policies and foreign trade. While the Flemish regional government oversees regional and community issues, the Walloon region is represented by both a Walloon regional and Walloon community government. Belgium was a founder member of the EEC in 1957. The ECHR has been incorporated into domestic law.

Labour Law

The highest court in Belgium in the *Cour de Cassation*, but it does not have the power to rule on the constitutionality of legislation. Below the highest court are five courts of appeal, 26 tribunals of first instance and 222 judicial cantons. There is a separate court for administrative matters. The Council of State undertakes the functions of judicial review. A Constitutional Court rules on matters of jurisdiction between national and regional levels, and on some constitutional matters involving the review of Acts of Parliament in the light of the constitutional principle of equality. There are labour courts consisting of a professional judge and two lay persons dealing with individual employment disputes over rights.

Due to the fact that Belgian businesses are overwhelmingly small in size (ie less than 50 workers), the country's system of industrial relations takes account of size in its structure. Works councils are only required in businesses of 100 workers or more, a Committee for Prevention and Protection at Work is only necessary in businesses of 50 workers or more, and a trade union committee is only required when 25–50 workers are employed in a business. Therefore, very few businesses have any worker representation at the enterprise level. Collective bargaining is entirely regulated by the Act of 5 December 1968 on Collective Bargaining Agreements, which deals with the coverage, form, content and binding force of agreements in considerable detail. Nonetheless, collective agreements for the private sector or certain industries can be drafted to cover all employers in either category. Employer organisations tend to be quite powerful and linked to the major political parties. While collective bargaining has historically been an independent process between the relevant parties, the Belgian government has become involved due to inflation concerns.

The hierarchy of sources that regulate employment relations are set out in an Act of 5 December 1968. These are: (i) the mandatory provisions of the law; (ii) collective bargaining agreements that are rendered generally binding (usually by Royal Decree) in the following order: (a) agreements concluded in the National Labour Council (composed of employer and employee representatives and presided over by a civil servant); (b) agreements concluded in a joint committee of industry; and (c) agreements concluded in a joint sub-committee; (iii) collective agreements that are not rendered generally binding in a defined order similar to the above; (iv) an individual agreement in writing; (v) company work rules; (vi) supplementary legal provisions; (vii) verbal contracts of employment; and (viii) customs.

Political Parties

Until the mid-1960s, the country's primary political entities represented Christian, socialist and liberal ideologies. However, once disputes developed between the Walloons and the Flemish, these ideologies differentiated further into distinct parties along the two cultural lines. The main Christian parties are the *Centre Democrate Humaniste* for the French-speaking population, and the *Christen-Democratsch en Vlaams* for the Dutch-speaking population. The Party of Liberal Progress is divided into *Le Mouvement Réformateur* for the Walloons and the *Vlaamse Liberalen en Democraten* for the Flemish. Finally, the Socialist Party ended up as the *Socialistische Parij Anders* for the Dutch community and the *Parti Socialiste* for the French community. There is an ultra right-wing *Vlaams Blok* Party. Governments are invariably coalitions.

Trade Unions

Belgium has three major trade unions, each corresponding to one of the major political parties. The main unions are the Confederation of Christian Trade Unions (ACV-CSC), the Socialist Trade Union Movement (ABVV-FGTB) and the far smaller Liberal Trade Union Movement (ACLV-CGSLB). These organisations have separate divisions for white-collar workers. Women comprise around half of the membership in unions. Overall unionisation has remained high (around 50%). White- and blue-collar workers are represented by separate organisations within each of the three trade unions. Freedom of association is legally provided for under the Act of May 1921, Article 1, but few prosecutions take place on this basis due to a high burden of proof. This Act also protects the right not to join a union. Benefits associated with union memberships are afforded in some sectors.

Britain (United Kingdom of Great Britain and Northern Ireland)

Territory and Population

The island of Great Britain comprises England (130,410 km^2), Wales (20,748 km^2) and Scotland (78,789 km^2). These territories, together with Northern Ireland (12,567 km^2), form the UK. The total population by 2004 was 59.5 million. Foreign workers (born outside the UK) comprise about 9% of the work force. Life expectancy was 76 (men) and 81 (women). In 2004 the GNI per capita was $US33,940 (€28,850).

Constitutional Development

Britain is a parliamentary monarchy. The Constitution will not be found in a basic document or set of documents as it has evolved over centuries and consists of Acts of Parliament and other legislation, judge-made common law and practices known as constitutional conventions. The most important feature of this constitution is parliamentary sovereignty. Parliament can enact any law on any subject and this can be changed by ordinary legislation. Although the ECHR was incorporated into domestic law by the Human Rights Act 1998, the courts are not empowered to strike down any primary Acts of Parliament that are in conflict with convention rights. Instead, they only have the power to declare that such a breach has occurred, and it is then up to Parliament to decide whether or not to correct the breach. Parliament consists of the elected House of Commons, and the largely appointed House of Lords, the latter having only a delaying power. The government consists of members of both Houses (mainly the Commons) and the Cabinet, headed by the Prime Minister, is collectively responsible to the Commons, and would have to resign if it lost a vote of confidence in the Commons. The Queen exercises only formal and ceremonial functions.

In 1999 a Scottish Parliament and a Welsh Assembly, with defined law-making powers, were set up. Acts of Parliament no longer apply to Scotland and Wales unless expressly stated to do so. In practice, nearly all labour legislation does apply to the whole of Great Britain. Employment and industrial relations are matters reserved to the UK (Westminster) Parliament and are therefore not devolved. A separate Northern Ireland Assembly was set up in 1998 as a result of the Belfast (Good Friday) peace agreement, but this was later suspended because of the failure of power-sharing arrangements between the Protestant (Unionist) and Roman Catholic (Sinn Féin) parties. Since then, Northern Ireland has been under direct rule by the central government, which usually extends labour legislation, with modifications, to that province. Britain became a member of the European Economic Community (EEC) in 1973, but did not join the Economic and Monetary Union (EMU).

English common law (all the law that is not legislation) is developed by the courts in England, Wales and Northern Ireland. Scots law is a hybrid system, with roots in the Roman (civil) law as well as being under the living influence of English law. The highest court for all these countries was the House of Lords (Judicial Committee).[2] The ordinary courts in all these jurisdictions have exclusive jurisdiction in respect of (i) actions in tort (delict), the most important of which for labour law are injunctions and damages for industrial action; and (ii) actions for damages for personal injuries and in respect of a person's death.

---

[2] From 2009 or 2010, the judicial functions of the House of Lords will be transferred to a new Supreme Court.

Labour Law

A system of tripartite industrial tribunals was established in 1965 (renamed employment tribunals in 1996) to deal with disputes arising under labour legislation. These have concurrent jurisdiction with the ordinary courts in respect of some claims for damages for breach of contract. Appeals on questions of law go to the tripartite Employment Appeal Tribunal, and from there to the Court of Appeal in England or the Northern Ireland Court of Appeal, or the Scottish Court of Session (Inner House). In very limited cases, there may be a final appeal to the House of Lords.

The traditional British system of industrial relations rested on a social consensus that the state's role should be minimal, characterised by Kahn-Freund as 'collective laissez-faire'.[3] There was a small amount of 'auxiliary' legislation designed to promote and support voluntary collective bargaining under which the terms and conditions of employment of nearly four-fifths of workers were determined. The primacy of voluntary bargaining meant that there was relatively little regulatory legislation laying down rules of employment on matters such as wages and hours. However, there was a significant amount of legislation on health and safety, an area beyond the reach of collective bargaining. This traditional system remained in place for the first 20 years after the Second World War, which also saw nationalisation of some key industries and the rapid growth of the welfare state following the Beveridge proposals of 1942.

The social consensus that had sustained this traditional system fell apart in the 1960s and 1970s. The pressure of full employment had contributed to a shift in power to the workplace, and shop stewards were increasingly identified by politicians as the cause of wage inflation. A Royal Commission (the Donovan Report) recommended that the informal shop stewards system should be brought under control. Two broad strategies were adopted: a series of ultimately unsuccessful incomes policies (no fewer than six from 1948 to 1979), and direct legal intervention to reform and restrict collective bargaining. These strategies were not consistently applied and were not infrequently discordant. In the period 1971–74, the Industrial Relations Act (introduced by Heath's Conservative government) tried to provide a legal structure for collective bargaining, with restrictions on the right to strike, and at the same time introduced new individual legal rights, notably the right not to be unfairly dismissed. The immediate cause of the failure of the Act was the defeat of the Heath government in the February 1974 election, which arose from a confrontation with the miners' union over incomes policy. However, even before the election the Trades Union Congress (TUC)'s policy of non-co-operation had rendered the Act virtually inoperable, and employers were reluctant to use the law. The Labour government (1974–79), following a 'social contract' with the TUC, repealed the Act and restored and clarified the traditional legal support for voluntary collective bargaining and the right to strike

---

[3] Kahn-Freund (1959).

including the right to take secondary industrial action. Labour also introduced an Employment Protection Act 1975, which created many new individual legal rights, and legislated against sex and race discrimination.

The death-knell of the voluntarist system was sounded in the 'winter of discontent' against government policies in 1979, when unemployment and inflation were both rising and public expenditure was being cut. In May 1979, a Conservative government led by Mrs Thatcher was elected to power. The policies and legislation of her administration fundamentally shifted the parameters of labour law. Her administration's solution to the problems of inflation and the politicisation of unions was influenced by the thinking of Hayek and other neo-liberals. They sought the restoration of 'free' markets and the common law. Trade unions and labour legislation were seen as a distortion of market relations; their power had to be weakened and there had to be 'deregulation'. This philosophy was reflected in the seven main pieces of labour legislation introduced by the Conservative Government between 1982 and 1996. The legislation pursued four specific policies: (i) workers' rights of self-help through collective organisation and strikes were effectively restricted to their own employment units; (ii) trade union funds were placed at risk through heavy fines and sequestration of their assets; (iii) contrary to the public policy of the previous 100 years, there was a clear commitment to restrict collective bargaining; and (iv) central to the whole policy was the control of labour through the market, including the abolition of all forms of minimum wage-fixing, the ending of tripartism in most regulatory bodies, and the restriction of unfair dismissal and other employment and welfare rights. This was accompanied by privatisation and outsourcing which also severely weakened the unions.

The New Labour government, led by Tony Blair, elected in 1997, consciously set about forging a 'Third Way' in labour law and industrial relations, distinct both from Thatcherite neo-liberalism and from Labour's corporatist social contract legislation of the 1970s. It introduced legislation to expand fundamental individual rights at work, such as a national minimum wage, new rights in respect of disability and other forms of discrimination, the incorporation of the ECHR into domestic law and 'family-friendly' measures to ease the entry of women into the work force. Some legislation, such as that on working time and health and safety, has been the direct result of EC Directives. The Blair administration also promoted union-recognition legislation, and (following EC Directives) new forms of workers' representation and participation. However, at the same time, it retained the key legal provisions enacted under the Conservatives to restrict industrial action and to outlaw the closed shop.

Political Parties

Since the Second World War, power has alternated between the Conservative Party and the Labour Party. The emergence in 1980 of a Social Democratic Party, which later merged with the Liberal Party to form the Liberal Democrats, has not changed the dominance of the two main parties. The political consensus on labour legislation began to break down in the 1960s, and there followed 25 years of intense conflict and shifts of legislation. However, since the election of New Labour under Tony Blair in 1997, a new centrist consensus has emerged on these matters.

Trade Unions

Aggregate union density was remarkably stable in the post-war years (around 40–45% membership), with a sharp rise to over 50% in 1979 under a Labour government. After 1979, with the election of Mrs Thatcher's Conservative government and the decline of manufacturing industry, this began to fall, so that by end of the 1990s less than 30% of the workforce were union members. Most of these were in the public sector. Employers' associations also declined in importance, with companies taking responsibility for their own industrial relations. Nearly all trade unions (also declining in number, as a result of union mergers) are affiliated to the TUC. The TUC exerted considerable political influence from the period of Second World War until 1970 and again from 1974 to 1979. Its status was severely undermined during 18 years of Conservative government, and this has not been greatly revitalised under the New Labour government since 1997. The TUC does not take part in collective bargaining with the main employers' organisation, the Confederation of British Industry, and it exercises only limited power over its affiliates.

Denmark

Territory and Population

Denmark (a Nordic country) has an area of 43,098 km^2 and, by 2004, a population of 5.4 million, with foreign workers comprising 2.8% of the labour force. Greenland and the Faroe Islands are self-governing dependencies within the Danish realm. By 2004, life expectancy was 75 years for men and 79 years for women; the GNI per capita was €34,550.

Constitutional Development

Denmark is a constitutional monarchy, with the current constitution coming into effect in 1953. The constitution has had little impact on labour law, although freedom of association, freedom of speech and assembly are guaranteed. Legislative power is shared by the monarch (whose role is purely formal) and Parliament, which consists of a single chamber. Since 1953 Cabinet responsibility has been a written rule of the Constitution. The courts can rule on the constitutionality of legislation. International treaties do not automatically become Danish law; they must be implemented by Acts of Parliament. Denmark became a member of the EEC in 1973. The ECHR has been incorporated into domestic law. The Crown appoints a 15-judge Supreme Court on recommendation from the government. Below this level are two high courts and around 100 local courts.

Labour Law

The industrial relation regime in Denmark is commonly referred to as 'the Danish model'. A distinctive feature of this model is that there is a high-trust tripartite co-operation between trade unions, employers' organisations and the government. There has been a long-standing consensus that the state should not interfere in the regulation of wages and other employment conditions, without a joint request from the social partners. The social partners have generally preferred regulation through collective agreements. Thus, legislation has traditionally played a minor role in the field of labour law. Another feature of the Danish model is that the social partners play a predominant role in the dispute settlement through industrial bodies, such as the Labour Court and industrial arbitration tribunals. The Labour Court (formerly the Permanent Court of Arbitration), first established in 1910, is now governed by an Act of 1973, amended in 1997. This Court, consisting of professional and lay judges appointed by the Minister of Labour, deals with disputes on the interpretation and breach of collective agreements. There is no right of appeal against its decisions. There is a specialist industrial arbitration tribunal appointed under the Basic Agreement (below).

   The basis for the industrial relation regime was laid down in the basic agreements between the social partners. The most important is the Agreement between the Danish Employers' Confederation (DA) and the Danish Confederation of Trade Unions (LO), originally concluded in 1899 (the September Compromise). The agreement was amended in 1960 and replaced by new one in 1973 (subsequently revised several times). These amendments have only contained minor changes of substance. There has been remarkable stability in the coverage of collective agreements—over 75% of the workforce—but with some sectoral differences. The last decades have witnessed a significant decentralisation of collective bargaining. From the 1950s to the late 1970s, LO and DA played a key role in wage setting. Since the 1980s, by contrast, the main wage agreements have been concluded at sectoral level. For a long time, however, wage agreements at sectoral level were closely coordinated, with wage agreements in certain sectors, most notably the metal industry, setting the trend. At the same time, the content of sectoral agreements has changed. Collective agreements based on the standard-wage system (*normalløn*), whereby the wage levels for different occupations are set at federal level without the possibility of local adjustment, have increasingly been replaced with a wage system in which actual wages are set at local level, and often for each employee individually. The tripartite approach is an integral part of labour market policy. The social partners take part in the drafting of regulations even on issues which are not subject to collective agreements but are instead regulated by law, such as the work environment, job placement services and unemployment insurance schemes. The social partners are regularly consulted on draft labour market legislation. The policy of all political parties is that labour legislation should be used only in exceptional circumstances, which means that very little such legislation has existed historically. Most labour standards are governed by collective agreements and judicial decisions, although EU membership has necessitated some legislation.

By international standards, employment legislation has been relatively restricted for a long time. Apart from the Annual Holidays Act (*Ferieloven*) and the White-Collar Workers Act (*Funktionærloven*), first adopted in 1938, the majority of statutes governing the relationship between employers and employees are a consequence of Danish membership of the EU. Nevertheless, the number of labour law statutes has increased dramatically during recent decades. Although there are some examples of purely national legislation, the bulk of new legislation has been introduced in order to transpose EC directives. The predominant issue in the evolution of labour law in Denmark during recent decades has been how to integrate EC labour law into the Danish model. EC Directives are implemented by transposing the Directive into national law, after which the legislator will adopt the statutes necessary to guarantee that every employee is ensured the rights in the Directives. Further, individual human rights have become more important. In 1997 the ECHR was incorporated into Danish law. The Convention has had a significant impact on the labour law debate (eg the questions on negative freedom of association and *locus standi* for individual employees).

Political Parties

The Danish Parliament consists of members from a relatively large number of political parties. The Social Democratic Party, which is usually the largest one, has traditional ties to the LO. However, it has shown signs of losing strength, falling out of power in the 1980s and again from 2001. Party goals include: improving social security rights, pensions, sickness and unemployment benefits, equalising incomes and democratising economic life. Other parties in Parliament have similar agendas but are more centrist or right; these include the Liberal Party and the Conservative Party. These parties would like to see reduced spending and employment in the public sector and a more limited growth in the social welfare and health arena, but, like the Social Democratic Party, they also support a modern welfare state. The Danish People's Party was formed in 1997 to push a new agenda against foreign immigration and for strong law enforcement. Having acquired around 15% of the vote, it has been able to play many of the other political parties off one another.

Trade Unions

Trade union membership has remained high throughout the period covered by this book, with more than 75% of workers being affiliated to unions. About 70% of these belong to unions affiliated to the LO. There is also a Salaried Employees and Civil Servants Confederation (FTF), representing white-collar employees and civil servants, and the Danish Confederation of Professional Associations (AC), representing graduate professionals. Over recent decades unions have increasingly been organised on sectoral or industry lines rather than according to occupation. Unions generally do not compete for the same members and they are not divided by political or other ideological beliefs. The main central organisation of employers is the DA.

Finland

Territory and Population

Finland (a Nordic country) has an area of 338,145 km^2, about two-thirds covered by forest and one-tenth by water, and by 2004 had a population of 5.2 million. The percentage of foreign workers in the labour force increased from 0.5 in 1990 to 3% in 2000. GNI per capita in 2004 was €27,870. Life expectancy was 75 (men) and 82 years (women). Finland has at times been part of Sweden and of Russia. Around 12% of the country was ceded to the USSR after the Second World War.

Constitutional Development

The old Swedish constitutional enactments were replaced in 1919 by a republican constitution. Constitutional provisions on fundamental rights were modernised in 1995, adding economic, social and cultural rights, and extending them to everyone within the jurisdiction of Finland, not only Finnish citizens. A new Constitution of Finland, consolidating all constitutional provisions, came into effect in 2000. Legislative power is exercised by the Parliament, whose position was enhanced by the new Constitution, and the President of the Republic, who can return an Act to Parliament for reconsideration. The country is divided administratively into provinces, reduced in number from 12 to 6 in 1997. Finland is a member of the Nordic Council and became a member of the EU in 1995.

Labour Law

The main models for the Finnish legal system have been taken from Sweden. The system has also been influenced by German legal science, but there is no systematically codified law. There is a three-tier system of regular courts dealing with civil and criminal matters. Labour law disputes outside the competence of the Labour Court (below) fall within the jurisdiction of the ordinary courts. These include disputes concerning the interpretation of individual employment contracts or employment legislation, claims for overtime compensation, holiday pay, and on hours of work etc, and prosecutions for violation of labour legislation. The Labour Court is a specialist court dealing with collective agreements. It is composed of a president and two other neutral members, four employers' and four employees' members, and four additional members for cases concerning public officials. Finnish labour law is a mixture of legislation, which establishes the basic framework, and collective agreements. Traditionally collective bargaining was highly centralised, but since the 1990s it has become increasingly decentralised. Individual contracts are governed by the Employment Contracts Act 2001, while collective agreements are in practice subject to the Collective Agreements Act 1946 (with separate legislation for civil servants).

Political Parties

In the period since the Second World War, Finland has mainly had coalition governments, first under Centre Party control and then under Social Democrats, with the concurrence of the small centrist parties.

Trade Unions

Trade union membership has remained high (about 80%) throughout the period. The largest body is the Central Organisation of Finnish Workers (SAK), with about one million members organised on industrial union lines, and also federations of public sector and transport workers. The second largest is the Finnish Confederation of Salaried Employees (STTK), and the third is the Confederation of Unions for Academic Professionals (AKAVA). There are four main organisations representing employers.

France

Territory and Population

France covers 543,965 km² and by 2004 had a population of 60.7 million. Foreign workers comprised about 6.3% of the labour force. GNI per capita in 2004 was €25,570. Life expectancy was 76 (men) and 83 years (women).

Constitutional Development

After the euphoria of the Liberation, France quickly fell back into its old divisions, rejecting, in a second referendum, a constitutional project adopted by the Constituent Assembly. Finally, in Autumn 1946, the fourth republic was born, bringing with it the same problems as the third: chronic governmental instability, aggravated by proportional representation, and legislative incapacity, which resulted in procedures to transfer difficult decisions to the executive branch.

However, the *coup de grâce* came not from within, but from Algeria, bringing General de Gaulle back to power in 1958, with a phalanx of traditional forces behind him. The new constitution, approved by a large popular majority, gave the executive, and in particular the President of the Republic, a dominant role, but the executive is still answerable to the deputies of the National Assembly. Parliament is made up of two chambers: the Chamber of Deputies, directly representing the electorate, and the Republican Council ('Senate'), whose role is more representative of local council level. De Gaulle's attempt to replace this second assembly with an 'economic' chamber in 1969 ended in failure; this project was too strongly reminiscent, for the French, of the corporate-style organisations convened during the war. One of the originalities of the fifth republic lies in its creation of a constitutional council, charged with overseeing constitutionality. Several laws have come to reinforce the role of local powers, transferring some decisions from national level to the old local collectivities (the departments and communes) and also to the regions. This gives France an unusually high number of local governance levels, in comparison to other countries. France was a founder member of the EEC in 1957.

There are two parallel hierarchies of courts, one judicial the other administrative. The judicial arm consists of *Tribunaux de Grande Instance*, appeal courts, with the *Cour de Cassation* at the top. The administrative arm is under the Council of State (*Conseil d'Etat*). Conflicts of jurisdiction are decided by the *Tribunal des Conflits*.

Labour Law

Any of the above courts may have to decide a dispute concerning labour and social law. However, the system of specialist labour courts (*conseils des prud'hommes*), started under Napoleon, has continued and was reformed several times during the period. They deal with individual disputes under employment contracts. Half the members are employers and half workers, with no professional judge. Throughout the period, legislation rather than collective bargaining was the predominant source of labour law. Most of the statutory rules are gathered together in a Labour Code (*Code du Travail*). They are often detailed and cover not only individual terms and conditions of employment, but also collective organisation and representation, including trade union organisation within the enterprise, collective bargaining and the conclusion and application of collective agreements, and employee representation within the enterprise. The law, often very generic and imprecise, is supplemented by ordinances, decrees, directives and orders, etc, which, notwithstanding the legal control exercised by the Council of State, sometimes redirect legislation to a great extent. Collective agreements, industrial agreements and professional codes of practice also bring specificities, developments and derogations. Private and public sector workers are frequently subject to different sets of regulations, as are workers in agriculture, public enterprises, those who work from home, sales representatives, sailors, miners, journalists, etc.

The first goal at the time of the liberation was to eradicate the decisions taken by the Vichy regime and give the trade unions back their position, and even to help the unions to collaborate with the industry committees, to try to make them into management controllers. Meanwhile, the government began to construct a modern system of social protection, inspired by the Beveridge report, which was, however, undermined by concerted opposition. Legislative activity was especially important in 1946: a constitution that recognised social rights and a complementary law on the economic council; texts on welfare and family benefits; elimination of forced labour in overseas territories; a general statute on civil servants and nationalisation laws modifying the position of employees; reorganisation of the collective conventions system; the establishment of medical and social services within industries, etc. The following years were naturally calmer, at least where large structures were already in place. The following should nevertheless be noted: the appearance of the Minimum Guaranteed Interprofessional Salary (1950) and its indexation, based on purchasing power (1952), but with the failure, in 1957, to systematically index-link all salaries; several texts on collective agreements and salary agreements, which prefigured the promotion of contractual politics; and better protection against both arbitrary dismissal and the financial consequences of unemployment, even if the public benefits system remained notoriously insufficient. Agreements between trade- and employers' organisations remained secondary, with the exception of the supplementary pension system, which favoured the managerial level (1947).

The Gaullist period was marked by a flurry of activity, both conventional and legislative. An idea very dear to General de Gaulle was the suppression of class conflict through improved integration of workers in their companies; this explains the texts concerning shares in profits derived from increased productivity (1960), benefits (1959, 1965) and the association for work-capital (1967), as well as an extension of the powers of industrial committees, which had previously been confined to the management of holiday camps and other undertakings (1966), and the introduction of trade union rights within companies (end of 1968). Additionally, there was an attempt to improve the situation of employees with regard to two significant risks: old age and unemployment. Supplementary pension schemes were very greatly extended, and a nationwide agreement was reached at the end of 1958, creating a system of insurance against unemployment to complement the public benefits system, managed by those whom it affected. However, a National Employment Agency (*Agence Nationale pour l'emploi*) was not organised until 1967. Even if the opposition parties and the unions denounced the inequitable distribution of the wealth resulting from growth, as well as an increase in employer control, especially with regard to Social Security (1967 ordinances), this decade did, however, mark an impressive advance which has allowed some to conclude that, even if it was not the golden age for the working class, it was at least a 'silver' one.

President Pompidou continued the policy of the integration of the working class through contractual policy, profit sharing and shareholding. However, this programme encountered a number of obstacles, amongst them certain salary-related turmoil around May 1968, uncontrolled inflation, the need for a painful reorganisation of industry and the first oil crisis. Important laws were adopted during this period (Minimum Interprofessional Growth Salary and workers' shareholding at Renault in 1970; a text on apprenticeships, technical training and especially ongoing training from 1971; generalisation of supplementary pensions in 1972; improvement of working conditions and enlargement of workers' participation in 1973), but the situation was far from being what had been called 'socialism applied only to assets', even if one takes into account contractual agreements concerning monthly payments (1970), or early retirement schemes at age 60 and benefits for partial unemployment (1972–74).

President Giscard d'Estaing initially attempted to launch a new programme for social development, including several benefits, such as the guarantee of 90% of maintenance benefits for workers made redundant for economic reasons and the generalisation of social security. However, the worsening economic crisis and budgetary difficulties curtailed the government's social agenda, with only one piece of legislation being approved, concerning retirement at 60 for women.

The Socialists' accession to power brought about large-scale labour laws in 1981 and 1982: a fifth week of paid leave, the limitation of the working week to 39 hours, a universal retirement age of 60, and the Auroux laws advancing the rights of workers and of their organisations within companies. All of this was accompanied by direct and indirect financial advantages, as it was expected that

consumerism would relaunch financial activity. However, the effect of this application of the brakes was rapid and brutal. A certain 'flexibility' in the approach to
social benefits was pursued, as well as reduced control over redundancies and
greater room for manoeuvre in terms of working hours, benefit packages for
those made redundant for economic reasons, early retirement, periods when salaries were frozen, etc. It was then indicated to the trade unions that they should
expect less from legislation, but rather attempt to obtain changes to the situation
of workers through contractual policies at company, branch or interprofessional
levels. However, labour relations changed not as a result of agreements, but as a
result of legislation. In the period after 1992, there was an 'explosion of complex
legislative techniques'.[4] From 1998 employers sought to modernise labour law by
restricting legislation to basic principles and leaving the rest to contract. From
2000, there were negotiations between MEDEF (employers) and the five nationally representantive unions on the theme of 'radical social reform' (*refondation
sociale*). The common position agreed in 2001 led to the Fillon reform of collective bargaining adopted into law in 2004. This is aimed at greater decentralisation
in collective bargaining and greater flexibility in negotiated rules.

Political Parties

The electoral systems selected by De Gaulle maintained several political parties.
The two-rounds majority vote, established in 1958, brought about the consolidation of left- and right-wing block alliances at the expense of a centre that many
would have liked to see reaffirmed. Another characteristic of this period was the
existence of parties rejecting institutions; these often had a strong popular
following. The communists were a force to be reckoned with for 50 years, in term
of both votes in legislative elections (up to 25% of the vote) and their presence in
the leadership of the communes, especially in the suburbs of the big cities.
However, except upon liberation and in the months following Mitterand's election in 1981, they were never in government.

   The fourth republic experienced a second opposition force, almost as systematic: the Gaullists of the Rassemblement du Peuple Francais (RPF), who, though
with a more modest electoral following, did much to paralyse the institutions,
with governments having to find a majority within the 60–70% of deputies who
did not oppose the political system. The rise of extreme right and left wing forces
contributed to creating a tense atmosphere. The extreme left was the first to react
aggressively, with the events of 1968 and its tumultuous consequences in the early
1970s. The *Front National* then took up the torch with some electoral successes,
but also influencing the more classical right wing ideology. The Gaullists changed
their name on several occasions (RPF, UDR, UD-Veme, RPR) and had limited
success at finding grassroots support; and the classic non-Gaullist right wing,

---

[4] Moreau in European Commission (2005) 292.

forced into formal unions because of the voting system, continued to struggle between several poles and leaders. The weakness of the parties originates more globally, in low levels of party membership and the lack of real public sponsorship of the parties.

Trade Unions

The most important unions are the General Confederation of Labour (CGT), the French Democratic Confederation of Labour (CFDT), the General Confederation of Labour-Workers' Force (CGT-FO), the French Christian Workers' Confederation (CFTC) and the General Confederation of Cadres (CGC). These five confederations are recognised at national level as having 'representative' status. At the time of liberation, the situation was straightforward, insofar as the General Confederation of Labour (GCL) found its unity within the resistance, and dominated the trade union sector, having an influence on labour relations, as well as the birth of the welfare state. The French Confederation of Christian Workers, drawing their inspiration from Christian social doctrine, and the General Confederation of Management, born in the aftermath of 1936, are but pale reflections of the GCL. However, the unity of the GCL was only a façade, and the beginning of the cold war reinforced tensions between the majority close to the Communist party and the minority, grouped around the magazine *Force Ouvrière*. Finally, with the support of American trade unions, and also pushed by the implosion of the government coalition, the GCL-FO was born in 1947, uniting all those opposed to the Leninist conception of trade unionism: anarcho-syndicalists, socialist militants and sympathisers, conservatives, and even strong reactionaries; the only common aspects were an aggressive secularism and instinctive anti-communist sentiment. This division was rejected by some professional groups, such as teachers, who organised themselves separately, forming the National Education Federation, and managed to maintain unity, albeit troubled by internal infighting. Other groups, often with a public character, or working alongside the public, developed autonomous syndicalism (railway workers, city public transport, electricians, etc).

Under the guidance of the RPF, militant Gaullists attempted to create company groups with political objectives, or independent trade unions. However, they never managed, even at the height of Gaullism, to have a significant presence, challenged on their own ground by groups further to the right of the political spectrum, which employers sometimes used as strike-breakers, not to mention the groups organised by the companies themselves (the in-house unions of Simca or Citroën).

The most interesting ideological evolutions took place at the heart of the Christian Trade Union Confederation, where modernising currents appeared especially amongst the members of the 'Christian Working Youth'. Their objective was to bypass the Leninist discourse of traditional leaders, to demarcate the limits of working-class collaboration and to seek a deeper democratisation of industry, as well as society. The rift was to be widened towards the mid-1950s with the great strikes (the metal workers of the lower Loire), when the Christian elements joined the General Confederation of Labour in the strike committees. It was only in 1964 that the separation took place and the French Democratic Confederation of Labour was born, a dynamic centre that was later to advocate self-management, which was followed by a contract-based policy. Thus French workers found themselves in a myriad of organisations that were weakened by their sheer number, the time spent in internal discussions, their dependence upon the political parties and their failures in recruitment, since the great majority of workers do not belong to any organisation. The rate of unionisation in France is the lowest in the EU.

On the side of the employers, things were simpler; the National Council of French Employers (NCFE) remained the great centre, even if its representation of the larger employers sometimes drove small and middle-sized companies to organise themselves beside, or even against, the NCFE. The General Confederation of Small- and Medium-sized Businesses is most often allied to the NCFE, but more radical elements express themselves through anti-state programmes, sometimes even with a fascist agenda.

Germany

Territory and Population

The Federal Republic of Germany covers 357,052 km^2 and by 2004 had a population of 82.5 million. Before unification on 3 October 1990, Germany was divided into the Federal Republic (FRG), with about three-quarters of the total German population, and the German Democratic Republic (GDR), with the other quarter. Foreign workers made up between 8 and 9% of the workforce. By 2004, the GNI per capita was $US 30,120 (€25,600). Life expectancy was 76 (men) and 81 (women).

Constitutional Development

In 1949, West Germany established a federal, republican, parliamentary democracy (FRG) while East Germany became a communist state (GDR). Both entities formed constitutions at this time, but the West did so with a European orientation and the East did so under the guidance of the USSR. When reunification occurred, the opportunity to devise a new constitution, or Basic Law, was foregone as the former GDR adopted the FRG Constitution. This process took place according to Article 23 of the Basic Law. Under this document, most power lies with the federal government, but the 16 *Länder* (states) have power in all areas not covered at the federal level.

Within the federal government, legislative power is vested in the Federal Parliament (*Bundestag*), which is elected every four years. The Federal Council (*Bundesrat*) is the second legislative body, consisting of members of the governments of the *Länder*. The consent of the *Bundesrat* is required for any legislation that affects the specific interests of the *Länder*. On recommendation from the Federal President, who is elected by the Federal Assembly, the *Bundestag* appoints a Federal Chancellor. The Constitutional Court is meant to protect fundamental rights and has the authority to assess the constitutionality of legislation and court decisions. It comprises two chambers, each with eight judges. Half of the judges are elected by the Federal Parliament and half by the Federal Council. The term for the Constitutional Court justices is 12 years, with no re-election possible. The court structure includes a high court of justice and more specialised courts in areas such as administration, finance and labour The FRG was a founder member of the EEC in 1957, and of the EMU from its beginning in 1999.

Labour Law

Collective agreements are generally concluded at regional level, but there has been an increasing trend towards single company agreements. Agreements cover about 63% of German workers. Works councils play a significant role in implementing collective agreements and, since the 1980s, making them more specific to the plant or enterprise, although collective agreements retain precedence. Labour courts have competence in both individual and collective labour disputes. The basic structure established in 1926 was revised in 1953 and again in 1979. The labour courts at first instance consist of a career judge and two lay judges one from an employer and one from an employee panel.

At the end of the Second World War, the Allies repealed Nazi labour law and widened workers' representation in plants, Social rights were developed in the new *Länder* constitutions. In the period from 1949 to the early 1960s the *Wirtschaftswunder* (German prosperity success story) was accompanied by an extension of individual labour law rights and restriction of collective articulation. The measures included the Co-determination (*Mitbestimmung*) Act for the iron and steel industries and the Works Constitution Act 1952, with relatively strong councillors' rights but largely excluding trade unions from the plant level. The Federal Labour Court recognised a 'liberty' (not a 'right') to strike, with a depoliticisation of the strike and the recognition of the lockout. The first economic crises and wildcat strikes led to restrictive emergency legislation (1968) and an integration of wage policies into economic planning (1969). The restructuring process was dominated by social democrats and coincided with 'economic democracy' and co-management strategies in the works councils (1972). The Co-determination Acts extended quasi paritarian co-determination in supervisory boards to companies with more than 2000 employees. After 1982 there was limited deregulation and, after 1989, unification of the two German labour laws on the basis of FRG laws. Deregulation in Germany never became mainstream; it concerned mainly atypical workers (fixed-term, agency work, part-time, self-employed) and working time, but left the 'standard employment relation' and the collective labour law framework mainly untouched. Sector-level collective agreements were 'opened' to plant agreements, beginning with working time (during the1980s) and later all fields of labour law in the course of concession bargaining. After 1998, the Red–Green coalition actively pushed austerity and flexibility programmes reducing employment protection. Social security reform was based on the Hartz proposals, involving a sharp cut in the public placement insurance and social assistance, and a smaller cut in old age pensions.

Political Parties

The major German political parties are the Social Democratic Party (SDP), the Christian Democratic Union (CDU) and the CDU's Bavarian sister party, the Christian Social Union (CSU). Other parties with a significant role include the Alliance 90/Greens, the Free Democratic Party and the Party of Democratic Socialism, which succeeded the former Communist Party.

There have been alternate right- and left-wing governments.[5]

Trade Unions.

The German Federation of Trade Unions (DGB) has existed since 1949 as a non-partisan and sectoral trade union body. After a number of mergers, by 2004 this federation consisted of eight single industry (sectoral) unions. The level of union membership has remained relatively stable, at around 30–35%. The Federal Union of German Employers' Federations (BDA) is the representative body of about 40–45% of all employers.

Greece (Hellas)

Territory and Population

Greece covers an area of 131,957 km^2 and by 2004 had a population of 11 million. By 2000, foreign workersmade up 3.8% of the labour force. Life expectancy was 76 (men) and 81 years (women). GNI per capita was €13,730.

[5] In 2005, a grand alliance of CDU, CSU and SDP formed the government.

Constitutional Development

Greece was a monarchy after the Second World War faced with a civil war until 1949. In 1967, Greece experienced a *coup d'état*. The result was a republican military regime that was then overthrown in 1974 and replaced with a new republic. The Constitution established in 1975 created a separation of powers. The legislature is composed of Parliament and a President; the executive incorporates the President and government, and there is an independent judiciary. General elections take place every four years. Amendments to the Constitution were made in 1986 and 2001. The court system includes a Supreme Court (*Areios Pagos*), with judges who have functional and personal independence. Below this court are administrative, civil and criminal courts established by special laws and with the power to disapply Acts they find to be inconsistent with the Constitution. The Council of State is the supreme administrative court and administers a judicial review function. It can annul Acts of the executive that are an abuse of power or violate the law. Greece became a member of the EEC in 1981, and of the EMU in 1999.

Labour Law

There is no separate system of labour courts, but individual disputes are subject to a special labour disputes procedure in the civil courts under Article 664 of the Civil Code. Collective disputes may be resolved by voluntary conciliation and mediation, or compulsory arbitration awards.

The Civil Code (1946) regulates individual employment relations. Various other Acts were passed regulating such matters as termination of the employment contract and collective dismissals (1955), the protection of union-elected representatives (1951) and collective disputes (1955). In 1967, the military dictatorship repealed all previous legislation on trade unions (1968, 1969, 1971 and 1974). After the re-establishment of Parliament and trade union freedom, the military regime's laws were repealed and previous legislation was revived as a first step towards new legislation. There followed a considerable body of labour legislation on trade inions, equality for women, works councils conditions of employment and social insurance. The Economic and Social Council (OKE) was established in 1994 as an advisory committee and central forum for social dialogue. In 1997, tripartite social consultations were introduced between the state, employers and trade unions aimed at securing consensus on legislative reforms to enable Greece to meet EMU criteria. A 'Confidence Pact' was reached between the government and social partners.

Political Parties

Having joined NATO, Greece was led by conservative governments under the

Greek Rally and its successor, the National Radical Union (ERE). From 1965, unstable coalition governments were in place. The 1967 military coup led Greece into a dictatorship under Colonel George Papadopoulos. Greece emerged from the dictatorship to be led by the newly formed and aptly named New Democracy. The major Greek political parties are: the Pan-Hellenic Socialist Movement (PASOK), New Democracy (ND), the Communist Party, and the Coalition of the Left and of Progress. After entering the EEC, the country's first socialist government came to power under the PASOK. The ND and the PASOK have subsequently alternated in power.

Trade Unions

The Greek General Confederation of Labour (GSEE), founded in 1918, is the only confederation of trade union organisations in a severely fragmented trade union movement. By 2004, it had 116 inter-sectoral or inter-professional organisations, 82 regional labour centres and 4,500 primary level unions organised on occupational lines. Industry-based organisation is an exception, and enterprise unions have grown only since the 1990s. Civil servants are represented by the Confederation of Civil Servants (ADEDY). Trade union density (by 2004) was about 23–25% in the private sector and 60% among civil servants. The Federation of Greek Industries (SEV), founded in 1907, signs about 80 sectoral collective agreements a year. There are also federations of small businesses and of other trades.

Ireland

Territory and Population

The Republic of Ireland (excluding Northern Ireland, which is part of the UK) covers 70,182 km² and by 2004 had a population of 4 million. Foreign workers comprised around 3% of the labour force. By 2004, life expectancy was 75 (men) and 80 years (women). GNI per capita was $US34,380 (€29,220).

Constitutional Development

There is a bicameral Parliament (*Oireachtas*), consisting of a directly elected lower house (*Dáil*) and an indirectly elected upper house (*Seanad*). The *Dáil* appoints and can dismiss the Taoiseach (Prime Minister). Ireland was neutral during the Second World War and became a member of the EEC in 1973.

Labour Law

During the Second World War wages were controlled by orders under the Emergency Powers Act 1938. In the early post-war period Irish labour law returned to the British tradition of local free collective bargaining. From the 1970s onwards the country moved towards a neo-corporatist model, in which the state actively participated in national tripartite wage agreements, in return for a commitment by trade unions not to engage in collective action. In the 1970s these agreements included provisions for basic pay, local bargaining in exchange for productivity agreements and provision for resolving disputes. Industrial action was not permitted unless the employer had refused, without reason, to observe a recommendation by the Labour Court. Between 1981 and 1987 this system of centralised pay bargaining broke down, and there was a return to decentralised collective agreements. There was a series of national social agreements from 1987 (1987–90, 1991–93, 1993–97 and 1997–2000). These included provisions for reducing taxation, improving social welfare payments, the elimination of discrimination in employment, increased investment in public services and the promotion of human rights. Trade union legislation from 1946 sought to reduce the number of unions through a licensing system that made it more difficult for new unions to be established, and by improving provisions for mergers. Industrial Relations Acts from 1990 established machinery for the prevention and settlement of trade disputes.

There is a multiplicity of institutions concerned with labour relations. A Labour Relations Commission was set up in 1990 to promote good industrial relations practices, and to provide conciliation services. The Labour Court was established in 1946 to resolve industrial disputes. The Court can make recommendations on the merits of an industrial dispute and the terms on which it should be settled. It operates on a voluntary basis; it also establishes joint labour committees for settling mandatory minimum rates of remuneration and other terms of employment for certain classes of workers; and it registers employment agreements with the consent of both parties. A registered agreement is binding on the parties and can be enforced through the Labour Court or by way of civil proceedings.

The Rights Commissioner has an important role in informal adjudication of disputes under most employment rights statutes, and can make non-binding recommendations to the parties. The Employment Appeals Tribunal, established in 1967, determines disputes under a wide range of employment statutes; it consists of a legally qualified chairman, a member from a panel nominated by trade unions and a member from an employers' panel. Since 1998 there has been a Director of Equality Investigations to adjudicate on discrimination claims, who may delegate these functions to equality officers and equality mediation officers. An Equality Agency promotes equality. The District Court has jurisdiction in contract-based employment cases (eg non-payment of wages, termination without due notice) where the amount in dispute is small. The Circuit Court has jurisdiction in cases involving larger amounts in respect of breach of contract or tort. It also has jurisdiction in certain disputes under employment equality legislation since 1998. The High Court has unlimited jurisdiction in civil matters. It is the only court that can grant a declaration, or a means by which a plaintiff may obtain a formal statement establishing the existence of a right, including a labour law right. It has exclusive jurisdiction in matters of judicial review.

Political Parties

The main political parties are Fianna Fail, Fine Gael, Labour, Progressive Democrats, Green Party, and Sinn Fein.

Trade Unions

The Irish Congress of Trade Unions was established in 1959 and includes unions in Northern Ireland. By 2004 there were 46 unions, and 37% of all employees were union members. The main employers' organisation, the Irish Business and Employers' Confederation, organises about 7000 companies.

Italy

Territory and Population

Italy has a land area of 301,277 km². At the end of 2004, the country had a population of 58.4 million. Foreign workers made up about 4.9% of the labour force. Life expectancy was 76.8 (men) and 82.9 years (women). It was estimated in 2003 that about 3.3 million people (15% of the workforce) were engaged in irregular work and activities. GNI per capita was €28,509.

Constitutional Development

A 1946 referendum in Italy established a parliamentary republic to replace the fascist regime The Italian Constitution, promulgated in 1948, abolished the monarchy and replaced it with a Parliament that maintains legislative power and oversees the general direction of the government. Elections determine the composition of two bodies, the House of Representatives and the Senate. These bodies have the same power. A Council of Ministers was created as the executive branch, and an independent judiciary was formed. The President of the Republic is elected by joint sittings of both Houses and three delegates from each region.

The office is a seven-year term and is responsible to Parliament. After the President chooses a Prime Minister, the latter then chooses other ministers. In October 2001 the Italian Constitution was amended by the Parliament in order to give more power to local authorities, especially the Regions. As a consequence of this reform, a distinction has been made between issues that are subjected to exclusive legislative power of the state, issues on which state and regions have concurrent powers and issues on which regions have exclusive power.[6] Italy was a founder member of the EEC in 1957 and a member of the EMU since 1999.

Labour Law

With regard to labour legislation, although statutes lay out a general minimum framework for working standards, collective agreements can be implemented to raise these standards. If they contradict labour legislation, they are considered void, and certain legislated rights are immutable. Most legislation consists of Acts of Parliament and decrees, with the latter format seeing increasing use. This approach has been criticised as an ineffective stop-gap measure for crisis management and weak governing coalitions. Court decisions are not supposed to constitute a source of law but in practice often greatly influence its application. Similarly, collective bargaining agreements have come to be legal sources in practice though not technically designated for the purpose. International law does not have automatic entry into the Italian legal system and must be integrated through legal processes.

The rules of legal origin governing employment relationships in Italy have never been enshrined in any unified code of laws; this is why, after the fall of the fascist regime (which, on the one hand, totally suppressed trade union freedom and, on the other, set some very rigid rules guaranteeing the workers minimum standards), the regulations, which dated back to Book V of the Civil Code and were enacted during the fascist regime in 1942, were first supplemented (and subsequently reinterpreted) only by those of the 1948 Constitution, which in Part III lays down principles such as on fair pay, maximum working hours, weekly and annual paid vacation (Article 36); on the protection of women and of minors on the job (Article 37); and on the social insurance for old age, illness, invalidity, industrial diseases and accidents (Article 38). At the same time, the right to organise was not only recognised as a basic collective right (see Article 39 on the freedom of association and Article 40 on the right to strike), but was also recognised as having a major role in the economic and social life on the country (see Section I, Articles 1–4). The resulting body of special legislation developed in the constitutional framework was directed, by imposing limits of varying kinds and intensity on individual private autonomy, at creating a system of protection for

---

[6] A subsequent reform that would have further increased regional powers and changed the parliamentary system towards a presidential one was voted for by Parliament but rejected by a general referendum in the spring of 2006.

the worker as the weaker of the two contracting parties. Therefore, in the 1950s and 1960s, by means of specific measures, the legislators endeavoured mainly to restrain the most glaring forms of exploitation of the labour force (laws on home-working and the subcontracting of labour; restrictions on fixed-term or temporary employment) or, as in Act 604 of 1966 (which implemented a collective agreement on the issue), to introduce limitations on the employer's freedom to dismiss. The peak of this first phase was the Workers' Statute (Act 300 of 1970), the aim of which was to protect the freedom and dignity of workers in the workplace, and to openly promote trade unions as representative agents at the enterprise level.

In the period of economic crisis starting from the late 1970s and early 1980s, the role of the law changed: on numerous occasions Parliament intervened not to impose norms of minimum protection that could be modified *in melius* by collective bargaining, but also to fix ceilings for bargaining, particularly as regards pay. At the same time, public authorities and the major political parties induced trade unions to co-operate and to behave consistently with the broader social and political plans considered necessary for overcoming the impact of the crisis on the economic and social welfare of the country (see Act 285 of 1977 on young people employment and Act 297 of 1982 on severance pay). More recently, the need to confront an employment crisis of vast dimensions compelled the legislators to take action on so-called atypical employment relationships, although the attitude shifted from the guaranteed or so-called 'assisted' flexibility during the 1980s to a more straightforward and radical flexibility during the 1990s (with the Temporary Employment in Act 196 of 1997).

Nevertheless, Italy's labour law—rightly described as 'alluvial' or 'stratified' in its formation—experienced a new flourishing during the 1990s, with regulations concerning the right to strike in public essential services (ie those relating to constitutional rights, such as life, health, freedom, safety and instruction; Act 146 of 1990), on collective dismissals (Act 223 of 1991), on equal treatment for men and women (Act 125 of 1991), on health and safety in the workplace (Decree 626 of 1994), and on parental leave (Act 53 of 2000). Among these provisions, Legislative Decree No 29 of 1993, regarding the privatisation of public sector employment relationships, completed a process of assimilation to the sphere of labour law by establishing that, with a few exceptions, the rules of the Civil Code and the laws regulating work under an employment contract in the private sector apply to the public employment relationship. The most recent legislation has confirmed two already established trends: on one hand, the increasing deregulation and individualisation of employment relationships (with new provisions on part-time work and fixed term contracts and with the radical reform of the labour market of Act 30 of 2003 and Decree 273 of the same year, which further liberalises temporary work and introduces new forms of employment like the job-sharing or job-on-call); and on the other hand, the growing importance of European labour law (especially in the shape of Directives) and its mandatory implementation in the Member States' legislation (eg Decree 66 of 2003 on working time). A similar course has been followed by Italian social security legislation, whose principles of social protection and solidarity were contained in Article 38 of the Constitution, which aimed to create a universalised system. Those principles were developed throughout the following decades with the setting up of the Social Fund in 1965, the launch of social pensions in the same year for over-65s without income, the launch of civil invalidity benefit in 1971 and the setting up, in 1978, of the National Health Service, which was for all citizens and was paid for by the state. From the second half of 1970s onwards, when public finances faced a serious crisis, the whole idea of welfare state began to be questioned, leading to a harmonisation of many different pension schemes and to a widespread reform of the pension system, completed in 1995 with Act 335 (introducing a flexible pension age and moving from a payback system to a contributory one). Last but not least, since 1993, Italy has introduced a comprehensive legislation concerning private additional pension schemes and occupational (pension) schemes within the framework of social security.

Political Parties

Italy traditionally has a plethora of political parties vying for office. The Christian Democratic Party has historically been a political force either on its own or in a coalition government. As of 1948, its primary opposition came from the Communists, but as of 1980s the Socialists have played the main opposing role. However, due to significant concerns of corruption and the fall of the USSR, the Socialists and Communists lost much of their power in the late 1980s. The decline of these parties opened up a political opportunity for the *Forza Italia*, a more free-market-oriented party than any of its predecessors, which became the leading party for the centre-right wing and, except for the period 1996–2001, held a relatively unstable grasp on power from 1994.[7]

Trade Unions

Freedom of association and of trade unions became important institutions in the wake of fascism's downfall. Following this transition, the main union, the General Confederation of Italian Workers (CGIL), built up a large membership, all three major political parties stated their support for unions and the Constitution enshrined the right to bargain collectively. However, political pressure forced a three-way split of the CGIL in 1948, the two new offshoots being the Italian Confederation of Workers Union (CISL) and the Union of Italian Workers (UIL). The union movement continued in this weakened state through the 1950s, until the political situation allowed greater solidarity among the three unions and

---

[7] A centre-left wing coalition, called *Unione* and led by the Democrats of the Left, regained control in the spring 2006 elections.

improved the strength of the movement. The government gave more leeway to industrial action and the collective bargaining process decentralised, leading eventually to the Workers Statute of 1970, which sought to increase union input in the bargaining process and thus increase their political strength. This approach was criticised as promoting an inappropriate power balance for the time, which resulted in a somewhat more limited role for unions in the 1980s and 1990s. During this time, some employees began to engage in individual bargaining, and public authorities made more use of legislation. By 2004, the CGIL, CISL, UIL and UGL combined represented about 35% of the workforce. Unions are free to organise themselves as they see fit, and the major union confederations are attempting to create both a vertical and a horizontal structure by sector. Vertical organisation covers aggregation by industry and horizontal organisation refers to geographic grouping. The result is that jurisdictional disputes are rare. Furthermore, regional unions became stronger at the same time that regional governments were gaining autonomy.

Luxembourg

Territory and Population

The Grand Duchy, tucked between Belgium, France and Germany, has a land area of 2,586 km^2 and by 2004 had a population of 454,960. Foreigners (half of these from Portugal) make up over 36% of the population. The country enjoys the highest standard of living in Europe (one of the highest in the world). GNI per capita was €64,498.

Constitutional Development

In spite of its neutrality, Luxembourg was occupied by Germany during the First and Second World Wars. In 1948, it gave up neutrality by joining various international organisations. It became a founder Member State of the EEC in 1957. The country is a constitutional monarchy, with the Grand Duke as Head of State. He has the right of initiative in legislative matters and must assent to all legislation. Together with the government the Grand Duke forms the executive organ of state. The government as a whole is responsible to the elected Chamber of Deputies. A Council of State deliberates on government bills and settles administrative disputes. The High Court of Justice consists of a Supreme Court of Appeal (Cour de Cassation) and a Court of Appeal, which hears appeals from district courts.

Labour Law

Luxembourg has enjoyed largely peaceful labour relations since the 1930s. Labour law has been heavily influenced by French and Belgian labour law, with which it has close connections. Since a major Act in 1989 on employment contracts, most legislation has been concerned with implementing EC Directives. The largest employers are in the steel industry and banking and finance. There were almost no strikes and no unemployment until the steel crisis of 1975. The so-called 'Luxembourg model', developed in response to the crisis, included agreed measures for 'partial' unemployment, ie reduced working hours without lay-offs, the hours lost being compensated by state subsidies, and extraordinary public work schemes. This was promoted by the *Comité de Conjuncture*, acting on behalf of bodies which represent employers. There is a tripartite Social and Economic Council, which advises the Cabinet, and also a Tripartite Co-Ordination Committee (since 1977), which deals with economic growth and employment policies.

There is a tradition of sector-based negotiation, the most important being in banking and insurance, representing 45% of jobs. Collective agreements are usually generally applicable. An Act of 12 June 1965 provides that only 'representative' trade unions have rights to sign collective agreements. After functioning effectively for 30 years, this gave rise to problems in the 1990s when the FEB split into sector-based unions, including ALEBA (below). In 1993, two unions that were under-represented in the banking and financial sector signed the collective agreement for this sector, denying ALEBA the right to negotiate. In 1999, however, ALEBA alone signed the agreement, and the Administrative Court accepted its representativity for those sectors in which it was strong. A Bill to amend the 1965 Act was introduced in 2002, with the aim of evaluating representativity quantitatively by sector and professional category. Since 2002 there has been an increase in unemployment and restructuring.

Political Parties

The ruling party is the Christian Social Party (24 seats in the Chamber of Deputies in 2004), the others being the Workers' Socialist Party (14 seats) and the Democratic Party (10 seats).

Trade Unions

There are three multi-sector and national unions (OGB-L, LVGB and FEB), all three being active in the banking sector. The FEB split into a number of sector-based unions, including ALEBA, which has a strong base in the banking and insurance sector.

The Netherlands

Territory and Population

The Netherlands covers 41,864 km^2 (almost 20% of which is water) and by 2004 had a population of 16.3 million. Foreign workers made up about 10% of the labour force. Life expectancy was 76 (men) and 81 years (women). The GNI per capita was €26,945.

Constitutional Development

The Netherlands has been a unitary kingdom since 1814, the power of the monarch having been limited by constitutional reforms since then to largely ceremonial and formal ones. Parliament is composed of the directly elected House of Representatives (*Tweede Kamer*), which controls the executive and can amend Bills, and the Senate (*Eerste Kamer*), indirectly elected by provincial councils, which can only endorse or veto a Bill. The impact of fundamental rights was very limited in labour law until the end of the 1960s. Since 1960, the Netherlands has ratified a growing number of international treaties which contain fundamental rights. These are directly enforceable. The Constitution was updated in 1983 with a more extensive list of fundamental rights, including social rights. The Netherlands was a founder member of the EEC in 1957 and of the EMU from 1999. Legislation takes a number of different forms, including royal orders, decrees, ministerial circulars and policy rules. Parliament can legislate on any constitutional matter, and conformity with constitutional principles is assessed by the Council of State. No constitutional court exists, so the courts do not rule on the constitutionality of domestic legislation, but they do assess legislative conformity with ratified international treaties. Although it is not a requirement to include social partners in the legislative process, this type of consultation occurs routinely. As such, legislation begins with Parliament, usually goes to social partners for comment, becomes a formal statutory instrument, and is finally signed and promulgated by the Queen. Collective agreements are an important source of labour law and often influence statutory law in this area.

Labour Law

All civil disputes concerning the contract of employment, collective agreements and strikes are dealt with in the ordinary courts. These are lower courts (*kantongerechten*), district courts (*arondissementsrechtbanken*) and the Supreme Court (*Hoge Raad*). Decisions of all courts are subject to review (*cassation*), and important rules of labour law have been established by the *Hoge Raad* through *cassation*. There are no labour courts.

At the end of the Second World War, the Netherlands developed what has become known as the 'Polder model', under which employers' organisations, trade unions and government closely co-operated. As a result, a private organisation of employers and trade unions, the Foundation of Labour (*Stichtung van de Arbeid*), was founded and developed a strategy of wage moderation in return for a social security system with a high level of protection. During the 1960s there were growing demands for increased wages, and in the index-linked compensation for price increases was introduced as a general principle in collective agreements. This contributed to high unemployment in the early 1980s. The Polder model came under increasing strain, leading to the 'Wassenaar Agreement' (named after the village where the meeting took place). The most important union (FNV) and employers' association (VNO) agreed to end the system of automatic compensation for inflation and to reduce working time to counter unemployment. As a result, the government took no measures to interfere in wage negotiations. The pressure for more flexibility in the 1990s was dealt with by centralised labour–management agreements under the Polder model, and wages have increasingly been determined by branch and company collective agreements. The comprehensive Dutch model of 'flexicurity' is reflected in the Flexibility and Security Act, in force since 1999, and the Work and Care Act 2001. The Social-Economic Council (*Sociaal Economische Raad*) was set up in the 1950s to advise the government on socio-economic matters, but the Foundation of Labour has remained the main avenue for central social dialogue. The basic legal framework for collective bargaining has remained largely unchanged since before the Second World War, but some provisions, such as the extension procedure for collective agreements, are increasingly being questioned at the beginning of the twenty-first century.

Political Parties

At the end of the Second World War, traditional ideological segregation of religious and political groups in political parties, as well as schools, unions and other organisations, was revived. However, since the 1950s religious influences have declined, with denominational parties and unions becoming far smaller. The Netherlands has always had coalition governments. These have mainly been dominated by Christian democrat parties, sharing power sometimes with social democrats, sometimes with liberals. Only in the period between 1994 and 2002 did the social democrats and liberals share power.

Trade Unions

With religion playing a declining role in both politics and labour relations, and with the Catholic and social democrat trade unions merging in 1977, the union movement developed a completely non-denominational structure by the 1990s. The Netherlands has a large number of unions, mainly concentrated into three major confederations: the Confederation of Dutch Trade Unions (FNV), with Catholic roots, the National Christian Confederation (CNV), with Protestant origins, and *Middelbaar en Hoger Personeel*, the latter consolidating a number of white-collar unions. All of these organisations are associated with the European Trade Union Confederation (ETUC). Generally, unions try to organise workers by economic sector, which lessens inter-union competition. The largest confederations have at least 15 unions as members and usually have full-time officers to conduct their administrative affairs. Unions usually have regional and local sections as well. The rate of unionisation declined from over 40% in 1950 to around 20% in 2004, although this statistic does vary by sector. This low rate of membership allegedly stems from a lack of union activity at the company level. Large and medium-sized employer organisations tend to affiliate with the VNO-NCW, while small and some other medium-sized companies ally themselves with the MKB-Nederland. Farmers are generally members of LTO-Nederland. These organisations promote a democratic structure by electing their leaders, and they manage to maintain a high rate of organisation.

Portugal

Territory and Population

Portugal covers 92,345 km^2 and by 2004 had a population of 10.5 million. Foreign workers made up about 2.2% of the work force. Life expectancy was 73 (men) and 80 years (women). GNI per capita was €12,195.

Constitutional Development

From 1926 until 1974 there was an authoritarian political regime and corporate state. After a two-year revolutionary military government, which had overthrown the Salazar regime, the Constitution of 1976 (subsequently revised) guaranteed fundamental rights. The President is elected by universal franchise and can dismiss the government only in prescribed circumstances after hearing the Council of State. There is a unicameral parliament (Assembleia da Republica) to which the government is responsible. The Supreme Court of Justice is the highest judicial body, and the Constitutional Court, which came into effect after 1982, has the duty of enforcing the Constitution. Portugal became a member of the EEC in 1986 and of the EMU in 1999.

Labour Law

There are specialist labour courts which fall within the system of ordinary courts and are run by professional magistrates. Their jurisdiction covers civil proceedings relating both the terms and conditions of work and collective agreements, strikes and trade union freedom, as well as work accidents. The labour courts also deal with criminal sanctions for breaches of statutory rules, and appeals against decisions of the general labour inspectorate. A Decree of 1947 regulated collective bargaining until 1969, and an Act of 1952 established the first specific legal regime of the individual labour contract in Portugal, until 1967. The substantial Decree 203/1974 (Provisional Government Programme) changed the whole labour law system after the fall of the dictatorship, with union freedom, new mechanisms for the solution of collective conflicts, minimum wage, etc; however, the legal reality is that the implementation of the reforms was not very vigorous. It has been the Constitution that has exercised the strongest influence on the institutions to change the patterns in areas like sex discrimination, unfair dismissals, periodical revision of the minimum wage, or regulation of the right to strike and prohibition of the lockout. Since 2003, a new Labour Code has replaced most of the earlier Acts.

Political Parties

After the downfall of the authoritarian regime in 1974, a two-party system emerged, with the Social Democratic Party (PSD) on the centre-left and the Socialist Party (PS) on the left as the main contenders. Other parties to the right and left of the main players include the more right-wing Social Democratic Center (CDS) and the Portuguese Communist Party (PCP). Historically, the PSD has been the most successful party in elections.

Trade Unions

During the corporatist period (1926–74) trade organisations were integrated at the bottom of the 'social and corporatist' regime (*organismos corporativos*). These bodies required recognition and approval by the government, and their activities were monitored by a government department. Since the Trade Union Act 1974 (LS), freedom of association has been respected. Portugal has two principal trade union confederations, the *Confederacao Geral dos Trabalhadores Portugueses—Intersindical National* (CGTP-IN), and the *Uniao Geral de Trabalhadores* (UGT), both of which have maintained their power since 1978. The CGTP was created in 1974 after the coup and maintains a special relationship at the international level with the FSM union. According to a study in 1993, 71% of trade union members are affiliated to the CGTP. The UGT was

established a few years later, in 1978, with the support of the Socialist Party and
the Popular Democratic Party (now the Social Democratic Party). It has about
23% of union members, its orientation is reformist, and it maintains special
connections at the international level with the International Confederation of
Free Trade Unions and the ETUC. The UGT is comprised of large industrial
unions with no affiliation to sectoral or regulatory groups. By contrast, the
CGTP-IN has a system of small unions which then join larger federations as
defined by their sectoral activity. The overall rate of unionisation by 2004 was
about 30%.

Spain

Territory and Population

Spain covers an area of 505,988 km², and by 2004 had a population of 44.1
million. Foreign workers make up about 8.3% of the workforce. Life expectancy
was 76 (men) and 83 years (women). GNI per capita was €18,030.

Constitutional Development

After the civil war (1936–39) an autocratic political system was established under
General Franco. Spain underwent a peaceful transition after 1977, a democratic
election leading to a new Constitution adopted on 31 October 1978. This established a parliamentary monarchy, with legislative power vested in the *Cortes
Generales*, consisting of two chambers, the Chamber of Deputies (*Congreso de los
Diputados*) and the Senate (*Senado*). Executive power is entrusted to the Council
of Ministers (*Gobierno*). At a political level, Spain has gone from being quite
centralised to a more devolved state. Article 2 of the Constitutions affords the
right to autonomy for nationalities and regions, but different regions maintain
different levels of autonomy. Provinces are the most important divisions within
regions and have some autonomy. They are governed by provincial councils. The
smallest territorial units are municipal districts. The autonomous regions elect a
legislative assembly and a government, but not the judges. A regional government
and premier are responsible to the Assembly. Each region has special rules, as
approved by the *Cortes Generales* on the proposal of the regional parliament.
The Constitution differentiates between regional and central duties. The Constitution guarantees personal rights and liberties, and states that the government
has a duty to protect its citizens, establish a civil society, and recognise work as a
right and a duty. Spain became a member of the EEC in 1986 and of the EMU
in 1999.

The judiciary provides a professional, independent hierarchy of judges led by a Supreme Court with five chambers. The fourth chamber hears labour cases. While Spain's system does not technically incorporate legal precedent, Article 1 of the Civil Code stipulates that 'a constant and uninterrupted line of decisions of the Supreme Court establishing a legal precedent is a rule of law'. The Constitutional Court issues two types of decisions—a declaration of an unconstitutional act and decisions on fundamental rights—both of which are binding on lower courts. The second category deals with a substantial number of social and labour issues.

Labour Law

Primary jurisdiction in individual and collective labour cases is vested in the labour courts. The higher courts have both primary and appellate jurisdiction. The *Ley de Contrato de Trabajo* 1944 (Contract of Employment Act) applied during the dictatorship period and even beyond it, until its substitution by the Workers' Statute, *Estatuto de los Trabajadores* 1980, regulated not only the contract of employment, but also collective agreements and workers' representatives. A new Act of 1985 regulated union activity, and with regard to the strike it maintained a 1977 Decree, revised by a decision of the Constitutional Court of 1981.

Huge modifications of the Workers' Statute in 1994 introduced a 'collective' flexibilisation' of the Statute, in order to transfer to collective agreements a substantial part of the legal and administrative competences. Other minor modifications have tended to adapt the Spanish legislation to the EC, especially since the mid-1990s. With regard to the labour market, the state monopoly of the employment services gave way to a flexibilisation in 1994 to permit private employment services as well as temporary work agencies. There was a revival of social consultation from 1996, which had been abandoned since the mid-1980s. Major inter-confederal agreements were signed, sometimes with government participation, resulting in labour reforms, which focused on improving working conditions (eg with respect to temporary work agencies and part-time work) in order to restore a balance with flexibility. However, after 2000, when the conservative government won an absolute majority, the inter-confederal agreement, which expired in 2001, was not renewed. The government proposed extensive reforms relating to contracts of employment, increasing jobseekers obligations and restricting their protection, but these proposals were modified in the law finally adopted (Law 45/2002)

Political Parties

Since 1978, Spain's two main political parties have been the *Partido Popular* (PP), which is centre-right, and the *Partido Socialista Obrero Espanol* (PSOE), to the left. These have alternated in government.

Trade Unions

Trade unions re-emerged in 1977 after a long, difficult and clandestine period under the fascist dictatorship. The Constitution, implemented by the Trade Union Freedom Act of 1985, guarantees trade union freedom and also the right to strike. The strongest employee confederations are the *Confederacion Sindical de Comisiones Obreras* (CC.OO) and the *Union General de Trabajadores* (UGT). Less significant organisations include the *Union Sindical Obrera* (USO), the *Confederacion de Sindicatos Independientes de Funcionarios* (CSI-CSIF) and the *Confederacion General del Trabajo* (CGT). All of these organisations operate at a national level and are open to all workers and unions. On a regional level, the important confederations are the *Solidaridad de Trabajadores Vascos* (ELA-STV) and the *Confederacion Sindical Gallaga* (CIG). Public as well as private employees are free to join unions, but public officials such as judges and state attorneys cannot. The overall rate of unionisation is 15%.

Sweden

Territory and Population

Sweden covers an area of 441,964 km^2, and by 2004 had a population of 8.9 million. Foreign workers make up about 4.8% of the work force. Life expectancy was 78 (men) and 83 years (women). The GNI per capita was €30,400.

Constitutional Development

The Constitution that was in force from 1809 until 1975 established a constitutional monarchy based on separation of powers. This developed into a parliamentary monarchy, leaving the monarch with a largely symbolic function. The developments were codified in the new Constitution, which was enacted in stages. According to Article 1 of this Constitution, all public power comes from the people, who elect the unicameral *Riksdag*. Ministers have few formal powers as head of government departments. The government acts collectively, represented by the Prime Minister, and the central administration is managed by independent administrative offices. The Constitution has been developed as to guarantee fundamental rights such as freedom of association, free assembly and the right to strike. In 1994, the ECHR was incorporated into domestic law.

Sweden's legal system does not have a systematic code. Most of the early code of 1734 has been replaced by statutes. The government puts legislation before the *Riksdag* for approval, but in some areas it can issue decrees and directives, or delegate this responsibility. Judge-made law is also important in Sweden. At the top is the Supreme Court. Sweden became a member of the EEC in 1995.

Labour Law

By the late 1930s, the view had developed in Sweden that regulation of the labour market was a matter for the social partners and that the government and Parliament should refrain from intervening with legislation. This idea was manifested in the Basic Agreement (the Saltsjöbaden agreement). Over the subsequent decades—the Saltsjöbaden epoch—both the legislator and the social partners accepted this distribution of roles. The legislation adopted was limited and aimed mainly at levelling differences between different groups of workers (eg Acts on holidays adopted in 1938, 1945, 1963 and 1977), extending holidays from two to five weeks. In 1920 the 48-hour week was introduced through legislation; this was lowered to 45 in 1957, 42.5 hours in 1969 and 40 hours in 1973. Further, there was an intense reform of social insurance legislation, with a general sickness insurance system and insurance for supplementary pensions for all employees and self-employed persons as the prime examples. By contrast, many issues became the subjects of collective agreements, including the influence of works councils and a degree of employment protection.

The legislator's reluctance to intervene came to an end in the 1970s with the adoption of a raft of new laws. Prominent among these were the Employment Protection Act 1974 and the Co-Determination Act 1976. The implementation of these new laws led to a considerable deterioration in the prospects for co-operation and joint responsibility of the social partners. The legislation adopted in the 1970s remains controversial. Especially after the recession that hit Sweden in the first half of the 1990s, the debate was focused on how labour market regulation, especially the Employment Protection Act, might be changed to provide greater flexibility and thereby create conditions for growth and reduced unemployment. Long-standing demands for de-regulation were met with a strong defence of the existing order. Despite wide-ranging discussion and reviews, significant legislative reforms were few and limited. However, the substance of collective agreements changed considerably, providing greater scope for regulation at the level of the company and the individual

Through successive legislative amendments (1965, 1976 and 1994), public employment relationships have been 'privatised' in the sense that, broadly speaking, the same rules apply to the private and public sectors. Since the late 1970s extensive anti-discrimination legislation has been developed. The first Equal Opportunities Act was adopted in 1979 and replaced by a new one in 1991. In addition, statutory protection has been widened to take in more grounds:

ethnic origin, disability and sexual orientation. Swedish legislators have tended to anticipate or have gone further than the requirements of EC anti-discrimination law.

Despite the growth in labour market legislation, collective agreements have remained the most important instrument for regulating wages and other employment conditions. Swedish collective agreements comprise virtually every aspect of an employment relationship, and 90% of employees are estimated to be covered by such agreements. Between the mid-1950s and 1981 the level of wage increases was agreed between the central organisations in the private sector (LO) and the private employers' organisation (SAF). These agreements were seen as setting the trend for other labour market sectors, ie the public sector and white-collar workers in the private sector. Since 1981, wage agreements are no longer concluded between LO and the Confederation of Swedish Enterprise (the successor of SAF). In the last decades, the evolution has generally been towards more decentralised collective bargaining. This decentralisation is evident in two developments. First, bargaining between the central organisations at national level has become less significant. Secondly, the nature of national sectoral agreements has changed from detailed regulation to a framework of process agreements, leaving greater scope for regulation at company level. Among the issues increasingly dealt with at company level are wages and working time. This trend is strongest for salaried employees.

There is a tripartite Labour Court first established by an Act of 1928, replaced by an Act of 1974. Under the Act a case goes exclusively to the Labour Court when the dispute concerns the relationship between parties to a collective agreement or relates to conditions of service of an employee who is a member of a trade union. A dispute between an unorganised employee and his employer goes to an ordinary district court in the first instance, but the appeal goes to the Labour Court, whose decision is final.

Political Parties

The Social Democratic Party was the largest party in Sweden and held power from 1932 until 1976, at times in coalitions. This party is closely linked to the trade unions. Between 1976 and 1982, and again between 1991 and 1994, Sweden had non-socialist governments, but they never had a strong majority. In 1994, the Greens got the necessary 4% of the vote to get some seats in the *Riksdag* for the first time. The Social Democratic government was re-elected in 1998 and 2002.

Trade Unions

Trade union freedom is enshrined in the 1970s Constitution, and the right to free association is covered in the Co-Determination Act (Article 7). Given the importance of collective bargaining, which is the primary means of setting labour standards, unions play an important role in Sweden. Legislation sets a political framework for labour standards, but collective agreements fill in the specifics. Employee representation is channelled exclusively through trade unions, apart from European Works Councils under EC legislation. The main union for manual workers is the Swedish Trade Union Confederation (LO). Although it has a smaller rival in the Central Organisation of Swedish Workers (SAC), more than 80% of manual workers are affiliated with the LO. The Central Organisation of Salaried Employees (TCO) and the Swedish Confederation of Professional Associations (SACO) are the principal unions representing salaried employees. Overall the rate of unionisation has remained high, over 80%. The main central organisation of employers is the Confederation of Swedish Enterprise (before 2001, *Svenska Arbetsgivareföreningen*, SAF).

Appendix II

Chronology of Labour Law 1945-2005

List of abbreviations

Austria	*Aut*
Belgium	*Be*
Britain and Northern Ireland (UK)	*GB/NI*
Denmark	*Den*
Finland	*Fi*
France	*Fr*
Germany	*Ger*
Greece	*Gr*
Ireland	*Ir*
Italy	*It*
Luxembourg	*L*
Netherlands	*Ne*
Portugal	*Po*
Spain	*Sp*
Sweden	*Sw*

Note This chronology is not comprehensive. It refers only to the most significant measures and generally does not include measures transposing EC Directives into domestic law.

1945

GB/NI   Wages Councils Act 1945 (institutional wage determination; completely abolished in 1983)

Fr   Ordinance of 22 February 1945 (establishment of works councils)

Gr   Emergency Law 539/45 (annual vacation enacted for several kinds of enterprises from 1947 on)

Ne   Extraordinary Decree on Labour Relations (introduces a system of prior control of dismissals, administrative permission needed for any dismissal)

1946

GB/NI   Trade Union Act (repeal of post-1926 strike legislation)

Fi   Hours of Work Act (succeeded by the Hours of Work Act of 1996)

Fi   Collective Agreements Act (rules on collective bargaining; modernised the former Collective Agreements Act of 1924, amended several times since)

Fi   Labour Court Act (instituting a specialised tripartite court for legal disputes concerning collective agreements; succeeded by a new Labour Court Act of 1974)

Fi   Act on Conciliation in Labour Disputes (amending the former Act on Conciliation in Collective Labour Disputes of 1925; introducing a duty to give advance notice of strikes and lock-outs and a duty to take part in conciliation; system further developed by the Act on Mediation in Labour Disputes of 1962)

Fr   Constitution of the Fourth Republic (Preamble guaranteed for the first time the individual and collective rights of the workers)

Fr   Act of 26 February 1946 (re-establishment of the principle of the 40-hour working week; limited to 39 hours by Ordinance of 16 January 1982)

Fr   Act of 16 April 1946 (establishment of workers' delegates/employee representatives)

Gr   Civil Code (containing rules on the individual employment contract)

Ir   Industrial Relations Act 1946 (establishment of the Labour Court as the institution charged with the resolution/settlement of industrial disputes; rules on collective bargaining, i.e. employment regulation orders and registered collective agreements)

1947

Aut Collective Agreements Act and Works Councils Act.

It	Italian Constitution (in force since 1 January 1948; containing eg trade union freedom, freedom of collective bargaining, right to strike)

1948

Aut	Act on the employment of children and juveniles (general prohibition of the employment of children under 12 years of age)
Be	Act of 20 September 1948 on Works Councils (concerning the organisation of industry in general and works councils in particular)
Den	White-Collar Workers Act (amendment of the former Act on legal relations between the white-collar worker and employer of 1938, has been amended several times since; rules on the content of the employment contract)

1949

Ger	Foundation of the Federal Republic of Germany (FRG) (*Grundgesetz* Constitution, principle of the welfare state/social market economy; re-establishment of the former collective labour law including trade unions and employers' associations, collective agreements, industrial action; special system of labour courts rebuilt) and of the German Democratic Republic (task of trade unions to guarantee the performance of the economic plan, close link to the political party; no employers' associations, no industrial action, no real collective agreements; 'right to work' guaranteed in the Constitution)
Ger	Act on Collective Agreements (FRG)
It	Act 264/1949 (prohibition of temporary work)

1950

Fr	Act of 11 February 1950 (establishment of a government-fixed minimum guaranteed wage, now SMIC)
Ne	Organisation of Industry Act (provided the legal framework for a corporatist organisation of business)

1951

Ger   Protection against Dismissal Act (statutory protection against unfair dismissal, introduction of reinstatement as the principal remedy, FRG)

Ger   Co-determination Act 1951 (Montan-Mitbestimmungsgesetz; introduced co-determination for undertakings of the mining, iron and steel industry, FRG)

1952

Ger   Act on Maternity Protection (FRG)

Ger   Works Council Act (workers' representation in the establishment, rights of information, consultation and participation; co-determination for undertakings not belonging to the mining, iron and steel industry; FRG)

1953

Den   Danish Constitution (eg right to associate, but no explicit rules with regard to the rights of trade unions or employers' associations; the right to strike is not secured)

Ger   Labour Courts Act (FRG)

Ger   Act on Disabled Persons (FRG)

1955

Gr   Act 3239/55 (law on collective bargaining, including arbitration; replaced later by Act 1876/90)

Gr   Act 3198/55 (on termination of labour contracts)

1956

Fr   Act of 27 April 1956 (express prohibition of union security clauses)

Ne   Act repealing the provision establishing a married woman's need for the consent of her husband to conclude a contract of employment

1958

Fi   Labour Safety Act (relating to occupational safety and health)

Fr   Constitution of the Fifth Republic (Preamble refers expressly to the Preamble of the Constitution of 1946 including the latter's provisions on individual and collective rights of workers)

Sp   Collective Bargaining Act (re-introduced the establishment of labour conditions through collective bargaining after a period of more than 20 years, in which trade agreements had been formally and legally unknown; Act replaced later by the Collective Bargaining Act of 1973, abolished in 1980 by the Employees' Statute)

1960

It   Act 604/1966 (prohibition of labour-only subcontracting)

1961

Den   Agricultural and Domestic Workers Act (specific rules for this category of employees; amended later by the Agricultural and Domestic Workers Act of 1994)

1962

It   Act 230/1962 (fixed-term contracts allowed only in exceptional cases and under conditions strictly determined by the law)

1963

GB/NI   Contracts of Employment Act 1963 (introduction of minimum periods of notice for dismissals)

Ger   Federal Holiday Act (first uniform rules in the federal republic on a minimum annual holiday of 18 business days; FRG)

Sp   Act introducing a system of minimum wage rates (government annually fixes the inter-professional minimum wage after consultation with the most representative employers' associations and trade unions)

1964

GB/NI   Industrial Training Act (industrial tribunals became part of the legal system

1965

Aut   Employees' Liability Act (reduced liability of employees)

Be   Act of 12 April 1965 concerning the protection of remuneration (including the principle of equal pay)

GB/NI   Redundancy Payments Act 1965 (introduced a claim for compensation in case of a dismissal for redundancy)

L   Act on collective agreements

Ne   Temporary Agency Work Act (introduction of a licence system)

1966

Fr   Act of 30 December 1966 on maternal protection

Gr   Act 4504/66 on Sunday rest, paid leave etc

It   Act 604/1966 on unfair dismissals (introduction of statutory protection against unfair dismissals; introduction of the principle of continuity of the employment contract in case of a transfer of the enterprise, modified several times since)

Ne   Act inserting provisions for a minimum paid holiday into the Dutch Civil Code

1967

Fr   Ordinance of 17 August 1967 (introduction of a system of compulsory profit-sharing accompanied by tax advantages)

Ir   Redundancy Payments Act 1967 (entitlement of dismissed employees to a redundancy payment)

1968

Be   Act of 5 Dec 1968 on Collective Agreements (rules on collective bargaining, gave real legal standing to the collective agreement)

Fr   Act of 27 December 1968 on union rights in the enterprise

Ne   Act on Minimum Wages and Minimum Holiday Allowances (introduces statutory minimum levels; minimum yearly holiday allowance of at least 8%t of the yearly wage)

1969

Aut   Hours of Work Act (on permissible working hours per day and week; obligation to make an addition over and above normal payment for overtime work)

Aut   Vocational Training Act (rules on apprenticeship)

Be   Act on the individual labour contract for blue-collar workers (introduced the concept of an abusive dismissal)

GB/NI   Employers Liability (Defective Equipment) Act 1969 (liability of the employer for defective equipment without fault)

GB/NI   Employment Liability (Compulsory Insurance) Act 1969 (insurance principle, formed by Workmen's Compensation Act 1897, now guaranteed to all employers)

Ger   Act on Vocational Training (FRG)

Ger   Act on Continued Payment of Remuneration (made the right to receive sick pay for six weeks be applicable to all employees, before only white-collar workers)

Po   Decree-Law 49408/69 (Labour Contract Act, legal system of the individual employment relationship)

1970

GB/NI   Equal Pay Act 1970

Fi   Employment Contracts Act (succeeding the Employment Contracts Act of 1922; introducing new principles such as non-discrimination, statutory protection against unfounded dismissals)

It   Act 300/1970 Workers' Statute (Statuto dei Lavatori, basic source of protection of trade union freedoms and workers' representation at plant level; on workers' and unions' rights in the enterprise, basic freedoms of expression and of concerted activity within the plant; shift of the system of remedies for unfair dismissals from compensation to reinstatement)

Ne   Determination of Wages Act (gave the social partners freedom in their wage policy by means of collective agreements, but left the door open for public-authority intervention)

Ne   Merger Code (introducing a right of trade unions to be informed and consulted about future mergers)

Sw   new Constitution Acts (passed gradually in the 1970s; insertion of provisions concerning industrial relations, eg freedom to associate, right to organise and to negotiate)

Sw   Act on Preferential Claims (employee is given priority over other creditors if employer has gone bankrupt)

Sw   Act on Governmental Wage Guarantees in case of Bankruptcy (creation of a national wage guarantee fund to which all employers have to pay contributions in proportion to their pay roll; Act later replaced by the Wages Guarantee Act 1992)

1971

Be   Labour Act of 16 March 1971 (on working time; succeeded the Act of 15 July 1964)

GB/NI   Industrial Relations Act 1971 (introduced protection against unfair dismissal; introduction of a statutory procedure for recognition of trade unions, later abolished by Employment Act 1980 and re-introduced by Employment Relations Act 1999)

Ir Trade Union Act 1971 (rules on registration and licensing of trade unions)

It Act 1204/1971 (special protection of women workers in cases of pregnancy and maternity)

Ne Act amending Dutch Company Law and introducing a right of inquiry (investigation into the policy and daily management of an enterprise)

Ne Structure Act (allows employees to have some influence over the composition of the top level of management of major enterprises)

Po Decree-Law 409/71 ('Length of Working Time Act')

1972

Aut Employee Protection Act (rules on health and safety)

GB/NI European Communities Act 1972 (UK joined the EC)

Den accession to the EC

Den Act of Arbitration (possibility for parties to an employment contract to agree to submit their dispute to an arbitration court)

Fr Act of 3 January 1972 on agencies of temporary employment

Fr Act of 22 December 1972 (equal pay)

Ger Agency Work Act (provides a minimum of protection for temporary employees; introduced the need for an administrative licence for commercial temporary work; since 1982, commercial temporary work totally banned in the building industry; FRG)

Ger Act on the Transfer of Undertakings (transfer of the establishment leads to a transfer of the employment relationship to the new owner)

Ir European Communities Act 1972 (accession to the EC)

Sw Act of Board Representation for Employees in Joint Stock Companies and Co-operative Associations (aimed at achieving employee influence in enterprise management; followed by several amendments, now Act on Board Representation of Private Employees of 1987)

1973

Den Labour Court Act (for cases concerning breaches of collective agreements; substituted the Labour Court Act of 1910, later amended by Labour Court Act of 1997)

Den   Seafarers Act (specific rules for this category of employees)

Fi   Annual Holidays Act

Fr   Act of 13 July 1973 (reform of the law of dismissals, introduction of a fixed procedure)

Fr   New Labour Code (applied since 22 November 1973)

It   Act 533/1973 (on settlement of labour disputes)

1974

Aut   Labour Regulation Act (rules on collective bargaining, works agreements, workers' representation, enforceable co-determination etc.)

Aut   Act guaranteeing sick pay to workers

Aut   Act on co-participation in Supervisory Boards (introduction of a one-third participation of employees in the internal controlling body of certain large undertakings)

GB/NI   Health and Safety at Work Act 1974 (industrial safety law)

GB/NI   Trade Union and Labour Relations Act 1974 (statutory protection for the closed shop; later, pre-entry closed shop prohibited by Employment Act 1990)

Ger   Act on the Improvement of Occupational Pension Schemes (claims to occupational pensions cannot be revoked after a certain length of service; insolvency insurance; FRG)

Gr   Legislative Decree 42/1974 (restored trade union freedoms)

Po   Decree 203/1974 Provisional Government Programme (changing labour law system after fall of dictatorship)

Sw   Employment Protection Act (introduced statutory protection against unfair dismissals, need for a dismissal to be founded on a just cause; fixed-term contracts allowed only in specific cases for a special purpose; replaced by a new Employment Protection Act of 1982 with few changes)

Sw   Act on Litigation in Labour Disputes ('Labour Disputes Act')

Sw   Act on the Position of a Trade Union Representative at the Work Place (Shop Stewards Act)

1975

GB/NI   Sex Discrimination Act 1975

GB/NI   Employment Protection Act 1975 (introduced maternity pay, right to return after pregnancy; introduction of the employer's obligation to consult with unions or elected employee representatives in certain cases of redundancy)

Den   Work Environment Act (uniting several, formerly separated Acts on health and safety)

Fr   Act of 3 January 1975 (reform of the law of dismissals for economic reasons; need for administrative authorisation; consultation of the workers' representatives)

Gr   National Constitution (eg freedom of trade unions, right to strike, freedom of collective bargaining)

Po   Decree-Law 215-B/75 (Trade Union Act, legal regime of trade union association)

Po   Decree-Law 215-C/75 (Employers' Associations Act, legal regime of employers' associations)

Po   Decree-Law 372-A/75 (Dismissal Act, rules on termination of employment; modified several times since)

1976

Aut   Holidays Act (uniform regulation of annual vacation rules previously contained in various acts)

GB/NI   Race Relations Act 1976 (introduced prohibition of discrimination, on grounds of colour, race, ethnic or national origins, in employment)

Ger   Act on the Protection of Youth Employment

Ger   Co-Determination Act 1976 (extension of co-determination to undertakings with more than 2000 employees; FRG)

Gr   Act 330/76 on Trade Unions

Ne   Notification of Collective Dismissals Act

Po   Constitution of the Portuguese Republic (eg express prohibition of dismissals without a just cause; right to form workers' committees in companies; establishment of union freedom; right to collective bargaining and to strike, expressly forbidding lock-out; revision of the Constitution later in 1982)

Po	Decree-Law 781/76 on fixed-term employment contracts
Po	Decree-Law 874/76 (holidays, public holidays and absences)
Po	Decree-Law 112/76 on Maternity Protection
Sp	Act creating a Warranty of Wages Fund (guarantees the payment of wages to the employee in cases of insolvency or bankruptcy of the employer up the four months preceding insolvency/bankruptcy; fund supported by a tax on wages (today at 0.4%) paid by the employers)
Sw	Co-determination Act (contains the fundamental rules on collective labour law including rules on industrial action; rules emanate from the former Collective Agreements Act of 1928 as well as from the Act on the Rights of Association and of Negotiation of 1936)
Sw	Industrial Injuries Insurance Act (concerning compensation for incapacity due to industrial accidents)

1977

Aut	Act on employees' interests in case of insolvencies (safeguarding employees' interests in the event of insolvency)
Ir	Unfair Dismissals Act 1977 (right to dismiss limited to be exercised only on one of a restricted set of grounds)
Ir	Protection of Employment Act 1977
Ir	Worker Participation (State Enterprise) Act 1977 (formal basis for worker participation on company boards)
It	Act 903/1977 (principle of non-discrimination between men and women)
It	Act 285/1977 on young people in employment
Po	Act 66/77 on the right to strike
Po	Decree-Law 353-H/77 (declaration of a firm in a difficult economic situation)
Po	Act 82/77 on the judicial organisation of labour
Sp	Trade Union Act 19/1977 (about the right to unionise; implied the recuperation of trade union freedom within the period known as 'political transition')
Sp	Labour Relations Royal Decree-Act 16/1977 on the right to strike
Sw	Working Environment Act (rules on health and safety, good environment in the workplace; protection of minors)
Sw	Vacation Act (links the right to leave and the right to vacation pay)

1978

Be   Act on Employment Contracts (rules on individual employment contracts, dismissals etc.)

Fi   Cooperation Within Undertakings Act (rules on representatives of the employees, participation; repealing the Shop Rules Act of 1922)

Fi   Seamen's Act

Fr   Act of 19 January 1978 (rules on sickness)

Sp   new Spanish Constitution (guarantees trade union freedom and pluralism, means a partial return to the pre-1939 situation; rights of employers' associations, collective bargaining, right to strike; Spain as a 'social and democratic state of law')

Sp   Royal Ordinances of Armed Forces (Act of 28 December 1978, absence of the right to unionise for military personnel)

1979

Aut   Act on equal pay/equal treatment (protection against sex discrimination widened later by an amendment in 1990)

Aut   Protection of Working Mothers Act (protection of pregnant women and after delivery)

Fi   Study Leave Act (right to study leaves after continuous full-time employment of one year minimum)

Fr   Act of 18 January 1979 (reform of the labour court system, *conseil des prud'hommes*)

Po   Act 40/79 (regime of the workers' committees)

Po   Act 68/79 (introducing a special system of protection against dismissals for workers' representatives)

Po   Decree-Law 519-C1/79 (Collective Labour Relations Act; legal framework for the collective labour relations)

Po   Act 16/79 (participation of the workers in the elaboration of labour legislation)

Sw   Act on equality between women and men at work (replaced later by the Equal Opportunities Act 433/1991)

1980

Ger	Act introducing the prohibition of sex discrimination and the principle of equal pay into the Civil Code; FRG)
Gr	Act 1082/80 on paid public holidays etc.
Sp	Workers' Statute (Estatuto de los Trabajadores; new amalgamated text approved by Royal Decree 1/1995)

1981

Be	Act on part-time work
GB/NI	Transfer of Undertakings (Protection of Employment) Regulations 1981
Den	Act introducing reinstatement as a remedy for dismissals
Fr	Act of 7 January 1981 (special protection of employees who are victims of work-related accidents)
Gr	accession to the EEC
Po	Decree-Law 272-A/81 on labour procedure

1982

GB/NI	Employment Act 1982 (removal of the blanket immunity of Trade Unions)
Fr	Representation of Employees Act of 28 October 1982 (on representativeness of unions; reform of works councils)
Fr	Act of 13 November 1982 (enhancement of collective bargaining; introduction of a duty to bargain at industry and enterprise level)
Fr	Ordinance 82-131 of 5 February 1982 (on the conditions for temporary work; extension of the rights of workers' representatives regarding temporary work)
Fr	Ordinance of 5 February 1982 on fixed-term contracts (authorisation of a limited set of situations; modified by Ordinance of 11 August 1986)
Fr	Ordinance of 16 January 1982 on paid vacation (five weeks)
Gr	Act 1264/82 (rules on trade unions and the right to strike)
Gr	Act 1302/82 on maternity protection

It	Act 297/82 on severance pay
Sp	Act on social integration of handicapped persons (including an explicit prohibition of discrimination)
Sw	Working Time Act

1983

Aut	Act on working times (Sunday rest and rest on public holidays)
Gr	Act 1346/83 (introduced the automatic price index re-adaptation of employees' income (ATA), abolished in 1991)
Gr	Act 1342/83 on equal pay
It	Act 266/1983 (fixed term contracts initially limited to specific sectors, here: radio-TV)
Ne	reform of the Dutch Constitution (now also including fundamental social rights, eg trade union freedom, freedom of collective bargaining, right to strike, right to equal treatment)
Po	Decree-Law 398/83 on the suspension of individual contracts of employment

1984

Fr	Act of 4 January 1984 (extension of the right to parental leave to all parents – mother or father – with one year's seniority)
Ger	Act on optional early retirement (promotion of early retirement in order to fight unemployment; later replaced by the Act on Part-time Retirement 1989; FRG)
Gr	Act 1414/84 on employment equality
Ir	Protection of Employees (Employers' Insolvency) Act 1984

1985

Aut	Wage Garnishment Act (limiting wages being subject to execution)
Fr	Law on the contract of employment
Ger	Act on the Improvement of Employment Opportunities (introduced the

> possibility to conclude a fixed-term contract without a justifying reason for 18 months maximum; principle of equal treatment of part-time and full-time employees; FRG)

Gr   Act 1568/85 on hygiene and safety

Po   Decree-Law 49/85 on minimum wages (fixing and updating of a national minimum wage occurred for the first time in 1974)

Sp   Trade Union Freedom Act 11/1985

1986

Aut   Labour Courts Act (fundamental reorganisation of the labour courts and their proceedings)

Fr   Law 86-987 on administrative authorisation of dismissal

Fr   Law 86-130 on dismissal procedures

Fi   Act on the Equality between Women and Men (prohibition of sex discrimination)

Po   accession to the EEC

Po   Act 17/86 on overdue wages)

1987

Aut   Act on agency/temporary work

Be   Act of 24 July 1987 on temporary work

1988

GB/NI   Employment Act 1988 (general unfairness of any dismissal for union or non-union membership)

Gr   Act 1767/88 on Works Councils (introduced works councils)

1989

Be   Act of 22 December 1989 (introduced the concept of maternity benefits covered by medical insurance/social security)

Fi   Associations Act (rules on trade unions and employers' associations, extended freedom of association to foreigners; succeeded the Associations Act of 1919)

Ir   Safety, Health and Welfare at Work Act 1989

1990

Aut   Act on occupational pensions schemes

Aut   Act extending the right to maternity leave to two years ant to the father as potential claimant

Fi   Act on the Representation of the Personnel in the Administration of Enterprises (applicable to employers with at least 150 employees; gives employees a say in the administration of enterprises)

Fr   Law 90-57 on vocational training

Ger   Unification Treaty (extension of all law of the original FRG to the territory of the former GDR; dissolution of trade unions of the former GDR, trade unions and employers' associations of the old FRG extended their scope of activity to the territory of the former GDR)

Gr   Act 1892/90 (on working time, part-time work and flexibility of working hours)

Gr   Act 1876/90 on collective agreements (extension of the right to collective bargaining to a single private employer)

Ir   Industrial Relations Act 1990 (conciliation service of the Labour Relations Commission)

It   Act 146/1990 on strikes in essential services

1991

Fr   Law 91-1405 on vocational training

Ir   Payment of Wages Act 1991 (introduced procedural pre-conditions for wage deductions)

Ir	Worker Protection (regulkar Part-Time Employees) Act
It	Act 223/1991 on collective dismissals
It	Act on equal treatment for men and women
Sw	Act 1047/1991 on sick pay

1992

Fr	Act of 2 November on sexual harassment
Ne	General Act on Equal Treatment (prohibition of unequal treatment irrespective of religion, political orientation, race, sex, nationality, sexual orientation or marital status, covering all aspects of behaviour on the labour market)

1993

Fr	Act of 27 January relating to restructuring plans
Fr	Five-year Act of 20 December relating to employment
GB/NI	TURERA 1993 (introduction of maternity leave)
It	Act 29/1993 (privatisation and introduction of common labour law rules and of collective bargaining in the public sector; abolishment of all pre-existing forms of co-determination in the public sector)
Sw	Act 440/1993 (legalised private employment agencies)

1994

Be	reform of the Belgian Constitution of 1831 (introduced provisions specifically relating to labour matters, guarantee of social rights, eg of collective bargaining)
GB/NI	Statutory Sick Pay Act 1994 (introduced statutory sick pay)
Ger	Working Time Act (replaced the former Working Time Act of 1938)
Gr	Act 2224/94 on paid leave after pregnancy
Ir	Maternity Protection Act 1994
It	Decree 626/1994 on health and safety in the workplace

Ne	Equal Treatment Act
Sp	Act 14/1994 on Temporary Work (need for a special administrative authorisation)
Sw	Act against Ethnic Discrimination (prohibition of discrimination on grounds of race, colour, national or ethnic origin or creed)

1995

GB/NI	Disability Discrimination Act 1995
Fi	constitutional reform concerning fundamental rights (modernisation of the provisions of the Constitution, introduction of new provisions on social rights)
Fi	accession to the EU
It	Act 335/1995 (major reform of the pension system, linking pensions more closely to the contributions paid by the employers and employees during working life)
Sp	Labour Risks Prevention Act 31/1995 (employer's obligations on safety organisation in the work place)
Sp	Royal Decree 1561/1995 (limitation on working time for works with special conditions of risk or stress; modification of the weekly rest system for specific activities)
Sp	Labour Risk Prevention Act 31/1995 (on information and consultation rights of employees' representatives in safety and hygiene matters)
Sw	accession to the EU
Sw	Parents' Right to Leave Act 584/1995

1996

Fr	Act of 5 July modifying parental leave
Fr	Act of 6 May relating to working hours
Fr	Act of 12 November relating to employee representation including the European works council.
GB/NI	Employment Tribunals Act
GB/NI	Employment Rights Act
Ger	Posted-Workers Act

Ir	Parental Leave Act 1996
Ir	Transnational Information and Consultation of Employees Act 1996
Ne	Working Time Act (statutory rules on working hours, increased flexibility; rules on the prohibition of child labour; prohibition of unequal treatment of part-time workers)
Po	Law 38/96 on dismissals
Sw	Act amending the Employment Protection Act (introduces a new type of fixed-term contracts for which no special purpose is needed for a total of 12 months)
Sw	Act 359/1996 on European Works Councils

1997

Be	Act of 17 February 1997 on Night Work (general prohibition of night work)
GB/NI	Treaty of Amsterdam (UK signed up to the EU Social Policy Agreement, i.e. the Social Chapter)
Ir	Organisation of working time Act 1997 (on working time and minimum holidays)
It	Act 196/1997 on employment promotion and labour market regulation (recognition of temporary work agencies; abolished the former prohibition of temporary work, but limits it to types of works not normally used in the enterprise; reduction of the working hours per week from 48 to 40 hours maximum)
Ne	new Dutch Civil Code (modernised version of the chapter on the contract of employment)
Ne	Act on European Works Councils
Po	Law 105/97 on equality and non-discrimination at work
Sp	Act 10/1997 on the information and consultation rights of employees' representatives in EU scope enterprises

1998

Fr	Act of 13 June on reduction of working time (*loi Aubry*)
Be	Act of 13 February 1998 on Collective Redundancies
Be	Act of 23 April 1998 on European Works Councils

GB/NI   Human Rights Act 1998 (incorporation of the ECHR into British Law)

GB/NI   Public Interest Disclosure Act 1998 (protection for employees who disclose confidential information in certain cases)

GB/NI   Working Time Regulations 1998 (introduction of minimum conditions for working time, rest periods, holidays, night work, etc)

GB/NI   National Minimum Wage Act 1998 (re-introduction of a basic minimum rate of pay per hour for all workers, covering all regions of the UK and all sectors of economy)

GB/NI   Employment Rights (Dispute Resolution) Act

Fi   Act on the Guaranteed Payment of Wages (payment of wages assured by the Government in the event of the employer's bankruptcy or insolvency)

Gr   Act 2639/98 on Temporary Work

Ir   Employment Equality Act 1998 (equal pay; general prohibition of sex discrimination and of discrimination on grounds of age)

Ne   Allocation of Employees by Intermediaries Act (introduced specific rules on temporary work agencies; abolished the former system of licences for private temporary work business)

Ne   Health and Safety at Work Act (aiming at human working conditions and the welfare of the workforce)

Sp   Act eliminating the difference in the minimum wage rates previously made between adults and workers being 16–18 years old (now only one minimum wage rate)

1999

Be   Act of 7 May 1999 on equal treatment of men and women in employment matters (eg access to employment, working conditions)

Be   Act of 26 March 1999 on shares with 'decode' stock options (financial participation of employees)

GB/NI   Scottish Parliament and Welsh Assembly established

GB/NI   Employment Relations Act 1999 (including rules on parental leave, dependant care leave)

GB/NI   Transnational Information and Consultation of Employees Regulations 1999 (implementation of the European Works Council Directive EC 94/95)

GB/NI   Disability Rights Commission Act

Fi   new Constitution of Finland (containing eg a constitutional right not to be dismissed from work without reasons; replaces the Finnish Constitution of 1919)

Gr   Law 2738/1999 established collective bargaining in public administration

L   Act on implementation of national employment plan

Ne   Flexibility and Security Act ('flexicurity programme'; expansion of the possibility to conclude temporary agency work contracts and to repeat fixed-term contracts; improved the rights of temporary agency workers; rules on labour on call; shortened the legal periods of notice)

2000

Fr   Act of 19 January on reduction of working time (*loi Aubry II*)

GB/NI   Part-Time Workers (Prevention of less favourable Treatment) Regulations 2000

Gr   Act 2874/00 on working time (abolition of overwork)

Ir   National Minimum Wage Act 2000 (introduction of a national minimum wage)

It   Act 61/2000 on Part-time Work (principle of non-discrimination)

It   Act 53/2000 on parental leave

Ne   Working Time Adjustment Act (gives employees the right to have their working hours increased or decreased at their request, provided that there are no serious objections on the grounds of company interests)

2001

Fr   Act of 9 May on professional equality

Fr   Act of 17 July on integration of unemployed people instituting PARE (return to work programme)

Fr   Act of 16 November on discrimination

Be   Act of 10 August 2001 concerning the reconciling between work and quality of life (provides for paternity leave and adoption leave)

Be   Act of 22 May 2001 on Participation of Employees in the Capital and the Profit of Companies (financial participation of employees)

Fi   Employment Contracts Act

Ir   Protection of Employees (Part-time work) Act 2001 (prohibition of discrimination)

Ir   Carer's Leave Act 2001

It   Act 368/2001 (liberalisation of fixed-term contracts, now allowed not only in specific cases, but in general, whenever they are justified by 'technical, organisational or substitutional reasons')

Ne   Work and Care Act

2002

Fr   Act of 17 January on social modernisation

Be   Act of 26 June 2002 on the closure of an enterprise (right of the employees to a compensation)

GB/NI   Fixed-term Employees (Prevention of less favourable treatment) Regulations 2002

GB/NI   Employment Act

Ger   Act reforming general Contract Law (eg law on standard contract terms now applicable to employment contracts)

L   Data Protection

Ne   Act prohibiting unequal treatment of workers on fixed-term contracts

2003

Fr   Act of 3 January on redundancy (*loi Fillon*)

Fr   Act of 17 January on reform of working time (RTT)

Fr   Act of 23 August on retirement

It   Act 30/2003 (further liberalisation of temporary work, allowed whenever it is justified by 'productive, technical, organisational or substitutional reasons'; introduction of the contract of intermittent work ('job on call') as a further kind of atypical contracts)

It   Act 66/2003 (minimum of four weeks annual vacation)

Po   Labour Code (replacing earlier Acts)

2004

Fr   Act of 6 January on collective bargaining

Bibliography

Aaron, B (ed) (1971) *Labor Courts and Grievance Settlement in Western Europe* (Berkeley, University of California Press).

—— (1978) 'Discrimination Based on Race, Color, Ethnicity and National Origin' in F Schmidt (ed), *Discrimination in Employment* (Stockholm, Almquist & Wiksell).

——(1985) 'Labour Courts and Organs of Arbitration' in B Hepple (ed), *International Encyclopedia of Comparative Law. Vol 15. Labour Law* (Tübingen, Martinus Nijhoff) ch 16.

Aaron, B and Farwell, DF (eds) (1982) 'Worker Participation in Management Decisions', International Society for Labor Law and Social Security, 10th International Congress, Reports and Proceedings 1 (Washington, DC, The Bureau of National Affairs).

Abrams, P (1982) *Historical Sociology* (Shepton Mallet, Open Books).

Adam, G, Reynaud, JD and Verdier, JM (1972) *La négociation collective en France* (Paris, Éditions Économie et humanisme).

Adlercreutz, A (1976) 'The Development of Swedish Labour Law 1973–1974' *Bulletin of Comparative Labour Relations* 7.

——(1998) 'Sweden' in R Blanpain (ed), *International Encyclopedia for Labour Law and Industrial Relations* (Deventer, Kluwer).

Ahlberg, K and Bruun, N (2005) 'Sweden: Transition through collective bargaining' in R Blanpain, T Blanke and E Rose (eds), *Collective Bargaining and Wages in Comparative Perspective* (The Hague, Kluwer) 117.

Albeda, W, Blanpain, R and Veldkamp, GM (eds) (1978) *Temporary Work in Modern Society. A Comparative Study. Part I. Temporary Work and the Law* (The Hague, Kluwer).

Albertyn, C (2007) 'Substantive Equality and Transformation in South Africa' 23 *South African Journal of Human Rights* 253.

Anderman, SD (1985) *The Law of Unfair Dismissal* (London, Butterworths).

Anker, R, Melkas, H and Korten, A (2003) 'Gender-based Occupational Segregation in the 1990s', Working Paper 16 (Geneva, International Labour Organisation).

Ardagh, J (1982) *France in the 1980s* (Harmondsworth, Penguin).

Arrigo, G (1998) *Il diritto del lavoro dell'Unione Europea. Tomo I* (Milano, Giuffrè).

Arthurs, H (2006). 'Who is Afraid of Globalisation? Reflections on the Future of Labour Law' in JDR Craig and SM Lynk (eds), *Globalisation and the Future of Labour Law* (Cambridge, Cambridge University Press).

Ashiagbor, D (2005) *The European Employment Strategy* (Oxford, Oxford University Press).

Atiyah, PS (1979) *The Rise and Fall of Freedom of Contract* (Oxford, Oxford University Press).

Baglioni, G and Crouch, C (eds) (1991) *European Industrial Relations, The Challenge of Flexibility* (London, Sage Publications).

Batygin, K (1972) *Soviet Labour Law and Principles of Civil Law* (Moscow, Progress).

Bakels, B (1981) 'Het Engels en Nederlands Arbeids-en Ontlagrecht', *Social Maandblad Arbeid* 36.

Banerjee, SB (2008) 'Corporate Social Responsibility: The Good, the Bad and the Ugly' 34 *Critical Sociology* 51.

Barnard, C (1996) 'The Economic Objectives of Article 119' in TK Hervey and D O'Keeffe (eds), *Sex Equality in the European Union* (Chichester, Wiley).

Barnard, C, Deakin, S and Morris, GS (eds) (2004) *The Future of Labour Law. Liber Amicorum Sir Bob Hepple QC* (Oxford, Hart Publishing).

Begg, I, Draxler, J and Mortensen, J (2008) 'Is Social Europe Fit for Globalisation?', Study for the EU Commission (Brussels, CEPS).

Bell, M (2002) *Anti-Discrimination Law in the European Union* (Oxford, Oxford University Press).

Bell, M, Chopin, I and Palmer, F (2007) *Developing Anti-Discrimination Law in Europe* (Brussels, European Commission).

Bendiner, B (1987) *International Labour Affairs* (Oxford, Clarendon Press).

Bentham, J (1843) 'Anarchical Fallacies: Being an Examination of the Declaration of Rights Issued During the French Revolution' in J Bowring (ed), *Collected Works of Jeremy Bentham* (Edinburgh, William Tait).

Bercusson, B (1996) *European Labour Law* (London, Butterworths).

Bercusson, B and Ryan, B (2005) 'The British Case: Before and After the Decline of Collective Wage Formation' in R Blanpain, T Blanke and E Rose (eds), *Collective Bargaining and Wages in Comparative Perspective* (The Hague, Kluwer) 49.

Bertrand, Lamoureaux and Vermel (1993) 'La gestion prévisionnelle des emplois et des compétences dans les PME' *Travail et emploi* 57.

Biagi, M (1990) 'Forms of Employee Representation at the Workplace' in R Blanpain (ed), *Comparative Labour Law and Industrial Relations in Industrialised Market Economies*, 4th edn, vol I (Deventer, Kluwer).

——(1993) 'Forms of Representational Participation' in R Blanpain and C Engels (eds), *Comparative Labour Law and Industrial Relations in Industrialised Market Economies* (Deventer, Kluwer).

Blanc-Jouvan, X (1971) 'The Settlement of Labor Disputes in France' in B Aaron (ed), *Labour Courts and Grievance Settlement in Western Europe* (Berkeley, University of California Press).

Blanke, T and Rose, E (2005) 'Erosion or Renewal? The Crisis of Collective Wage Formation in Germany' in R Blanpain, T Blanke and E Rose (eds), *Collective Bargaining and Wages in Comparative Perspective* (The Hague, Kluwer) 5.

Blanke, T et al (1975) *Kollektives Arbeitsrecht*, vol II (Reinbek, Rororo-studium).

Blankenburg, E and Rogowski, R (1986) 'German Labour Courts and the British Industrial Tribunal System. A Socio-legal Comparison' 13 *Journal of Law and Society* 67.

Blanpain, R (1973) 'Security of Employment. Comparative Study' *Bulletin of Leuven Institute of Labour Relations* 4.

——(1994) 'Representation of Employees at Plant and Enterprise Level' in B Hepple (ed), *International Encyclopedia of Comparative Law. Vol XV. Labour Law* (Tubingen, Möhr) ch 13.

——(1998, 2004) 'European Works Councils' in R Blanpain (ed), *International Encyclopedia for Labour Law and Industrial Relations* (The Hague, Kluwer).

Blanpain, R and Graham, R (eds) (2004) *Temporary Agency Work and the Information Society*, special issue of *Bulletin of Comparative Labour Relations* 50.

Blanpain, R and Kohler, E (eds) (1988) *General Report. Legal and Contractual Limitation to Working Time in the European Community Member States* (Deventer, Kluwer).

Blanpain, R et al (2007) *The Global Workplace. International and Comparative Employment Law. Cases and Materials* (Cambridge, Cambridge University Press).

Blasco, JG and Val Tena, A de (2004) 'Collective Bargaining in Spain' in Spanish Ministry of Labour, *Collective Bargaining in Europe* (Madrid, Ministry of Labour) 1975.

Blomeyer, W (1967) 'Der befristete Arbeitsvertrag als Problem der Gesetzesinterpretation', *Recht der Arbeit.*

Boeri, T et al (ed) (2001) *The Role of the Unions in the Twenty-First Century* (Oxford, Oxford University Press).

Bonell, MJ (1983) *Partecipazione operaia e diritto dell'impresa* (Milano, Giuffrè editore).

Borenfeund, G (1998) 'Les syndicats forcent les protes de l'enterprise: la loi du 27 décembre 1968 relative a l'exercise du droit sydnical dans l'enterprise' in Le Crom, JP (ed) *Deux siècles de droit du travail* (Paris, Les éditions de l'atelier).

Brown, W (ed) (1981) *The Changing Contours of British Industrial Relations* (Oxford, Basil Blackwell).

Brown, W, Deakin, S, Nash, D and Oxenbridge S (2000) 'The Employment Contract, From Collective Procedures to Individual Rights' *British Journal of Industrial Relations* 38.

Browne, J (2006) *Sex Segregation and Inequality in the Modern Labour Market* (Bristol, Policy Press).

Brunhes, B (2003) 'Le droit du licenciement collectif: les humeurs d'un praticien' *Droit Social* 1.

Bruun, N and Hellsten, J (eds) (2001) 'Collective Agreements and Competition Law in the EU', Report of the COL COM Project (Helsinki, Kauppakaari Oyj).

Bruun, N and Veneziani, B (1999) 'The Right or Freedom to Transnational Industrial Action in the European Union' in 'A Legal Framework for European Industrial Relations', Report by the ETUI Research Network on Transnational Trade Union Rights (Brussels, ETUI) 77.

Bruun, N, Flodgren, B, Halvorsen, M, Hydén, H and Nielsen, R (1992) *The Nordic Labour Relations Model* (Aldershot, Dartmouth).

Burkett, BW (2006) 'The International Labour Dimension: An Introduction' in JDR Craig and SM Lynk (eds), *Globalisation and the Future of Labour Law* (Cambridge, Cambridge University Press).

Camerlynck, GH (1962) 'Syntesis report' in AA, VV (eds), *Il contratto di lavoro nel diritto dei paesi membri della Ceca* (Milano, Giuffrè).

——(1978) 'France' in R Blanpain (ed), *Temporary Work in Modern Society: a Comparative Study. Part I* (The Netherlands, Kluwer).

Carby-Hall, J (2003) 'New frontiers of Labour Law: dependent and autonomous workers' in AA, VV (eds), *Du travail salarié au travail indépendant: permanences et mutations* (Bari, Cacucci) 249.

Caruso, B (2004) 'Flexibility in Labour Law: the Italian Case' in B Caruso and M Fuchs (eds), *Labour Law and Flexibility in Europe. The Cases of Germany and Italy* (Milan, Giuffré) 11.

Casado Lopez, ML (2005) 'Inmigración y políticas de regularización en Europa' in *III Seminario Inmigración y Europa* (Barcelona, Fundació CIDOB).

Castells, M (2000) *The Rise of the Network Society: The Information Age, Economy, Society and Culture*, vol 1 (London, Blackwell).

Cerami, A (2006) *Social Policy in Central and Eastern Europe* (Berlin, LIT Verlag).

Chauchard, JP (2003) 'Entre travail salarié et travail indépendant: L'emergence du travail autonome' in AA, VV (eds), *Du travail salarié au travail indépendent: permanences et mutations* (Bari, Cacucci) 14.

Chlepner, BS (1972) *Cent ans d'histoire sociale en Belgique* (Bruxelles, Éditions de l'Université de Bruxelles).

Clauwaert, S et al (2004) 'Social Dialogue and Coordination of Collective Bargaining at European Level' in Spanish Ministry of Labour, *Collective Bargaining in Europe* (Madrid, Ministry of Labour) 301.

Cohen, GA (2000) *If You're an Egalitarian, How Come You're So Rich?* (Cambridge MA, Harvard University Press).

Collins, H (2000) 'Justification and techniques of legal regulation of the employment relation' in H Collins, P Davies and R Rideout (eds), *Legal Regulation of the Employment Relation* (London, Kluwer and Institute of Advanced Legal Studies).

Commission Des Communautes Européennes (1981) *Economie Europèenne. Rapport économique annuel 1981–1982*, 10.

Contouris, N (2007) *The Changing Law of the Employment Relationship. Comparative Analyses in the European Context* (Aldershot, Ashgate).

Cordova, E (1985) 'Collective Bargaining' in R Blanpain (ed), *Comparative Labour Law and Industrial Relations* (Deventer, Kluwer).

——(1986) 'De l'emploi total au travail atypique: vers un virage dans l'évolution des relations de travail' *La Revue internationale du Travail* 715.

Cousins, M (2005) *European Welfare States* (London, Sage Publications).

Coussey, M (2002) *Tackling Racial Equality: International Comparisons*, Home Office Research Study 238 (London, Home Office).

Cr., F (1959) 'L'integration des handicaps dans la vie sociale et economique' *Revue du Travail* 4.

Craig, JDR and Lynk, M (2006) *Globalisation and the Future of Labour Law* (Cambridge, Cambridge University Press).

Creighton,WB (1979) *Working Women and the Law* (London, Mansell).

——(2004) 'The Future of Laboru Law: Is There a Role for International Labour Standards' in C Barnard, S Deakin and GS Morris (eds), *The Future of Labour Law: Liber Amicorum Sir Bob Hepple QC* (Oxford. Hart Publishing).

Crouch, C (1979a) *The Politics of Industrial Relations* (Manchester, Manchester University Press).

——(1979b) 'Inflation and the Political Organisation of Economic Interests' in P Davies and MR Freedland (eds), *Labour Law: Text and Materials* (London, Weidenfeld & Nicholson).

Daniel, WW and Millward, N (1983) *Workplace Relations in Britain. The DE/PSI/SSRC Survey* (London, Heinemann).

D'Antona, M (1979) *La reintegrazione nel posto di lavoro* (Padova, Cedam).

Däubler, W (1994) *Derecho del Trabajo* (Madrid, Ministry of Labour and Social Assistance).

——(2008) 'Kündigungsschutz durch Gesetz, durch Tairfvertrag, durch Betriebsvereinbaring und durch Arbeitsvertrag' in M Kitner, W Däubler, B Zwanger (eds), *Kündigungsschutzrecht* (Frankfurt, Bund Verlag).

Davidov, G and Langille, B (2006) *Boundaries and Frontiers of Labour Law* (Oxford, Hart Publishing).

Davies, P and Freedland, MR (1979) *Labour Law: Text and Materials* (London, Weidenfld and Nicholson).

——(1993) *Labour Legislation and Public Policy* (Oxford, Clarendon Press).

——(2006) *Towards a Flexible Labour Market: Labour Legislation and Regulation since the 1990s* (Oxford, Oxford University Press).

De Broeck, G (1973–74) 'L'évolution des relations professionnelles en Belgique' *Reflets et Perspectives de la Vie économique.*

De Riemaecker-Legot, M (1960) 'Le Fonds Social européen' *Revue du Travail* 2.

De Schutter, O (2007) 'Positive Action' in D Schiek, L Waddington and M Bell (eds), *Cases, Texts and Materials on National, Supranational and International Non-discrimination Law* (Oxford, Hart Publishing).

De Vos, M (ed) (2003) *Nationale Arbeidsraad 50 jaar* (Brugge, Dalloz).

Deakin, S (1998) 'The Evolution of Contract of Employment *1900–1950*' in N Whiteside and R Salais (eds), *Governance, Industry and Labour Markets in Britain and France* (London, Routledge) 221.

——(2001), *The Contract of Employment: a Study in Legal Evolution*, Working Paper 203 (Cambridge, ESRC Centre for Business Research).

——(2002) 'The Many Futures of the Contract of Employment' in J Conaghan, RM Fischl and K Klare (eds), *Labour Law in an Era of Globalization* (Oxford, Oxford University Press).

Deakin, S and Morris, G (1998) *Labour Law*, 3rd edn (London, Butterworths).

——(2005) *Labour Law*, 5th edn (Oxford, Hart Publishing).

Deakin, S and Wilkinson, F (2000) 'Labour Law and Economic Theory' in C Collins, P Davies and R Rideout (eds), *Legal Regulation of the Employment Relation* (London, Kluwer and Institute of Advanced Legal Studies).

——(2005) *The Law of the Labour Market—Industrialization, Employment and Legal Evolution* (Oxford, Oxford University Press).

Dederichs, E and Kohler, E (1991) *Part-time Work in the European Community: Laws and Regulations* (Dublin, European Foundation for the Improvement of Living and Working Conditions).

Degryse, C (2006) 'Historical and Institutional Background to the Cross-industry Social Dialogue' in A Dufresne, C Degryse and P Pochet (eds), *The European Sectoral Social Dialogue. Actors, Developments and Challenges* (Brussels, Peter Lang SALTSA).

Desai, M (2005) *Marx's Revenge: The Resurgence of Capitalism and the Death of Statist Socialism* (London, Verso).

Despax, M (1966) *Traîté de Droit du Travail. Tome 3. Conventions Collectives* (Paris, Dalloz).

Despax, M and Rojot, J (1987) 'France' in R Blanpain (ed), *International Encyclopaedia for Labour Law and Industrial Relations. Monographs and Legislation* (Deventer, Kluwer).

Dickens, L and Neal, AC (2006) *The Changing Institutional Face of British Employment Relations* (Alphen aan den Rijn, Kluwer Law International).

Di Pasquale, V (2002) 'New Law Passed on Temporary Agency Work' *Euronline* 4 December.

Dolado, JJ (2002) 'Los nuevos fenómenos migratorios: retos y políticas' (Barcelona, CREI, Universidad Carlos III, Departamento de Economía), available at: http://docubib.uc3m.es/WORKINGPAPERS/DE/de021303.pdf (accessed December 2008).

Dore, R (2004) 'The concrete meanings of Labour Law flexibility' in JP Laviec, M Horiuchi and K Sugeno (eds), *Work in the Global Economy* (Tokyo, International Labour Organisation) 26.

Doyle, B (1995) *Disability Discrimination and Equal Opportunities: a Comparative Study of the Employment Rights of Disabled Persons* (London, Mansell).

Dorssemont, F, Jaspers, T and Hoek, A van (eds) (2007) *Cross-border Collective Actions in Europe: A Legal Challenge* (Oxford, Hart).

Dufresne, A, Degryse, C and Pochet, P (eds) (2006) *The European Sectoral Social Dialogue. Actors, Developments and Challenges* (Bruxelles e al., Peter Lang SALTSA).

Durand, P and Rouast, A (1957) *Droit du travail* (Paris, Dalloz).

Dworkin, R (2000) *Sovereign Virtue: the Theory and Practice of Equality* (Cambridge MA, Harvard University Press).

Edström, Ö (2002) 'Co-determination in Private Enterprises in Four Nordic Countries' in P Wahlgren (ed), *Stability ad Change in Nordic Labour Law* (Stockholm, Stockholm Institute of Scandinavian Law).

Eichengreen, B (2007) *The European Economy since 1945* (Princeton, Princeton University Press).

Ellis, E (1991, 1998) *EC Sex Equality Law* (Oxford, Clarendon Press).

Engblom, S (2001) 'Equal Treatment of Employees and Self-employed Workers', 17 *International Journal of Comparative Labur Law and Industrial Relations* 211.

Epstein, R (1984) 'In Defense of Contract at Will' 51 *University of Chicago Law Review* 947.

——(1995) *Forbidden Grounds: The Case Against Employment Discrimination Law* (London, Harvard University Press).

Esping-Andersen, G (1990) *The Three Worlds of Welfare Capitalism* (Cambridge MA, Princeton University Press).

EU Network of Independent Experts on Disability Discrimination (2004) 'Baseline Study in Disability Discrimination Law in the Member States', available at: www.euroblind.org/fichiersGB/synfinquinn.htm (accessed 23 July 2008).

European Commission (1974) *Preliminary Draft of the Transfer of Undertakings Directive*, COM (74) 351/final2, 21 June 1974, OJ C/104/1, 13 September 1974.

——(1993) *European Social Policy: Options for the Union* [Green Paper] COM(93) 551 (Brussels, EC).

——(1994a) *European Social Policy: a Way Forward for the Union* [White Paper] COM(94) 333 (Brussels, EC).

——(1994b) *Growth, Competitiveness, Employment: The Challenges and Ways Forward into the 21 Century* [White Paper] (Brussels, EC).

——(1996) 'For a Europe of Civic and Social Rights', Report of the Comité des Sages [Chair: M de Lourdes Pintasilgo] (Brussels, EC).

——(1999) 'Applying Fundamental Social Rights in the European Union', Report of the Expert Group on Social Rights [Chair: S Simitis] (Brussels, EC).

——(2000) *Social Policy Agenda* (Brussels, EC).

——(2005) *The Evolution of Labour Law (1992–2003). Vol 2. National Reports* (Brussels, EC).

——(2008) *Gender Mainstreaming of Employment Policies: A Comparative Review of 30 countries* (Brussels, EC).

——(various years) *Employment in Europe* (Brussels, EC).

Fahlbeck, R (2002) 'Industrial Relations and Collective Labour Law: Characteristics, Principles and Basic Features' in P Wahlgren (ed), *Stability and Change in Nordic Labour Law* (Stockholm, Stockholm Institute for Scandinavian Law).

Fakiolas, R (1988) 'The Greek Trade Unions: Past Experience, Present Problems and Future Outlook' in G Spyropoulos (ed), *Trade Unions Today and Tomorrow* (Maastricht, PIE) 123.

Ferner, A and Hyman, R (1998) *Changing Industrial Relations in Europe*, 2nd edn (Oxford, Blackwell).

Ferrera, M (2005) *The Boundaries of Welfare—European Integration and the New Spatial Politics of Social Protection* (Oxford, Oxford University Press).

FitzRoy, FR and Kraft, K (2005) 'Co-determination, Efficiency, and Productivity' 43 *British Journal of Industrial Relations* 233.

Fox, A (1974) *Beyond Contract: Work, Power and Trust Relations* (London, Faber).

Fraile, L (1999) 'Tightrope: Spanish Unions and the Labour Market Segmentation' in A Martin and G Ross (eds), *The Brave New World of European Labour* (New York, Berghahn Books) 269.

Fredman, S (1999) 'A Critical Review of the Concept of Discrimination in UK Anti-Discrimination Law', Working Paper No 3 (Cambridge, Centre for Public Law).

——(2004) 'The Ideology of New Labour Law' in C Barnard, S Deakin and GS Morris (eds), *The Future of Labour Law: Liber Amicorum Sir Bob Hepple QC* (Oxford, Hart Publishing) 9.

——(2005) 'Disability Equality, A Challenge to the Existing Anti-Discrimination Paradigm' in A Lawson and C Gooding (eds), *Disability Rights in Europe. From Theory to Practice* (Oxford, Hart Publishing).

——(2008) *Human Rights Transformed* (Oxford, Oxford University Press).

Freedland, M (1976) *The Contract of Employment* (Oxford, Clarendon Press).

——(2003) *The Personal Employment Contract* (Oxford, Oxford University Press).

——(2004) 'Otto Kahn-Freund (1900–1979)' in J Beatson and R Zimmermann (eds), *Jurists Uprooted* (Oxford, Oxford University Press).

——(2007) 'Application of Labour and Employment Law beyond the Contract of Employment' 146 *International Labour Review.*

Freedland, M, Craig, P, Jacqueson, C and Kountouris, N (2007) *Public Employment Services and European Law* (Oxford, Oxford University Press).

Freeman, RB and Lazear, EP (1995) 'An Economic Analysis of Works Councils' in J Rogers and W Streeck (eds) *Works Councils. Consultation, Representation, and Cooperation in Industrial Relations* (Chicago, University of Chicago Press).

Frieden, JR (2007) *Global Capitalism. Its Fall and Rise in the Twentieth Century* (New York, WW Norton).

Friedman, W (1964) *Law in a Changing Society* (Harmondsworth, Penguin).

Galenson, W (1952) *The Danish System of Labour Relations* (Cambridge MA, Harvard University Press).

Gaudu, F (2004) 'Deregulation and Labour Law' in JP Laviec, M Horiuchi and K Sugeno (eds), *Work in the Global Economy* (Tokyo, International Labour Organisation) 55.

Geddes, A and Guiraudon, V (2004) 'Britain and France and EU: Anti-discrimination Policy: the Emergence of an EU Policy Paradigm' 27 *West European Politics* 334.

Ghera, E (2000, 2003) *Diritto del Lavoro* (Bari, Cacucci).

Ginsborg, P (1990) *A History of Contemporary Italy, Society and Politics, 1943–1988* (Harmondsworth, Penguin).

Giugni, G (1971) 'The Settlement of Labor Disputes in Italy' in B Aaron (ed), *Labour Courts and Grievance Settlement in Western Europe* (Berkeley, University of California Press).

——(1984, 1992, 2001) *Diritto Sindacale* (Bari, Cacucci Editore).

Gregory, F (1951) *Population Changes in Europe since 1919* (Geneva, International Labour Organisation).

Grunfeld, C (1980) *The Law of Redundancy* (London, Sweet and Maxwell).

Gumpert, A (1961) 'Arbeitsrechtliche Sonderbestimmungen für Saison- und Kampagnebetriebe', *Betriebsberater* I.

Hakim, C (1996) *Key Issues in Women's Work* (London, Athlone).

Hall, PA and Soskice, D (eds) (2001) *Varieties of Capitalism. The Institutional Foundations of Comparative Advantage* (Oxford, Oxford University Press).

Hanami, T and Monat, J (1987) 'Employee Participation in the Workshop, in the Office and in the Enterprise' in R Blanpain (ed), *Comparative Labour Law and Industrial Relations*, 3rd edn (Deventer, Kluwer).

Harris, DJ and Darcy, J (2001) *The European Social Charter*, 2nd edn (Ardsley NY, Transnational Publishers).

Hasselbalch, O (2002) 'The Roots—The History of Nordic Labour Law' in P Wahlgren (ed), *Stability and Change in Nordic Labour Law* (Stockholm, Stockholm Institute for Scandinavian Law).

Hasselbalch, O and Jacobsen, P (1999) *Labour Law and Industrial Relations in Denmark* (The Hague, Kluwer).

Havinga, T (1994) 'Labour Office and Collective Dismissal in The Netherlands' in R Rogowski and T Wilthagen (eds), *Reflexive Labour Law: Studies in Industrial Relations and Employment Regulation* (Deventer, Kluwer).

Hay, D (2000) 'Master and Servant in England. Using the Law in the Eigtheenth and Nineteenth Centuries' in W Steinmetz (ed), *Private Law and Social Inequality in the Industrial Age. Comparing Legal Cultures in Britain, France, Germany and the United States* (Oxford, Oxford University Press).

Hayek, F (1980) *Law, Legislation and Liberty* (London, Routledge).

Hepple, B (1970) *Race, Jobs and the Law in Britain*, 2nd edn (Harmondsworth, Penguin Books).

——(1976) 'Recent Developments in British Labour Relations Law 1974–1975' *Bulletin of Leuven Institute of Labour Relations* 7, 13.

——(1981) 'A Right to Work?'10 *Industrial Law Journal* 65.

——(1982) 'Security of Employment' in R Blanpain and F Millard (eds), *Comparative Labour Law and Industrial Relations* (Deventer, Kluwer).

——(ed) (1986) *The Making of Labour Law in Europe: A Comparative Study of Nine Countries up to 1945* (London, Mansell).

——(1988) 'Labour Courts: Some Comparative Perspectives' 41 *Current Legal Problems* 169.

——(1990) 'Discrimination and Equality of Opportunity—Northern Irish Lessons' 10 *Oxford Journal of Legal Studies* 408.

——(1992) 'The Fall and Rise of Unfair Dismissal' in W McCarthy (ed), *Legal Intervention in Industrial Relations: Gains and Losses* (Oxford, Blackwell).

——(1995) 'Social Values and European Law' 48 *Current Legal Problems* 39.

——(1996) 'Equality and Discrimination' in P Davies, A Lyon-Caen, S Sciarra and S Simitis (eds), *European Community Labour Law: Principles and Perspectives* (Oxford, Clarendon Press).

——(1997) 'European Rules on Dismissal Law'18 *Comparative Labor Law Journal* 204.

——(1999) 'Can Collective Labour Laws be Transplanted' 20 *Industrial Law Journal* [*South Africa*] 1.

——(ed) (2002) *Social and Labour Rights in a Global Context: International and Comparative Perspectives* (Cambridge, Cambridge University Press).

——(2003) 'Four Approaches to the Modernisation of Individual Employment Rights' in R Blanpain and M Weiss (eds), *Changing Industrial Relations and the Modernisation of Labour Law* (The Hague, Kluwer).

——(2004) 'Race and Law in Fortress Europe' 67 *Modern Law Review* 1.

——(2005) *Labour Laws and Global Trade* (Oxford, Hart Publishing).

——(2006) 'The European Legacy of *Brown v Board of Education*', *University of Illinois Law Review* 605.

——(2008) 'The Aims of Equality Law' 61 *Current Legal Problems* 1.

Hepple, B and Fredman, S (1986, 2002) 'Great Britain' in R Blanpain (ed), *International Encyclopaedia of Labour Law and Industrial Relations* (Deventer, Kluwer).

Hepple, B and Hakim, C (1997) 'United Kingdom' in R Blanpain, E Köhler and J Rojot (eds), *Legal and Contractual Limits on Working Time in the European Union* 2nd edn (Leuven, Peeters).

Hepple, B and Napier, BW (1978) 'Great Britain' in R Blanpain (ed), *Temporary Work in Modern Society* (The Netherlands, Kluwer).

Hepple, B, Coussey, M and Choudhury, T (2000) *Equality: A New Framework: Report of the Independent Review of the Enforcement of UK Anti-discrimination Legislation* (Oxford, Hart Publishing).

Hervey, T and O'Keeffe, D (eds) (1996) *Sex Equality Law in the European Union* (Chichester, Wiley).

Horion, P (1965) 'Il contratto di lavoro nel diritto belga' in G Boldt, G Camerlynck, P Horion, A Kayser, MG Levenbach and L Mengoni, *Il contratto di lavoro nel diritto dei paesi membri della Ceca* (Milano, Giuffrè).

Hueck, A and Nipperdey, HC (1963) *Lehrbuch des Arbeitsrechts*, Part 1 (Berlin, Franz Vahlen).

Humblet, P and Rigaux, M (eds) (2004) *Aperçu du Droit du Travail Belge* (Brussels, Bruylant).

International Labour Conference (ILC) (1951) 'Equal Remuneration for Men and Women Workers for Work of Equal Value', 33rd Session, Report V(1) (Geneva, International Labour Organisation).

——(1958) 'Discrimination in the Field of Employment and Occupation', Report VII (2) (Geneva, International Labour Organisation).

——(1994) 'The Role of Private Employment Agencies on the Functioning of Labour Markets' 81st session, Report VI (Geneva, International Labour Organisation).

International Labour Organisation (ILO) (1959a) 'Informe en materia de compensaciones de mano de obra entre los países de Europa Occidental', *International Labour Review* (Spanish version).

——(1959b) *Social Aspects of European Collaboration*, Studies and Reports (New Series) No 46 (Geneva, International Labour Organisation).

——(1977) 'Tripartite Declaration' in R Blanpain (1994) 'Representation of Employees at Plant and Enterprise Level' in B Hepple (ed), *International Encyclopedia of Comparative Law. Vol XV. Labour Law* (Tübingen, Mohr) ch 13.

Jacobi, O (1988) 'New Technological Paradigms, Long Waves and Trade Unions' in R Hyman and W Streeck (eds), *New Technology and Industrial Relations* (Oxford, Blackwell).

Jacobi, O et al (eds) (1986) *Economic Crisis, Trade Unions and the State* (London, Croom Helm).

Jacobs, A (1986) 'Collective Self-Regulation' in B Hepple (ed), *The Making of Labour Law in Europe: a Comparative Study of Nine Countries Up to 1945* (London, Mansell).

——(1995) *Labour Law and Social Security in The Netherlands* (Den Bosch, Book World Publications).

——(2004a) *Labour Law in The Netherlands* (The Hague, Kluwer).

——(2004b) 'European Social Concertation' in Spanish Ministry of Labour, *Collective Bargaining in Europe* (Madrid, Ministry of Labour) 347.

——(2005) 'The Netherlands: In the Tradition of Intersectoral Pacts' in R Blanpain, T Blanke and E Rose (eds), *Collective Bargaining and Wages in Comparative Perspective* (The Hague, Kluwer) 89.

——(2006) 'Revitalising Board-level Employee Representation' in A Höland et al (eds), *Arbeitnehmerentwicklung in einer sich globalisierenden Arbeitswelt. Liber Amicorum Manfred Weiss* (Berlin, BWV).

Jamoulle, M (1994) *Seize leçon sur le droit du travail* (Liège, Ed Collection Scientific de la Fac de Liège).

Jandl, M, Kraler, A and Stepien, A (2003) *Migrants, Minorities and Employment: Exclusion, Discrimination and Anti-Discrimination in 15 Member States of the European Union* (Luxembourg, European Monitoring Centre on Racism and Xenophobia).

Javillier, JC (1996) *Droit du Travail* (Paris, LGLJ).

Jeammaud, A (1988) 'L'emploi périphérique' in *Les sans-emploi et la loi*, Actes du colloque-Nantes juin 1987 (Bretagne, Calligrammes) 176.

——(1993) *Le licenciement* (Paris, Dalloz).

Jepsen, M and Serrano, A (eds) (2006) *Unwrapping the European Social Model* (Bristol, Policy Press).

Jessup, B (2002) *The Future of the Capitalist State* (Cambridge, Polity).

Judt, T (2005) *Postwar: A History of Europe since 1945* (London, Heinemann).

Kaelble, H (2007) *Sozialgeschichte Europas. 1945 bis zur Gegenwart* (München, CH Beck).

Kaelble, H and Schmid, G (eds) (2006) *Das europäische Sozialmodell* (Berlin, Sigma).

Kahn-Freund, O (1926) 'Das Soziale Ideal des Reichsarbeitsgerichts', reprinted in T Ramm (ed) (1966) *Arbeitsrecht und Politik* (Berlin, Neuwied).

——(1952) 'Report on some Fundamental Characteristics of Labour Law in Great Britain', Atti del primo congress internazionale di diritto del lavoro, Trieste 24–27 maggio 1952 (Trieste,University of Trieste) 193.

——(1954) 'Legal Framework' in A Flanders and H Clegg (eds), *The System of Industrial Relations in Great Britain* (Oxford, Blackwell).

——(1959) 'Labour Law' in M Ginsberg (ed), *Law and Opinion in England in the Twentieth Century* (London, Stevens).

——(1966) 'The Personal Scope of English Labour Law, "Servant", "Employee", "Workman"' in *Studi in Memoria di Ludovico Barassi* (Milano, Giuffré) 515.

——(1972) *Labour and the Law* (London, Stevens).

——(1974) 'On Uses and Abuses of Comparative Law' 37 *Modern Law Review* 635.

——(1976a) 'The Impact of Constitutions on Labour Law' *The Cambridge Law Journal* 269.

——(1976b) 'Rapport général' in Centre d'études juridiques comparatives (ed), *La participation. Quelques expériences étrangères, Colloque tenu à la Sorbonne les 4 et 5 juin 1976* (Paris, Centre d'études juridiques comparatives).

——(1981) *Labour Law and Politics in the Weimar Republic* (Oxford, Blackwell).

Kahn-Freund, O and Hepple, B (1972) *Laws against Strikes* (London, Fabian Society).

Kaufmann, F-X (2001) 'Der deutsche Sozialstaat im internationalen Vergleich' in Bundesministerium für Arbeit und Sozialordnung und Bundesarchiv (eds), *Geschichte der Sozialpolitik in Deutschland seit 1945. Vol 1. Grundlagen der Sozialpolitik* (Baden-Baden, Nomos).

Kenner, J (2003) *EU Employment Law: from Rome to Amsterdam and Beyond* (Oxford, Hart Publishing).

Kerckhofs, P (2006) *European Works Councils—Facts and Figures* (Brussels, ETUI-REHS).

Kerr, A (2004) 'A Note on Further Irish Developments in 2003', Annex III, in European Commission, *The Evolution of Labour Law, Irish Report* (Brussels, European Union) 4.

Kilpatrick, C (2001) 'Gender Equality: a Fundamental Dialogue' in S Sciarra (ed), *Labour Law in the Courts: National Judges and the European Court of Justice* (Oxford, Hart Publishing).

——(2002) UK Report for the Project to Study Conciliation, Mediation and Arbitration, available at: http://ec/europa.eu/social/BlobServlet?docId=2476&langlId=en.

Kilpatrick, C, Novitz, T and Skidmore, P (eds) (2000) *The Future of Remedies in Europe* (Oxford, Hart Publishing).

Klare, K (2002) 'The Horizons of Transformative Labour and Employment Law' in J Conaghan, M Fischl and K Klare, *Labour Law in an Era of Globalisation* (Oxford, Oxford University Press).

Kravaritou, Y (1988) 'Formes nouvelles d'emploi: leurs effets en droit du travail et de la sécurité sociale dans les États membres de la Communauté Européenne' Rapport general (Luxembourg, European Foundation for the Improvement of Living and Working Conditions) 23.

Kritsantonis, RD (1998) 'Greece: From State Authoritarianism to Modernisation' in A Ferner and R Hyman (eds), *Changing Industrial Relations in Europe*, 2nd edn (Oxford, Blackwell) 601.

Kruger, J, Nielsen, R, and Bruun, N (1998) *European Public Contracts in a Labour Law Perspective* (Copenhagen, DJØF Publishing).

Kumlien, M (2004) *Continuity and Contract: Historical Perspectives on the Employee's Duty of Obedience in Swedish Labour Law* (Stockholm, Institutet för rättshistorisk forskning).

Landes, DS (1969) *The Unbound Prometheus: Technological Change and Industrial Development in Western Europe from 1730 to the Present* (Cambridge, Cambridge University Press).

Laulom, S (2003) 'Administrative Processes' in J Malmberg (ed), *Effective Enforcement of EC Labour Law* (The Hague, Kluwer).

Le Crom, J-P (ed) (1998a) *Deux siècles de droit du travail* (Paris, Les éditions de l'atelier).

——(1998b) 'La profession aux professionnels: la loi du 4 octobre 1941 sur l'organisaion sociale des professions, dite Charte du travail' in J-P Le Crom (ed), *Deux siècles de droit du travail* (Paris, Les éditions de l'atelier).

——(1998c)' Une révolution par la loi? L'ordonnance du 22 février 1945 sur les comités d'entreprise' in J-P Le Crom (ed), *Deux siècles de droit du travail* (Paris, Les éditions de l'atelier).

Le Goff, J (2002) *Droit du travail et société, Les relations collectives de travail* (Rennes, Presses Universitaires).

Le Grand, J (1991) *Equiy and Choice: an Essay in Economics and Applied Philosophy* (London, Harper Collins).

Lester, A and Bindman, G (1972) *Race and Law* (Harmondsworth, Penguin Books).

Lind, J (1988) 'Crisis and Conflict between the State and the Trade Union Mouvement: The Danish Experience' in G Spyropoulos (ed), *Trade Unions Today and Tomorrow* (Maastricht, PIE) 59.

Linsenmaier, W (2004) 'Von Lyon nach Erfurt—Zur Geschichte der deutschen Arbeitsgerichtsbarkeit', *Neue Zeitschrift für Arbeitsrecht* 401.

Lødemel, I and Trickey, H (2001) *An Offer You Can't Refuse. Workfare in International Perspective* (Bristol, Policy Press).

Macdonald, I and Blake, N (1995) *Inmigration Law and Practice in the United Kingdom* (London, Butterworths).

Magnusson, L (1999) 'Preface' in P Pochet (ed), *Monetary Union and Collective Bargaining in Europe* (PIE, Peter Lang).

——(2000) *An Economic History of Sweden* (London, Routledge).

Magrez-Song, G (1983) 'Le droit conventionnel du travail' in *Liber Amicorum F Dumon* (Antwerp, Kluwer Rechtswetenschappen) 597.

Mallet, S (1963) *Le nouvelle classe ouvrière* (Paris, Éditions du Seuil).

Malmberg, J (2002) 'The Collective Agreements as an Instrument for Regulation of Wages and Employment Conditions' in P Wahlgren (ed) *Stability and Change in Nordic Labour Law* (Stockholm, Stockholm Institute of Scandinavian Law).

——(ed) (2003) *Effective Enforcement of EC Labour Law* (The Hague, Kluwer).

Marsh, A, Hackmann, M and Miller, D (1981) *Workplace Relations in the Engineering Industry in the UK and in the Federal Republic of Germany* (London, Anglo-German Foundation).

Martin, A and Ross, G (1980) 'European Trade Unions and the Economic Crisis, Perceptions and Strategies' in J Hayward (ed), *Trade Unions and Politics in Western Europe* (London, Frank Cass) 33.

Martin, R (1992) *Bargaining Power* (Oxford, Clarendon Press).

McCarthy, C (1977) *Trade Unions in Ireland, 1894–1960* (Dublin, Institute of Public Administration).

McCrudden, C (1986) 'Rethinking Positive Action' 15 *Industrial Law Journal* 219.

——(1993) 'The Effectiveness of European Equality Law: National Mechanisms for Enforcing Gender Equality Law in the Light of European Requirements' 13 *Oxford Journal of Legal Studies* 320.

Meager, N (1992) 'Le travail indépendant et la politique de l'emploi dans la Communauté européenne' 38 *InforMissep* 24.

Mergits, B (1975) *De interprofessionele akkoorden 1960–1975* (Brussels, VUB).

Merlin, L (1993) 'Les accords de GPE: une coopération ambivalente' 57 *Travail et emploi* 33.

Mermet, E and Hoffmann, R (2001) 'European Trade Union Strategies and Europeanisation of Collective Bargaining—An Overview' in Schulten and Binspich (eds) *Collective Bargaining under the Euro. Experiences from the Metal Industry* (Brussels, ETUI) 37.

Meulders, D, Plasman, R and van der Stricht, V (1993) *Position of Women on the Labour Market in the European Community* (Aldershot, Dartmouth).

Milner, S (1995) 'The Coverage of Collective Pay-setting Institutions in Britain' 33 *British Journal of Industrial Relations* 70.

Monteiro Fernandes, A (2004) *Direito do Trabalho*, 12th edn (Coimbra, Almedina).

Moreau, M-A (2004) 'National Report. Changes in French Labour Law between 1992 and 2003' in European Commission, *The Evolution of Labour Law* (Brussels, EC)10.

——(2006) *Normes sociales, droit du travail et mondialisation* (Paris, Dalloz).

Mückenberger, U (1973) *Arbeitsrecht und Klassenkampf. Der große englische Dockarbeiterstreik* (Frankfurt, EVA).

——(1982) 'Streikrecht und Staatsgewalt in Polen' in 15 *Kritische Justiz* 44.

——(1986a) 'Die Krise des Normarbeitsverhältnisses' 31 *Zeitschrift für Sozialreform* 415.

——(1986b) 'Labour Law and Industrial Relations' in O Jacobi et al (eds), *Economic Crisis, Trade Unions and the State* (London, Croom Helm).

——(1988) 'Juridification of Industrial Relations: A German–British Comparison' 9 *Comparative Labor Law Journal* 526.

——(1989) 'Non-standard Forms of Work and the Role of Changes in Labour and Social Securitiy Regulation' 17 *International Journal of Sociology of Law* 381.

——(2003) 'German Industrial Relations in a Period of Transition' in B Burchell et al (eds), *Systems of Production. Markets, Organisations and Performance* (London, Routledge).

——(2004) 'Towards Procedural Regulation of Labour Law in Europe: The Case of Social Dialogue' in L Magnussen and B Strath (eds), *A European Social Citizenship? Preconditions for Future Policies from a Historical Perspective* (Brussels, Lang).

——(2007) 'Alternative Mechanisms of Voice Representation' in C Estlund and B Bercusson (eds), *Regulating Labour in the Wake of Globalisation: New Challenges, New Institutions* (Oxford, Hart Publishing).

Mückenberger, U and Deakin, S (1989) 'From Deregulation to a European Floor of Rights: Labour Law, Flexibilisation and the European Single Market' 3 *Zeitschrift für ausländische und internationales Arbeits- und Sozialrecht* 153.

Mückenberger, U and Duhm, R (1983) 'Computerisation and Control Strategies at Plant Level' 4 *Policy Studies Review* 261.

Napier, BW (1979) 'The French Labour Courts—An Institution in Transition' 42 *Modern Law Review* 270.

Napoli, M (1980) *La stabilità reale del rapporto di lavoro* (Milano, Franco Angeli).

Nevin, S (ed) (1984) *Trade Unions and Change in Irish Society* (Dublin, Mercier Press for Radio Telefis E´ireann).

Nielsen, R (2002) 'Europeanisation of Nordic Labour Law' in P Wahlgren (ed), *Stability and Change in Nordic Labour Law* (Stockholm, Stockholm Institute for Scandinavian Law).

Ó Móráin, S (2000) 'The European Employment Strategy—A Consideration of Social Partnership and Related Matters in the Irish Context' 16 *International Journal of Comparative Labour Law and Industrial Relations* 85.

O'Higgins, P (1997) 'Labour is not a Commodity: An Irish Contribution to International Labour Law' 26 *Industrial Law Journal* 226.

——(2002) 'The Interaction of ILO and Council of Europe, and European Union Labour Standards' in B Hepple (ed), *Social and Labour Rights in a Global Context: International and Comparative Perspectives* (Cambridge, Cambridge University Press).

Organisation for Economic Co-operation and Development (OECD) (1976) 'Guidelines for Multinational Enterprises' in R Blanpain (1994) 'Representation of Employees at Plant and Enterprise Level' in B Hepple (ed), *International Encyclopedia of Comparative Law. Vol XV. Labour Law* (Tübingen, Mohr) ch 13.

——(2004) *Labour Force Participation of Women: Empirical Evidence of the Role of Policy and other Determinants in OECD Countries* (Paris, OECD).

——(2005) 'Pensions at a Glance', available at: http://www.oecd.org/document/6/0,3343,en_2649_33933_34814598_1_1_1_37419,00.html (accessed December 2008).

——(2006) 'Employment Outlook 2006', cited from the Spanish translation, *Perspectivas del Empleo 2006* (Madrid, MTAS).

Ojeda Aviles, A (1980) 'El final de un principio (la estabilidad en el empleo)' in *Estudios de Derecho del Trabajo en memoria del profesor Gaspar Bayón Chacón* (Madrid, Tecnos).

——(ed) (1990) *La concertación social tras la crisis* (Barcelona, Ariel).

——(2002) 'Il diritto del lavoro oltre il contratto di lavoro' subordinato' *DLRI* 464.

Parekh, B (2000) *The Future of Multi-ethnic Britain* (London, Profile Books).

Paton, RP (1977) 'La Reivindicacion obrera: La cogestion. Los consejos de impresa' in *Estudios sobre derecho laboral. Homenaje a Rafael Caldera*, vol 2 (Caracas, editorial sucre).

Pedrazzoli, P (1999), 'Dai Lavori Autonomi al Lavoro Subordinati' in *Studi in Onore di Gino Giugni* (Bari, Cacucci).

Pélissier, J et al (1998) *Droit de l'emploi* (Paris, Dalloz).

Pélissier, J, Supiot, A and Jeammaud, A (2000, 2004, 2006) *Droit du Travail* (Paris, Dalloz).

Pelling, H (1979) *A History of British Trade Unionism* (Harmondsworth, Penguin).

Pierson, C (2006) *Beyond the Welfare State* (Cambridge, Polity).

Pierson, C and Castles, F (2006) *The Welfare State Reader*, 2nd edn (Cambridge, Polity).

Pinto, M (1991) 'Trade Union Action and Industrial Relations in Portugal' in G Baglioni and C Crouch (eds), *European Industrial Relations, The Challenge of Flexibility* (London, Sage Publications) 243.

Plantegna, J and Remery, C (2006) *The Gender Pay Gap—Origins and Policy Responses. A Comparative Review of 30 European Countries* (Brussels, EC).

Pochet, P (2006) 'A Quantitative Analysis' in A Dufresne, C Degryse and P Pochet (eds), (2006) *The European Sectoral Social Dialogue. Actors, Developments and Challenges* (Bruxelles, Peter Lang SALTSA).

Prodzynski, F von (1992) 'Ireland: Between Centralism and the Market' in A Ferner and R Hyman (eds), *Industrial Relations in the New Europe* (Oxford, Basil Blackwell) 69.

Ramm, T (1971) 'Labor Courts and Grievance Settlement in West Germany' in B Aaron (ed), *Labor Courts and Grievance Settlement in Western Europe* (Berkeley, University of California Press).

——(1979) 'Federal Republic of Germany' in R Blanpain (ed), *International Encyclopedia of Labour Law and Industrial Relations* (The Netherlands, Kluwer).

——(1986) 'Workers' Participation, the Representation of Labour and Special Labour Courts' in B Hepple (ed), *The Making of Labour Law in Europe. A Comparative Study of Nine Countries up to 1945* (London, Mansell).

——(1989) *Per Una Storia della Constituzione del Lavoro Tedesca* (Milan, Giuffré).

Rawls, J (1971) *A Theory of Justice* (Cambridge MA, Harvard University Press).

Redenti, E (1906) *Massimario delle Giurisprudenze dei Probiviri* (Rome, Giappichelli).

Reneau, L (1960) 'Réflexions sur le problème du chômage en Belgique' 4 *Revue du Travail.*

Rhodes, M (1993) 'The Social Dimension after Maastricht: Setting a New Agenda for the Labour Market' 4 *International Journal for Comparative Labour Law and Industrial Relations* 314.

——(2005) 'Employment Policy. Between Efficacy and Experimentation' in H Wallace et al (eds), *Policy-making in the European Union*, 5th edn (Oxford, Oxford University Press).

Rhodes, RAW (1991) 'The Hollowing Out of the State: The Changing Nature of the Public Service in Britain' *Political Quarterly Review* 65.

Roberts, BC (1973) 'Multinational Collective Bargaining—A European Prospect' 9 *British Journal of Industrial Relations* 1.

Roberts, JM and Devine, F (2003) 'The Hollowing Out of the Welfare State and Social Capital', 2 *Social Policy & Society* 309.

Rocella, M and Treu, T (1995) *Diritto del lavoro della Comunità Europea* (Padova, CEDAM).

Rodríguez Garcia, D (2005) 'From Emigration to Immigration: Changing Trends in International Migration in Europe and the Case of Spain' in CERIS (Joint Centre of Excellence for Research on Immigration and Settlement), Public Seminar, Toronto, available at: http://ceris.metropolis.net/events/seminars/2005/January/Jan05_Dan.htm   (accessed December 2008).

Rodríguez-Pinero Royo, MC (2004) 'Developments in Labour Law in Spain between 1992 and 2002—National report' in European Commission, *The Evolution of Labour Law* (Brussels, EC).

Roe, MJ (1996) 'Chaos and Evolution in Law and Economics' 109 *Harvard Law Review* 641—68.

Rogers, J (1995) 'United States: Lessons from Abroad and Home' in J Rogers and W Streeck (eds), *Works Councils. Consultation, Representation, and Cooperation in Industrial Relations* (Chicago, University of Chicago Press).

Rogers, J and Streeck, W (eds) (1995) *Works Councils. Consultation, Representation, and Cooperation in Industrial Relations* (Chicago, University of Chicago Press).

Rojot, J and Plotino, MF (2007) 'I servizi d'impiego in Francia' in *Nuove povertà, nuove priorità. Ripensare l'inclusione sociale. Annali Fondazione Giuseppe di Vittorio 2006* (Roma, EDIESSE).

Rosenau, J (2003) *Distant Proximities. Dynamics beyond Globalization* (Princeton, Princeton University Press).

Rousseau, M (1993) 'Les pratiques des entreprises en matière d'anticipation des qualifications' 57 *Travail et emploi* 8.

Royal Commission on Trade Unions and Employers' Associations (1968) Report, Cmnd 3623 (London, HMSO).

Rubin, N (2005) *Code of International Labour Law: Law, Practice, Jurisprudence* (Cambridge, Cambridge University Press).

Rudolf, S (1993) 'Direction of Changes in the Employee participation System in Poland' in R Blanpain and M Weiss (eds), *The Changing Face of Labour Law and Industrial Relations. Liber Amicorum for Clyde W Summers* (Baden-Baden, Nomos) 261.

Rudyer, A and Spencer, S (2003) 'Social Integration of Migrants and Ethnic Minorities: Policies to Combat Discrimination', conference jointly organised by European Commission and OECD, 21–29 January 2003, available at: www.oecd.org.

Sainsaulieu, R (ed) (1992) *L'Entreprise une affaire de société* (Paris, Presses de la Fondation Nationale des Sciences Politiques).

Sassen, S (2006) *Territory—Authority—Rights. From Medieaval to Global Assemblages* (Princeton, Princeton University Press).

Sauvy, A (1948) 'La situation économique', *Droit Social* 4.

Savatier, R (1959) *Les métamorphoses économiques et sociales du droit privé d'aujourdui* (Paris, Dalloz).

Schiek, D, Waddington, L and Bell, M (eds) (2007) *Cases, Materials and Text on National, Supranational and International Non-discrimination Law* (Oxford, Hart).

Schmidt, F (ed) (1978) *Discrimination in Employment* (Stockholm, Almquist & Wicksell).

Schmidt, M (2004) 'Part-time Work in Germany' in B Caruso and M Fuchs (eds), *Labour Law and Flexibility in Europe. The Cases of Germany and Italy* (Milan, Giuffré) 97.

Scholten, GH (1968) *De Sociaal-Economische Raad en de Ministeriële Verantwoordelijkheid* (Meppel, Boom).

Schumpeter, J (1943) *Capitalism, Socialism and Democracy* (London, Allen & Unwin).

Sciarra, S (ed) (2001) *Labour Law in the Courts: National judges and the European Court of Justice* (Oxford, Hart).

——(2004a) *General Report. The Evolution of Labour Law (1992–2003)* (Brussels, EC).

——(2004b) 'The "Making" of EU Labour Law and the "Future" of Labour Lawyers' in C Barnard, S Deakin and GS Morris (eds), *The Future of Labour Law: Liber Amicorum Sir Bob Hepple QC* (Oxford, Hart Publishing).

Sefert, A (2003) 'Le contrat de travail en droit allemand' in Chauchard, JP, Hardy-Dubernet A-C (eds), *La subordination dans le travail* (Paris, La Documentantion française).

Sen, A (1992) *Inequality Re-examined* (Oxford, Clarendon Press).

Serrano Pascual, A (ed) (2004) *Are Activation Policies Converging in Europe? The European Employment Strategy for Young People* (Brussels, European Trade Union Institute).

Servais, JM (2005) *International Labour Law* (The Hague, Kluwer).

——(2008) *Droit Social de l'Union Européenne* (Brussels, Bruylant).

Simitis, S (1994) 'The Rediscovery of the Individual in Labour Law' in R Rogowski and T Wilthagen (eds), *Reflexive Labour Law: Studies in Industrial Relations and Employment Regulation* (Deventer, Kluwer).

Simitis, S and Lyon-Caen, A (1996) 'Community Labour Law: A Critical Introduction to its History' in P Davies et al (eds), *European Community Labour Law: Princples and Perspectives* (Oxford, Clarendon Press).

Slomp, H (1990) *Labour Relations in Europe. A History of Issues and Developments* (New York, Greenwood Press).

Smith, SC (1991) 'On the Economic Rationale of Codetermination Law' 12 *Journal of Economic Behaviour and Organization* 261.

Sobczak, A (2003) 'Rapport comparé' in AA, VV (eds), *Du travail salarié au travail indépendant: permanences et mutations* (Bari, Cacucci) 316.

Spyropoulos, G (1998) *Labour Relations. Developments in Greece, Europe and International Sphere* (Athens, A Sakkoulas Editions).

——(ed) (1988) *Trade Unions Today and Tomorrow* (Maastricht, PIE).

Steinberg, HG (1991) *Die Bevölkerungsentwicklung in Deutschland im Zweiten Weltkrieg: mit einem uberblick uber die Entwicklung vonm 1945 bis 1990* (Bonn, 1991).

Steiner, HJ and Alston, P (1996) *International Human Rights in Context* (Oxford, Clarendon Press).

Strasser, R, Grillberger, K and Rebhahn, R (1982) 'Austria' in R Blanpain (ed), *International Encyclopaedia of Labour Law and Industrial Relations* (Deventer, Kluwer).

——(1992) *Labour Law and Industial Relations in Austria*, vol 3 (Wien, Manz).

Streeck, W and Schmitter, P (1992) 'From National Corporatism to Transnational Pluralism: Organised Interests in the Single European Market' *Politcs and Society* 142.

Stuby, G (1978) 'Das Recht auf Arbeit als Grundrecht und als Internationales Menschenrecht' in U Achten (ed), *Recht auf Arbeit—eine politische Herausforderung* (Darmstadt, Neuwied).

Summers, CW (1998) 'Exclusive Representation: A Comparative Inquiry into a "Unique" American Principle' 20 *Comparative Labor Law & Policy Journal* 47.

Supiot, A (1987) *Les juridictions du travail* (Paris, Dalloz).

——(1998) 'Autopsie du "citoyen dans l'entreprise": le rapport Auroux sur les droits des travailleurs' in J-P Le Crom (ed), *Deux siècles de droit du travail* (Paris Les éditions de l'atelier).

——(1999a) 'Wage Employment and Self-employment' in *Reports to the 6th European Congress for Labour Law and Social Security* 129.

——(1999b) *Au–delà de l'emploi. Transformation du travail et devenir du droit du travail en Europe. Rapport pour la Commission Européenne* (Paris, Flammarion).

——(2001) *Beyond Employment: Changes in Work and the Future of Labour Law in Europe* (Oxford, Oxford University Press).

Suviranta, A (1976) 'Recent Developments in Finnish Labour Law' 7 *Bulletin of Comparative Labour Relations.*

——(2000) *Labour law in Finland* (The Hague, Kluwer).

Syrpis, P (2007) *EU Intervention in Domestic Labour Law* (Oxford, Oxford University Press).

Szell, G (ed) (2001) *European Labour Relations*, vol 2 (Aldershot, Gow).

Tálos, E (ed) (1999) *Atypische Beschäftigung. Internationale Trends und sozialstaatliche Regelungen* (Wien, Manz).

Tawney, RH (1964) *Equality* (London, Unwin Books).

Trades Union Congress (TUC) (1973) 'Industrial Democracy', Interim Report by the TUC General Council (London, TUC).

Teubner, G (ed) (1987) *Juridification of Social Spheres: A Comparative Analysis in the Areas of Labor, Corporate, Antitrust, and Social Welfare Law* (Berlin, De Gruyter).

——(2001) 'Legal Irritants: How Unifying Law Ends Up in New Divergences' in PA Hall and D Soskice (eds), *Varieties of Capitalism: The Institutional Foundations of Comparative Advantage* (Oxford, Oxford University Press) 417.

Tremblay, DG and Le Bot, D (2000) 'The German Dual Apprenticeship System: An Analysis of its Evolution and Present Challenges', paper presented at the Fourth Annual Conference of the Labour Education & Training Research Network (Vancouver), available at: http://eric.ed.gov/ERICWebPortal/custom/portlets/recordDetails/detailmini.jsp?_nfpb =true&_&ERICExtSearch_SearchValue_0=ED461048&ERICExtSearch_SearchType_0 =no&accno=ED461048 (accessed December 2008).

Treu, T (2004) 'Italy' in R Blanpain (ed), *International Encyclopaedia for Labour Law and Industrial Relations* (Deventer, Kluwer).

Valverde, AM, Rodriguez-Sanudo Gutierrez, F and Garcia Murcia, J (1991) *Derecho del trabajo* (Madrid, Tecnoc).

Van Acker, G (1977) *30 jaar Belgische Arbeidsverhoudingen* (Deventer, Kluwer).

Van der Heijden, P (1994) 'Post-industrial Labour Law and Industrial Relations in The Netherlands' in Lord Wedderburn, M Rood, G Lyon-Caen, W Däubler and P van der Heijden, *Labour Law in the Post-industrial Era* (Aldershot, Dartmouth).

Van der Ven, JJM (1986) 'Social Law in The Netherlands' in MG Rood et al, *Fifty Years of Labour Law and Social Security* (Deventer, Kluwer).

Van Parijs, P and Vanderborght, Y (2006) *La renta básica. Una medida eficaz para luchar contra la pobreza* (Barcelona, Paidós).

Van Peijpe, T (1998) 'Employment Protection Under Strain' 33 *Bulletin of Comparative Labour Relations* (The Hague, Kluwer).

——(2003) 'Industrial Relations Processes' in J Malmberg (ed), *Effective Enforcement of EC Labour Law* (The Hague, Kluwer).

Van Voss, GH (1999) 'The "Tulip" Model and the New Legislation on Temporary Work in The Netherlands' 15 *International Journal of Comparative Labour Law and Industrial Relations* 419.

——(2000) 'Deregulation and Labour Law in the Netherlands' in R Blanpain (ed), *European Labour Law* (The Hague, Kluwer).

Veneziani, B (1986) 'The evolution of the contract of employment' in B Hepple (ed), *The Making of Labour Law in Europe, a Comparative Study of Nine Countries up to 1945* (London, Mansell) 35.

——(1987) 'New Technologies and the Contract of Employment' in Lord Wedderburn, B Veneziani, S Ghimpu (eds), *Diritto del Lavoro in Europa* (Milan, Angeli).

——(1993) ' The New Labour Force' in R Blanpain, C Engels (eds), *Comparative Labour Law and Industrial Relations in Industrialised Market Economies* (Deventer, Kluwer).

——(2004) 'Collective Bargaining in Italy' in Spanish Ministry of Labour, *Collective Bargaining in Europe* (Madrid, Ministry of Labour) 155.

Verdier, J-M, Coeuret, A and Souriac, M-A (2007) *Droit du travail*, 14th edn, vol II (Paris, Dalloz).

Vergara Del Rio, M (2005) *Empresas de trabajo temporal* (Madrid, CES).

Vigneau, C and Sobczak, A (2005) 'France: The Helping Hand of the State' in R Blanpain, T Blanke and E Rose (eds), *Collective Bargaining and Wages in Comparative Perspective* (The Hague, Kluwer) 31.

Vigneau, C, Ahlberg, K, Bercusson, B and Bruun, N (eds) (1999) *Fixed-term work in the EU—A European Agreement against Discrimination and Abuse* (Stockholm, National Institute for Working Life).

Vis, B (2007) 'States of Welfare or States of Workfare? Welfare State Restructuring in 16 Capitalist Democracies 1985–2002' 35 *Policy and Politics* 105.

Visser, J (2004) 'Patterns and Variations in European Industrial Relations' in European Commission (ed), *Industrial Relations in Europe* (Brussels, EC) 11.

Vogel-Polsky, E (1986) 'The Problem of Unemployment' in B Hepple (ed), *The Making of Labour Law in Europe* (London, Mansell Publishing).

Vom Beyme, K (1980) *Challenge to power* (London, Sage).

Vranken, M (1987–88) 'Specialisation and Labour Courts: a Comparative Analysis', *Comparative Labor Journal* 497.

Wahlgren, P (ed) (2002) *Stability and Change in Nordic Labour Law* (Stockholm, Stockholm Institute of Scandinavian Law).

Walters, D (ed) (2002) *Regulating Health and Safety Management in the European Union: A Study of the Dynamics of Change* (Brussels, PIE. Peter Lang).

Wank, R (1980) *Das Recht auf Arbeit im Verfassungsrecht und im Arbeitsrecht* (Königstein, Athenäeum).

Warner, J (1984)' EC Social Policy in Practice: Community Action on Behalf of Women and its Impact on Member States' 23 *Journal of Common Market Studies* 141.

Weber, M (1954) *Max Weber Law in Economy and Society*, edited by M Rheinstein (Cambridge MA, Harvard University Press).

Wedderburn, KW (Lord) (1971) *The Worker and the Law*, 2nd edn (Harmondsworth, Penguin).

——(1972) 'Multi-national Enterprise and National Labour Law' 1 *Industrial Law Journal* 12.

——(1987) 'Labour Law: From Here to Autonomy' 16 *Industrial Law Journal* 1.

——(1991) 'The Italian Workers' Statute: British Reflections on a High Point of Legal Protection' in *Employment Rights in Britain and Europe* (London, Lawrence & Wishart) 236.

——(1992) 'Inderogability, Collective Agreements and Community Law' 21 *Industrial Law Journal* 249.

——(1995) *Labour Law and Freedom. Further Essays in Labour Law* (London, Lawrence & Wishart).

Wedderburn, KW and Davies PL (1969) *Employment Grievances and Disputes Procedures in Britain* (Berkeley, University of California Press).

Wedderburn, Lord, Veneziani, B and Ghimpu, S (eds) (1987) *Diritto del lavoro in Europa* (Milano, Franco Angeli).

Weekes, B, Mellish, M, Dickens, L and Lloyd, J (1975) *Industrial Relations and the Limits of the Law: The Industrial Effects of the Industrial Relations Act* (Oxford, Basil Blackwell).

Weiss, M (1992) 'Immigration Policy and the Labour Market in Germany' 2 *International Journal of Comparative Labour Law and Industrial Relations*, special edition.

——(1996) 'Workers' Participation in the European Union' in P Davies et al (eds), *European Community Labour Law—Principles and Perspectives* (Oxford, Clarendon Press).

——(2004) 'The Future of Workers' Participation in the EU' in C Barnard, S Deakin and GS Morris (eds) (2004) *The Future of Labour Law. Liber Amicorum Bob Hepple QC* (Oxford, Hart Publishing).

——(2007) 'Convergence and/or Divergence in Labor Law Systems? A European Perspective' 28 *Comparatie Labor Law and Policy Journal* 469.

Weiss, M and Schmidt, M (2000) *Labour law and Industrial Relations in Germany* (The Hague, Kluwer).

Williams, K (1988) *Industrial Relations and the German Model* (Aldershot, Avebury.

Windmuller, JP (1969) *Labour Relations in the Netherlands* (Ithaca, NY, Cornell University Press).

Windmuller, JP and Gladstone, A (1984) *Employers' Associations and Industrial Relations—A Comparative Study* (Oxford, Clarendon Press).

Wrench, J and Modood, T (2000) 'The Effectiveness of Employment Equality Policies in Relation to Immigrants and Ethnic Minorities in the UK', International Migration Papers 38 (Geneva, International Labour Office).

Yannakounou, S (2004) *The Evolution of Labour Law in the EU 1992–2003, Country Study on Greece* (Brussels, EC).

Zachert, U (1999) 'A Change of Paradigm in German Labour Law—An Inspiration for Other Countries?' *International Journal for Comparativ Labour Law and Industrial Relations* 21.

Zambarloukou, S (2006) 'Collective Bargaining and Social Pacts: Greece in Comparative Perspective' 12 *European Journal of Industrial Relations* 211.

Zappalà, L (2004) 'Fixed Term Contracts in Italy' in B Caruso and M Fuchs (eds), *Labour Law and Flexibility in Europe. The Cases of Germany and Italy* (Milan, Giuffré).

Zweigert, K and Kötz, H (1998) *An Introduction to Comparative Law*, 3rd edn translated by T Weir (Oxford, Clarendon Press).

Index